Digital Religion, Social Media
and Culture

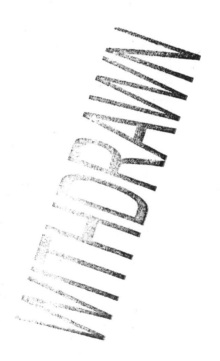

Digital Formations

Steve Jones
General Editor

Vol. 78

The Digital Formations series is part of the Peter Lang Media and Communication list.
Every volume is peer reviewed and meets
the highest quality standards for content and production.

PETER LANG
New York • Washington, D.C./Baltimore • Bern
Frankfurt • Berlin • Brussels • Vienna • Oxford

Digital Religion, Social Media and Culture

Perspectives, Practices and Futures

Edited by Pauline Hope Cheong,
Peter Fischer-Nielsen, Stefan Gelfgren,
and Charles Ess

PETER LANG
New York • Washington, D.C./Baltimore • Bern
Frankfurt • Berlin • Brussels • Vienna • Oxford

Library of Congress Cataloging-in-Publication Data

Digital religion, social media, and culture: perspectives, practices,
and futures / edited by Pauline Hope Cheong ... [et al.].
p. cm. — (Digital formations; v. 78)
Includes bibliographical references and index.
1. Computers—Religious aspects—Christianity. 2. Social media.
3. Information technology—Religious aspects—Christianity.
4. Christianity—Computer network resources. 5. Christianity and culture.
I. Cheong, Pauline Hope.
BR115.C65D54   230.00285—dc23   2011051546
ISBN 978-1-4331-1475-5 (hardcover)
ISBN 978-1-4331-1474-8 (paperback)
ISBN 978-1-4539-0569-2 (e-book)
ISSN 1526-3169

Bibliographic information published by **Die Deutsche Nationalbibliothek**.
Die Deutsche Nationalbibliothek lists this publication in the "Deutsche
Nationalbibliografie"; detailed bibliographic data is available
on the Internet at http://dnb.d-nb.de/.

The paper in this book meets the guidelines for permanence and durability
of the Committee on Production Guidelines for Book Longevity
of the Council of Library Resources.

Table of Contents

Part III: Historical and Theological Examinations

Foreword: Practice, Autonomy, and Authority in the Digitally Religious and Digitally Spiritual

STEWART M. HOOVER, PH.D.

The digital revolution has brought with it a nearly overwhelming discourse of change. Across a range of disciplines and industries, it has been commonplace for the past two decades to think and talk about the changes that these devices are bringing about. Underlying much of this talk is a kind of moral panic about the way that these new media are threatening to undermine important settled social and cultural arrangements. It is as though the digital media hold within them a nearly unparalleled power to undo all of what we value about *Gemeinschaft*.

This conversation pervades domains from business to the family. For the former, particularly for those businesses we call "news," digitalization has displaced some important received areas of value and practice. At the same time that important new kinds of journalism have emerged through these media, voices in the discourse decry digitalization as the end of journalism, or even as the advent of a new era of " . . . fact-free journalism . . ." (as one journalism professor has put it). For the family, digital media join most other media of the modern era in being seen by cultural leaders as threatening, even dangerous, to domestic life. Just as "dime novels," then cinema, then radio, then television, then homevideo, were each seen as potentially undoing childhood, family, and—importantly—parental authority, digital media are seen to threaten the same values, only in more seductive and dangerous ways.

Much of this discourse is driven by a generational gulf between those who grew up with these media and those who did not. For emerging generations of practitioners, digital cultures are nothing more than new, complex, and satisfying ways of doing many of the things we've always done. They enable new forms of social relations, new ways of networking, and new ways of organizing social, cultural, and political life. They enable new forms of entertainment, artistic expression, consumption, and journalism. For those threatened by these developments, these media seem to shake the very foundations of professional practice, aesthetic performance, and reception. This generational divide underlies—and provides some essential *frisson* to—all discourse about these "new media."

Any new social arrangement must be described in terms familiar to the arrangements that preceded it, and will naturally be seen and understood with reference to that past. What makes something new is of course its variation on past practice, and when what is changing is the technology that constitutes much of our social relations in modernity, then it is natural that a wide range of "changes" will be seen and talked about. So, it makes sense that people in various professions will think and talk about new media in relation to what went before.

Religion has entered this discourse about emergent digital culture in two ways. First, these changes in media do actually affect religion, the practice of religion, and the understanding of religions and spiritualities. The second way is a bit more esoteric. It seems that when we are thinking about larger, even epochal, changes in the culture, the term "religion" can stand for "tradition," or "culture," or "established practice," or "authenticity," in a way that nothing else can. This is, of course, a function of the settled discourses of secularized late modernity where, for many, religion has ceased to occupy an organic space at the center of cultural life, but has instead come to represent a past of received practice and authority. Thus, in a way, what happens to "religion" in the digital age is less important on its own terms. What is discursively important to this line of argument is to describe the changes wrought by digitalization as particularly deep, portentous, or significant. "If this is happening to something like *religion*," the argument might go, "imagine what it might be doing elsewhere?"

This means that a great deal of what has passed for discussion of the impact of digitalization on religion out there in public culture has actually been about something else. It has actually been commentary on the importance of digital change for tradition, authority, authenticity, and "the received." This is obvious to astute observers who look at such commentary and coverage for insights into religion and find that the understanding of religion therein is often superficial, misplaced, or actually misleading.

This all describes a situation where digital media have evolved with important, even world-changing implications for religion, but with a need for a broadened scholarly and lay discourse of digital religion. And two important dimensions of this discourse are clear. First, to account for these changes in ways that will actually contribute to knowledge and to the evolution and understanding and critique of practice, this discourse must understand religion. This means that it must account for religion in ways outside the formalism and essentialism that typify much garden-variety commentary about it. Religion is actually a range of things, many of which have little to do with what received discourse suggests constitutes it. It is far more than the doctrines or histories or truth claims of any particular faith tradition. It is more than the symbolic and narrative resources approved or promoted by clerical authority. It is even more than a quest for "the numinous" or for transcendence. As contemporary religion scholarship has learned, we must try to understand it through its practices, through the aspirations of its adherents and—most importantly—through the cultural "work" being performed through its practice, and what is therefore accomplished and in what domains.

The second way discourse about digital religion must move ahead is in its appreciation of how religion (in the range of valences I've just suggested) is, in fact, being expressed, understood, and performed through digital media. This is a complex and challenging task, not least because it must account for religion in all the ways it is significant in, and to, modern globalized cultures. Such work must be smart and sophisticated about media change, but also about religious change. It must understand the religion "object" in a way that can account for, and hold in tension, the impulses and meanings surrounding it, in ways that can chart the contribution it makes to digital media and that it receives from these media practices. Media are doubly articulated into such social spaces, contributing important things to both the way we do things and to the way we think about the things we do. As a cultural dimension deeply connected with consciousness and identity, religion therefore is uniquely implied by changes in ways of knowing, seeing, and communicating.

This is all a tall order. This volume is an important and substantive waypoint on the quest for better understanding. The contributions here address both of the dimensions I've raised above. Religion is well understood here on its own terms, and these authors understand that the questions are not about the impact of digitalization on some received notion of religion-as-tradition or religion-as-past, but are instead about how religion is constituted today in new ways through digital cultures. These works are therefore well-placed to be able to address the primary goal of helping us understand the actual contribution that "the digital" is making to "the religious." They are impressive for their range of inquiry. Some address large theoretical themes, others look at particular and specific settings. The question of digital religion is a large and complex question, and that fact is well-represented by the range of work here.

This work will thus prove valuable as a landmark in this field. The most convincing evidence of this is that its works contain within them provocative markers of the way forward, both directly and in the intriguing questions they leave unanswered. Because of their substance and success, we can use this occasion to think about some of the larger themes that are implied here and that will increasingly occupy us as this scholarly discourse moves forward.

From my privileged position of having had an advance peek at these pages, I'd like to point to a few of these themes.

First, there is the issue of "the new." Because, as many have noted, all religions are mediated in a variety of ways, entirely fresh and novel forms seem to have particular importance and potential. While we should not essential-ize religion, as I have said, and certainly should not essentialize the notion of mediation in relation to religion, we do nonetheless need to understand the extent to which new forms of mediation have real affordances and potentiali-ties. There is a self-fulfilling dimension to this. Communication and mediation are processes that are open to all of us. It is the nature of human community. So reflection and awareness about communication and mediation is also open to all of us, and some of the "effect" of "the new" comes from practices that adopt it or accommodate to it because it *is* new. We also tend to think that authority, particularly religious authority, will be resistant to the new. But the situation is often more complex. As the introduction here notes in relation to the much-touted "Confession App" for iOS devices, rather than rejecting this idea outright, clerical authority in Catholicism found a way to negotiate a version of it that it found acceptable.

Second, there is the issue of the scale of change that accompanies these developments. Much of the early work on digital, web, and internet religion assumed that the most important implications were in the wholesale remak-ing of religion or in the emergence of entirely new religious movements and expressions in online environments. As is also demonstrated in these pages, important changes can be underway at entirely different scales or levels. And, more important, perhaps, is the insight that we might best look for reformu-lation of existing practices rather than more radical change.

Third is an issue that I have already mentioned, but that is not explicitly addressed in these pages: the problem of authenticity. Implicit in our sense of the religious is a persistent concern about the "authentic," and about what of the "authentic" (Durkheim's "mechanical solidarity") might be traded away as technologies interpose themselves in social relations, identity practices, community, ritual practices, and framings of "the sacred." It is true that for our knowledge- and theory-building on religion and media (and by extension, on religion and digital media) to advance in recent years, it has been necessary to leave this question aside. And, I am certainly not saying that there is some essential "authenticity" that should be the mea-sure by which emergent practices are judged. But at the same time, there are good intellectual reasons to wonder about how, and under what cir-cumstances, senses of "the authentic" are formed, stabilized, circulated, and enforced, and the ways that new media forms condition these processes.

Fourth, there is a whole package of issues under the general heading of *reflexivity*, or *self-consciousness*. The work here persuasively demonstrates that much of what makes digital practices of "the religious" possible is the reflexive engagement of those practitioners. We are active in creating and inhabiting our senses of the religious and the spiritual, and we work to maintain those conditions, symbols, boundaries, and practices. There are abundant examples of this here. The whole sense that it is the "affordances" of these media implies that we are "hailed" into subjectivities which articulate with them.

I'd like to tease out some dimensions of this issue of reflexivity that appear here. These are what McLuhan used to call "probes:" not completely fleshed out, but provocative and indicative. There is a sense that reflexive engagement here is not just about individual action and motivation, or about individual identity, but is also a public act. The way that digital media are used in ways that "frame" symbols, values, or truth claims is an example of this. Even more important is the way that, like the older "screen" media, digital media can be seen to be used to project religious claims and values into a public sphere, and through that, a sense of ascendance for those particular claims and values may result.

There is also the sense that whatever work is about self and identity here, we are hailed into a subjectivity of empowerment and autonomy by the nature of digital practice. That we are encouraged to think of ourselves as "produsers" has a number of important implications. It is clearly not just about solipsistic self-absorption and cultural isolation. The contributions here also underscore a different perspective on the issue of the "privatization" or "de-privatization" of religion. Often, it is assumed that public culture and commodification have resulted in a kind of involuntary "de-privatization" of the purely religious. At least in digital culture, what we tend to see instead is a voluntary, affirmative impulse to what has been called "public-ization." We seem to want to share what we have made, culturally, out of our media practices, and the technology conditions such sharing.

There is, finally, a sense here that religious and spiritual practices in digital culture reflexively involve negotiated subjectivities that are both autonomous and submissive to various forms of authority. At the same time that digital culture enforces a discourse of autonomy and prosumption, we can also see evidence of consumption that is positioned to subject itself to authority. Websites sponsored by conventional religious bodies that clearly articulate those bodies' values and goals, nonetheless encourage a conditional autonomy. It's a negotiation, and one where practice can alternatively evidence autonomous action and submission to history, doctrine, or authority. So, it's not only one or the other, and it is a self-conscious, reflexive negotiation that makes either work.

Fifth, this brings us to the question of authority itself, a topic that deserves several volumes of its own. These chapters ably demonstrate many manifest and latent ways that authority is clearly challenged by emergent digital cultures. I use the term "cultures" here advisedly in that the implications for authority lie not in structural concerns (i.e., who actually owns and controls these proliferating media channels) though those are important. Digital media contest authority because they enable, encourage, and interact with a wide range of social and cultural contexts and practices. They are coming to be integrated into personal, economic, civic, educational, and public life. They modulate and condition the ways that many legacy media work. Thus, their implications transcend simple questions of which channels are used by whom with what effect.

Instead, their implications are becoming broadly cultural. Doctrinal authority thus faces new forms and sources of symbolic and narrative resources. Clerical authority faces new locations, communities, and means of practice. But the fundamental challenge to authority lies more subtly and broadly in the reflexivity I've noted as a fundamental feature of the situation. Both of Weber's categories of "traditional" and "charismatic" authority depend to an extent on the complicity of adherents and communities of practice. That is, publics must in a sense choose to take up subject positions in relation to authority. This is, of course, an entirely modernist reading of tradition, but one that is more obvious to us now in part because of our social experience with the new means of communication that have emerged since the 19th Century.

In the digital age, adherents, audiences, listeners, communities of shared practice and shared memory, and various "publics" are now active in the production, circulation, imbrication, selection, and re-making of "the religious" and "the spiritual." It's not just that authority faces competition from new sources, it's that the whole mode of practice that defines cultural participation today operates on logics that put authority in a different place than in the past. The inventory of resources and practices through which religion and spirituality are known and done today is an increasingly "horizontal" inventory, where the traditional sources exist alongside a range of other ones. But, more importantly, those who turn to that inventory are increasingly finding themselves empowered to both contribute to it in new ways and to think critically about who is responsible for each of those resources.

This is not to say that tradition and doctrine are no longer important. In some ways they are more important than ever. Indeed, as we see in these pages, many people look to imputed "authentic" resources as particularly valuable for their authenticity, history, and tradition. It's just that those resources are today consumed conditionally and within a context of practice that puts power in the hands of the interpretive and active communities of the digital age.

That is the fundamental reality of the religious and the spiritual in an age increasingly defined by the new means of communication. There is much more to be learned and known about the implications of all of this, and this book lays critical groundwork for scholarship on digital religion and digital spirituality.

1. Introduction: Religion 2.0? Relational and Hybridizing Pathways in Religion, Social Media, and Culture

Pauline Hope Cheong and Charles Ess

Religion 2.0?

"Religion 2.0" can be aptly introduced by the example of *Confession: A Roman Catholic App* for the iPhone and iPad (Little i Apps, 2011). For the relatively modest price of $1.99, *Confession* invites users to confess, and keep track of, their sins. As we will discuss in this chapter, it is enormously significant that *Confession* is *not* marketed as a complete and virtual replacement for a central rite in the Roman Catholic tradition. Rather, as the *Confession* description on iTunes carefully points out:

> The text of this app was developed in collaboration with Rev. Thomas G. Weinandy, OFM, Executive Director of the Secretariat for Doctrine and Pastoral Practices of the United States Conference of Catholic Bishops, and Rev. Dan Scheidt, pastor of Queen of Peace Catholic Church in Mishawaka, IN. The app received an imprimatur from Bishop Kevin C. Rhodes of the Diocese of Fort Wayne—South Bend. It is the first known imprimatur to be given for an iPhone/iPad app. (ibid.)

In this way, *Confession* is careful to make explicit how far it is integrally interwoven with both the traditions and relevant authoritative hierarchy of the Roman Catholic Church. Moreover, *Confession* users are reminded that in order to receive absolution for their sins, they will still need to take the matter up with a real priest in a real church. *Confession* is hence clearly still rooted within the ancient practices and structures of the Roman Catholic Church, and, if anything, seeks to reinforce and enhance those structures and practices rather than call them into question, much less seek to overturn them.

Confession represents and exemplifies larger trends that emerge across the course of this volume on digital religion, new media, and culture. Here, we and our contributors examine how far "religion"—meaning, minimally, the individual and institutionalized practices, values, and beliefs that make up specific religious traditions—interacts with the multiple affordances and possibilities of computer-mediated communication, most especially those affiliated with Web 2.0. We understand these to include social media especially, such as social networking sites (Facebook), blogs and micro-blogs (Twitter), sites featuring user-generated content (YouTube and Wikipedia), and virtual worlds and online games (*Second Life* and *World of Warcraft*). Most broadly, *contrary* to 1990s' theory and rhetoric that emphasized radical distinctions between the (online) virtual and the (offline) real—so that, for example, some might argue that a virtual church or a virtual practice such as *Confession* could fully *replace* their offline, real-world counterparts and connection points— Religion 2.0 by and large represents an amalgamation and assemblage of real- and virtual-world practices. To be sure—and in keeping with much of the hype surrounding Web 2.0 as ostensibly ushering in a new age of radical individualism and thereby greater freedom, equality, and democracy— the affordances and practices of Web 2.0 media in many ways profoundly challenge more traditional structures, norms, and practices. At the same time, however, these challenges—with few but notable exceptions—issue less in radical revolution, and more in transformation and reconfiguration of existing practices, beliefs, and infrastructures. These findings, moreover, are consistent with similar patterns noted in the broader fields of new media and intercultural communication (Cheong, Martin, & Macfadyen, 2012) and Internet Studies (Ess & Consalvo, 2011). So it is, then, that *Confession* seeks to complement and amplify, but ultimately reinforce—not replace—an ancient religious practice.

To see how this is so, we begin with a brief note on the origins of this volume, as an entrée into the larger conceptual matters and issues that constitute the frameworks of the volume. We will then briefly introduce the chapters themselves, as organized into three sections: "Theorizing Digital Religion," "Empirical Investigations," and "Historical and Theological Examinations." Following this, we will explicate three major themes that cut across the organizational boundaries of the sections, namely, *identity, community*, and *authority*. Specifically, we articulate a dialectical perspective in digital religion and culture, by identifying central tensions and highlighting multiple interdependent links that are characteristic of what Schement and Stephenson (1996) noted as "unavoidable frictions" and "endemic tensions" in mediated religious practice. We will explore how specific chapters contribute to these relational and hybridizing dynamics with the three major themes, as part of our developing a broader understanding of Religion 2.0.

Origins

Our volume has its beginnings at the Church and Mission in a Multireligious Third Millennium conference, held at Aarhus University, Denmark (January 27–29, 2010). The co-editors of this book collaborated on the organization and presentation of a paper session and a panel, entitled *Church in Cyberspace* and *Church and Social Media*, respectively, in which we emphasized attention—theoretical, theological, and empirical—to social media and religion in particular. Inspired by both Knut Lundby's keynote for the conference— included here in revised form—as well as by our initial findings as collected in the panel presentations, we thought it might be time for an anthology focusing on what we now call Religion 2.0, i.e., the manifold interactions between, on the one hand, diverse expressions and institutions affiliated with religious traditions and practices around the globe, and, on the other, the equally diverse and rapidly changing affordances and possibilities of Web 2.0. Our thoughts on the timeliness of such an anthology were reinforced by the fact that it has now been over seven years since the appearance of a major volume dedicated to religion and CMC (Computer Mediated Communication). Happily, Mary Savigar and Steve Jones at Peter Lang agreed that a collection on Religion 2.0 would be worth pursuing as part of their Digital Formations series. And so, in addition to encouraging panel contributors to develop their presentations into suitable chapters, we issued an open call for papers and also invited key figures in the field of religion and CMC to participate. Very happily, the result is what we like to think of as a symbiosis between younger and more seasoned scholars and researchers.

The first section, "Theorizing Digital Religion," begins with a revised version of Knut Lundby's keynote speech, *Dreams of Church in Cyberspace*. Lundby took up a media sociological perspective, one that focused more closely on the *content* of messages rather than their medium. Lundby was thereby able to critique more enthusiastic claims for cyberspace, virtual communities, etc., in ways that are directly relevant to the Church's interest in mission.

Bernie Hogan and Barry Wellman echo and reinforce Lundby's critiques by way of a larger historical overview of Internet Studies. As the title suggests, "The Immanent Internet Redux" argues against 1990s' claims of a radical divorce between the real and the virtual, the offline and the online—a divorce that would otherwise issue a "transcendent Internet." While instances of such a divorce can be found, the prevailing trends are in the opposite direction— again, as our opening example of *Confession* suggests—towards complementary relationships and resonance between offline and online.

Pushing beyond familiar notions of Web 2.0, Bala A. Musa and Ibrahim M. Ahmadu seek to build a more complex and holistic model of contemporary communication. Their "New Media, Wikifaith and Church Brandversation" focuses specifically on "Wikifaith" as "people-centered, people-cultivated," vis-à-vis specific processes of "brandversation," i.e., the diverse processes that shape specific churches and their sense of identity, as they perceive the need to establish themselves as brands in a market-oriented, pluralistic society. One of their central questions is how far the church can learn to sell itself in this new environment—but without selling out entirely and becoming simply another commodity shaped entirely by the casual needs and interests of "prosumers" (p. 75). It is worth noting here that Peter Fischer-Nielsen and Stefan Gelfgren highlight precisely this theme of ever-growing commercialization as a major point of concern and research in their concluding chapter.

In her "How Religious Communities Negotiate New Media Religiously," Heidi Campbell raises these and related core issues concerning how religious institutions—and individuals—can retain something of their traditions and identities in contemporary (and, as Musa and Ahmadu remind us, increasingly commercialized and commercializing) communication environments. Rather than addressing these questions head on, Campbell instead gives us an account of her "religious-social shaping of technology" theory, a framework developed to illuminate the complex interactions between religious communities and new communication technologies. These foundations thereby reinforce—now at a theoretical level—our broader theme of how far online religion is shaped by its offline points of origin and return.

Jørgen Straarup takes up some of the most intriguing possibilities of new media and Web 2.0—what he calls "avatar religion." His analysis in "When Pinocchio Goes to Church: Exploring an Avatar Religion" suggests that despite the revolutionary potential of new media, even avatars seek community—community that appears to require precisely the (sometimes very) traditional, real-world communities and practices that serve as the origins and destinations of their virtual counterparts.

As its title "Empirical Investigations," suggests, chapters in the second section intend to balance and complement our theoretical beginnings with what can be known empirically about contemporary practices and patterns. So, we begin with Peter Fischer-Nielsen, whose "Pastors on the Internet: Online Responses to Secularization" summarizes his extensive analysis of how Danish pastors respond to the communicative possibilities of Web 2.0. Fischer-Nielsen's research highlights three possible strategies for responding to the challenges new media and Web 2.0 bring in their wake—most bluntly, in terms of a threat of secularization (a threat already felt strongly in highly secular Denmark, where only ca. 4% of the population attend a church on a regular basis).

Contra the tendencies, even today, to hype new media as *new* and thereby *revolutionary*, Lorenzo Cantoni and his colleagues approach the appropriation of new media by the Roman Catholic Church as a "normal stage" in the development of the Church's activities. Their study, utilizing an international survey, is distinctive, as they interrogate precisely the primary representatives of the church hierarchy—namely, priests and bishops—regarding their understandings of, and responses to, new media. Their quantitative analysis thereby nicely complements the more external analysis of Catholic media usage provided by Campbell.

In "Voting 'Present': Religious Organization Groups on Facebook," Mark D. Johns examines how individuals interact with Facebook groups initiated by diverse religious organizations. Contrary to the hopes of some—i.e., that the more interactive media of Web 2.0 might "empower" individuals to shape, and participate more extensively in, the lives of institutions, including congregations—Johns finds instead that those who join such groups usually just stop there. That is, their action amounts to little more than hitting the "join" or "like" button in Facebook; no further engagement follows. While these actions are of symbolic significance, as they mark and index individuals' religious identity, Johns' findings also serve as a reality check for those institutions that hope that if they make themselves apparent online via such groups, more engagement with their real-world communities will follow.

In their case study, Stine Lomborg and Charles Ess reinforce and complement Johns' findings. The title of their chapter, "'Keeping the Line Open and Warm': An Activist Danish Church and Its Presence on Facebook," quotes a young pastor who deftly uses the social networking site to maintain and refresh extant relationships with congregants. But, as we will discuss more fully below, church leaders and congregants have responded to the various ways that such media may challenge traditional authority and hierarchies with a renegotiation process that takes on board some of the affordances of the new media, but only insofar as these complement and reinforce the real-world community.

Pauline Hope Cheong's "Twitter of Faith: Understanding Social Media Networking and Microblogging Rituals as Religious Practices" focuses on how believers seek to appropriate and exploit micro-blogs such as Twitter for a variety of community-building purposes, including evangelism, mediation, and prayer. Echoing the thematic of "church as brand," Cheong finds that blogging practices contribute to the construction of "faith brands," as such practices encourage both loyalty to church leadership as well as church growth through evangelism. The chapter also discusses some of the potential advantages of microblogging as a religious practice, as well as its more shady side, and suggests multiple areas for future research.

The last chapter in this section, by Tim Hutchings, represents one of the most extensive investigations into online churches through participant-observation methodology that we know of. His "Creating Church Online:

Networks and Collectives in Contemporary Christianity" begins with a solid historical overview of research in these domains, and then turns to close inquiry into five of the best-known examples of online church. Echoing many of the chapters in this volume, as well as, as we have begun to see, larger trends in Internet Studies over the past decade or so, Hutchings finds that "These online groups may be viewed as communities, but also as components in wider collectives of digital and local religious activity, and as connections in the self-constructed religious networks of their visitors" (p. 221).

Our third and last section, "Historical and Theological Examinations," broadens our attention out to the longer histories of media and religion, and to careful efforts to examine both historical and contemporary interactions between religion and media in theological terms. We open with Stefan Gelfgren's " 'Let There Be Digital Networks and God Will Provide Growth?' Comparing Aims and Hopes of 19th-Century and Post-Millennial Christianity." Gelfgren's comparison between expectations, hopes—and fears—surrounding the introduction of new media in the 19th century (e.g., printed tracts) and those familiar from more recent times, as inspired by the emergence of social media, is a salutary counter to early claims about the latter as, for example, perhaps the most revolutionary event since the invention of fire (John Perry Barlow, 1996). Gelfgren further expands on the attention we've seen paid to how churches are goaded to negotiate new media use within a highly commercialized, consumer-driven marketplace that demands branding and competition (Musa & Ibrahim; Cheong).

Peter Horsfield's " 'A Moderate Diversity of Books?' The Challenge of New Media to the Practice of Christian Theology" turns us directly towards theology. Horsfield uses the now well-known framework of communication theory that we have drawn on from the outset—as developed by the likes of McLuhan, Innis, and Eisenstein, and especially Walter Ong—so as to approach human cultural history in terms of four primary communication technologies, namely *orality*, *literacy*, and *print*, and then the *secondary orality* of electric media (cf. Ess, 2010). Horsfield draws a picture of how Christian theology is transformed in foundational ways as theology itself begins in the oral culture of the earliest Christian message, and then makes its way through the succeeding shifts. Connecting his account focusing on theology, and the broader account we develop here, would indeed be a most useful and interesting exercise for the reader.

Sam Han helpfully takes up a different media theory—that of Friedrich Kittler—vis-à-vis the specific Christian notion of human beings as *imago Dei*, the image of God. Focusing specifically on the computer as the site for developing and extending artificial intelligence, Han argues that the upshot will be an "immanentization" of the *imago Dei*.

Lynne Baab concludes this section with theological attention to the three specific topoi identified in her title, "Toward a Theology of the Internet: Place, Relationship, and Sin." In particular, her observation that the individualism otherwise hyped as an unalloyed good in the rhetoric surrounding Web 2.0 (as well as Web 1.0) intersects with traditional theological concerns about sin—e.g., addictive, and other, destructive behaviors potentially facilitated through the affordances of Web 2.0 as the medium of the networked *individual*—is a sobering counterpoint that helps deflate such hype with a more critical view. At the same time, Baab's discussion provides us with yet one more instance of how new media fosters at least certain kinds of individualism that directly challenge more traditional claims of religious institutions.

The concluding chapter by Peter Fischer-Nielsen and Stefan Gelfgren takes up the work collected in this volume as both grounds and springboard for six trajectories of future research. Among these is the thematic concern with how the increasingly commercialized environments of Web 2.0 interact with our expectations and uses of new media. Such concerns, we can note, are not limited to frameworks, values, and practices shaped solely by religious institutions and traditions. Rather, several noted researchers in the broader fields of Internet Studies have raised similar concerns in recent years—most notably, perhaps, as Sonja Livingstone puts it, with regard to how our increasing engagements in proprietary SNSs and other new media environments leads not simply to our giving away our data for the sake of commercial interests, but, more fundamentally, to our collaborating in processes of *commodifying* ourselves and our identities according to the prevailing market categories and tastes that "sell" (Livingstone, 2011, p. 354; cf. Baym, 2011, pp. 399f.; van Dijck, 2010). Such commodification would seem to warrant the attention and concern of both the secular and religious alike. In addition, Fischer-Nielsen and Gelfgren highlight several other developments that inspire further research, such as the rise of ever more mobile and personalized digital media, which provide more sophisticated and interactive infrastructures, and the globalization of digital religion.

Religion in the Age of Web 2.0—An Initial Survey

As an initial effort to develop a larger understanding of what the work collected here may suggest more broadly regarding Religion 2.0, we begin with a provisional understanding of Web 2.0. We take this rubric as intending to denote a qualitative jump (from Web 1.0, ca. 1992–2005) to new levels of interactivity and individual expression, and the emergence of the hybrid producer-consumer or "produser" (Bruns, 2008) as facilitated by a range of technological advances (such as ever-increasing and ever more widely available bandwidth and mobility of computational devices, most notably Internet-enabled mobile phones and tablets), ongoing developments in new/digital media (including the convergence of digital photo- and video-cameras in said mobile phones), and in computer-mediated communication itself. The latter typically include sites that feature, and ostensibly foster, user-generated content in diverse forms, such as YouTube; social networking sites (SNS); blogs and micro-blogs, such as Twitter, that invite ongoing, potentially instantaneous interaction between posters; new arrays of virtual worlds such as Second Life and Massively Multiplayer Online Games (MMOGs) such as World of Warcraft; and a bewildering and ever-growing array of variations on these, ranging from "citizen journalism" as interwoven with more traditional news formats (and their still well-known corporations), to the use of social media in so-called "soft revolutions" (and some not so soft revolutions, as are currently being battled in the Middle East), and everything in between (e.g., sites and interactive venues dedicated to specific interests and hobbies, ranging from knitting to music to child pornography to racist hate groups). Along the way, our smartphones use GPS technology not only to connect efficiently to our mobile networks for the sake of an SMS or even a phone call, but also—whether voluntarily (as in Foursquare, or Google's Latitude) or involuntarily (as in Apple's recently unveiled practice of collecting our locations in a hidden file, ostensibly for the purposes of greater efficiency)—to constantly update our physical location.

All of this is made even more complicated by the rapid growth and diffusion of the internet and the web world-wide. At the time of writing, nearly two billion people or ca. 29% of the world's population now enjoy some form of internet access (Internet World Stats, 2011). In the face of the harsh realities of our contemporary world—often brought to us with unedited immediacy and clarity precisely by mobile phones recording history in the making—the 1990s' utopian language of "an electronic global village" is heard less frequently. Rather, the global diffusion of these new media has made cross-cultural encounters all but inevitable—and, as the Mohammed Cartoon Crisis of 2006 demonstrates (Ess, 2009), not all of these encounters are peaceful and salutary.

In sum, in the age of Web 2.0 we are "always on" (Baron, 2008) and interconnected globally and cross-culturally. And in the midst of all of this—again, as the 2006 Cartoon Crises exemplifies—"religion" (another difficult and contested term) is often deeply at work and in play. In particular, specific characteristics of Web 2.0 technologies are lifted up as affordances that will surely challenge traditional institutions—including religious institutions. Most centrally: to begin with, the *interactivity* of Web 2.0 applications—the capacity of ordinary users to respond to, and indeed create, new media expressions on their own—is often claimed to lead us in the direction of greater freedom of expression and equality, and thereby greater democracy. This means, in particular, that tensions emerge as these affordances, insofar as they are realized, challenge traditional forms of authority as top-down and hierarchical.

These claims in turn lead to central thematic questions in the latest phase of research on religion online, such as, as the use of CMC becomes increasingly de rigueur, and an expected, if not major, component of how religious institutions communicate with congregants—most especially young people—will not the various forms of *identity, community,* and *authority* necessarily be called into radical question? The 15 chapters in our book formulate such questions from a variety of theoretical, historical, and theological contexts, and provide empirical investigations in a variety of specific ways. Collectively, these chapters contribute stimulating insights into the dialectics of digital religion as they intertwine with emergent tensions in the contested areas of individual and relational identity, community networks, and authority performances and paradoxes.

Identity: Individual, Ephemeral and Relational Selves

It is often claimed that functionalities highlighted under Web 2.0 apparently foster greater interactivity, equality, and democracy. But it is worth reconsidering how these functionalities in turn rest upon—and perhaps influence foundational transformations in—our sense of *self,* or identity.

To be sure, these claims for Web 2.0 are familiar to those of us who remember the rhetoric and debate of the 1990s (Ess, 2011; Wellman, 2011, pp. 17–20). And so, with the beginnings of what Wellman identified as the "third age" of Internet Studies (ibid., 21f.), we find the initial suggestions of how our interactions with CMC technologies were issuing in new conceptions of self and identity. Captured in notions of "networked individualism"—findings from Castells (2001) and Wellman (2001), as highlighted by Knut Lundby in his opening chapter here—and in what Wellman and Haythornthwaite identified as "the networked individual" (2002), these notions represent something of an amalgam between modernist notions of the individual self (especially as affiliated with *literacy* and *print* as media technologies), and postmodern notions of multiple, fluid, but also ephemeral selves, with the latter, especially, documented in the work of Sherry Turkle (1984, 1995, 2010) and often argued to be fostered by CMC venues, beginning with the MUDs and MOOs whose denizens Turkle closely studied.

As Lundby points out, such individualism, however moderated and/ or amplified by ever increasing networked interactivity, facilitates direct challenges to traditional religious institutions—certainly, within the

Christian traditions, those of the Roman Catholic Church. Even Protestant churches—historically, those built on giving the individual "greater voice," as Lundby puts it—"are definitely being challenged." The upshot, as Lundby points out succinctly, is that "Churches as institutions are in trouble" (this volume, p. 36).

At the same time, however, several studies in this volume also highlight both individual and institutional *resistance* in various forms to these challenges—as we will see below, when we turn to the theme of *authority*. Here, however, we can point out, to begin with, that in their study of a progressive Danish Lutheran church, Lomborg and Ess document both a strong individual and institutional commitment to the traditional Protestant values of equality and individualism. In part, it was this commitment that encouraged the church's ministers and some enthusiastic laity to pursue the development of a Facebook page. Yet both ministers and at least one informant made clear that they also wanted to preserve a good deal of the traditional hierarchy and boundary between the ministers, as professionals and authorities representing the institutions and roles of the traditional church, and congregants. In light of the question of *identity* in Religion 2.0, this would suggest that whatever the affordances of Web 2.0, at least some of its users wish to maintain something of the traditional boundaries and structures of the church—boundaries that appear to delimit the authority of the individual as a member of a religious community and institution.

On the one hand, these findings are in keeping with other research and analyses that suggest that the shifts we appear to be witnessing towards more relational or networked selves—shifts that are fostered precisely by networked technologies, and most especially several of the venues characteristic of Web 2.0, such as SNSs, micro-blogs, and virtual worlds (Cheong & Gray, 2011; Ess, 2010; Gergen, 2011)—are nonetheless neither inexorable nor unlimited. That is, such shifts towards more networked or relational selves do *not* automatically mean (as they did for some 1990s pundits) the end of the modernist conception of the individual (Rodogno, 2011). Rather, what may be emerging is some sort of hybrid notion of identity, one that conjoins a modernist understanding that emphasizes individual rationality and autonomy with a "post-post-modernist" understanding that emphasizes relationality, multiplicity, affect, and ephemerality. And, as we have indicated from the outset, such a hybrid self would be in keeping with the larger patterns discerned over the past decade (and more) in Internet Studies. That is, as Klaus Bruhn Jensen concisely notes, "Old media rarely die, and humans remain the reference point and prototype for technologically mediated communication" (2011, p. 44). And thereby, insofar as our use of diverse media technologies can be correlated with distinctive notions of selves—i.e., a modernist notion of the rational individual as affiliated with the technologies of *literacy* and *print*, vis-à-vis a post(post)modernist notion of the self as fluid, multiple, and ephemeral, as affiliated with what Walter Ong characterized as the "secondary orality" of "electric media" (meaning: radio, movies, TV, and, at least to some degree, CMC)—our learning to conjoin literacy and print with secondary orality would correlate with just such a hybrid self (Ess, 2010).

On the other hand, as Baab's analysis suggests, one of the key questions to emerge here is what *kind* of individualism is fostered in Web 2.0? At the risk of oversimplification—but reflecting central dialectical tensions in the emergence of the modern self (cf. Taylor, 1989, pp. 495–521)—we can distinguish between two emphases of individualism, namely, a more rationally oriented autonomy vis-à-vis a more emotive (and, perhaps, more relational) individualism. The more rationally oriented, autonomous individual is highlighted in modernity, both in affiliation with modern conceptions of democratic-liberal regimes, and in Protestant and Catholic traditions that have been deeply influenced by the critical rationalism of modern Enlightenment. Such individuals, finally, seem to depend upon the technologies of literacy and print—including writing, which was described by the late Foucault as a "technology of the self" (Bakardjieva & Gaden, in press). By contrast, as the secondary orality of electric media and CMC brings about a return of a more complete human sensorium—including sight and sound—it is thereby able to powerfully appeal to our emotions in ways that are more difficult for texts (Turkle, 2010).

Indeed, Cheong (2010) discusses how microblogging rituals may create a new textual and visual sensorium by restructuring wired believers' consciousness, and generating a heightened awareness of relationship between the I, You, and the Thou, which opens up possibilities for revitalised religiosity to counteract claims of secularisation in technologically advanced and developed countries. In this light, it may not be accidental that those Protestant traditions that emphasize emotive experiences—e.g., of being "born again"—are characteristically among the early adopters and adapters of electric media and CMC technologies, in contrast with the comparatively conservative approaches to these media in the more rationally oriented Protestant and Catholic traditions (cf. Bernice Martin, 1998, 2001, cited in Straarup, this volume, p. 106). Insofar as these correlations hold, then, a key question for religious communities is, what *kind* of individuals and individualism do we wish (or need) to foster, and how do we use both traditional and new media to do so?

More broadly, however, the internet and the web have been with us for less than 20 years. It is by no means clear whether resistances such as those we see documented here indicate long-term trends, or simply suggest generational differences that will pass as the older generations take their leave of this good Earth—and with them, older, more modernist notions of the individual may also pass away.

Community: Networked Individualism, Sociality and Collectivism

Of course, as the (re)emergence of the networked and relational self in conjunction with the emergence of networked media emphasizes, our notions of self and identity are inextricably interwoven with our basic understandings and assumptions regarding how such selves may and/or must relate to larger communities. These interrelationships begin with human communities, ranging from the family, through national communities, to humanity at large. At the same time, religious traditions and frameworks stress how such communities and relationships further include, one way or another, the natural order and the sacred (whether as *transcendent*, as is stressed in most versions of the Abrahamic traditions of Judaism, Christianity, and Islam, or *immanent*, as is thematic of many Confucian, Buddhist, and Hindu traditions, for example). Very clearly, digital media facilitate and mediate social relations, including peoples' notions of relationship, patterns of belonging, and community—and in doing so, digital media thus immediately intersect with, and significantly impact, central religious concerns with (re)establishing right relationship or harmony in these various communities. Hence, several contributions within this book analyze the culture, connection, and activity emerging within particular online groups, as well as their role within wider religious networks and fields of activity.

So, to begin with, online churches have been historically studied as classic examples of "virtual communities," constituted as such by stable patterns of social meanings and personal relationships and largely self-contained as bounded groups with distinctive cultures. Equally historically, however, much of the rhetoric (if not simply hype) surrounding such virtual communities in the 1990s, celebrating how such communities would replace their real-world counterparts, has now been toned down. Empirical findings towards the end of the 1990s to the present have documented how far such virtual religious communities were intertwined with their offline communities (Cheong, Poon, Huang, & Casas, 2009; Ess, 2011). As part of these developments, the emergence of conceptions of the networked individual thereby highlighted both online and offline connections with larger communities.

In particular, Jørgen Straarup points out in this volume that even avatars seem to prefer community as rooted in real-world locations and practices. At the same time, as Knut Lundby suggests, our drive for community connections rests in part on a (somewhat Romantic) conception of *Gemeinschaft*, as defined by Tönnies ([1957] 1988; Lundby, this volume, p. 30). In this sense, another central tension thus emerges between the networked individual who—as Hogan and Wellman point out here—emerges as the portal seeking to control information flows and connections, and the communities of diverse relationships (often initially analyzed in terms of the contrast between weak-tie and strong-tie relationships) that such individuals thereby intercon-nect with. Hogan and Wellman's analysis of survey data over the past decade prompts the question: what are the implications of networked individualism for the definition and enactment of religious communities?

Tim Hutchings provides some initial insight as he documents several examples which indicate "the presence of a fluid, loosely networked sphere of Christian activity in Second Life, within which individuals circulate freely to find the people, places, and activities that appeal to them" (this volume, p. 218). Hutchings compares these circulation patterns with those described by Nancy Baym (2007) in terms of a "networked collectivism" in music fandom. As Baym (2007) put it, a form of digital sociality emerges here that lies "between the site-based online group and the egocentric network, distributing them-selves throughout a variety of sites in a quasi-coherent networked fashion . . . members move amongst a complex ecosystem of sites, building connections amongst themselves and their sites as they do." For Hutchings, this pattern "applies easily to the Christian population of Second Life," as "a kind of 'net-worked religious collective' that incorporates a wide array of often short-lived locations" (this volume, p. 218).

The ephemerality of such online relationships, as apparently discon-nected from offline, real-world communities (religious or otherwise), resonates with a second phenomenon described by Mark D. Johns in his wide-ranging exploration of religious groups on Facebook—or more spe-cifically, global groups on Facebook registered in the category of "religious organizations." Members were observed to join such groups as a way of voting affirmation for the group, its goals, and/or its creator, but almost no interaction took place within the groups. The research suggests that joining a Facebook group is a symbolic act for the purpose of declaring a religious identity for the user to those outside the group. Implications for faith groups include a warning that use of social networks also needs to focus on building relationships, not merely on building large lists of fans or followers. Yet the observation here about little interaction also raises a larger question about the nature of online religious collectives: in what ways and from what vantage points do we characterize the evolving nature of religious community, from the locus of Facebook group pages and/or individual Facebook pages?

A third insight offered here is found in Cheong's (2010) examination of the relatively recent phenomenon of religious microblogging. Cheong exam-ines the ways in which Twitter is appropriated by faith users to develop inno-vative and interactive forms of evangelization, prayer, and meditation, and discusses the implications of these new sociotechnical practices, termed here as "microblogging rituals," for religious community building. Specifically, Cheong argues that the creation and circulation of microblogging rituals, including "faith memes," functions to constitute and fuel the stream of lived sacred experiences, thereby ideologically connecting Twitter believers. Moreover, microblogging rituals facilitate the promotion of organized religion, as churches construct distinctive "faith brands" to publicize their mission and encourage loyalty to church leadership, and church growth.

In this way, Cheong's (2010) findings reinforce our opening examination of *Confession* as an example of contemporary media that is rooted in, and seeks to reinforce, real-world traditions and practices, not to replace them. These examples in turn stand in tension with the countervailing patterns highlighted by Hutchings and Johns that emphasize the ephemerality of online collectives and groups that are not otherwise rooted in real-world, offline communities. As with our initial findings concerning self and identity, the only thing we can say with assurance, as based on these investigations and insights, is that our notions of self, identity, and thereby interactions are not settled. Rather, we seem to see patterns of online interaction and media use that fit both a more (postmodern) sense of self, and thereby community, as multiple, fluid, ephemeral, and emotive, as well as a hybrid sense of self and community that encompasses both more modernist and traditional conceptions in (more or less) comfortable alliance with more postmodernist and contemporary conceptions and behaviors. In other words, the central dialectic between the freedom of the networked individual to engage in multiple but short-lived engagements online, vis-à-vis our clear interest to thereby *connect* with others in community, including in more stable, geographically located, and defined offline communities, is a tension still fully open, allowing and requiring further exploration.

We see this same tension, finally, in terms of our third and last theme.

Authority: Communicative Performances and Paradoxes

Religious authority can be understood and studied as a quality of communication, which in an electronic era, may be media-derived, discursively constructed, and dynamically constituted across digital media (Cheong, Huang, & Poon, 2011). A review by Cheong (in press) on studies exploring the relationships between the Internet and religious authority highlights that early studies in religion online conceptualized the Internet as a distinct and convivial space for spiritual interaction, and, as such, new flows of religious information and knowledge posed corrosive effects on the influence and jurisdiction of traditional religious authorities. The dominant logic associates offline religious authority with more static models of legitimation, and views the internet as promoting informational diversity and social fractures that are disruptive to the status quo. In lieu of traditional authorities, and within virtual communities, newer forms of web-based religious authorities such as web masters and forum moderators were proposed. Yet a more recent and alternative perspective is stimulated by the growing recognition of situating religious authority among older media and faith infrastructures. The internet may have, to some extent, facilitated changes in the personal and organizational basis by which religious leaders operate, but strategic practices by some clergy, including their engagement with digital and other forms of media, enable them to regain the legitimacy and trust necessary to operate in the religious ken.

Several of our chapters contribute to these contemporary themes and threads of authority research specifically, as they document how religious leaders are actively harnessing and appropriating new and social media for their individual cultivation and organizational practices. At the same time, in part just as new and social media challenge—as promised—traditional hierarchies and patterns of authority, religious leaders are caught up in an often complex and dynamic process of re-negotiating the authority they now seek to exercise in online, as well as offline, spheres, including possibly new institutional structures.

Here, some findings are in fact consistent with claims regarding Web 2.0, i.e., more of its interactive, ostensibly democratizing, features are made use of by comparatively less-hierarchical traditions, while more hierarchical traditions are better at resisting those democratizing features precisely in an effort to preserve traditional institutional structures of authority. As an example in this volume, Heidi Campbell documents here (building on her earlier work, including her analysis of "the Kosher cellphone" as developed for use within Ultra-orthodox Jewish communities: 2010, pp. 179–193) how more conservative religious traditions—specifically, the Roman Catholic Church—while embracing new media up to a certain point, at the same time seek to set clear boundaries on such media use so as to preserve foundational values, practices, and beliefs that would otherwise potentially be brought into question. So Campbell describes how the Catholic Church has shaped its uses of web-based communication technologies in line with the Church's formal hierarchy and clerical caste led by the Pope. On the one hand, yes, the Vatican website will generate automated email responses on the Pope's behalf. On the other hand, Vatican officials either disabled or removed such hallmark Web 2.0 features as the ranking function and comment mode on the Vatican YouTube channel, in order to preserve the Vatican's image and control of new media. More broadly, the Vatican site has historically functioned mostly as a massive text archive, one that thereby follows a "top-down," one-to-many broadcasting model. This usage highlights, perhaps not accidentally, the capacity of the web to serve as a text archive for the important documents of the Church, and thereby how far CMC remains close to the modernist conjunction of *literacy* and *print*. Such usage contrasts with the more fluid, if ephemeral (and emotive), "secondary orality" highlighted by Ong as characteristic of electric media and, up to a point at least, the more interactive dimensions of Web 2.0 as we have seen exemplified in changing, perhaps hybridizing, notions of self, identity, and community.

Indeed, as Campbell further points out, these more conservative uses of the Internet and the Web contrast with what we might characterize as more aggressive uses among, especially, Evangelical communities,[1] including SNSs, micro-blogs such as Twitter, etc., as these make greater use of interactive features. And betwixt and between these diverse institutional and denominational trends and patterns, more recent scholarship has proposed redefinitions of the constitutions and practices of religious authority to account for fresh ways in which it is flourishing in increasingly integrated new and social media platforms.

In our volume, Peter Horsfield documents one of the major directions or trends of Web 2.0, namely, that the "distributed and decentralized patterns of new media communication have increased the potential for a diversity of voices rather than an authorized few to project themselves and their opinions into the marketplace." Consequently, "the previously recognized criteria of religious authority, such as formal qualifications or institutional position, are changing to more fluid characteristics applied by audiences, such as a person's charisma, accessibility, and perceived cultural competence" (this volume, p. 225). In this sense, there appear to be temporal changes in the modes of authority production as some religious leaders expand the scope of their calling and restructure their roles to use social media such as Twitter to extend their outreach and influence (Cheong, 2011). Other contributors here likewise highlight how religious institutions and authority figures manage to both take up new communication possibilities while simultaneously retaining much of their earlier authority and status.

As a first example, Peter Fischer-Nielsen shows how far Google, Facebook, and YouTube have been integrated into the working lives of pastors. In an analysis of results from a survey completed by 1040 pastors of the Evangelical Lutheran Church in Denmark, he found that 95% of the pastors are online daily, and a significant proportion (94% of the pastors aged between 25 and 39 years) regard the Internet as having a positive influence on their work. But this is in part, it would seem, insofar as these new media work to complement and reinforce traditional practices, rather than challenge or overturn them. So: two-thirds of the respondents reported that the Internet had "caused more frequent contact with parishioners," and most endorsed "flesh and blood" "real church practice" in lieu of cyberchurch rituals and Web-based services (this volume, p. 127). The creators of *Confession* would be pleased.

Indeed, Cheong, Huang, and Poon (2011) have documented some of the complex processes that follow on churches taking up Web 2.0 media that initially facilitate challenges to traditional hierarchies and conceptions of authority. Significantly, their investigations highlight dialectical tensions in authority related to the countervailing tendencies in digital media negotiations. While online knowledge sources can provide laity with alternative resources that may encourage them to question their ministers' claims, beliefs, etc., these same sources also serve as a source of education that enhances a priest's epistemic authority, as the latter is able to move beyond dictating, to mediating between texts, i.e., Scripture as interpreted by the priest or minister, and alternative interpretations gleaned from Internet sources. In other words, "a paradox of epistemic authority is that it may be more effective when followers possess some level of knowledge that enables them to evaluate the legitimacy of clergy's knowledge" (2011, p. 1163). In still broader terms, these findings can be seen to suggest a hybridization of *literacy-print*, on the one hand, and secondary orality of electric media on the other hand. That is, in these re-negotiations of authority, a minister's knowledge of the Bible—the premier artifact of the printing revolution and, as increasingly available through print in standardized form to ever more readers, a main driver of the Protestant Reformation—at least on occasion still serves as a "stopper" vis-à-vis competing claims or views drawn from electronic (and thus more multiple but also more fluid) epistemic sources.

A last chapter from our volume also makes this point, in the Danish context. Stine Lomborg and Charles Ess note in their case study of an activist Danish church how the presence of the church on Facebook was praised in terms of its "brand value," signaling that the church is "progressive" (and thereby instantiates the "brandversation" described here by Musa and Ibrahim). But even as Facebook friendships may be relationally rewarding for leaders seeking to build closer relationships with their members, these leaders also highlighted tensions in the negotiation of authority; it is "a delicate balance to strike as this strategic presentation of the pastor as an ordinary person also possibly entails a risk of jeopardizing the professional respect and authority so important for a pastor in his work and leadership within the community" (this volume, p. 178). And so it is that the church leaders have come to recognize how far they can go in terms of blurring the boundary between clergy and laity via Facebook and other forms of electronic communication—and how far they must reinforce traditional roles and relationships, e.g., in part through continued use of traditional, print-based media in worship, beginning precisely with standard Bible readings and hymns as sung from traditional psalm books.

In these ways, we note in closing, these dialectics in the renegotiations of authority appear to correlate with parallel emergences of hybrid senses of self and identity, as we have examined above. That is, there clearly are many "hyperindividuals" who, as facilitated by networked communication media, prefer to spend much of their life online (often for very good reasons), exploring, developing, and then abandoning networked relationships that thus befit more postmodernist senses of selfhood as multiple, fluid, and ephemeral—and largely as disconnected with, and to the exclusion of, real-world relationships and identities. At the same time, however, just as religious institutions are learning to renegotiate traditional authority and structures of hierarchy in the face of the multiple ways Web 2.0 technologies facilitate challenges to these, so many congregants are apparently learning how to be both traditional selves (i.e., as marked by more singular, enduring, rational, selfhood and autonomy, as affiliated with literacy-print) and contemporary selves (as more multiple, fluid, ephemeral—and, perhaps, more emotive— as affiliated with new and digital media technologies).

In Vivo Religion 2.0 and Beyond

In closing, we note that the placement of a question mark behind the nomen-clature of digital religion evinces our reconsideration of the wholesale embrace of Web 2.0 on the one hand, and the critical examination of emerging and hybridizing patterns of change with regard to mediated faith practices on the other hand. The question mark is also, to use a customary expression, a journey, in which the ongoing enterprise begins here to make sense of how new and emerging practices of religion emend our comprehension of Religion 2.0 and beyond; as a process that encompasses the dynamic nature of cultural processes. And this is a significant journey that we undertake, together with our contributors, fueled by new technological vistas and the fertile landscape of prior scholarship. As Stewart Hoover and Knut Lundby (1997) presciently observed, we require more thoughtful attention toward a triadic understanding of media, religion, and culture, as these areas are "interpenetrated by one another" (p. 6). This volume thereby represents a cross-disciplinary venture to refine our understanding of the burgeoning social web of digital religion, with insights into the varied meanings of technology, in different cultural grounds. Humbly, the view here is that the road of learning and discovery goes on—the only certainty is that everything is in flux. But through these contributions, as now illuminated in terms of larger patterns and findings in contemporary Internet Studies, we hope our readers come away with at least a reasonably grounded theoretical and empirical (if not also theologically informed) understanding of how Religion 2.0 appears to work and function in the contemporary world.

Finally, we wish to express our deep thanks to our colleagues and families. It has been a mount of hard work, and a joy to work as an international editorial team. Of course, no single researcher or editor can hope to develop anything even approximating a clear and comprehensive picture of the vast and constantly changing landscape of digital religion, especially as a globally distributed phenomenon. But we are heartened by the results of this transnational and cross-cultural collaboration. That is not to say that we believe the results of our collaboration achieve completeness: it is to say that we believe our collective work results in a much broader view, one shaped by a much greater diversity of perspectives and experiences, than any of us could have achieved on our own. Such collaboration, of course—across diverse cultures, time zones, and disciplines—brings its own set of challenges as well. We wish to acknowledge with gratitude how enjoyable—and, at times, downright fun —this collaboration has been, thanks to the patience, perseverance, and good humor of each of our co-editors. It is our privilege to introduce this inspiring multidisciplinary volume to you.

Note

1. Readers should remember here that "Evangelical" in the U.S. context usually refers to those traditions— often also characterized as charismatic or Pentecostal—that highlight not simply mission (evangelism) but also emotive experiences of "being saved" as primary signs of religious authenticity, etc. By contrast, "Evangelical" in the European context usually refers to churches in Protestant, often specifically Lutheran, traditions. In the northern European context in particular, these churches rather stress modernist conceptions of rationality as critical elements in religious identity and reflection—again, as such rationality (and individual autonomy) correlates with the emphasis on literacy and print in modernity. (This is not to say that Evangelicalism—whether in the U.S., Europe, or elsewhere—is thoroughly modernist: on the contrary, Evangelicalism began in part in reaction against various expressions of modernity, including a pitting of personal-felt experience of the Divine (and fideism, more broadly) against critical-rational approaches (including, e.g., historical-critical approaches to interpreting Scripture).

References

Bakardjieva, M., & Gaden, G. (in press). Web 2.0 technologies of the self [Special issue]. *Philosophy & Technology, 24,* doi: 10.1007/s13347-011-0032-9

Barlow, J. P. (1996). A declaration of the independence of cyberspace. Retrieved from https://projects.eff.org/~barlow/Declaration-Final.html

Baron, N. (2008). *Always on: Language in an online and mobile world.* Oxford, England: Oxford University Press.

Baym, N. (2007). The new shape of online community: The example of Swedish independent music fandom. *First Monday 12*(8). Retrieved from http://firstmonday.org/htbin/cgiwrap/bin/ojs/index.php/fm/article/view/1978/1853

Baym, N. (2011). Social Networks 2.0. In M. Consalvo & C. Ess (Eds.), *The handbook of Internet Studies* (pp. 384–405). Oxford, England: Wiley-Blackwell.

Bruns, A. (2008). *Blogs, Wikipedia, Second Life, and beyond: From production to produsage.* New York, NY: Peter Lang.

Campbell, H. (2010). *When religion meets new media.* London, England: Routledge.

Castells, M. (2001). *The internet galaxy: Reflections on the internet, business, and society.* Oxford, England: Oxford University Press.

Cheong, P. H. (2010). Faith tweets: Ambient religious communication and microblogging rituals. *M/C Journal: A Journal of Media and Culture, 24(2)*. Retrieved from http://journal.media-culture.org.au/index.php/mcjournal/article/viewArticle/223

Cheong, P. H. (2011). Religious leaders, mediated authority and social change. *Journal of Applied Communication Research, 39*(4), 452–454.

Cheong, P.H. (in press) Authority. In H. Campbell (Ed.). *Digital religion: Understanding religious practice in new media worlds.* New York, NY: Routledge

Cheong, P. H., & Gray, K. (2011). Mediated intercultural dialectics: Identity perceptions and performances in virtual worlds. *Journal of International and Intercultural Communication. 4*(4), 265–271.

Cheong, P. H., Huang, S., & Poon, J. P. H. (2011). Religious communication and epistemic authority of leaders in wired faith organizations. *Journal of Communication, 61,* 938–958.

Cheong, P.H., Huang, S.H., & Poon, J.P.H. (2011). Cultivating online and offline pathways to enlightenment: Religious authority in wired Buddhist organizations. *Information, Communication & Society, 14* (8), 1160–1180.

Cheong, P. H., Martin, J. N., & Macfadyen, L. (2012). Mediated intercultural communication matters: Understanding new media, dialectics and social change. In P. H. Cheong, J. N. Martin, & L. Macfadyen (Eds.), *New media and intercultural communication: Identity, community and politics* (pp. 1–20). New York: Peter Lang.

Cheong, P. H., Poon, J. P. H., Huang, S. H., & Casas, I. (2009). The Internet highway and religious communities: Mapping and contesting spaces in religion-online. *The Information Society, 25*(5), 291–302.

Ess, C. (2009). *Digital media ethics.* Oxford, England: Polity Press.

Ess, C. (2010). The embodied self in a digital age: Possibilities, risks, and prospects for a pluralistic (democratic/liberal) future? [Special issue]. *Nordicom Review.* Retrieved from http://www.nordicom.gu.se/common/publ_pdf/320_10%20ess.pdf

Ess, C. (2011). Self, community, and ethics in digital mediatized worlds. In C. Ess & M. Thorseth (Eds.), *Trust and virtual worlds: Contemporary perspectives* (pp. 3–30). Oxford, England: Peter Lang.

Ess, C., & Consalvo, M. (2011). Introduction: What is "Internet Studies"? In M. Consalvo & C. Ess (Eds.), *The handbook of Internet Studies* (pp. 11–16). Oxford, England: Blackwell.

Gergen, K. (2011). *Relational being: Beyond self and community.* Oxford, England: Oxford University Press.

Hoover, S. M., & Lundby, K. (1997). Introduction: Setting the agenda. In S. M. Hoover & K. Lundby (Eds.), *Rethinking media, religion and culture* (pp. 3–14). Thousand Oaks, CA: Sage.

Internet World Stats. (2011). Retrieved from http://www.internetworldstats.com/stats.htm

Little i Apps. (2011). Confession: A Roman Catholic app [iPhone app]. Retrieved from http://itunes.apple.com/us/app/confession-a-roman-catholic/id416019676?mt=8#

Livingstone, S. (2011). Internet, children, and youth. In M. Consalvo & C. Ess (Eds.), *The handbook of Internet Studies* (pp. 348–368). Oxford, England: Wiley-Blackwell.

Martin, B. (1998). From pre- to postmodernity in Latin America: The case of Pentecostalism. In P. Heelas (Ed.), *Religion, modernity and postmodernity* (pp. 102–146). Oxford, England: Blackwell.

Martin, B. (2001). The Pentecostal gender paradox: A cautionary tale for the sociology of religion. In R. K. Fenn (Ed.), *The Blackwell companion to sociology of religion (Blackwell companions to religion)* (pp. 52–66). Oxford, England: Blackwell.

Rodogno, R. (2011). Personal identity online [Special issue]. *Philosophy & Technology, 24,* doi: 10.1007/s13347-011-0020-0

Schement, J. R, & Stephenson, H. C. (1996). Religion and the information society. In D. A. Stout & J. M. Buddenbaum (Eds.), *Religion and mass media: Audiences and Adaptations* (pp. 261–289), Thousand Oaks, CA: Sage.

Taylor, C. (1989). *Sources of the self: The making of the modern identity.* Cambridge, MA: Harvard University Press.

Turkle, S. (1984). *The second self: Computers and the human spirit.* Cambridge, MA: MIT Press.

Turkle, S. (1995). *Life on the screen: Identity in the age of the internet.* New York, NY: Touchstone.

Turkle, S. (2010). *Alone together: Why we expect more from technology and less from each other.* New York, NY: Basic Books.

van Dijck, J. (2010). Users like you? Theorizing agency in user-generated content. *Media, Culture & Society, 31*(1), 14–58.

Wellman, B. (2001). Physical place and cyberplace: The rise of personalized networking. *International Journal of Urban and Regional Research, 25*(2), 227–252.

Wellman, B. (2011). Studying the Internet through the ages. In M. Consalvo & C. Ess (Eds.), *The handbook of Internet Studies* (pp. 17–23). Oxford, England: Blackwell.

Wellman, B., & Haythornthwaite, C. (Eds.). (2002). *The Internet in everyday life.* Malden, MA: Blackwell.

Part I: Theorizing Digital Religion

2. Dreams of Church in Cyberspace

KNUT LUNDBY

Dreams of Church in Cyberspace

This chapter critically examines notions of church and mission in a Christian tradition that emerge from contemporary practices on the internet. In these circles, the metaphor of cyberspace is frequently evoked.[1] How valid is this metaphor and what are the implications of it for online and offline religious practices? How do new forms of digital communication challenge church and mission?

Theologians would say that "The Church Is Mission" (Hauerwas, 2010), implying that the Christian churches constantly have to find new ways of communicating when "engaging plurality" (Mortensen & Østerlund Nielsen, 2010). Internet certainly invites a plurality of voices.

With a few exceptions, my examples are taken from Christianity. However, the theoretical argument should be of relevance for "digital religion" springing from other traditions as well. The critical discussion of "cyberspace" and "virtual" forms of communication are of importance not just to church people and mission thinkers, but also just as much to scholars of social media and internet culture.

This chapter analyses religious organizations and their relation to cyberspace and the internet. Hence, it has an institutional perspective. As part of the "networked individualism" (Castells, 2001, pp. 125–129; Wellman, 2001) of Western modernity, seeking individuals are much quicker to manoeuvre on the Net than established institutions like churches. These "users" will be brought into the argument towards the end of the chapter, in the response to moves taken by the churches.

I apply a media sociological perspective in my struggle with the above questions. This implies that I focus on the *context* of communication and not the *conduits* of church and mission.

Cyberspace and Virtuality

Cyberspace as a concept indicates a context of communication. This space may pose promises as well as threats to those approaching it. For agents and organizations involved in Christian mission it may appear as a space of opportunities. For the inner life of Christian churches it may also be perceived as a competing space they cannot control.

I regard the concept of cyberspace as a misleading construction to tempt us to think that there is another realm out there. Like the officer in Shakespeare's *Hamlet* who had just seen the ghost of Hamlet's father, the late king of Denmark, I feel the ghost of cyberspace. Just as he said "Something is rotten in the state of Denmark" I think there is something rotten about this concept of cyberspace.

The concept was coined in 1984 by the science fiction author William Gibson. In the novel *Neuromancer,* he described cyberspace as a world of connected computers, a decade before the World Wide Web on the internet was made easily accessible by the Netscape Navigator browser. In Gibson's cyberspace the actors undertake "bodiless" experiences away from the "flesh" (Gibson, 1984). Gibson's cyberspace is a world governed by the matrix: the synthesis of the data banks of every existing computer in the human system (Lechte, 2002). *Neuromancer* constructed cyberspace as fiction.

Cyberspace is a "place" metaphor. New, digital media are not *channels* but more akin to *places* where information is *made available* rather than *transferred,* the media philosopher Johnny Hartz Søraker (2011) argues. Spatial metaphors such as cyberspace have arisen because one tries to denote an environment that constitutes and contains information that does not seem to exist in the regular physical world and only can be accessed by the use of special equipment. Instead of through the image or analogy of cyberspace, this phenomenon should be approached by the concept of virtuality, Søraker (2011, pp. 46–47) proposes. He defines the virtual as a generic term with a range of applications compared to the other, place-bound metaphor (2011, p. 45).

Within the range of this metaphor, the virtuality of cyberspace can be understood in three ways, based on different paradigms, the media scholar Lars Qvortrup (2002) proposed: Cyberspace has frequently been conceptualized as a parallel world, based in a dualistic paradigm. Cyberspace has also been understood as a representation of the real world drawing on a positivistic paradigm. Both these options must be rejected, I concur. Qvortrup advocated a third way that we could try: Virtuality, then, should be conceptualized as representations of the space experiences of human beings. This is a phenomenological paradigm where the phenomenon "space" is constituted by the observer's practical experience of space (2002).

The Virtual and the Real

The concept of virtuality has roots that can be traced back to the High Middle Ages. The philosopher and theologian John Duns Scotus (1265/66–1308) applied the Latin term *virtualiter* to bridge the gap between the reality we define by our conceptual expectations on the one hand, and our actual and diverse experiences on the other. Referring to Scotus, Michael Heim defined virtual as a philosophical term meaning not actually, but just "as if." Virtual space—as opposed to natural bodily space—contains the informational equivalent of things. Virtual space makes us feel as if we are dealing directly with physical or natural realities (Heim, 1993, pp. 132–133).

"Today, we call many things virtual," Heim (1998, p. 3) pointed out, but the use of the term is rather unspecific. Marianne Richter (2011) takes this up from a philosophy of virtuality point of view. While reality is a generic term, the virtual is used in different ways: "Like fiction, 'virtuality' is defined with regard to its generation (making up something, simulating something) as well as with regard to the corresponding product or complementary effect (e.g., fictional world, virtual world)." In the first sense, Richter (2011, p. 41) argues, "'virtual' qualifies something that *is not* real or actual in the sense of being made-up another way, appearing differently or referring to a different mode of being" (emphasis in original). Then it works as a generic term. But in the second sense, as with an ideal or possible state of "virtual reality," the virtual also works as a modal term. This is a "significant incoherency" (2011, p. 41).

The virtual worlds that the novel *Neuromancer* depicted in 1984 are closer to realizing a quarter of a century later. The dichotomy between the real and the virtual is untenable in light of the advances in simulation and communication technologies, the technology philosopher Susan Stuart (2008) argued. Today, one can be fully immersed in a multimodal setting "in which we can feel ourselves walking around and manipulating objects, whilst at the same time feeling the warmth of the sun on our face, smelling the newly mown grass, and hearing the dog next door barking." In this context a person, or "agent," enacts a dynamic coupling with her environment (Stuart, 2008, pp. 258, 255).

However, as Søraker reminds us: Although virtuality in terms of interactive computer simulation is possible, at the same time "there are clearly differences between the virtual and the physical, precisely because a computer simulation is a necessary condition for the existence of the virtual world" (Søraker, 2011, p. 55).

Virtual and Digital

Søraker (2011) brings the conceptual discussion of virtuality into the digitized setting where church and mission try to enter. Most talk of cyberspace may be more about dreams of one's own expansion into the internet, I suggest, than of real virtuality. Dreams of church in cyberspace may be repetitions of hopes for missionary expansion through any new medium, as I will come back to.

With dreams of cyberspace it is the digital and network media based on computers that matters: It is the computer that underpins the virtual world and "makes virtual worlds *similar* to the physical world and dramatically *different* from dreams," Søraker underlines (2011, p. 55, emphasis in original).

Søraker clarifies the levels of concepts when one looks at the virtual in "new media": Everything virtual is ultimately digital, but many forms of digital technology are not related to media. And there are digital media, such as digital radio or digital cameras, that are not virtual. So, "digital" is a wider category than "virtual" (2011, pp. 46, 65).

Søraker (2011) defines "virtuality," and the adjective "virtual" as interactive computer simulations. Both the capacity for simulation in computer-created "environments" and the possibility for interactivity in these simulated settings are necessary to make it virtual. Interactive computer simulations provide a technological base for various forms of virtuality, more strictly defined:

- *Virtual Environments* are the general form of computer-simulated virtuality in which one is represented by an avatar. An avatar is a virtual entity that you control, and use to interact with other virtual entities in this computer-shaped environment.
- *Virtual Worlds* are environments where several players or users have access to and play or interact with each other in the same "virtual community." Multi-user virtual worlds are always three-dimensional, whereas virtual environments need not be.
- *Virtual Reality* implies that a computer-simulated virtual environment is experienced from within, with a first-person view. This immerses the participant in the virtual environment (Søraker, 2011).

Obviously, most of what churches and other religious organizations do online does not fit these precise definitions of virtuality.

What Goes on Out There?

So what do churches do out there? Some church-related sites on the internet may be distinctly different from their offline mother organizations; others are direct offspring of the parent body. There is no complete overview of how Christian churches and groups use the Net. Here are some examples:[2]

Official sites providing information about church families such as Roman Catholic (www.vatican.va), Anglican (www.anglicancommunion.org), or Lutheran (www.lutheranworld.org/lwf) are mostly non-interactive "home pages." The same goes for the global World Council of Churches (www.oik-oumene.org) as well as official sites for national and local denominations and churches. There is some, limited, interactivity, but, for example, although the Church of Scotland (www.churchofscotland.org.uk) invites visitors to its site to "Worship on the web," the website comprises nothing more than worship material and resources for hymns, prayers, readings, and reflections, with no virtual worship.

Online churches may offer a minister to chat with or write to, prayers, and other religious practices. They may develop within or outside of church traditions (Hutchings, 2010). For example, *The Church of Fools* (http://churchoffools.com), established in 2004, was an experimental, virtual—and short lived—site where you could enter a 3D-designed church, select a cartoon-like avatar to represent you in this virtual church, and take part in services, praying, singing hymns, and greeting people, and walk around (Kluver & Chen, 2008, p. 116). The bishop of London, and the Methodist Church in Britain both sponsored this initiative. To quote the site's initiator, Simon Jenkins: "Just as the Methodist church leader John Wesley took his preaching out of churches and into the fields and streets in the 18th century, we wanted to take church to where people are in the 21st century—on the Net" (2008, p. 100). *The Church of Fools* was non-denominational. However, the creators stuck to Anglican, Celtic, and other liturgies in their virtual services. (See also Tim Hutchings's chapter in this volume.)

In the virtual environment that is *Second Life* there are real ministries and churches to be found (Radde-Antweiler, 2008b, pp. 183–189), and even an Anglican cathedral (Hutchings, 2010). However, the online churches in *Second Life* also have relations that was then termed the regular "'First Life'" (Miczek, 2008).

Blogging with day-to-day comments and notes on events has become an extensive activity within the Christian realm. Usually these blogs have a base in networked individualism, creating an alternative space (Teusner, 2010, p. 125) to established institutions. *Christianblog.com*, which claims to be the "world's leading Christian Blogging website," is a website "where you can be blessed and bless others." Two more examples are *Christian Blog Evangelism* (www.internetevangelismday.com/blogging.php) and *ChristiaNet* (http://christianblogs.christianet.com) which bills itself as "The Worldwide Christian Community."

In *social networking*, Christian alternatives to the regular sites are introduced.

SpaceFaith (http://spacefaith.com) used to present itself as a "Christian MySpace" but has—among heavy adverts—retreated to advertising itself as "the best place to find Christian MySpace layouts." Another example, *Your-ChristianSpace* (Yourchristianspace.com) connects to Facebook, while *Jesus Klub* (Jesusklub.com) offers "Christian Networking."

YouTube, the video-sharing site, turns up millions of hits if you search for "Jesus." However, an alternative Evangelical GodTube with "Christian Videos" was launched in 2007 on Godtube.com and after a period re-branded as *Tangle,* encouraging Christians to get tangled up with the new technologies "to support and promote their beliefs in the world of the internet" (Campbell, 2010, p. 191).

Although there are significant examples (Heidbrink & Miczek, 2010; Radde-Antweiler, 2008a), the three forms of virtuality Søraker defines are pretty marginal in the online activities of church and mission.

The Dream of Virtual Community

A loose form of virtual community seems to be the form of virtuality most frequent in Christian settings. This meaning of virtuality is the one closest to the dreams of church in cyberspace, I suggest.

The concept of "virtual community" was coined by Howard Rheingold ([1993] 2000). However, the origin of this concept is not that virtual, having a very specific location in time and space. Fred Turner (2006) tells the story of how Rheingold created the concept from 1987 onwards. Rheingold, then a freelance journalist, took his point of departure as the *Whole Earth Catalog* that was established as part of the Californian counterculture in 1968. This publication helped young people who were heading "back to the land." In 1985 the *Whole Earth Catalog* was developed into a Bulletin Board System (BBS) known as the *Whole Earth 'Lectronic Link* (the WELL). When Rheingold "describes virtual community as a way to restore a 'cooperative spirit' that has been lost, it's hard not to hear him pining in part for the very particular cooperative spirit abroad in the counterculture of the 1960s," Turner (2005) held.

In a broader perspective, this dream of a virtual community was part of a romantic longing for community that Tönnies ([1957] 1988) called *Gemeinschaft.* This search for close bonds is countered by the observations of a "networked individualism" (Castells, 2001, pp. 125–129; Wellman, 2001). Lori Kendall concludes on this tension in her overview of studies of "Community and the internet" that "we need more studies of the kinds of commitments and connections people form and the ways that these relationships intersect communications technologies" (Kendall, 2011, p. 323). This brings us down to earth, in terms of social relations and material conditions.

Down to Earth

Cyberspace is certainly a physical reality, if taken as being a network of computers and file sharing. Cyberspace and virtual communities are based in material and historical realities. They are not just "out there," but also part of life and structures here. Cyberspace is something real in terms of the connectivity available with the internet as well as on cell phone networks. I subsume them both under "the Net."

Examining the relationship between church, mission, and the new Net media, we need to make clear in which directions the influences go. It may be tempting to think that technology shapes religion, like Marshall McLuhan and his followers have proposed (McLuhan, 1999; Meyrowitz, 2008).

Heidi Campbell, in her book, *When Religion Meets New Media* (2010), challenged such simple determinism. She asked rather how religious communities shape the technologies. Her references are the established traditions of Judaism, Christianity, and Islam. In their immediate interaction with the technologies, religious communities enter into negotiation processes with new media, which could lead either to rejection and resistance or to reconstruction and innovation, where the technology is reshaped to enhance the community. The negotiations may also lead to acceptance and appropriation, where the new media are embraced as a neutral tool for outreach and internal purposes. Campbell observed several patterns of appropriation of the new digital and Net-based media. They can be used:

- for purposes of proselytizing and proclamation. The e-vangelism of evangelical groups is the most prominent example (Campbell, 2010, pp. 137–144);
- to facilitate global networking, as in the Emerging Church (Campbell, 2010, pp. 150–156);
- as a tool for agenda setting among the believers and to publicize beliefs, as visible in the official web sites of denominations or churches (Campbell, 2010, pp. 144–150);
- to digitize or technologize religious rituals (Campbell, 2010, pp. 127–131).

It works in both directions: New media technologies will influence the way churches work, but religious communities also help shape the technologies. The social formations of religious practices should be regarded as strong factors.

The church in cyberspace is to be taken down to earth (which should be reasonable for a church that believes in incarnation, i.e., that God became man). The church in cyberspace is church in the world, simply, because Net communication has become part of everyday life. The development of social media helps to explain this.

Social Media and Social Networks

With the so-called "Web 2.0," the space or the infrastructure of the internet offers not just information from websites or "home pages" but interaction between users of the web. We have got "social networking" in "social media."

Again, something is rotten: Basic forms of social life are being projected into cyberspace. However, social networks have been linking people since the inception of humanity. In this sense "Web 2.0" is not offering us anything new. Internet gives other opportunities for community formations (Kendall, 2011) and for personal connections (Baym, 2010), but this still does not add up to more than what Nancy Baym (2011) terms "Social Networks 2.0." It is still about shaping and keeping social relations.

The concept of social networks, however, is fairly recent. Some 60 years ago the anthropologist John Barnes went to the "island parish" of Bremnes on the west coast of Norway, where the fisheries were great. It is told that he sat contemplating the fishing nets hanging up to dry in the wind, and came to think of such a net, with its nodes and threads, as a suitable metaphor of the social life he was observing. He wrote:

> Each person has a number of friends, and these friends have their own friends; some of any one person's friends know each other, others do not. I find it convenient to talk of a social field of this kind as a *network*. (1954, p. 43)

His description could fit the networks of "friends" on social networking sites such as Facebook. Barnes, in a footnote, informs us that he earlier used the term *web* for such links but that became too much of a two-dimensional spider's web for him, while he wanted to "form an image for a multi-dimensional concept" (1954, p. 43) of social relations.

What is new is that the Net further extends social networks by linking face-to-face interactions with interactions on the Net. Online and offline life is linked together. This brings internet and mobile networks into everyday life (Bakardjieva, 2005, 2011; Baym, 2010, 2011; Wellman & Haythornthwaite, 2002).

Into Everyday Life

For the church there is no reason to retreat into putative dual existence. The overall findings of the authors in the recent *Handbook of Internet Studies* (Consalvo & Ess, 2011) simply finds any strong distinction between "virtual" and "real" as, at best, quaint, and at worst, simply not relevant to how people use the internet these days, i.e., as interwoven into the fabric of everyday life.

There is no parallel cyberspace world. Neither is there a need to project the representations of the church into the social media on the Net. These two conceptualizations of cyberspace are rejected. We have to go for the third option and explore the new possibilities for practical experience of space through the social interaction that the Net and the social media encourage—as extensions of social relations by other means, face-to-face or mediated by other media.

The countries of Scandinavia—with small populations, a high degree of social equality, and highly developed Net infrastructure as public goods—are like windows or laboratories for these extended social networks across the online-offline interface, working in a three-way interchange of culture, medium, and message according to the "cultural grammar of the internet" (Finnemann, 2005) and the social, economic, and political patterns of the society.

In Norway, nine out of 10 citizens have access to the internet. Four out of 10 of all Norwegians, including those without internet access, are on Facebook every day. Six out of 10 of the entire population use Facebook on a weekly basis in their communication with others. Among the young, aged 15–29 years, this is the case with nine out of 10. Facebook has a larger share of users than the main radio channel and the biggest newspaper in Norway. However, the two main television channels in Norway still have more daily users than Facebook.[3]

Digital divides will persist, but access to the Net will expand all over the globe, to a larger extent from mobile devices, connecting people on the move in their daily interactions. More of the daily social networking among people and institutions will take place on the Net. People—and especially the young—move back and forth between face-to-face and mediated communication. It is like an extension of making a phone call in former days, which gave an experience of a shared space between the two "on the line"—or, these days, like writing emails. The repertoire of "personal media" (Lüders, 2008) available today invites a range of such spaces to be set up between people, be it in the exchange of pictures, text messages, and smileys or other emoticons on your cell phone, or on social networking sites.

Church and mission are social movements, involved in social networks. When the media become "social" it matters for church as well as for mission. Three new features of social media are of special relevance to church and mission:

- *connectivity* (although large parts of the world are not yet "wired");
- *immediacy* (you can interact with others as if you were next to each other);
- *sharing culture* (it is easy to do, and you are encouraged to share ideas on the Net).

Before the adoption of a statement on mission at the 2005 Synod of the Church of Norway, youth delegates formulated that mission in the footsteps of Jesus, today means *dialogue, sharing,* and *presence.* This fits with the connectivity, immediacy, and sharing culture of the Net, linking communication, exchange, and social interaction offline with activities online.

Who Uses Church Sites?

Who uses the websites and services produced by the churches and Christian groups? Roughly speaking, the users are those already active in churches and religious organizations. Of course there are visitors who are just passing by or looking in, but the general tendency, from research, is that these sites primarily attract those already committed and active.

A survey from the renowned Pew Internet & American Life Project in 2004 showed that nearly two thirds of all Americans had "done things on the internet that relate to religious or spiritual matters," but this could be no more than sending or receiving an electronic greeting card related to religious holidays. The "online faithful" are more likely to be connected to religious institutions and practices than other internet users. Half of them go to church at least once a week and many of them describe themselves as evangelicals. The researchers concluded that "Faith-related activity online is a *supplement* to, rather than a *substitute* for offline religious life" (Hoover, Clark, & Rainie, 2004).

Mia Lövheim confirmed this from studies among teenage internet users in much more secular Sweden. Internet seems for them to be a significant context for exploring religion—and to stay in touch with the likeminded—particularly for the "offline faithful" (Lövheim, 2008, p. 214).

The internet is a significant arena, a rapidly growing site for information and interaction. However, even in highly networked societies, people still spend more time in front of the television than on the internet, and religious books and magazines continue to be important for the faithful.

It is not just that people watch television more than they go on the internet. In research I have done on a representative sample of the Norwegian population, only 12 percent said they had been in touch with questions on faith and religion on the internet during the last 12 months. In contrast, 49 percent said that they had seen questions on faith and religion on television during the last year (Lundby, 2010). Similar results have come up in Denmark and Sweden (Hjarvard, 2008; Lövheim, 2008). And the main public radio channel in Norway, the P1 from the Norwegian Broadcasting Corporation, still gathers nearly 10 percent of the adult population for Sunday worship transmissions, as well as daily short devotions.

Other Voices as Well

For every new media technology there has been a new optimism for Christian mission. The printing press gave people a chance to read the Bible themselves as well as launching a wave of religious books and pamphlets. However, others also made use of the print technology. For every new medium invented there have been more outlets for Christian mission, but there is also more "competition," more voices. Stefan Gelfgren's chapter in this volume on 19th century Evangelical uses of print media is a case in point.

Today, with the abundance of the internet, there are more mediated voices than ever. The Christian churches are visible but definitely not alone. It is not really possible to know the number of web sites in the world. Internet services and statistics company Netcraft (http://netcraft.com) found 255 million sites (December 2010), of which some 100 million are active. Quite a rise since the very first website was built less than 20 years ago. Each site was counted to have 273 web pages per site on average.[4]

A Google search on some keywords indicates the activity of church and mission on the internet:[5]

"Christianity"—about 31 million hits ("Christian"—330 million)
"Protestantism"—2 million ("Protestant" including "Protestantism"—
    17 million)
"Anglican"—6 million ("Lutheran"—17 million)
"Church"—323 million

To compare with other religious traditions:

"Buddhism"—about 13 million hits ("Buddhist"—23 million)
"Islam"—143 million ("Muslim"—86 million)
"Mosque"—17 million

In his recent book *iMuslims*, Gary R. Bunt (2009) explored how the House of Islam is being "rewired." The activity in "digital Islam" is extensive and creative. The "traditional paradigm of a Muslim community, or *ummah*, has, on one level, itself shifted online with the development of social-networking software leading to alternate forms of affiliation and friendships," he concluded (2009, p. 288).

Challenge to Authorities

Muslim authorities have their say online. However, the virtual *ummah* bypasses the traditional channels of knowledge and authority of Islam. The same goes for Jewish communities and Christian churches (Campbell, 2007, 2010). The Net helps to bypass old authorities, and to give rise to new ones. This point is made in several of the chapters in this volume (and also in other articles by Pauline Hope Cheong) and is therefore only covered in passing here.

Those who can programme and operate the internet and World Wide Web emerge as new authorities—often unknown and anonymous but capable of directing searches and communication traffic. New kinds of authority are built from the bottom up by technical knowledge of the web.

The Catholic Church tries to control and keep the authority of the Pope and the Vatican on the Net but there will always be alternatives for those who want to find them or make them. The Protestant churches are to a greater extent encouraging the individual voice. However, the Protestant church structures are definitely being challenged. Churches as institutions are in trouble.

Secularization, globalization, individualization, and multireligiosity make significant elements in the context for the "church in cyberspace." These cultural forces all infuse the Net, and from there influence the authority and life of the churches and their mission. Youth are leaving churches; people want to define their own way. This fits with the capabilities of the Net.

Challenges to the Institutional Understanding of Church

Can church and congregational communities be built in cyberspace? Yes, as supplements or extensions to church institutions "offline" (Campbell, 2005, 2010, 2011). But these constructions do not easily attract newcomers other than those who were already there before, as noted above.

In 1960 Eugene A. Nida, Executive Secretary of the American Bible Society, published *Message and Mission: The Communication of the Christian Faith*. He was aware that communication has to relate to the social structure. He knew the "Mysterious Power of Symbols." However, his conceptualization of communication was linear, "communication is designed to convey information, and by this means to influence or control the behavior or attitudes of others," he wrote (1960, p. 4). The media of the times were the big mass media, and the church a sender institution. Those days are gone. An understanding of mission as proclamation inspired this approach. The transportation model "was seen as a form of communication with profoundly religious implications. This movement in space was an attempt to establish and extend the kingdom of God, to create the conditions under which godly understanding might be realized," wrote the communication scholar James Carey (1989, p. 16). When science and secularization gained ground, "the religious metaphors fell away and the technology of communication itself moved to the center of thought" (Carey, 1989, p. 17).

Well before the advent of the web, Carey (1989) formulated an alternative "ritual model" of communication, aimed at the representation of shared symbols and beliefs, similarly rooted in religious metaphors of communion and community (1989, p. 18). This is still a relevant perspective. However, with the new reality of the Net, large ritual circles of communication are fragmented into a range of smaller ones. Such smaller circles or communities online, with their offline anchoring, may represent counter movements to the authority of traditional religious institutions.

The church as institution, with its material structure and bureaucracy, will be under constant challenge from individualised moves with the connectivity, immediacy, and sharing culture of the Net. New forms of church and networked religion may appear.

In an essay on the understanding of the church, the Norwegian practical theologian Harald Hegstad stated that the "real church" is not the one defined by theological dogma but rather the *empirical* church, the community people experience when they gather in the name of Jesus, with its hopes and faults (2009, p. 197). This is close to the phenomenological conceptualization of virtuality that I have advocated. A person experiences space in the physical proximity of a congregation, and may add a practical experience of space during virtual or not so virtual participation on the Net. In that case, the virtual experience is part of the empirical "real church."

Hegstad (2009) reminded us, from his theological point of view, that the social formation and appearance of the church is crucial for the credibility of its mission. The quality of virtual and other Net church expressions, I will argue, becomes crucial if they add to the experience of a "real church" for people.

Conclusions

The quality of church in virtual space and on the internet depends on the relevance and credibility of its ongoing day-to-day interactions in that realm. The Net is becoming a natural part of the daily environment for more and more people, such as for the half of the Norwegian population that goes on Facebook at least once a week as part of their communication with others. People switch "seamlessly" between social interaction on the Net and social interaction face-to-face. The offline and the online make one reality, one environment. This reality is highly mediated. If the church wants to be in mission it simply has to be there.

The internet offers new alternatives to traditional approaches to mission. However, some of the most fancy artificial applications may not go home. The concept of cyberspace is rotten. It carries with it, for me at least, connotations of something different, of a sci-fi parallel world. I suggest scrapping that concept. Net interaction has to be felt naturally by those who live much of their lives on the Net, if it is to make up part of the empirical "real church" and its mission for them.

Church hierarchy representatives cannot do this alone. The established church will have to let go, and invite its young, Net-creative membership—and even non-members—to take part and be on the Net on behalf of the church. Developers, writers, artists, and multimedia designers should be encouraged, professionals and amateurs alike. Let them shape church.

Church leaders, pastors, and ministers also have to be online, to interact with people as they would, or should, do offline. In a similar way in which social relations require ethical considerations, there is a need for an extension into cyber ethics (Hamelink, 1999) or digital media ethics (Ess, 2009).

More and more of the lives of churches and people will be hooked up to the Net. To end with another *Hamlet* statement: To be, or not to be *online:* that is *not a* question.

Notes

1. This was also the case at the international scholarly conference for theologians and missiologists on "Church and Mission in a Multireligious Third Millennium" at Aarhus University, Denmark, 29 January 2010. This chapter is a revised and expanded version of a keynote on the given topic of "The Church in Cyberspace." Thanks to Charles Ess for comments and suggestions on this chapter as it was further developed after the conference presentation.
2. All sites referred to in this section have been visited and found to be active as of 10 January 2011.
3. www.tns-gallup.no/medier, figures from the first quarter of 2010.
4. www.boutell.com/newfaq/misc/sizeofweb.html, accessed 10 January 2011. The figures comparing the number of pages with the netcraft.com data are from 2005.
5. Figures as they came out in Norway January 2011. Compared to January 2010 there was a decrease for the named church institutions/traditions and an increase in the terms related to individuals' religious belonging. There was a steep increase in the number of sites on"Muslim" as well as on "Islam." The number of hits came out higher when I did comparable searches from the US than in Norway.

References

Bakardjieva, M. (2005). *Internet society. The internet in everyday life.* London, England: Sage.

Bakardjieva, M. (2011). The internet in everyday life: Exploring the tenets and contributions of diverse approaches. In M. Consalvo & C. Ess (Eds.), *The handbook of Internet Studies* (pp. 59–82). Malden, MA: Wiley-Blackwell.

Barnes, J. A. (1954). Class and committees in a Norwegian island parish. *Human Relations, 7*(1), 39–58.

Baym, N. (2010). *Personal connections in the digital age.* Cambridge, England: Polity Press.

Baym, N. (2011). Social networks 2.0. In M. Consalvo & C. Ess (Eds.), *The handbook of Internet Studies* (pp. 384–405). Malden, MA: Wiley-Blackwell.

Bunt, G. R. (2009). *iMuslims. Rewiring the house of Islam.* Chapel Hill, NC: The University of North Carolina Press.

Campbell, H. (2005). *Exploring religious community online. We are one in the network.* New York, NY: Peter Lang.

Campbell, H. (2007). Who's got the power? Religious authority and the internet. *Journal of Computer-Mediated Communication, 12*(3), 1043–1062.

Campbell, H. (2010). *When religion meets new media.* London, England: Routledge.

Campbell, H. (2011). Internet and religion. In M. Consalvo & C. Ess (Eds.), *The handbook of Internet Studies* (pp. 232–250). Malden, MA: Wiley-Blackwell.

Carey, J. W. (1989). *Communication as culture. Essays on media and society.* Boston, MA: Unwin Hyman.

Castells, M. (2001). *The internetgalaxy: Reflections on the internet, business, and society.* Oxford, England: Oxford University Press.

Consalvo, M., & Ess, C. (Eds.). (2011). *The handbook of Internet Studies.* Malden, MA: Wiley-Blackwell.

Ess, C. (2009). *Digital media ethics.* Cambridge, England: Polity.

Finnemann, N. O. (2005). The cultural grammar of the Internet. In K. B. Jensen (Ed.), *Interface://Culture—The World Wide Web as a political resource and aesthetic form* (pp. 65–89). Frederiksberg, Denmark: Samfundslitteratur/NORDICOM.

Gibson, W. (1984). *Neuromancer.* New York, NY: Ace Books.

Hamelink, C. (1999). *The ethics of cyberspace.* London, England: Sage.

Hauerwas, S. (2010). Beyond the boundaries: The Church is mission. In V. Mortensen & A. Østerlund Nielsen (Eds.), *Walk humbly with the Lord: Church and mission engaging plurality* (pp. 53–69). Grand Rapids, MI: Wm. B. Eerdmans.

Hegstad, H. (2009). *Den virkelige kirke. Bidrag til ekklesiologien [The real church. Contributions to ecclesiology].* Trondheim, Norway: Tapir Akademiske Forlag.

Heidbrink, S., & Miczek, N. (2010). Introduction to the special issue: Religions on the internet—Aesthetics and the dimensions of the senses. *Online—Heidelberg Journal of Religions on the Internet, 4*(1), 1–11. Retrieved from http://online.uni-hd.de

Heim, M. (1993). *The metaphysics of virtual reality.* New York, NY: Oxford University Press.

Heim, M. (1998). *Virtual realism.* New York, NY: Oxford University Press.

Hjarvard, S. (2008). The mediatization of religion. A theory of the media as agents of religious change. In S. Hjarvard (Ed.), *The mediatization of religion* (pp. 9–26). Bristol, England: Intellect.

Hoover, S. M., Clark, L. S., & Rainie, L. (2004). *Faith online.* Retrieved from http://www.pewinternet.org/Reports/2004/Faith-Online.aspx

Hutchings, T. (2010). The politics of familiarity. Visual, liturgical and organisational conformity in the online church. *Online—Heidelberg Journal of Religions on the Internet, 04*(1), 63–86. Retrieved from http://online.uni-hd.de

Jenkins, S. (2008). Rituals and pixels. Experiments in online church. *Online—Heidelberg Journal of Religions on the Internet*, *03*(1), 95–115. Retrieved from http://online. uni-hd.de

Kendall, L. (2011). Community and the internet. In M. Consalvo & C. Ess (Eds.), *The handbook of Internet Studies* (pp. 309–325). Malden, MA: Wiley-Blackwell.

Kluver, R., & Chen, Y. (2008). The church of fools: Virtual ritual and material faith. *Online—Heidelberg Journal of Religions on the Internet*, *03*(1), 116–143. Retrieved from http://online.uni-hd.de

Lechte, J. (2002). Cyberspace. *Key contemparary concepts. From abjection to Zeno's Paradox* (pp. 51–52). London, England: Sage.

Lövheim, M. (2008). Rethinking cyberreligion? Teens, religion and the internet in Sweden. *Nordicom Review, 29*(2), 205–217.

Lüders, M. (2008). Conceptualizing personal media. *New Media & Society, 10*(5), 683–702.

Lundby, K. (2010). Medier som ressurs for religion [Media as resource for religion]. In P. K. Botvar & U. Schmidt (Eds.), *Religion i dagens Norge. Mellom sekularisering og sakralisering [Religion in contemporary Norway. Between secularization and sacralization]*, pp. 111–131. Oslo, Norway: Universitetsforlaget.

McLuhan, E., & Szklarek, J. (Eds.). (1999). *The medium and the light. Reflections on religion*. Niagara Falls, NY: Stoddart.

Meyrowitz, J. (2008). Medium theory. In W. Donsbach (Ed.), *The international encyclopedia of communication, Vol. VII.* (pp. 3055–3061). Malden, MA: Blackwell.

Miczek, N. (2008). Online rituals in virtual worlds. Christian online service between dynamics and stability. *Online—Heidelberg Journal of Religions on the Internet, 03*(1), 144–173. Retrieved from http://online.uni-hd.de

Mortensen, V., & Østerlund Nielsen, A. (Eds.). (2010). *Walk humbly with the Lord: Church and mission engaging plurality*. Grand Rapids, MI: Wm. B. Eerdmans.

Nida, E. A. (1960). *Message and mission. The communication of the Christian faith*. New York, NY: Harper & Row.

Qvortrup, L. (2002). Cyberspace as representation of space experience: In defence of a phenomenological approach. In L. Qvortrup (Ed.), *Virtual space: Spatiality in virtual inhabited 3D worlds* (pp. 5–24). New York, NY: Springer.

Radde-Antweiler, K. (2008a). Religion is becoming virtualised. Introduction to the special issue on religion in virtual worlds. *Online—Heidelberg Journal of Religions on the Internet, 03*(1), 1–6. Retrieved from http://online.uni-hd.de

Radde-Antweiler, K. (2008b). Virtual religion. An approach to a religious and ritual topography of Second Life. *Online—Heidelberg Journal of Religions on the Internet, 03*(1), 174–211. Retrieved from http://online.uni-hd.de

Rheingold, H. ([1993] 2000). *The virtual community. Homesteading on the electronic frontier*. Cambridge, MA: The MIT Press.

Richter, M. (2011). "Virtual reality" and "virtual actuality": Remarks on the use of technical terms in philosophy of virtuality. In C. Ess & M. Thorseth (Eds.), *Trust and virtual worlds: Contemporary perspectives* (pp. 31–43). New York, NY: Peter Lang.

Stuart, S. A. J. (2008). From agency to apperception: Through kinaesthesia to cognition and creation. *Ethics and Information Technology, 10*(4), 255–264.

Søraker, J. H. (2011). Virtual entities, environments, worlds and reality: Suggested definitions and taxonomy. In C. Ess & M. Thorseth (Eds.), *Trust and virtual worlds: Contemporary perspectives* (pp. 44–72). New York, NY: Peter Lang.

Teusner, P. (2010). Imaging religious identity: Intertextual play among postmodern Christian bloggers. *Online—Heidelberg Journal of Religions on the Internet, 04*(1), 111–130. Retrieved from http://www.online.uni-hd.de/

Turner, F. (2005). Where the counterculture met the new economy: The WELL and the origins of virtual community. *Technology and Culture, 46*(3), 485–512.

Turner, F. (2006). *From counterculture to cyberculture. Stewart Brand, the Whole Earth Network, and the rise of digital utopianism.* Chicago, IL: The University of Chicago Press.

Tönnies, F. ([1957] 1988). *Community & society: (Gemeinschaft und gesellschaft).* New Brunswick, NJ: Transaction.

Wellman, B. (2001). Physical place and cyberplace: The rise of personalized networking. *International Journal of Urban and Regional Research, 25*(2), 227–252.

Wellman, B., & Haythornthwaite, C. (Eds.). (2002). *The internet in everyday life.* Malden, MA: Blackwell.

3. *The Immanent Internet Redux*[1]

BERNIE HOGAN AND BARRY WELLMAN

The Transcendent Internet

The internet has descended from an awesome part of the ethereal firmament to become immanent in everyday life. As it descended, the internet developed, mutated, and proliferated, providing a multitude of computer-mediated options for people to communicate. The stand-alone capital-I "Internet" has become the more widespread and complex small-i "internet."

Although the technological nature of the immanent internet does not determine social behavior, it provides both opportunities and constraints for social relationships. The internet has become intertwined with a larger paradigm shift in how people are connected: from relatively homogenous, broadly embracing, densely knit, and tightly bounded groups to more heterogeneous, specialized, sparsely knit, and loosely bounded social networks. Although the transformation began in the pre-internet 1960s, the proliferation of the internet both reflects, and by design further facilitates, this shift in social organization to networked individualism.

Utopian Dreams and Dystopian Fears

The internet was originally viewed as a dazzling light shining above everyday concerns. In the 1990s, when the internet moved from the arcane scholarly world to homes and offices, it was heralded as the gateway to a new, illuminating Enlightenment. The very term "Internet" became used for any snazzy new electronic activity. Early adopters congratulated themselves on being progressive elites, and techno-nerds rejoiced in newfound respect and fame. Bespectacled, nerdy Microsoft founder Bill Gates was as much a superstar as rock singers and professional athletes (Turner, 2006). Special newspaper internet sections were created in the boom to capture dot-com ads and reader interest. All things seemed possible. The internet had astounded and mesmerized the world. The cover of the millennial December 1999 issue of *Wired* magazine (the *Vogue* of the internet world) graphically represents the optimism of the times. It shows an Icarian cyberangel leaping from a cliff to reach for the ethereal sun. The angel's graceful posture points upward, placing boundless faith in an unfettered cyberfuture.[2]

In the euphoria, much early writing of the impact of the internet was unencumbered by data and informed only by conjecture and anecdotes. Most writers were entranced by this emerging network of digital information. It was easy to make the leap from bits moving instantly across the planet to people (in spirit if not in body) moving across the planet as well. Early interactions on the internet were the domain of obscure in-groups and hackers, cultish tribes with their own slang, cultural symbols, and internal coherence. For example, sociologist Lori Kendall showed in *Hanging Out in the Virtual Pub* how a crowd of (mostly) guys in the "BlueSky" virtual community formed supportive bonds that gave them a strong sense of solidarity.

Travelers' tales from *internet incognita* abounded. The analyses were often utopian: extolling the internet as egalitarian and globe-spanning, and ignoring how differences in power and status might affect interactions on- and offline. In many writings, the internet was seen as an ethereal manifestation of Teilhard de Chardin's noosphere (1964), providing the technological means for the collective consciousness of the world. Philosopher Eric Raymond makes this transcendent connection clear in his *Homesteading in the Noosphere* (1998), showing how open-source hackers stake their claims on the frontier of programming ideas, and approach their projects simultaneously as property and gift.

Communication was the internet's main use during these early years. Ironically, given the emphasis on instantaneity, this interaction was predominantly asynchronous, person-to-person email. Nevertheless, it was the synchronous chat groups, multi-user simulations (MUDs, MOOs), and, beginning in 1997, instant messaging, which captured the imagination of internet pioneers.[3] Some seers felt that it would not be long before all would be connected to all, transcending the boundaries of time and space. As John Perry Barlow, songwriter, founding member of the Electric Frontier Foundation, and fellow of Harvard's Berkman Center for Internet and Society, wrote in 1995:

> With the development of the Internet, and with the increasing pervasiveness of communication between networked computers, we are in the middle of the most transforming technological event since the capture of fire. I used to think that it was just the biggest thing since Gutenberg, but now I think you have to go

back farther (p. 36). . . . In order to feel the greatest sense of communication, to realize the most experience, . . . I want to be able to completely interact with the consciousness that's trying to communicate with mine. Rapidly . . . We are now creating a space in which the people of the planet can have that kind of communication relationship. (p. 40)

While utopian at the time, the course of internet events has been moving in that direction. Barlow has since walked back his most aggressively utopian claims, but at the time his sentiment was hardly a departure from the cultural Zeitgeist. His sentiment epitomized a widespread wish that we could untether our minds from our bodies, transcend this earthly plane, and commune as beings of pure information and thought.

This fantasy was aptly romanticised in early cyberpunk novels, which promoted the notion of the body as essentially a host for the superhighway-cruising mind. Early writers of cyberpunk set the terms through with characters who "jacked in" to a separate and more engaging reality. The novels *Neuromancer* (Gibson, 1984) and *Snow Crash* (Stephenson, 1992) played a substantial part in shaping this cultural fantasy, with Gibson's "cyberspace" term becoming a metaphor for life on the internet. Sherry Turkle's non-fiction *Life on the Screen* (1995) portrayed the internet as fracturing a person's unified sense of identity, and aligned with then-vogue post-modern notions of the multiple self, bricolage, and deconstruction. As one of her respondents says "RL [Real-Life] is just one more window . . . and it's not usually my best one" (p. 13).

Yet Turkle's continued, highly focused observations (such as her 2011 *Alone Together* book) have led some pundits to mistake the leaves for the trees and forests. Extrapolations from her tiny sample of early adopters to the population at large popularized the perception of a transcendental life-consuming internet.[4] Rather than seeing denizens of virtual communities as a special minority, pundits often pointed to them as precursors of the future, linked in a Borgian meta-mind (Berman & Pillar, 1995) as "connected intelligence" (De Kerckhove, 1997) and "collective intelligence" (Levy, 1997). Yet Turkle's work has been based on the notion of a distant and transcendent internet, where identity play happens with strangers in anonymous chat rooms. In reality, for almost all users, the immanent internet is networked, part of their everyday lives (Schiano & White, 1998). They no longer think "I'm using the internet" than they think "I'm using the telephone lines." It is a tool that is there, often used unconsciously.

Many people lost their perspective in their euphoria and became parochial and presentist. In their *presentism*, they forgot that long-distance ties had been flourishing for generations, using automobiles, telephones, airplanes, and even postal (snail) mail. Others had no perspective to begin with, and just jumped on the internet bandwagon to find fame and fortune. Like

Barlow, they thought that the world had started anew with the internet (see the review in Wellman & Gulia, 1999).

Parochially, many pundits and computer scientists assumed that only online phenomena are relevant to understanding the internet. They realized that computer-mediated communication—in the guise of the internet—fostered widespread connectivity, but they insisted on looking at online phenomena in isolation. They committed the fallacy of *particularism*, thinking of the internet as a lived experience distinct from the rest of life. This approach often shaded towards *elitism*, as only the small percentage of the technologically adept had the equipment, knowledge, time, and desire to plunge so fully into cyberspace.

To be sure, there was scholarly research, much of it good, but it was mainly laboratory experiments, well summarized in Sproull and Kiesler's *Connections* (1991) or ethnographic accounts such as Turkle's. The media were permeated with traveler's tales of journeys to the exotic internet, written with the same gusto and apprehension as early travelogues of the American frontier. For example, the tagline on the cover of Mary Dery's cultural study of the internet suggests the book is "an unforgettable journey into the dark heart of the information age" (1995, book cover). Enthusiastic computer scientists filled meetings of "CSCW" (computer supported cooperative work) and "CHI" (computer-human interaction) conferences with reports of their amazing new applications. All of these accounts provided rich detail and a sense of process, but their particularity created the danger of inaccurate generalization. While it was true that some people were immersed online, most were not.

The dystopians had their say too. They similarly assumed the future would find humanity engulfed by the internet, but found this proposition distressing. By assuming a strong distinction between the online and offline worlds, the dystopians were able to first suggest that online interaction was inauthentic, and consequently, that time spent online is wasted, or worse, corrupting.

Populist Texas broadcaster Jim Hightower summarized this sentiment well by suggesting that "while all this razzle-dazzle connects us electronically, it disconnects us from each other, having us 'interfacing' more with computers and TV screens than looking in the face of our fellow human beings" (quoted in Fox, 1995, p. 12).

Notions of inauthenticity vary, from the flat-out rejection of the online world as a space of legitimate interaction, to one where deception runs rampant. Anecdotes of gender deception were told and retold (Van Gelder, 1985; Turkle, 1995; Dery, 1997; selections from Bell & Kennedy, 2000) They led to the oft-quoted, parodied, and updated *New Yorker* cartoon featuring two dogs in front of a screen, one barking to the other "on the internet, no one knows you're a dog" (Steiner 1993). One of the authors' favorite parodies shows a screen with purchases for dog food and squeaky toys, with a message saying "it looks like you're a dog, would you like to meet other dogs."

With every new affordance, site, or tabloid story, these concerns about authenticity are renewed. One of the latest trends is to assert that social networking is not merely inauthentic interaction but may actually have adverse health effects. This notion, put forth separately by Sigman (2009) and Greenfield (2009), suggests that because in-person contact is good for our health, and social network sites substitute for this contact, these sites therefore have adverse health effects.

More recently, Turkle has released another volume of cyber-dystopianism (2011). Taking a 180-degree turn from the problems of the fragmented self in chat rooms, it is a work focused on the concerns of performing a consistent and persistent self on social network sites. Again, this work rests on the assumption that online interaction is a problem because it pushes people away from "real" interaction offline. Undoubtedly, she raises fair issues about the pressure to constantly perform and maintain an online expression of self (boyd, 2006), but this might have less to do with the online world being an inauthentic performance compared to the real world (Hogan, 2010) and more to do with the constant need to cope with persistent content and a social network that rarely forgets this content.

Soothsayers of the internet age do not simply warn us about the false idols of online interaction, but consider it a site of unparalleled temptation. Consequently, a mini-industry has emerged to deal with internet pathologies. Several psychologists claimed to treat people with "internet addiction" (e.g., Young, 1998). One psychologist's diagnostic tool was adapted from a gambling addiction questionnaire, with "Internet" substituted for gambling (Greenfield, 1999).

In February 2004, a Toronto reporter asked one author (Wellman) to comment on the deaths of four "cyber-addicts" who spent much time online in virtual-reality milieus. When Wellman pointed out that other causes might be involved and that "addicts" were probably a low percentage of users, the reporter lost interest. Nor are such pathologies necessarily the result of internet use. As one disheveled man points out to a bar-mate in another *New Yorker* cartoon, "I was addicted to porn before there was an internet" (Vey, 2004).

This is not to dismiss these concerns entirely. Even one of the authors published a scale of email overload (Hogan & Fisher, 2006). But in that case, as one would hope in other work, the real issue is not the internet, but the extent to which the internet facilitates undesirable social relations, like an expectation that one be "always on" (Baron, 2008; Quan-Haase & Collins, 2008; McEwen, 2009). Many of the above approaches ignore the positive benefits of being involved with the internet: Compare a statement such as

"I am gambling too much" with one such as "I am communicating too much." In this case, one is demonizing the medium rather than questioning the social relationships that underpin this activity.

Fueling this fear, one scholarly report showed that adolescent heavy internet users were more alienated than other teens from their households (Kraut et al., 1998). This was trumpeted in newspaper headlines that neglected to report that the differences were only a few percentage points and occurred only among a small minority of internet users. Despite its limitations, at least this research was a pioneer of field-based systematic research with a representative sample. It was a marked improvement from the 1990s attempts of pundits and computer scientists alike to get a handle on what was happening without taking account of social science knowledge.

Frustrated with the prevalence of presentism and parochialism, one of the authors wrote an article arguing that the internet was not the coming of the new millennium (Wellman & Gulia, 1999). Rather, it was a new computer-mediated technology following the path of other promoters of transportation and communication connectivity, such as the telegraph, railroad, telephone, automobile, and airplane. The article showed how community dynamics continued to operate on the internet. There was no disconnection between the "virtual world" and the "real world." Rather, online communications have become—and probably always were—immanent parts of the real world of flesh and computers. Again, this is not to suggest the internet is business as usual. The internet has had a huge impact on the routines of daily life as well as the ways in which individuals find each other, maintain personal ties, work, and so forth. But in each case, we can point to specific mechanisms whereby the internet "reconfigures accessibility" (Gennaro & Dutton, 2007) rather than acts of its own accord to distance people from each other. Without this focus on the reconfiguring of access, it is possible to fall prey to the same utopian visions that ensnared those in the dot-com bubble.

Amazon.com was an early success story for the online world. By selling more books than any store could hold, and making recommendations based on crowd sourcing similar books (i.e., collaborative filtering) it cemented its business model. Amazon leveraged the stream of clickthrough and shopping information in creative and useful ways. By contrast, sites such as Pets.com simply assumed that the internet was "different" and thus transferring brick and mortar offerings to a digital world was sufficient. It was not, because the internet is not simply a different world out there, but a means for wielding digital information in ways that cannot (or usually are not) done offline. While some understood this notion, many did not. Only a year after *Wired* published its digital Icarus' daring leap forward, the dot-com bubble came crashing down.

The dot-com stock market bust of 2000 brought expectations down to earth. It curbed media enthusiasm and tempered the polarized rhetoric of utopian hope and dystopian fear. Special newspaper sections shrank in the wake of instantly vanishing dot-com vanity ads. The pages of *Wired* magazine, the internet's greatest cultural champion, shrank 25 percent from 240 pages in September 1996 to 180 pages in September 2001, and another 22 percent to 140 pages in September 2003. Revenue and subscription rates followed suit, with *Wired* editors noting ruefully that their magazine "used to be as thick as a phone book" (*Wired*, 2004, p. 23). By September 2010, the situation had stabilized, with a partial rebound of 20 percent to 168 pages.

This situation has started to shift again, however, as the internet has entered a new phase of sophistication about identity. Where there used to be a web for consuming content, and a set of media (email and instant messenger, etc.) for communicating with friends, now the two are becoming increasingly hybridized. In the seven years since the original publication of "The Immanent Internet," several trends have sprung up that can be recast in the mold of utopianism and dystopianism, testing our sense of authentic experience and reigniting moral panics about stranger danger, anonymous crowds, and alienation in modern life. In particular, social network sites, ubiquitous connectivity, and online mobilization have risen in prominence. The explosive growth of smartphones has made always-on connectivity the new normal. They *are* having a transformative effect, and in the Middle East and North Africa, they have contributed to revolutions. But again, it is important to look at the social relations underpinning these actions. These revolutions, for example, were also structured by political groups and the complex relations of the U.S. government with regimes and armed forces. Such a grounded attitude enables us to consider Wikileaks as contemporary descendants of Woodward and Bernstein, who initiated Watergate using old-fashioned audio tapes. It allows us to revisit social movement theories of McAdam, Tarrow, and Tilly (2001), Hedstrom (1994) and others, rather than assume Twitter creates mass discontent from apathetic nothingness. It allows us to consider that six degrees of separation bound people together before they could surf the friends of their friends on a social site.

The Immanent Internet

Despite the dot-com meltdown, both the number of internet users and their frequency of use have increased. The internet's growth meant it no longer stood apart from the rest of life, if it ever had. The internet has become embedded in everyday life, a routine appliance for communicating and being informed. Indeed, many people do not even think they are on the internet when they are instant messaging or chatting. For example, the Telus Canadian national survey found in 2009 that 35 percent of Canadians thought the internet was good for their family communication, while only 7 percent thought it was bad. But the other 58 percent had no opinion or did not care (Wellman, Garofalo, & Garofalo, 2009). For them, the internet is just something they do, and not a privileged form of communication to get excited about. As Susan Herring put it, the internet is now "slouching toward the ordinary" (2004, p. 26).

This is reminiscent of the transformation in the use of the telephone. Where our great-grandparents used to shout at the telephone receiver during a local call, and our grandparents were reluctant to make expensive long-distance calls, almost all residents of the developed world use the telephone routinely, without any consciousness of the technological marvels that sustain it. Moreover, young people apparently feel undressed without their mobile phones—so much so that it can become their "third skin" after biological skin and clothing (Fortunati, Katz, & Riccini, 2003). In cafés in Europe, automobiles in North America, and railroads in Japan, mobile phones come out as soon as people sit down. The use of mobile phones is so habitual that people often talk into them without any apparent awareness that their conversations impinge on the comfort of nearby listeners (Ling, 2004, 2008).

In retrospect, it is easy to see how early diffusion patterns had fostered the emergence of the ideology of internet as a transcendent force. When the internet connected few members of society it was likely that a disproportionate time online would be spent connecting with strangers, often living far away. Something as prosaic as a neighborhood message board is unthinkable when only three people on the street are online. As the network effect of this technology took hold, people adopted it because others they already knew were online. Communication was not primarily with far-flung mysterious others in virtual worlds, but with the people whom users already cared about most: family, friends, and workmates (Quan-Haase et al., 2002; Boneva & Kraut, 2002). And now neighborhood message boards, such as iNeighbors (www.i-Neighbors.org), are common (Hampton, 2007).

As the internet has become immanent in everyday life, its uses have kept multiplying and democratizing. The initial killer application of email is now routinely accompanied by interactions via chat rooms, instant messaging, and smartphones. Pictures, streaming video, music, and data files of all sorts now accompany text. The web is now comprehensive, usable, and often aesthetically pleasing. Search engines, such as Google, have developed clever algorithms to shift web surfing from a cognoscenti's game of memorizing arcane URLs and IP addresses to successful surfing through a few well-suggested words. Blogs have moved web creation beyond institutional designers' expertise to everyperson's soapbox, while 140 character "tweets" and smartphone texts cater to the short-winded. Desktop computers have been joined by much smaller laptops, netbooks, tablets, and smartphones as the quest for a universal, portable personal appliance continues. Indeed, many computers are so interwoven into life that they are not generally recognizable as "computers": some examples are GPS location systems, bank terminals, factory control systems, restaurant order-takers, and cash registers. With the advent of IPv6, these devices are indeed becoming networked, as the internet of things (Greenfield, 2006).

Although a majority of people in developed countries have access to the internet, the digital divide persists. For one thing, access does not necessarily mean use, as people have real or imagined reasons and fears about why they do not use the internet. They are more apt to use mobile phones. In most countries it is the economically privileged or educated (typically men) who are the early adopters. Racial minorities, the economically disadvantaged, and those who do not read English, use the internet less than others. This has serious social consequences as companies and government agencies place more services exclusively online (Chen & Wellman, 2004).

Once the issue of access is resolved, the issues of digital skills and cultural barriers emerge as dominant concerns. The quality of the internet experience is a key concern for reducing social inequality. First, the ability to perform a complex and efficient search is not a skill learned by osmosis, but through experience and openness to the potential of the technology (Hargittai & Shafer, 2006). Second, bloated software can inundate users with ambiguous options and icons. Third, there are time lags in informed use between experienced early adopters, late adopters, and newbies. These populations can have significantly different expectations about what to do online, and how to do it. Fourth, many sites are available only in English, a language not read by most of the world. Fifth, there are network effects: If one's network members are not online, there is less need to use the internet.

The digital divide is narrowing in developed countries, so that old as well as young, rich as well as poor, are frequently online. As time wears on, both women and the less privileged typically log on (often getting the computer because of its perceived benefit to their children). The gender gap is disappearing in developed countries, with women coming to use the internet as much as men. However, the socioeconomic gap persists in most countries even with increasing use because poorer folks are not increasing their rate of use as much as wealthier, better-educated ones. And the global digital divide remains wide, as internet use in developed countries remains much higher than in developing countries.

Although the demographic trends show that internet use is converging within countries, the character of internet use can differ widely between countries. For example, Catalans mostly use the internet for acquiring information and shopping—train schedules, theatre tickets—and less for communicating by email. Correspondingly, Catalonia is a local society in a salubrious climate where people gather in cafés to chat face-to-face (Castells et al., 2003).

To take another example, teens in developed countries communicate more by mobile phone and instant messages than by email (Ling, 2004). In Japan, the proliferation of web-enabled phones means that two hitherto separate communication media are becoming linked: Japanese teens and young adults frequently exchange emails on their mobile phones, or use their PCs to send short text messages to mobile friends (Miyata et al., 2004; Ito, Matsuda, & Okabe, 2004). The extent to which such media as email or instant messaging are used depends on the complex interplay of people's tastes, financial resources, culture, geographic location, location in the social structure, and national infrastructure.

Pundits have often claimed that the internet is yet another way in which the world is being recast as a "global village" (McLuhan, 1962, p. 31). The metaphor implies that the role of place is deprecated due to the speed of electronic communication. Yet, the internet is a social phenomenon, and for many reasons, one's social network remains at least partially rooted in locality (Mok, Wellman, & Carrasco, 2010). In Catalonia, when email is used, it is usually to contact someone nearby. In the wired Toronto suburb of "Netville," those residents with always-on, super-fast internet access knew the names of three times as many neighbors as their unwired counterparts, spoke with twice as many, and visited the homes of 1.5 times as many (Hampton & Wellman, 2003). A Toronto and a Chicago study each found that coworkers were more likely to use the internet when they worked in the same building, in part because they had more tasks and concerns in common (Koku, Nazer, & Wellman, 2001; Quan-Haase & Wellman, 2004). People often use the internet to communicate quickly with nearby others without the disturbance of a phone call or in-person visit. Even many long-distance ties have a local component, such as when former neighbors or officemates use the internet to remain in touch, or distant ties arrange a get-together in "meatspace" (i.e., in the flesh).

Nevertheless, the globe-spanning properties of the internet are real, as in the electronic diasporas that connect émigrés to their homeland. The internet enables diasporas to aggregate and transmit reliable, informal news back to often-censored countries (Miller & Slater, 2000; Mitra, 2003). The internet supports co-presence as well as long-distance communication, which we refer to as *glocalization* (Wellman & Hampton, 1999). In the community and at work, the internet facilitates physically close local ties as well as physically distant ties.

Interestingly, glocalization has not led to a reduction in levels of communication, for the internet actively supports all forms of contact: interpersonally, within organizations, and between organizations. Far from pulling people apart, the internet often brings them closer together. Controlling for demographic factors, internet users are more likely than non-users to read newspapers, discuss important matters with their spouses and close friends, form neighborhood associations, vote, and participate in sociable offline activities. The more they meet in person or by telephone, the more they use the internet to communicate. This "media multiplexity" suggests that the more people communicate by one medium, the more they communicate overall. For example, people might phone to arrange a social or work meeting, alter arrangements over the internet, and then get together in person. Rather than only connecting online, in person, or by telephone, many relationships are complex dances of serendipitous face-to-face encounters, scheduled meetings, telephone chats, email exchanges with one person or several others, and broader online discussions among those sharing interests (Haythornthwaite, 2005; Rainie & Wellman, 2012).

Neither the utopian hopes nor the dystopian fears have been borne out. Despite hopes, the internet has not brought a utopia of widespread global communication and democracy. Despite fears, high levels of internet use have not lured people away from in-person contact. To the contrary, the more people use the internet, the more they see each other in person (distance permitting) and talk on the telephone (Wellman & Haythornthwaite, 2002; Mok, Wellman, & Carrasco, 2010). This may be because the internet helps arrange in-person meetings and maintain relationships in between meetings. Mobile phones have become key in arranging get-togethers among people who frequently move between social roles and physical sites (McEwen, 2009). Although it is too early to provide a definitive interpretation of these findings, they suggest that internet users are shifting their contact from being based on demographic homophily to being based on common interests and values.

The Social Affordances of the Internet

Social scientists have repeatedly shown that technological changes do not determine social behavior (e.g., Oudshoorn & Pinch, 2004). For example, communication scientists mistakenly thought in the 1980s and early 1990s that the lower "media richness" of the internet would preclude emotional and social conversations. Yet psychological research has shown that individuals tend to invest emotionally in their computers and in lean media such as chat (Reeves & Nass, 1996; Joinson, 2002).

To this end, we see the internet as providing a set of "affordances," and, especially, "social affordances": "the possible actions a person can perform on an object" (Norman, 2011, p. 228). In their original use, affordances refer to environmental (typically visual) cues that signal a path for action. This has been a popular notion in design, as it focuses on a clear mapping between form and function, and does not refer to a necessary constraint but a gentle guidance. It also suggests that some people may never pick up on the affordance (or will only pick up on it subconsciously).

Some analysts have expanded the affordance to consider not merely motion and simple actions but, more abstractly, affordances for *social* action. That is, technology can provide cues about the social world, and guide social action as well as movement (Bradner & Kellogg, 1999). This is especially relevant in an age of burgeoning "social" software. Facebook, Twitter, LinkedIn, and their ilk are really a set of social affordances, providing cues such as "retweets," "likes," "friending," and "friends of a friend," all of which give individuals actionable cues about their social world. But stepping back from the new hype of social-everything, social affordances are bundled into virtual communication media. Email, for example, affords multi-party messages simply by addressing multiple people, rather than simple one-to-one messaging. IM affords a cue about accessibility through the "status" showing whether people are available, busy, occupied, and so forth (Quan-Haase & Collins, 2008).

Affordances move in tandem with infrastructure. Facebook needed high-powered servers and sophisticated scalable databases in order to provide a sufficient level of service. But this infrastructure could have been used in a multitude of ways. For example, learning who looks at one's Facebook profile is an affordance that Facebook explicitly *prevents*. By contrast, this affordance ("gaze transparency") is extremely important for dating sites, and is the basis of LinkedIn's business model (i.e., knowing which potential client looks at one's profile is useful for maintaining the right relationships). In the same vein, webcam videos require a certain bandwidth in order to be feasible. But above that, there are a multitude of design considerations and social cues that enable a variety of potential uses and activities online.

The use of technology is socially malleable. Different cultures use the internet in a wide variety of ways that map on to their existing social patterns. For example, Catalans have a convivial culture that is not amenable to online interaction (Castells et al., 2003). As such, they use it most often for coordination and information retrieval. The Japanese send many more short text messages by mobile phones than do Americans, but they use PCs less (Miyata et al., 2004).

Globalized ubiquitous connectivity is another affordance. Inexpensive, rapid internet communication helps immigrants with many long-distance ties to maintain their connections back home. On the other hand, the digital divide between and within countries means that only the technologically well-connected can be socially well-connected to loved ones abroad. But ubiquitous does not merely refer to who one can access but also where. Mobile phones are rapidly shifting to smartphones, and the internet is not only untethered from the desktop, but travels with people in the car, the train, and across the country.

Personalization is an emerging affordance. Users can have their own settings, email accounts, and desktop aesthetics. Accounts, such as email, are for the person rather than for the household. Coupled with ubiquitous computing, personalization means that whenever people log on to communications devices, the device knows who they are, where they are, and what settings they prefer. Such personalization is fostering societal shifts from place-to-place connectivity—a particular telephone or computer wired in place—to person-to-person connectivity—a particular user's mobile phone or internet account, wherever located (Rainie & Wellman, 2012).

Towards Networked Individualism

A funny thing happened on the way to the embedding of the internet in everyday life. The nature of everyday life changed for many people, from group-centric to network-centric. Much social organization no longer fits the group model. Work, community, and domesticity have moved from hierarchically arranged, densely knit, bounded groups to social networks. In networked societies boundaries are more permeable, interactions are with diverse others, linkages switch between multiple networks, and hierarchies are flatter and more recursive.

The shift to a ubiquitous, personalized, wireless world fosters personal social networks that supply sociability, support, and information, and a sense of belonging. Individuals are becoming switchboards between their unique sets of ties and networks. Rather than holding membership in a few broadly supportive groups, people are separately operating their specialized ties to obtain resources. Although people remain connected and supportive, individuals in unique networks have supplanted the traditional organizing units of the household, neighborhood, kin group, and work group.

The technological development of computer networks and the societal flourishing of social networks are affording the rise of networked individualism in a positive feedback loop. Just as the flexibility of less bounded and spatially dispersed social networks creates demand for collaborative communication and information sharing, the rapid development of computer-communications networks nourishes societal transitions from group-oriented societies to a society of networks.

Rather than fitting into the same group as those around him or her, each person has his or her own personal network. Household members keep separate schedules, with family get-togethers—even common meals—on the decline in North America (Putnam, 2000; Rainie & Wellman, 2012). Instead of belonging to two stable kinship groups, people are just as likely to have complex household relations with stepchildren, ex-marital partners (and their progeny), and multiple sets of in-laws. Communities—both in the flesh and in the ether—are far-flung, loosely bounded, sparsely knit, and fragmentary. Most people operate in multiple, partial communities as they deal with shifting, amorphous networks of kin, neighbors, friends, workmates, and organizational ties. Their activities and relationships are informal rather than organizationally structured. Only a minority of network members are directly connected with each another. Most friends and relatives live in different neighborhoods; many live in different metropolitan areas. At work, people often work *with* distant others and not those sitting near them.

The internet has been fostering this transformation by affording people the possibility of obtaining information when they want, and of communicating with anyone else connected to the internet, regardless of place. Coupled with asynchronous media, people can also communicate with others regardless of time of day. Furthermore, this is coupled with person-specific accounts that distribute custom-curated information of personal relevance (Hogan, 2010). This is the societal turn away from groups and toward networked individualism: People connected to each other as individuals rather than as members of households, communities, kinship groups, workgroups, and organizations. Yet the internet did not start or predetermine the shift to a network-centric society: The transformation began earlier. Even before the advent of telephones and airplanes, some ties with friends and relatives stretched long distances. In the developed world, the flourishing of person-to-person connectivity has been fostered since at least the 1960s by social changes such as dual-career (and dual-schedule families) and liberalized divorce laws reducing household size, and by technological changes that have increased personal mobility and communication. Low-cost airplane and expressway trips have enabled in-person get-togethers at distance. Low-cost local and long-distance telephone—and now internet—communication enables rapid connectivity, constrained more by time zone differences than by space (Takhteyev, Gruzd, & Wellman, 2011).

As a result, people probably maintain more long-distance ties with friends, kin, and workmates than ever before. It is easy for internet users to search for, and be actively involved in, far-flung communities of shared interests that are thinly represented on the ground. Groups may have declined (Putnam, 2000), but connectivity has not. People have more friends than before, and heavy internet users have the most (Wang & Wellman, 2010; Rainie & Wellman, 2012).

Networked individualism is having profound effects on *social cohesion*. Rather than people being a part of a hierarchy of encompassing groups like nesting Russian dolls, they belong to multiple, partial communities. It is not a matter of moving from place to place, but from person to person. Networking person to person means concerning oneself with support on a one-by-one basis.

Even as social networks have become less dense, *social linkages* have increased. Internet connectivity adds on to in-person and telephone contact; almost all people had stopped writing letters long before (Wellman & Haythornthwaite, 2002). As email can be stored until accessed, it helps facilitate contact with long-distance relationships. Furthermore, social network sites provide a communication route to people who might have otherwise been inaccessible as they drifted over time. This is how the internet is reconfiguring the notion of a "latent tie" from a friendship that might never have been easily accessible to one that is now conveniently available when needed (Haythornthwaite, 2005). Moreover, the velocity of internet contact approaches the speed of light, meaning that the only significant delay in email interaction is the time lag set by the user's attention. Additionally, email, Facebook postings, and texting are seen as less intrusive than telephone calls or in-person meetings. It is often the medium of choice for practical, socially considerate reasons. In short, there is probably more interpersonal contact among more people than ever before.

Although increasing *specialization* of tastes and combination of roles is not a product of the internet, the culturally rooted design of the internet in a specific brand of individualism considers the person regardless of place and regardless of a socially imposed structure such as a kinship network. Consider how email messages and mobile phone calls arrive sequentially, without inherent regard to the place of reception or to their relationship to the preceding or following messages. Work messages are followed by postings from interest group lists and communication among family members.

While this has led to concerns about "task switching" with one's private email, it has become an even larger issue on social network sites. This focus on the individual, regardless of role or situation, has been referred to as the collapsing of context (Marwick & boyd, 2010). Such a situation leads to new social tensions—it seems that almost every day a tabloid story of naughty pictures, drinking pictures, complaints about work, and relationship troubles are all vented in these flat spaces online to the detriment of those submitting or featured in this content. People are now so accustomed to the internet as a third space for casual chatting that many behave as if it were a site of social support even if that social support means complaining about the boss (also a Facebook friend), students (also following one on Twitter), or the spouse (also viewing this content).[5]

The ethereal internet light that previously dazzled has now dimmed to a soft glow permeating everyday concerns. We have moved from a world of internet wizards to a world of ordinary people routinely using the internet. The internet has become an important part of people's lives, but not a special part. It has become the utility of the masses rather than the plaything of computer scientists. It has become the infrastructure for a variety of computer-supported communications media, and not just the specialized conveyor of e-mail, Facebook, or any specific digital medium.

The change began before the coming of the internet, but the immanent internet has accelerated this change and helped shape its nature. Connectivity is up; cohesion is down. Journalists often ask us: "Is this a good thing or a bad thing?" Our answer is, "It is just a thing." It will have good and bad outcomes. However, while the internet is immanent, its effects are not technologically predetermined nor sociologically predestined. They are evolving, and humans shape their uses.

Notes

1. A revised and updated version of "The Immanent Internet" by Barry Wellman and Bernie Hogan (2004) in *Netting Citizens*, edited by Johnston McKay. St. Andrews, Scotland: University of St. Andrews Press. Our research has been supported by the DINS project of the GRAND Network Centre for Excellence, and the Social Sciences and Humanities Research Council of Canada. We appreciate the help of Julie Wang, Annie Shi, and Lilia Smale. Both authors contributed equally to this article.
2. See www.wired.com/wired/archive/7.12/full.html
3. Search engines for finding information had not yet reached their Googlean ease of use, and producing web content still required the knowledge of computer code. Most businesses did not think that a web presence was crucial until the late 1990s.
4. Howard Rheingold's *The Virtual Community* (1993) is a classic statement, although he markedly tempers his outlook in the second edition (2000). For other recent and more balanced ethnographies see Kendall (2002) and Chayko (2002).
5. A simple search on http://openfacebooksearch.com for something like "hate my boss" will show how cavalier people are becoming with content that was previously meant to be restricted to a select group of peers.

References

Barlow, J. P. (1995). Property and speech: Who owns what you say in cyberspace? *Communications of the ACM, 38*(12), 19–22.

Baron, N. (2008). *Always on: Language in an online and mobile world.* Oxford, England: Oxford University Press.

Bell, D., & Kennedy, B. M. (2000). *The cybercultures reader.* London, England: Routledge.

Berman, R. (Writer), & Piller, M. (Writer). (1995). *Star Trek: Voyager.* [Syndicated television series]. Los Angeles, CA: Paramount Television.

Boneva, B., & Kraut, R. (2002). Email, gender, and personal relationships. In B. Wellman & C. Haythornthwaite (Eds.), *The internet in everyday life* (pp. 372–403). Oxford, England: Blackwell.

boyd, d. (2006). Friends, friendsters and top 8: Writing community into being on social network sites. *First Monday 11*(12). Retrieved from http://firstmonday.org/htbin/cgiwrap/bin/ojs/index.php/fm/article/view/1418/1336

Bradner, E., & Kellogg, W. (1999, May). *Social affordances of BABBLE.* Presented at the CHI Conference, Pittsburgh, PA.

Castells, M., Tubella, I., Sancho, T., Diaz de Isla, I., & Wellman, B. (2003). *The network society in Catalonia: An empirical analysis.* (Universitat Oberta Catalunya, Barcelona, Spain). Retrieved from http://www.uoc.edu/in3/pic/esp/icl.html

Chardin, T. (1964). The formation of the noosphere. In *The future of man* (pp. 149–178). New York, NY: Harper & Row.

Chayko, M. (2002). *Connecting: How we form social bonds and communities in the internet age*. Albany, NY: State University of New York Press.

Chen, W., Boase, J., & Wellman, B. (2002). The global villagers: Comparing internet users and uses around the world. In B. Wellman & C. Haythornthwaite (Eds.), *The internet in everyday life* (pp. 74–113). Oxford, England: Blackwell.

Chen, W., & Wellman, B. (2004). Charting the Multiple Digital Divide. in W. Dutton, B. Kahin, R. O'Callaghan, & A. Wyckoff (Eds.), *Transforming Enterprise: The Economic and Social Implications of Information Technology* (pp. 467–497). Cambridge, MA: MIT Press.

De Kerkchove, D. (1997). *Connected intelligence: The arrival of the web society*. Toronto, Canada: Somerville House.

Dery, M. (1997). *Escape velocity: Cyberculture at the end of the century*. New York, NY: Grove Press.

Di Gennaro, C., & Dutton, W. (2007). Reconfiguring friendships: Social relationships and the internet [Special issue]. *Information, Communication & Society 10*(5), 591–618.

Fortunati, L., Katz J., & Riccini, R. (Eds.). (2003). *Mediating the human body: Technology, communication, and fashion*. Mahwah, NJ: Lawrence Erlbaum.

Fox, R. (1995). News track. *Communications of the ACM, 38*(8), 11–12.

Gibson, W. (1984). *Neuromancer*. New York, NY: Ace Science Fiction.

Greenfield, A. (2006). *Everyware: The dawning age of ubiquitous computing*. Berkeley, CA: Peachpit Press.

Greenfield, D. N. (1999). Psychological characteristics of compulsive Internet use: A preliminary analysis. *Cyberpsychology & Behavior: The impact of the internet, multimedia and virtual reality on behavior and society 2*(5), 403–412. Retrieved from http://www.ncbi.nlm.nih.gov/pubmed/19178212

Greenfield, S. (2009, February 25). Facebook: "Environment influences connections in brain" [Audio]. *The Guardian*. Retrieved from http://www.guardian.co.uk/technology/audio/2009/feb/25/greenfield-facebook

Hampton, K. (2007). Neighborhoods in the network society: The e-neighbors study. *Information, Communication, and Society 10*(5), 714–748.

Hampton, K., & Wellman, B. (2003). Neighboring in netville: How the internet supports community and social capital in a wired suburb. *City & Community, 2*(4), 277–311.

Hargittai, E., & Shafer, S. (2006). Differences in actual and perceived online skills: The role of gender. *Social Science Quarterly 87*(2), 432–448.

Haythornthwaite, C. (2005). Social networks and internet connectivity effects. *Information, Communication & Society 8*(2), 125–147.

Hedström, P. (1994). Contagious collectivities: On the spatial diffusion of Swedish trade unions, 1890–1940. *American Journal of Sociology 99*(5), 1157–1179. Retrieved from http://www.journals.uchicago.edu/doi/abs/10.1086/230408

Herring, S. (2004). Slouching toward the ordinary: Current trends in computer-mediated communication. *New Media & Society 6*(1), 26–36.

Hogan, B. (2010). The presentation of self in the age of social media: Distinguishing performances and exhibitions online. *Bulletin of Science, Technology & Society 30*(6), 377–386. Retrieved from http://bst.sagepub.com/cgi/doi/10.1177/0270467610385893

Hogan, B., & Fisher D. (2006). *A scale for measuring email overload* (MSR-TR-2006-65). Redmond, WA: Microsoft Research.

Ito, M., Matsuda, M., & Okabe, D. (Eds.). (2004). *Personal, portable, pedestrian: Mobile phones in Japanese life*. Cambridge, MA: MIT Press.

Joinson, A. N. (2002). *Understanding the psychology of internet behaviour: Virtual worlds, real lives*. New York, NY: Palgrave Macmillan.

Kendall, L. (2002). *Hanging out in the virtual pub: Masculinities and relationships online*. Berkeley, CA: University of California Press.

Koku, E., Nazer, N., & Wellman, B. (2001). Netting scholars: Online and offline. *American Behavioral Scientist 44*(10), 1750–1772.

Kraut, R., Patterson, M., Lundmark, V., Kiesler, S., Mukopadhyay, T., & Scherlis, W. (1998). Internet paradox: A social technology that reduces social involvement and psychological well-being? *American Psychologist 53*(9), 1017–1031.

Lévy, P. (1997). *Collective intelligence: Mankind's emerging world in cyberspace*. Cambridge, MA: Perseus Books.

Ling, R. (2004). *The mobile connection: The cell phone's impact on society*. San Mateo, CA: Morgan Kaufmann.

Ling, R. (2008). *New tech, new ties: How mobile communication is reshaping social cohesion*. Cambridge, MA: MIT Press.

Marwick, A. E., & boyd, d. (2010). I tweet honestly, I tweet passionately: Twitter users, context collapse, and the imagined audience. *New Media & Society, 13*(1), 114–133. Retrieved from http://nms.sagepub.com/cgi/doi/10.1177/1461444810365313

McAdam, D., Tarrow, S., & Tilly, C. (2001). *Dynamics of contention*. Cambridge, England: Cambridge University Press.

McEwen, R. (2009). *A world more intimate: Exploring the role of mobile phones in maintaining and extending social networks* (Ph.D. dissertation). Faculty of Information, University of Toronto, Canada.

McLuhan, M. (1962). *The Gutenberg galaxy: The making of typographic man*. Toronto, Canada: University of Toronto Press.

Miller, D., & Slater, D. (2000). *The internet: An ethnographic approach*. Oxford, England: Berg.

Mitra, A. (2003). Online communities, diasporic. In K. Christensen & D. Levinson (Eds.), *Encyclopedia of community, Vol. 3* (pp. 1019–1020). Thousand Oaks, CA: Sage.

Miyata, K., Boase, J., Wellman, B., & Ikeda, K. (2004). The mobile-izing Japanese: Connecting to the internet by PC and webphone in Yamanashi. In M. Ito, M. Matsuda, & D. Okabe (Eds.), *Personal, portable, pedestrian: Mobile phones in Japanese life* (pp. 143–164). Cambridge, MA: MIT Press.

Mok, D., Wellman, B., & Carrasco, J. A. (2010). Does distance matter in the age of the internet? *Urban Studies 47*(13), 2747–2783.

Norman, D. A. (2011). *The design of everyday things*. New York, NY: Basic Books.

Oudshoorn, N., & Pinch, T. (2004). *How users matter: The co-construction of users and technology.* Cambridge, MA: MIT Press.

Putnam, R. (2000). *Bowling alone: The collapse and revival of American community.* New York, NY: Simon & Schuster.

Quan-Haase, A., & Collins, J. (2008). "I'm there, but I might not want to talk to you." *Information, Communication and Society 11*(4), 526–543.

Quan-Haase, A., & Wellman, B. (2004). Local virtuality in a high-tech networked organization. *Analyse und Kritik 26(1),* 241–257.

Quan-Haase, A., & Wellman, B. (with Witte, J., & Hampton, K). (2002). Capitalizing on the net: Social contact, civic engagement, and sense of community. In B. Wellman & C. Haythornthwaite (Eds.), *The internet in everyday life* (pp. 291–324). Oxford, England: Blackwell.

Rainie, L., & Wellman, B. (2012). *Networked: The new social operating system.* Cambridge, MA: MIT Press. Manuscript in preparation.

Raymond, E. S. (1998). Homesteading the noosphere. *First Monday 3*(10), 1–28.

Reeves, B., & Nass, C. (1996). *The media equation: How people treat computers, television, and new media like real people and places.* New York, NY: Cambridge University Press. Retrieved from http://portal.acm.org/citation.cfm?id=236605

Rheingold, H. (1993). *The virtual community: Homesteading on the electronic frontier.* Reading, MA: Addison-Wesley.

Rheingold, H. (2000). *The virtual community: Homesteading on the electronic frontier.* (Revised ed.). Cambridge, MA: MIT Press.

Schiano, D. J., & White, S. (1998). The first noble truth of cyberspace: People are people (even when they MOO). In *Proceedings of the SIGCHI conference on human factors in computing systems* (pp. 352–359). New York, NY: ACM Press.

Sigman, A. (2009). Well connected? The biological implications of "social networking." *The Biologist 56*(1), 14–20.

Sproull, L., & Kiesler, S. (1991). *Connections: New ways of working in the networked organization.* Cambridge, MA: MIT Press.

Steiner, P. (1993, July 5). On the internet, nobody knows you're a dog [Cartoon]. *The New Yorker.*

Stephenson, N. (1992). *Snow crash.* New York, NY: Bantam.

Takhteyev, Y., Gruzd, A., & Wellman, B. (2011, February). The imagined geographies of Twitter. NetLab Working Paper.

Turkle, S. (1995). *Life on the screen: Identity in the age of the internet.* New York, NY: Simon & Schuster.

Turkle, S. (2011). *Alone together: Why we expect more from technology and less from each other.* New York, NY: Basic Books.

Turner, F. (2006). *From counterculture to cyberculture: Stewart Brand, the Whole Earth Network, and the rise of digital utopianism.* Chicago, IL: University of Chicago Press.

Van Gelder, L. (1985, October). The strange case of the electronic lover. *Ms.,* 94–104, 117–123.

Vey, P. C. (2004, February 2). I was addicted to porn before there was an Internet [Cartoon]. *The New Yorker.*

Wang, H., & Wellman, B. (2010). Social connectivity in America: Changes in adult friendship network size from 2002 to 2007. *American Behavioral Scientist 53*(8), 1148–1169.

Wellman, B., & Hampton, K. (1999). Living networked on and offline. *Contemporary Sociology 28*(6), 648–654.

Wellman, B., & Gulia, M. (1999). Net surfers don't ride alone: Virtual communities as communities. In B. Wellman (Ed.), *Networks in the global village: Life in contemporary communities* (pp. 331–366). Boulder, CO: Westview.

Wellman, B., & Haythornthwaite, C. (Eds.). (2002). *The internet in everyday life*. Oxford, England: Blackwell.

Wellman, B., Garofalo A., & Garofalo, V. (2009). The internet, technology and connectedness. *Transition 39*(4), 5–7.

Wired. (2004, February) Hypelist. Retrieved from http://www.wired.com/wired/archive/12.02/start.html

Young, K. S. (1998). *Caught in the Net: How to recognize the signs of internet addiction—and a winning strategy for recovery*. New York, NY: Wiley.

4. New Media, Wikifaith and Church Brandversation: A Media Ecology Perspective

BALA A. MUSA & IBRAHIM M. AHMADU

Introduction

Today's information revolution and the general notion that we live in a (new) media age is an acknowledgment of how our relationship with communication technology has become fundamental to the essence of our society and being. The act of gathering, storing, and sharing information is not only an essential function and aspect of our culture, it has become the culture. It is our defining way of life. In previous eras, communication and information technology was the key player in the economic, cultural, political, and social sphere. Today, it is the arena and environment in which all these occur (Straubhaar & LaRose, 2008).

From earliest advances in communication technology, philosophers, communication scholars, sociologists, and political economists have sought to understand the nature of the relationship between a society's mode of communication and its norms and institutions. In the Western tradition, attempts to map the force field of communication technology and social change date back to earliest times. Plato and Aristotle postulated on the consequences of writing on society (Postman, 1992). Every new phase in the evolution of communication technology has witnessed a rekindling and intensifying of the debate over the impact, if any, of the new technology on society. The debate is often framed at multiple levels. At one level, the debate focuses on the question of whether advancements in communication technology and modes of communication are causes or effects of a larger sociological transformation. At another level, a question that often accompanies the dawn of each new communication technology is whether the new technology is good or bad for society. This has always been the case, whether it is the invention of paper, the printing press, radio, television, or the internet. And the effects of new modes of communication have always been part of these debates.

At one time the controversy surrounded papyrus (or paperspace); much later, it revolved around radio and television. Now, the question is about the danger posed by cyberspace or cybermedia communication. While the media forms have evolved, the central concerns have remained the same. At the heart of it all is the question of whether (communication) technology is neutral or deterministic. Various schools of thought have taken various positions, ranging from the all-powerful magic bullet media theory to passive audience, mass society, minimal-effect, active audience, and selectivity theories (Hoover, 2006; Hosseini, 2008).

This discourse does not assume a simplistic cause-effect view or one-way deterministic effect of new technology. Instead, it rests on the premise that the interface between new communication technology and society has profound mutually transformational results. The specific nature and direction of such effects has engaged prophetic voices on both sides of the technology utopia-dystopia debate, including, notably, McLuhan (1994), Ellul (1967), Ong (1982), Postman (1985, 1992), and Christians (1997, 2002), among others. Despite the preponderance of functional perspectives, there is limited holistic theoretical analysis of church public conversation. This discourse joins the call and search for relevant theoretical and conceptual models that examine the emergent realities of new media and church *brandversation*, i.e., the conversation and interaction that shapes the identity and perception of a brand (Thurlbeck, 2003, p. 276). It builds on the idea that in pluralistic and democratic societies, each religious organization is a cultural brand and needs to distinguish itself from the crowd by articulating its identity and its unique selling proportion (Einstein, 2008; Musa, 2000; Parente, 2004).

Using a historical, cultural-critical approach, the research identifies the relevant trends, issues, and challenges facing the church in a post-relevation, post-modern, epistemic environment. It addresses the need to go beyond the prevailing didactic, dialogic, trialogic, and triadic communication models (Woodward, 2000; DeVries, 2009). Instead, it argues that in the new Web 3.0 environment, triadic-transactional and evolutionary network theories of communication provide more holistic understandings of the emerging role of new media in church brandversation (Woodward, 1996; Monge, Heiss, & Margolin, 2008). In essence, the research calls for a media ecological analysis, one that examines the dynamic interaction between the institutions of new media and other cultural institutions, in this case, the church (Forsberg, 2009; Hosseini, 2008; Cooper, 2006; Christians, 2002). It looks at the implications for a people-centered, people-cultivated faith, which we call *wikifaith*, for church doctrine, identity, community, and governance.

Media Ecology: A Technology and Culture Perspective

"The word 'ecology' implies the study of environments: their structure, content, and impact on people. Media ecology is the study of media as environments" (Salas, 2007, p. 63). According to Lum, "media ecology is the 'study of how changes in communication media facilitate fundamental, large-scale or ecological changes in culture . . ." (cited in Salas, 2007, p. 65). Media ecology combines semiotic, cybernetic, phenomenological, and other communication theories (Craig, 1999). Postman (1975) believed media ecologists are not specialists; rather they are "generalists and connectionists" (in Salas, 2007, p. 63). This approach assumes that both message (content) and medium (technology) shape the communication experience.

Media ecology connects functional, interpretive, cultural, and critical theories into a holistic relationship between media and society. It pays attention, not only to language, message, and meaning, but also to technology and context. It looks at the effect of the media environment on people's behavior as well as its impact on socio-cultural norms. It examines the interaction between media environment and political, economic, religious, and cultural norms, for instance. According to Forsberg (2009):

> Media ecologists seek to discover how our thinking and behavior changes as we move from oral to scribal, to print, and electronic cultures. Media ecologists are interested in discovering how various forms of communication influence our moral, physical, social, intellectual, and spiritual development. . . . Some media ecologists are particularly interested in discovering how our media and technologies influence our values, our religious sensitivities, and our basic theological understandings. (p. 138)

The school of media ecology traces its roots to scholars such as Ong (1982), Ellul (1967), McLuhan (1994), Postman (1993), and Christians (1994), to mention but a few. Together they have provided a rich multi-perspectival critique of media communication and change in society in general, and in religion in particular. These multidisciplinary approaches involving sociologists, historians, linguists, theologians, psychologists, etc., converge in the field of communication studies to give a somewhat holistic understanding in the growing area of media ecology.

Media ecology perspective sees a close connection between the *mediascape* (Appadurai, 1990, p. 23), namely the complex mix of information communication technology (ICT) environment, and the culture at large (see also Rao & Johal, 2006). This approach views language and technology as semantic and cybernetic environments that structure and transform our experience as we move from one communication environment to another (Forsberg, 2010); "Media ecologists want to know what kind of environment we enter when we talk on the telephone or watch television or read a book" (Postman, 1974,

p. 76, cited in Frosberg, 2010, pp. 145–146). The mediasphere (world of media) is conceived of as a reality different from the natural environment. In other words, when we enter the world of media, we are entering a new time-space reality (Strate, 2010). According to Frosberg (2010), the mediasphere is a language-media-culture force field that structures our thinking, feeling, and behavior differently from the way in which the natural environment does. There-fore, transition from one form of communication to another always marks the dawn of a new era, a new reality, and a new way of life. As Postman (1993) put it: "A new technology does not add nor subtract, it changes everything" (p. 24).

New Media Ecology, the Church, and Wikifaith

This research seeks to address the question of how cyberspace, the new noo-sphere of communication, affects communication and culture in general, and church brandversation in particular (Krüger, 2007). Media ecology conceives of the internet in a primordial way. Krüger (2007, p. 143) asserted that the internet, or cyberspace, is not just another leap in the advancement or evolution of com-munication technology. Instead, it is organic to the noosphere, the ontological order of being. In Pesce's (2000, p. 170) view, the internet is "an organic part of the earth, destined to come into existence as part of the natural evolutionary process" (cited in Krüger, 2007, p. 143). The emergence of the internet and new media is integral to the created order of things, in which society and creation have evolved from discrete communal to organic global. "The medium now becomes part of a superior cosmic process, apparently unfettered by human influences. In an age that lacks one common myth, the medium itself becomes the master narrative—die Meistererzahlung—of the media society" (Krüger, 2007, p. 167).

The church is not immune to the power of the environment in which it is embedded to become the defining master narrative. Sam Pascoe (2010) pressed this point when he observed that:

> Christianity started out in Palestine as a fellowship; it moved to Greece and became a philosophy; it moved to Italy and became an institution; it moved to Europe and became a culture; it came to America and became an enterprise. (Quotations section, para. 1)

How are cyberspace and cyberculture acting as master narratives on faith and church brandversation? The web is an environment like no other, and yet like any other. It has features that can impact, and be impacted by, what goes on there. Dawson and Hennebry (1999) opined that "Like any 'envi-ronment,' the web acts back on its content, modifying the form of its users or inhabitants" (p. 31). The question, then, is what influence, if any, is the new media environment exerting on the institution of the church, and on the practice of Christianity, and vice-versa?

Attempts to answer this question have ranged from conservative skepticism to liberal utopianism. One school argues that religion and media exist in separate realms (Hall, 2008; Kerr, 2003; Postman, 1985). It is easy to assume the dichotomy between the two. After all, they say, religion concerns the spiritual, supernatural, metaphysical, and hypereal. The only mediation it requires is divine revelation and inspiration. On the other hand, media technology belongs to the temporal, physical, material, and natural realm. It is no accident that the dominant term for new media technology is social, not spiritual, media. From a philosophical perspective, religion and theology point people toward musing, meditation, and transcendence, while media technology has mostly been associated with amusement, entertainment, or anti-muse.

Another school argues that media can serve both secular and spiritual ends (Hoover, 2006; Schultze, 2000; Tipler, 1994; Cobb, 1998). This school believes religion and media not only exist in the same realm, but that they are inseparable. To them, the works of God are demonstrated in the physical laws of the universe, including advances in technology and science. Hoover (2006) also opined that:

> Media and religion have come together in fundamental ways. They occupy the same spaces, serve many of the same purposes, and invigorate the same practices in late modernity. Today, it is probably better to think of them as related than to think of them as separate. (p. 9)

Bugeja (2005) and Schultze (2000) extend the role of the media in religion and spirituality to that of prophet, priest, and idol.

The dichotomous and deterministic perception of (communication) technology has led the Amish and some ultra-orthodox Jewish groups, for instance, to reject modern or high technology, if not in daily life, certainly in religion (Campbell, 2005; Krüger, 2007). The Deeper Life Christian Church, a holiness church movement, which began in Nigeria in the 1970s, and now has a global followership, was strongly opposed to its members owning or watching a television. Even as some of these groups have modified their views about media, they find it necessary to spiritualize or sanctify these media to make them sacred enough for religious purposes.

The dominant view of media technology among American evangelicals is mostly utopian and sanguine. This is evidenced in the eagerness with which mainstream evangelicals have embraced every new communication media as a means for propagating the gospel. They point to how the media is used both to propagate faith by some and to promote immoral and anti-Christian values by others (Schultze & Woods, 2008; Schultze, 2000). Morgan (2002) observed that "antebellum evangelicals regarded the printed and distribution of the Bible and tracts as the appropriately modern instrument for universal evangelization" (p. 39).

The close ties between religion and media go back in time. The first notable use of the printing press by Johannes Gutenberg was to print the Bible. Likewise, every new medium that came along was immediately deployed to the service of religion, from the telegraph to radio, television, and now the internet.

The internet is saturated with the presence of religious sites and resources. The "church online" is alive and proliferating. *Beliefnet,* a website and blog on Christianity, culture, writing, and doubt, described the phenomenal followership of preachers such as John Piper and Rob Bell, who are influencing the internet through their tweets, Facebook pages, and blogs. Site host Jason Boyett describes how one posting by Bell and response tweet from Piper attracted 20,000 Facebook recommendations and 1,000 comments (Boyett, 2011). He observed that the phenomenal online followership generated by these Christian leaders put the Christian subject of their tweet in "the top 10 trending topics, which is usually reserved for Middle East unrest, dead celebrities, and Justin Biebers" ("Thoughts about Rob Bell," para. 8).

That religion is prevalent in cyberspace or that Christians and other religious groups have adopted cybermedia as a medium of communication is no longer a hot news item, but it is worth examining the nature of the relationship and its manifest consequences.

Hosseini (2008) differentiated between mediated religion and religious media. The former "is the religion and its exclusive teachings and doctrines, which uses the media as a mere tool for the transmission of messages." The latter is "the utilization of media through its unique identity, to achieve religious objectives, ultimate goals, and divine aspirations rather than the monopolistic teachings and beliefs of religion" (p. 67). Cybermedia serve to mediate religion. Established religious groups as well as up-and-coming groups have used the internet to recruit members, disseminate information, instruct, and build community.

Krüger (2007) spoke of cyberutopia. Just as with other preceding media, cyberspace has been viewed as a revolutionary medium with the potential to change society as we know it, mostly for the better. Cyberspace has been described "as an unlimited space for the development of the intellectual, spiritual and emotional potentials of humanity (Krüger, 2007, p. 143; see also, Cobb, 1998). The religious and spiritual potentials of cybercommunication are indeed unlimited.

Interface of Faith and Cybermedia

For the purpose of this discourse, we will focus on the phenomenon we describe as *wikifaith,* and its bearing on the Church. Wiki-culture is a cultural phenomenon and institution that is illustrative of community and communication in the virtual media environment. As observed earlier, as the Christian faith advanced from Palestine to Greece, the Roman Empire, England and the United States, it not only transformed those societies, it also took on some of the distinctive colorations of those cultures. The contention here is that church has not faired any differently in the cybermedia environment, or *wiki-land,* if you like.

Faith in the new media environment has taken on the markings of wiki-culture. Christianity is not immune to this. The word *wiki,* the root word for Wikipedia, is Hawaiian for "quick" (Lih, 2009). What Lih calls the "wiki culture" (p. 59) is both a product of, and the driving force behind the new social media communication environment. Among its characteristics are quick, fast-paced, multi-sourced exchange and updating of data. Wikipedia provides user-generated content, and is "the encyclopedia that anyone can edit" (p. 4). It is an information source that is "free, open, neutral, timely, and social" (p. 5). An environment of this sort would seem susceptible to confusion, misinformation, low quality, and anarchy. While that potential exists, its popularity and growth suggest the reverse. It "has evolved from being simply a no-cost alternative into being a superior resource in its own right. Over the years, it has become deeper, broader, and more up-to-date than its traditional rivals" (p. 5). It has the fingerprints of all other institutions that have evolved alongside it, and vice-versa.

One can speak of faith relative to place and time because faith impacts, and is impacted by, its environment. Just as reference can be made to American, European, Latin American, first-century, medieval, or twenty-first century Christianity, the idea of wikifaith speaks of faith in the new environment. Wikifaith is faith with the markings of wiki-culture. It is characterized by the many dialectical tensions that result from the pull between medium and message and function and essence, as well as social and spiritual. These tensions translate into specific attributes of faith expression in cyberspace, to be examined subsequently.

Centripetal-centrifugal

Christianity and all theistic religions are, by their very nature, revelation-based. Each theistic faith subscribes to certain fundamental revealed truths about the existence of the creator God or the divine being, and about how humans are to relate to the creator, to one another, and to the universe around them. The truths to which believers subscribe are deemed divinely inspired and transmitted. Such truths are usually contained in the teachings, sacred texts, or cannons of these religions. They are the core beliefs and faith-rituals that have been handed down over time and the generations. Implied in the idea of revelation is transmission or mediation. In Christianity, the vehicles of mediation have included the scriptural teachings which convey the knowledge of

God, the sacraments and rituals which give expression to belief or faith in this knowledge, and the communities or institutions that embody this faith. Christianity and the existence of the church has been inherently tied to what Ong (1982) called the "The Technologizing of the Word." Mediation is the means by which the ethereal word becomes flesh or takes on physical presence. The Word, which, as John the Apostle described, has existed for all eternity (John 1:1), now takes on finite, physical, temporal, human form by entering into specific time and place. The vehicle or medium through which the message is transmitted becomes a packaging and transformational environment. Where there is a message, there is supposed to be a messenger. In the church, the message has come down through prophets and prophetesses in antiquity, through Christ and his apostles, and subsequently through Christian ministers over the years.

Revelation and transmission of faith point to authority. Christ is the head of the church. His authority is believed to have been delegated to others who exercise it on God's behalf. That is to say, that the church is centripetal in nature. Authority is centralized in the anointed leader(s). Many newer evangelical and Pentecostal church denominations have embraced the Presbyterian and congregational leadership approaches, by giving more voice to the laity in church governance. In wiki-culture, it's the people who are the source of knowledge and authority, not a centralized authority. "Those who log onto cyberspace may tend to gravitate to religious denominations that emphasize centrifugal rather than centripetal force, just as the medium that is carrying them does. Authority loses its trappings and force on the net . . ." (Zaleski, 1997, pp. 111–112, cited in Dawson & Hennebry, 1999, p. 34).

Lih (2009) observed that one dominant element of the Wikipedia Revolution is peer-production by Net natives who have grown up in an environment of egalitarian democratic participation. They see themselves not just as consumers but "prosumers" of information, goods and services, popular culture, etc. According to Lih, they don't expect it to be otherwise when it comes to the exercise of their faith. They want to be active participants, not just passive recipients, in the construction of their faith.

Permeable boundaries

According to Caron and Caronia (2007) cyberspace as environment is characterized by the simultaneous experience of *delocalization* and *multilocalization*; one that lacks "territorial anchorage" (p. 14). It is an environment where people are able to maintain synchronous contact via mobile phones, e-mail, Facebook, MySpace, Twitter, Skype, etc. It is possible to be physically distant, yet be virtually present with another person at the same time. In wikiworld, space does not disappear. It is transcended. In the new media environment, community is no longer conceived entirely in geographic sense. In digital space, one can be present at, and impact, more than one location at a time. Technically, it seems so, since one can be in the presence of one person while texting, and be talking with another who is physically removed from the present location. Space and territory in the virtual world are more psychological than physical (Bugeja, 2005).

This new reality has significant implications for faith and culture. In traditional society, space and boundaries were real. Distance and place dictated interactions. Location defined one's communication and interaction partners. Choosing to be or not be at a location also meant a choice about whom or what one encountered. In a world of fluid boundaries, individuals can be exposed to multiple, sometimes divergent, groups, ideas, beliefs, values, etc., simultaneously.

Much about faith in cyberworld is akin to today's wiki-culture, a "prosumer" culture where the boundary between sender and receiver, author and audience, and producer and consumer is blurred or non-existent. The ecology of the media and theology have revealed significant parallels between how information, ideas, and knowledge flow in cyber-environment, and how faith is formed, nurtured, and circulated in the new media environment. Contemporary narratives of how people come to faith, and identify with and express their faith today, show a significant departure from biblical and historical faith journey narratives (Haynes, 1999). For example, in the Pauline epistle, Timothy was said to have "inherited" his faith from his mother who had, in turn, received it from her mother. The Book of Acts is filled with stories of whole families and communities converting to Christianity. Most of Paul's epistles were addressed to communities of believers in specific geographic locations as opposed to anonymous, disconnected individuals. However, these days:

> With the appropriate knowledge and minimal computer hardware and software, anyone can sample a wide array of alternative religious views, and, if they so choose, just as easily hide their exposure or consumption of such views from the prying eyes of others (e.g. parents, partners, friends, or employers). In fact, the net opens surprising new opportunities to even start one's own religion. (Dawson & Hennebry, 1999, pp. 18–19; see also Cheong & Poon, 2009)

Media technology has always enabled preachers and religious leaders to disseminate their teachings to people far and wide. Religious books, gospel tracts, and Bible correspondence courses enabled people in far away places to receive teachings from other sources beyond their localities and local pastors. The coming of radio and television made it possible to listen, in real time and on a regular basis, to one's favorite preacher, whom one may never have met in person. With the internet and social media, the opportunity has increased exponentially. Countless sources of teachings and beliefs are at one's fingertips. Parishioners and congregants receive spiritual teachings from their local leaders as well as from others outside their local congregation and denomination, and sometimes even outside their professed faith.

Within the organized religious system, one often requires lengthy education, vetting, and ordination processes to become a member of the clergy. Today, websites such as *Get Ordained Online* (www.openministry.org), *Become a Minister Today* (www.ministerregistration.org), and *Get Ordained Today* (www. getordainedtoday.com), offer instant ordination. Some couples have asked their friends to get instant online ordination in order for those friends to officiate at the couples' weddings. What may be considered fringe practices and religions in mainstream culture seem common in the new media environment.

Stability and chaos

Wikifaith can be said to be characterized by stability and change, order and chaos, if you will. Traditional churches were structured similarly to traditional society. They were characterized by strong hierarchies, and valued order and stability over change and flexibility. Wikipedia is to the new mediascape and cyberculture what the French Encyclopedia (circa 1750–1780) was to traditional society. Encyclopedia meant complete or "rounded education" (Lih, 2009, p. 14). It was deemed to contain the full body of knowledge and information available to a generation or group. Wikipedia reflects a culture of openness, change, and transition. That means that the information is changing all the time. In many new faith communities, people are not only open to new ideas, but are more embracing of different perspectives. Faith in the new environment is more of a process than an end state.

In the past, faith gave a person his or her sense of identity. Today, a person's religion is one of many elements that make up the person's sense of self. Research has shown "that a great number of young in the US, despite their claim of a 'religious' identity, might be classified . . . as 'marginal members'" (Clark, 2003, p. 23). At the level of the individual, the image is that of multiple selves, in which faith is only one piece of the puzzle.

Writing about a particular set of the wiki generation, whom they referred to as Mosaics (born between 1984 and 2002), Kinnaman and Lyons (2007) observed that spirituality is important to them, "but many consider it just another element of a successful, eclectic life" (p. 23). This generation's membership of a faith group is somewhat on the same footing to them as their membership of a fitness club, an environmental action group, etc. They have more faith identification than identity.

The Net generation "view life in a nonlinear, chaotic way, which means they don't mind contraction and ambiguity" (Kinnaman & Lyons, 2007, p. 23). To the traditionally minded observer, the *wikifaith* Christian may appear like a disorderly hybrid, one who is rebellious, irreverent, or even irreligious. The young person's religious language is usually "detribalized" and "de-ethnicized," again a function of not being confined to one box, category, community, or source of religious instruction (Clark, 2003). As in Wikipedia, wiki-culture and wikifaith members':

> systematic use of words belonging to different cultures and their creative appropriation, integration, and fusion in discourse create a specific language strongly characterized by heteroglossia. The interpretation of different voices speaking "other languages" weaves together different cultural frames of reference and reflects the multiple, heterogenic nature of these teenagers' cultural belonging. (Caron & Caronia, 2007, p. 140)

Usually, they are more apt to see and communicate spiritual truths through popular media content and characters than biblical or scriptural narratives. This is not evidence of lack of faith or spirituality. It is, rather, that their spiritual instruction and language comes from multiple sources, texts, and contexts, just as a Wikipedia entry would. This group's trans-cultural language "crosses not only the borders of ethno-linguistic communities but also those of different communities of [religious] practices" (p. 140).

The internet serves up a cacophony of voices and diversity of menu, yet it makes sense to the netizen. Today's young adult Christian may not express his or her spirituality the way the older generation did, yet they are not necessarily faithless or less devout. The proliferation of mega-churches, increasing popularity of religious media (Christian music in particular), and abundance of religious resources online, are all evidence of this.

De- and retribalization

As shown in the preceding discourse, the proliferation of, and ease of access to, multiple faith resources online has compounded the transformation of religious communities into consumption communities. Church websites serve to further the church brand as they "transform mundane products into 'holy' icons" (Schultze, 2000, p. 115). Church T-shirts, bracelets, mugs, etc., help extend the religious brand experience.

People can circumvent local restrictions to their faith expression (Cheong & Poon, 2009; Musa, 2000). Online media, because it can be private and discrete, has been able to penetrate communities where legal restrictions exclude missionaries or traditional media.

Schultze and Woods (2008) stated that God "created humankind with the ability to form tribelike religious communities that differentiate themselves from other religious and nonreligious communities. . . . Tribes give us a place to stand, beliefs to affirm, values to hold, friends for fellowship" (p. 22).

Bricks-and-mortar church congregations have expectedly served these functions, that local tribes serve, for their members. However, there are circumstances under which some people don't find that connection, or don't feel that sense of belonging to their local congregations. Online religious communities have served to fill the void where people are unable to, or choose not to, belong to a local congregation. Moreover, data has shown that in many parts of the Western world, church membership and attendance has been in decline since the mid-1900s, while at the same there has been an increase in people's quest for spirituality (Heelas & Woodhead, 2005). For many who seek alternative communities in order to nurture and express their spirituality, virtual media provide such opportunity.

Virtual communities help individuals detribalize and retribalize (Krüger, 2007, p. 153; Fortner, 2007, p. 167). It was predicted that the dawn of the electronic age would revert society and social relations toward a secondary orality culture reminiscent of oral, tribal, and communal societies (McLuhan, 1992; Ong, 1984). This prophetic vision has come true as people huddle in the electronic sheds of the blogosphere and the twittersphere. People are detribalized by escaping the trapping of their local groups, while retribalizing by joining other groups. By the mid-2000s, reports showed that of the three million people who surfed the web for religion, 67 percent sought information about their own faith, while 50 percent searched for information about other faiths (Einstein, 2008).

Expression of faith online removes limitations of tradition and local standards. Individuals can choose which rituals and practices they want to participate in, while still having a feeling of belonging. However, online communities often lack some of the elements that communities in real life offer to their members. Some believers have found spiritual home online who, otherwise would not. At the same time, others who could use the support of local communities or could be of service to their local community may resort to online spiritual community for the anonymity and convenience, or out of a desire to avoid accountability.

New Media and Church Brandversation

As with any brand, how the church defines itself, its mission, its membership, its methods, etc., to the world, and how society engages, shapes, and defines the church as a cultural brand in the brave new world of social media, is a form of conversation.

Religious tribes, be they faith or denominational groups, use boundaries, rituals, and labels to distinguish members from non-members, and insiders from outsiders. This process and ultimate goal is similar to that used in product and service branding, which is why religious communities have been compared with brand communities (Einstein, 2008). As brands, church denominations seek to be identifiable, distinguishable, appealing, competitive, accepted, and useful. The qualities of wikifaith, or faith in the wiki environment, constitute opportunities as well as threats to these goals. New and social media can help churches engage their audience in dialogue or in a conversation about their brands. That is the process of "brandversation" (Thurlbeck, 2003, p. 276).

Brandversation has evolved alongside generations of new media technology. Thurlbeck (2003) noted that earlier stages of brandversation, versions 1 and 2, were characterized by one-way information dissemination. Churches at this level operate their websites as electronic bulletins and notice boards for posting information. Third Generation (3G) social media technologies have allowed organizations not only to offer information, but also to contextualize their brand. Brandversation versions 3 and 4 now involve linking "touchpoints throughout the user's experience, making the experience more rewarding" (p. 278).

If church membership is declining, new media is blurring the boundaries between faiths and denominations, and it is becoming increasingly harder to distinguish between believers and non-believers, there may be a need for churches to reposition their products through effective brand communication. If others cannot distinguish between the spirituality of the Christian faith and that of other faiths, it is a failure of how the churches' story is being told in the new environment of multiple voices and sources.

The church has long used marketing and public relations techniques in selling itself to the public (Einstein, 2008). To suggest that the gospel message be presented in a way that will make it distinguishable, appealing, and inviting, raises concerns because of previous attempts that have been perceived as not only selling, but also selling out the church (Kenneson & Street, 1997).

In the wikifaith environment, the church no longer has a corner in the marketplace of ideas, or faiths, for that matter. It does not even have command of telling its story, as any person can reach the world audience with its narrative about Christianity, about a particular denomination or minister. Christians and non-Christians alike have their own opinions about churches, opinions formed largely by secular media.

Einstein (2008) argued that faith branding is necessary because religion is a commodity product, and competes with other products. Churches are becoming nondenominational and denominations (church brands) are becoming indistinguishable, and others, including opposers, have the capacity to hijack the narrative of the church. In such an environment, "branding faith becomes the shorthand for reaching the new religious consumer" (p. 13). The challenge for the church is how to harness the rich resources of new and social media toward affording its consumers, or prosumers, a rich and rewarding brand experience.

Many resourceful churches have embraced social media in full, just like they did with earlier generations of mass communication technology. Uses range from comprehensive information about various aspects and activities of church, to live streaming of services and opportunities to follow the church or its ministers on Twitter, Facebook, YouTube, etc. Even many less media-rich nations in Africa have embraced new media as a means of disseminating information about their churches and ministries, and they also make it possible to access teachings, order products, and donate to the church online. Through communication, churches create taste communities and followers who are attracted by a particular style of preaching, music, worship, leadership, experience, etc. (Fornter, 2007). The church then sees the need to maintain the brand-customer relationship. Churches in the West, who are in the era of Web 3.0, are able to give their audiences what Thurlbeck (2003) called brand-versation version 3.0 and version 4.0. The defining characteristic of this is:

> a profound change that has refocused many corporations [if one may add, churches] from a Webcentric perspectic to one that is customer-centric. . . . The consumer wants more, demands more, and is being given more, and this puts more pressure on the brand promise. (p. 278)

Churches in the West are able to immerse their audience and members in a digital bubble of interactive religious experience, typical of Web 3.0 cultures offering brandversation version 3.0 and version 4.0. In Africa and other Third World countries the experience is rather limited. Most are barely entering the Web 2.0 media environment. Nigeria, the most populous country in Africa, is still attempting to lay fiber optic cable to enable it to provide broadband internet to its citizens. While cell phone diffusion in the society is over 100 percent among adults (because many people carry two or even three cell phones because of service interruptions, variation in price, and intra-network prices—Bailard, 2009), computers and supporting infrastructure limit access. Some ministers do text or tweet devotions to their members, but e-mails and web surfing are still expensive luxuries. Many urban churches have skeletal websites, but most serve as electronic brochureware and bulletin boards; typical of brandversation version 1.0 and version 2.0.

Conclusion

As Wayne (2008) put it, "Theology is done in conversation" (p. 100). New media can serve as tools for conversation about the church as a particular community or brand. This dialogue about the church's brand, or this brandversation, involves brand promise, communication, and experience. Wayne (2008) argued that theological blogging, for instance, can widen the community and, therefore, our perspective, but should not change how we do theology.

In other words, the church's brand promise should be non-negotiable. The church throughout all generations stands for one thing: to propagate the gospel and bring people to the knowledge of the truth. However, its communication style must adapt to the environment in which it finds itself. Today's new mediascape environment impacts every institution in its horizon, the church included. When it comes to communicating the church's brand, we must beware of the potential of new media technology to both help and harm our theology (Wayne, 2008). A medium can easily serve its user, as it uses those it serves. Churches must understand this dialectic in order to effectively adapt their communication technique to the new media environment without losing control of their message. In a highly competitive new media environment, with multiple messages and voices, churches must pay attention to the brand experience customers get through church social media. The media can be used to set the community's agenda but, on the other hand, the media can also set the agenda for the community.

References

Appadurai, A. (1990). Disjuncture and difference in the global cultural economy. *Public Culture, 2*(2), 1–23.

Bailard, C. S. (2009). Mobile phone diffusion and corruption in Africa. *Political Communication, 26*(3), 333–353.

Boyett, J. (2011, February 28). Thoughts about Rob Bell, John Piper, and Justin Taylor [Web log post]. Retrieved from http://blog.beliefnet.com/omeoflittle-faith/2011/02/thoughts-rob-bell.html

Bugeja, M. (2005). *Interpersonal divide: The search for community in a technological age.* New York, NY: Oxford University Press.

Campbell, H. (2005). Spiritualizing the internet: Uncovering discourses and narratives of religious internet usage. *Online—Heidelberg Journal of Religions on the Internet, 1.1.* Retrieved from http://archiv.ub.uni-heidelberg.de/volltextserver/volltexte/2005/5824/pdf/Campbell4a.pdf

Caron, A. H., & Caronia, L. (2007). *Moving cultures: Mobile communication in everyday life.* Montreal, Canada: McGill-Queen's University Press.

Cheong, P. H., & Poon, J. P. H. (2009). Weaving webs of faith: Examining internet use and religious communication among Chinese Protestant transmigrants. *Journal of International and Intercultural Communication, 2*(3), 189–207.

Christians, C. G. (1997). Technology and triadic theories of mediation. In S. M. Hoover & K. Lundby (Eds.), *Rethinking media, religion and culture* (pp. 66–67). London, England: Sage Publications.

Christians, C. G. (2002). Religious perspectives on communication technology. *Journal of Media & Religion, 1*(1), 37–47.

Clark, L. S. (2003). The 'funky' side of religion: An ethnographic study of adolescent religious identity and the media. In J. Mitchell & S. Marriage (Eds.), *Mediating religion: Studies in media, religion and culture* (pp. 21–32). New York, NY: T & T Clark.

Cobb, J. J. (1998). *CyberGrace: The search for God in the digital world.* New York, NY: Crown.

Cooper, T. W. (2006). The medium is the mass: Marshall McLuhan's Catholicism and catholicism. *Journal of Media and Religion, 5*(3), 161–173.

Craig, R. T. (1999). Communication theory as a field. *Communication Theory, 9*(2), 119–161.

Dawson, L. L., & Hennebry, J. (1999). New religions and the internet: Recruiting in a new public space. *Journal of Contemporary Religion, 14*(1), 17–39.

DeVries, B. A. (2009). The evangelistic trialogue: Gospel communication with the Holy Spirit. *Calvin Theological Journal,* 49–73.

Durkheim, E. (1995) [1912]. *The elementary forms of religious life.* Translated by Karen E. Fields. New York, NY: Free Press.

Einstein, M. (2008). *Brands of faith: Marketing religion in a commercial age.* New York, NY: Routledge.

Ellul, J. (1967). *The technological society.* New York, NY: Vintage.

Forsberg, G. E. (2009). Media ecology and theology. *Journal of Communication and Religion, 32,* 135–156.

Forsberg, G. E. (2010, April). Alfred Korzybski: A founding figure in media ecology. *ETC: A Review of General Semantics, 67*(2), 144–148.

Fortner, R. (2007). *Communication, media and identity: A Christian theory of communication.* Lanham, MD: Rowman & Littlefield Publishers.

Hall, G. P. (2008, January/April). Choosing life or second life? Discipleship and agency in a mediated culture. *International Review of Mission, 97*(384/385), 7–20.

Haynes, J. (1999). Religion and political transformation. In T. Skelton & T. Allen (Eds.), *Culture and global change* (pp. 223–239). New York, NY: Routledge.

Heelas, P., & Woodhead, L. (2005). *The spiritual revolution: Why religion is giving way to spirituality.* Malden, MA: Blackwell Publishing.

Hoover, S. M. (2006). *Religion in the media age.* New York, NY: Routledge.

Horsfield, P., & Teusner, P. (2007). A mediated religion: Historical perspectives on Christianity and the internet. *Studies in World Christianity, 13*(3), 278–295.

Hosseini, S. H. (2008). Religion and media, religious media, or media religion: Theoretical studies. *Journal of Media and Religion, 7*(1–2), 56–69.

Kenneson, P. D., & Street, J. L. (1997). *Selling out the church: The dangers of church marketing.* Nashville, TN: Abingdon Press.

Kerr, P. A. (2003). The framing of fundamentalist Christians: Network television news, 1980–2000. *Journal of Media and Religion, 2*(4), 203–235.

Kinnaman, D., & Lyons, G. (2007). *unChristian: What a new generation really thinks about Christianity . . . and why it matters.* Grand Rapids, MI: Baker Books.

Krüger, O. (2007). Gaia, God, and the internet: The history of evolution and the utopia of community in media society. *Numen-International Review for the History of Religions, 54*(2), 138–173.

Lash, S., & Featherstone, M. (2001). Recognition and difference: Politics, identity, multiculture. *Theory, Culture & Society, 18*(2–3), 1–19.

Lih, A. (2009). *The Wikipedia revolution: How a bunch of nobodies created the world's greatest encyclopedia.* New York, NY: Hyperion.

McLuhan, M. (1994). *Understanding media: The extensions of man.* Cambridge, MA: MIT Press.

Mellor, P. A. (2004). Religion, culture and society in the 'information age.' *Sociology of Religion, 65*(4), 357–371.

Monge, P., Heiss, B. M., & Margolin, D. B. (2008). Communication network evolution in organizational communities. *Communication Theory, 18*(4), 449–477.

Morgan, D. (2002). Protestant visual practice and American mass culture. In S. M. Hoover & L. S. Clark (Eds.), *Practicing religion in the age of the media: Explorations in media, religion, and culture* (pp. 37–62). New York, NY: Columbia University Press.

Musa, B. A. (2000). Pluralism and prior restraint on religious communication in Nigeria: Policy versus praxis. In J. Thierstein and Y. Kamalipour (Eds.), *Law, religion, and freedom: A global perspective* (pp. 98–111). Westport, CT: Greenwood Press.

Ong, W. (1982). *Orality and literacy: The technologizing of the word.* New York, NY: Routledge.

Parente, D. (2004). *Advertising campaign strategy: A guide to marketing communication plans* (3rd ed.). Mason, OH: South-Western.

Pascoe, S. (n. d.) Quotations [Web post]. Retrieved from http://www.religioustolerance.org/christ.htm

Pesce, M. (2000). *The playful world: How technology is transforming our imagination.* New York, NY: Ballantine Books.

Pite, S. (2003). *The digital designer.* New York, NY: Thomson-Delmar Learning.

Postman, N. (1985). *Amusing ourselves to death: Public discourse in the age of show business.* New York, NY: Penguin.

Postman, N. (1992). *Technopoly: The surrender of culture to technology.* New York, NY: Vintage Books.

Rao, S., & Johal, N. S. (2006). Ethics and news making in the changing Indian mediascape. *Journal of Mass Media Ethics, 21*(4), 286–303.

Salas, A. (2007). Media ecology comes into its own. *Education Digest: Essential Readings Condensed for Quick Review, 72(8),* 62–66. Condensed from Salas, A. (2006). *The Hispanic Outlook in Higher Education, 17,* 24–26.

Schultze, Q. J. (2000). *Communicating for life: Christian stewardship in community and media.* Grand Rapids, MI: Baker Academic.

Schultze, Q. J., & Woods, R. H. (2008). Getting the conversation going about media and culture. In Q. J. Schultze & R. H. Woods (Eds.), *Understanding evangelical media: The changing face of Christian communication* (pp. 19–32). Downers Grove, IL: InterVarsity Press.

Strate, L. (2010). On the binding biases of time: An essay on general semantics, media ecology, and the past, present, and future of the human species. *ETC: A Review of General Semantics, 67(4),* 360–388.

Straubhaar, J., & LaRose, R. (2008). *Media now: Understanding media, culture, and technology.* Belmont, CA: Thomson-Wadsworth.

Thurlbeck, K. L. (2003). Brand experience. In S. Pite (Ed.), *The digital designer: 101 graphic design projects for print, the web, multimedia, and motion graphics* (pp. 276–281). New York, NY: Thomson Learning.

Tipler, F. (1994). *The physics of immortality: Modern cosmology, God, and the resurrection of the dead*. New York, NY: Doubleday.

Wayne, D. (2008). Theological blogging. In J. M. Reynolds & R. Overton (Eds.), *The new media frontier: Blogging, vlogging, and podcasting for Christ* (pp. 97–112). Wheaton, IL: Crossway Books.

Woodward, W. (1996). Triadic communication as transactional participation. *Critical Studies in Mass Communication, 13*(2), 155–174.

Woodward, W. D. (2000). Transactional philosophy as a basis for dialogue in public relations. *Journal of Public Relations Research, 12*(3), 255–275.

World News (1997, April 1) [Television programme] *ABC News*.

Zaleski, J. (1997). *The soul of cyberspace: How new technology is changing our spiritual lives*. New York, NY: HarperCollins.

5. How Religious Communities Negotiate New Media Religiously

HEIDI CAMPBELL

In a world where digital, mobile technologies increasingly play a fundamental role in facilitating and mediating our relationships, religious groups are faced with unique challenges. The communicative affordance offered by new media, such as faster and far-reaching interactions or ministry opportunities, requires religious communities to consider both the benefits and challenges offered by these technologies. They must balance the possibilities offered by the internet and Web 2.0 technologies and the new communicative desires and patterns they create for members against their established spiritual goals and beliefs. Religious groups are forced to consider how new technologies generate certain cultural and behavioral expectations, which may run counter to traditional structures of authority, social interaction, and ritual engagement. These complexities raise questions for many groups as to what extent new technologies should be embraced, resisted, or reconfigured in light of the beliefs of their community.

These are not easy questions to answer, and it is the task of this chapter to offer a framework for reflecting on these issues. I argue that there is a need for a new theoretical and methodological approach that helps both scholars and religious practitioners examine religious communities' engagement with new forms of media. This is described as the religious-social shaping of technology, which is based on the social shaping of technology perspective that technology is embedded in a set of social practices and constraints of particular user communities. This chapter provides a theoretical synopsis of the argument put forth in *When Religion Meets New Media* (Campbell, 2010). Here the religious-social shaping of technology was described and contextualized in light of previous scholarship on religious communities' use of media. Then it was applied by briefly exploring Catholic use of digital media and their strategies in order to demonstrate that this approach can offer valuable insights about religious engagement, especially that with digital technologies.

Religious Communities' Response to New Forms of Media

Scholars who have studied religious groups' engagement with media technology have often focused on the utilization strategies that different groups employ related to these media choices. Hoover (1993), for example, in his study of Anabaptist responses towards televangelism, argued that Christian churches typically use media in one of five ways: (a) evangelism and/or proselytization, (b) celebration or corporate worship, (c) public or secular validation, (d) social transformation or "civil religion," (e) the sacralization of civil society. This range demonstrates that religious groups' engagement is informed by motivations grounded not only in their beliefs about media, but also in the nature of their community and core values. Other scholars have approached media technology in light of how religious or theological orientation guides different groups' responses to media. Strom (2008), for instance, suggested Christian groups often approach the relationship between media and culture by taking one of a number of different roles, such as: the separator, avoider, reformer, acceptor, and vain religionist. These approaches suggest media may be seen by some religious groups as an extension or tool of mainstream, secular culture and thus the relationship is informed by larger models and beliefs about how one should engage with culture (i.e., Niebuhr, 1951). This demonstrates the need to take into account a religious community's beliefs about media and modernity alongside their religious values and boundaries.

Ferre (2003) presented a helpful range of religious groups' common beliefs about media that can be used to consider both of these issues simultaneously. He suggested that most groups see media either as a conduit mode of knowing or as a social institution. Groups that conceive of the *media as a conduit* perceive of media as a neutral instrument that can be good or evil, dependent on the manner in which it is used. Technology is seen as simply an avenue for delivering a message, so religious users are able to view media as a gift from God to do the work of the community. Religious users who see the media as a conduit can easily embrace it for innovative uses, without ideological conflict, as the media is presented as a clear conduit for the delivery of religious information and outcomes. Some scholars have taken this approach in arguing that organized religion has always depended on some form of media in order to communicate its message (Walsham, 2000) and that our information-based society has further cemented this dependence (Schement & Stephenson, 1997). Protestant Evangelicals historically took this approach as they readily embraced new forms of technology that enabled them to publicize their message. The phenomenon of appropriating media for religious purposes has led to unique religious genres and markets (Clark, 2007). It is also clearly seen in the rise of the e-vangelism movement online, which has sought to frame and promote the image of the internet as a vital field for missionary work (Careaga, 1999; Wilson, 2000). Seeing the media as a conduit promotes a pro-technology discourse for religious groups, allowing them to embrace new technologies because it is the content that determines the nature of the technology.

Ferre (2003) suggested, however, that some religious groups see media as a *mode of knowing*, emphasizing that media messages are closely intertwined with the medium itself. This becomes problematic because media technology is presented as having its own set of biases and values based on its history and production processes. Ellul (1964), for instance, argued that human society has become dominated by "technique" or science, and the values of the scientific system of progress and efficiency have created a value system that promotes a dependence on technology. Sometimes this perspective has been referred to as technological determinism, as the nature of technology itself is seen to determine its outcomes and impacts. This belief encourages a cautious, if not negative, response by individuals to the media. A number of religious scholars of communication have promoted this perspective, arguing that media has a mode of knowing separate from its users, and so serves as a powerful shaper of culture. Media as a mode of knowing encourages users to fear new forms of media or at least to treat them with suspicion. Informed by the writings of Ellul (1964), McLuhan (1964) and Postman (1993), some scholars of religion and media technology have focused their energies on critiquing the idea that technology is value-neutral and simply a tool that can be used to accomplish religious goals. Christians (2002) argued that new communication technology must be unmasked to reveal the value-laden "philosophical underpinning of these (technological) routines" (p. 37). Similarly, Schultze (2002) asserted that the internet promotes a technologized culture, which works against Christian values of community, truthfulness, and reciprocity. Religious users are encouraged to be suspicious of media, lest they cultivate or unknowingly promote values through their interaction with the media that run counter to their faith.

Media as a conduit or a mode of knowing suggests religious groups are left only with the choice of either accepting or rejecting technology. Ferre (2003) suggested that between the embrace and rejection of media there is a third option. *Media as a social institution* focuses religious groups' attention on media in terms of their systems of production as well as the users' reception of their form and content. Here, both "content and technology matter, but neither is determinative" (p. 89). This encourages a reflective response towards the media, focusing on the social construction of the media by its users. The media as a social institution, therefore, advocates religious groups should not shy away from media, because a community can purposely shape and present media content in light of its own beliefs. Yet it also requires that the religious community critically reflect on how the nature of media technology may impact their community. It is this perspective that underlies the religious-social shaping of technology approach set forth in this chapter. The internet is seen as a social, as well as a technological, system, so internet use is informed by the social context and boundaries of the community in which it emerges. This requires religious communities to be both technologically savvy and able to discern the long-range implications of their choices.

Ferre's (2003) range of approaches highlights that there are very different points of orientation for religious communities regarding their views of digital technologies. Media as a social institution is the least developed in scholarship on the study of religious communities' engagement with media. Thus, this chapter points to the need for a more human-centered, rather than technology-centered, analysis to the study of digital media.

The Social Shaping of Technology

Ferre's (2003) notion of media as a social institution is very close to the social shaping of technology approach found in Science and Technology studies and in the Sociology of Technology. Here, technology is presented as a product of the interplay between different technical and social factors in both design and use (MacKenzie & Wajcman, 2001). Technology use is seen as a social process. Social groups shape technologies towards their own ends, rather than the character of a technology determining its use and outcomes. Scholars taking this approach examine how social processes within a particular group influence user negotiations with different technologies. It acknowledges that groups employ a given technology in distinctive ways, so a group's technology use is unique, and their appropriation reinforces valued patterns of community life or practice.

I suggest the "religious-social shaping of technology" provides a methodological and theoretical framework for studying how religious communities and individuals negotiate their choices related to new forms of media technology. The religious-social shaping of technology approach seeks to give an account of the specific conditions influencing a user's negotiations with a technology, which can lead to changes in use or belief within a given social context. It also attempts to explain responses to new technology in socio-technological terms. In other words, the success, failure, or redesign of a given technology by a specific group of users is based not simply on the innate qualities of the technology, but on the ability of users to socially construct the technology in line with the moral economy of the user community or context. It recognizes that individuals and groups of actors within particular social situations see their choices and options constrained by broader structural elements of their worldview and belief system.

Applying a Religious-Social Shaping of Technology Approach

A key premise underlying the religious-social shaping of technology is the idea that religious communities typically do not reject new forms of technology outright, rather they often undergo a sophisticated negotiation process, in which members or leaders determine what effect technology might have on their community. If a religious community sees a new technology as valuable, but notes its use may promote beliefs or behaviors that run counter to their community's values, members must carefully consider the effects of its appropriation, and what aspects of that technology may need to be resisted. This resistance often leads to the reconstruction of the technology, in either how it is used or discussed within the community. It may even lead to innovation, where technical aspects or structures are modified so that they are more in line with the community's social and religious life. It is important to note that this negotiation is informed by the contemporary cultural setting in which the group is located, so that similar groups in different contexts may engage or respond differently to technological choices. In order to study how religious communities and users negotiate their responses to new forms of media technology, I argue that it is vital for researchers to investigate four core areas. These include studying the: (a) history and tradition of the community, (b) its core beliefs and patterns related to media, (c) the specific negotiation processes it undergoes with a new technology, and finally (d) the communal framing and discourses created to define and justify their technology use. Together, these form the basis of the religious-social shaping of technology theoretical approach to the study of religious communities' use of media, which is described below.

Taking a religious-social shaping of technology approach begins with studying the *History and Tradition* of a given religious community in relation to its media use. Here, researchers start by carefully considering the historical context of the specific religious community under study to see how a religious community's positions toward, and use of, different media have emerged over time, and what decisions or events in the community history might have shaped these decisions.

It is important to note that decisions made regarding texts, one of the earliest forms of media, often serve as a template for future negotiation with other media. In this phase of study, researchers should pay attention to how history and tradition form standards and a trajectory for future media negotiations. This leads to investigating religious communities' *Core Beliefs and Patterns*, where attention is paid to how these specific communities live out their core social values. While beliefs are often derived from a historically grounded tradition, they must always be contextualized and applied anew to the social, cultural, and historic context in which a given community finds itself. Researchers should identify how a community's dominant social and religious values are integrated into patterns of contemporary life, and how these might influence their interactions with contemporary technologies. In an age of digital technologies, close attention must be paid to how core beliefs guide communal decision making processes related to media use, and what patterns of use this encourages and discourages.

These two areas set the stage for the study of the *Negotiation Process* that religious communities undergo when faced with a new form of media. Religious communities must consider in what respect the new form of media mirrors past technologies so that old rules can be applied. If qualities, outcomes, or social conditions created by the technology are significantly unique, the community must enter into a rigorous negotiation process to see which aspects of the technology can be accepted, and which ones might need to be rejected or reconstructed. Innovation takes place if a technology is viewed as valuable, but possesses problematic qualities requiring it to be altered in order to be more in line with community beliefs and practices. Researchers consider how the previous phases inform a community's choices and responses to the new technology when considering the ways in which a new technology is accepted, rejected, and/or reconstructed. Key to this stage is the community's positions towards authority roles and structures, which can indicate who has the right to govern media decision-making and involvement in innovation.

Finally, attention must be paid to *Communal Framing and Discourse* resulting from the adoption of the new form of media. This is a stage often overlooked in studies of the social-shaping of technology, yet it plays an important role for religious communities in their internal justification for their approach to media. Researchers should consider how new technologies may require amendments to previous language about media, or how official policies regarding technology are constructed and publicized. The negotiation and adoption of new technologies requires the religious group to create public and private discourses that validate their technology choices in light of established community boundaries, values, and identities. The communal discourse can also serve as a tool for reaffirming traditions and past standards, as well as for setting a new trajectory for the future use of, or negotiation of, technology. Thus, it is important for researchers to pay attention to the language used by a religious community to frame technology and prescribe communal use. Together, these four levels of inquiry make up the religious-social shaping of technology approach to show how multiple social and structural processes influence religious groups' responses to media.

Catholic Negotiation of the Internet in Light of the Religious-Social Shaping of Technology

The importance of exploring the multiple factors that guide traditional religious communities' perception and use of new technologies is briefly discussed here through looking at the Catholic Church's response to the internet. Using the religious-social shaping of technology to read the Catholic approach to the internet demonstrates that a religious group's response to new forms of media can only be fully understood if it is considered within a broader historical social lens than is often employed in current studies of such phenomena.

Catholic Church history and media tradition

Research should start by looking at how a community's history and tradition create certain practices or standards that influence beliefs about media. A full exploration of the historical development of the Catholic tradition is beyond the scope of this brief investigation. However, it is argued that a religious community's conceptions of several key concepts—namely community, authority, and text—inform their views of media. This is true when we consider the grounds of the Catholic media tradition. The Catholic Church can be described as the original Christian church, from which all other branches of Christianity have been derived. The Catholic notion of community is closely tied to its notion of Church membership (Smith, Funkenstein, & Marty, 1972). Members connect themselves to the community through their participation in key initiation rituals or sacraments such as baptism, confirmation, and the sacraments of marriage/holy orders, through acceptance of core beliefs such as the salvation of humanity by faith as authenticated by good deeds, and through a recognition of key Catholic doctrines such as transubstantiation, purgatory, and the veneration of Mary and other saints. Through the ritual of baptism, and adherence to key sacraments and beliefs, members become part of a corporate community. This global communion is strongly linked to the Catholic understanding of church authority. The Catholic Church is a strong hierarchy, considered to be a "holy government," whereby it sees itself functioning as a divine institution here on earth. To this end, the church presents itself as the single accurate and authoritative source for the interpretation of scripture for its members. The church is led by the Bishop of Rome, the Pope, who oversees the ecclesiastical structure of the church, which was created to guide and regulate church practices and doctrinal understandings. The Vatican is at the center of this ecclesiastical monarchy. Led by the Pope, this governmental seat of authority for the church is complemented by a complex system of oversight groups and structures: From the College of Cardinals to the Episcopal conferences of specific nations or regions, they oversee the life of the Catholic community around the world. The important aspects to stress about Catholic views of community and authority are that community is based on membership obtained through official rites and confessions, and is overseen through regulated structures of a hierarchical authority system.

These factors influence Catholic social patterns and religious practices. One area where this can be clearly seen to shape the Catholic media tradition is its response to religious texts. The canonization of the Bible, or official selection of which documents would be recognized and included, took place over a 400-year process. This process involved numerous debates and official discussions led by church leaders (i.e., Councils of Laodicea, Carthage, and Hippo) during the 4th and 5th centuries to determine which books of the Hebrew Scriptures should be recognized and included in the final canon. It was not until the mid 5th century that the base of the Old and New Testaments was accepted into the form which most Christians today recognize (Smith, Funkenstein & Marty, 1972). The Great Schism of 1054 over issues of ecclesiastical authority, stemming from some of this history, resulted in the formation of the Eastern Orthodox Church and solidified the unique identity and structure of the Catholic Church. One outcome of this separation, later further reinforced through the division created by the Protestant Reformation, was enforcement of the primacy of Catholic hierarchy as a divine structure created for the shepherding of church life and doctrine. This top-down structure shaped the church's relationship to texts. For instance, in the Middle Ages, Biblical and religious manuscripts were written by hand, often crafted in the scriptoria of monasteries and overseen by specially trained scribes who copied the text with precision and supervision to maintain accuracy. The expense of creating these texts and regulating this process meant that Bibles were primarily the property of the Catholic Church, or of the very rich. Bibles were written in Latin, so only the educated or church-trained could read or have access to them. This allowed church officials to keep tight control over the meaning of the scripture, with priests serving as official interpreters for the unlearned laity. The printing press marked a turning point for church control over this text. It is important to note that while scholars have argued that the Catholic Church viewed the printing press primarily with suspicion and contempt (Cotter, 2003); it was not initially condemned by the Catholic Church (Eisenstein, 1980). Instead, it was lauded for its facilitation as a "divine art" of writing, and as an invention that could be used to extend glory to God through the production of religious material (Loach, 1986, p. 135). Catholics saw technology as a tool to be used for divine work, but within the oversight of the church. Catholics as well as Protestants utilized the technology to print training materials and religious propaganda to promote their convictions. The printing of Bibles in the vernacular languages of the people ended the Catholic Church's absolute control over the text, yet it also showed that they were not against technological innovation as long as it could be co-opted within recognized social and authority structures of the church. This shows that it is vital to pay close attention to a religious community's understanding of community and authority, and how this shapes historical relationships and engagement with text as an early form of media. These become important indicators of how the Catholic Church has developed its distinctive media tradition.

Catholic Church core beliefs and values in relation to media

Next, it is important to highlight a religious community's social and religious values, which influence their interactions with contemporary media. The Catholic Church has a strong tradition of reflecting on the theology of communication and the social implication of mass media. This has been done through the establishment of official church structures to advocate and monitor media usage and promotion. The Pontifical Commission for the Study and Ecclesiastical Evaluation of Films on Religious or Moral Subjects was launched in 1948 with the aim of exploring the pastoral and religious education challenges being posed by the audio-visual era, as well as issues that were being raised for the church by the growing media entertainment industry. Forty years later, the commission was elevated to the Pontifical Council for Social Communications, with the aim of exploring "questions regarding the means of social communication, so that, also by these means, human progress and the message of salvation may benefit secular culture and mores" (http://www.catholic-hierarchy.org/diocese/dxsco.html). Over the years, the commission, and then council, have issued numerous statements, including those dealing with cinema, the audio-visual representation of the mass, the use of media for training priests, and the ethics used in advertising. The heart of its work is to advise the church in how different forms of media can best be used to further the work of the Catholic Church, and how media in general can serve to spread the Christian message and spirit. The council's current mandate is to address questions that deal with social communications, and to show how to use these means to spread the message of salvation to humanity. One of its main roles has been to act as an advisor for the Catholic Church in how the institution and its members should interact with the media world.

One of the council's foundational documents is *Communio et Progressio* (PSCS, 1971), pastoral instructions written by order of the Second Vatican Council and proclaimed on the Fifth World Communication Day in 1971 to outline the church's official stance on social communication. It covers, in sequence: doctrinal principles; contribution of the communications media to human progress; training of recipients and communicators; opportunities and obligations of both; co-operation between citizens and civil authorities; collaboration among all believers and men of good will; the commitment of Catholics in the media; public opinion and closer communication in the life of the church; activity of Catholics in the fields of writing, movies, radio, television, theater, equipment, personnel, and organization; urgency of the need, because forces that are neither Catholic nor Christian are coming to dominate the media. The Catholic social communications tradition is clearly set out in the document and can be summed up as, "The Church sees these media as 'gifts of God' which, in accordance with His providential design, unite men in brotherhood and so help them to cooperate with His plan for their salvation" (PCSC 1971).

This document is foundational to the Catholic view of media, as it lays out a strong social justice agenda as well as theological instruction and justification for mass media appropriation and engagement. *Communion et Progressio* is evoked in later documents emerging about the church's prescribed use of the internet (PCSC, 2002). This shows that the Pontifical Council on Social Communication plays an influential role in guiding church practice, by creating policy related to the role of the media in human society and how media should be used within religious education, and by offering guidance related to media literacy and ethics. Research on the Catholic Church must carefully consider the role of the council and its statements in setting Catholic doctrine regarding the role of the media in society and in church practice.

Catholic negotiations with digital media

After considering how a religious community's history, tradition, and core beliefs create a platform for its media use, the negotiation process with new forms of media can be contextualized. This provides a basis for understanding and interpreting what aspects of a new technology will be accepted, rejected, and even reconfigured, in light of the community's ethos. As seen above, the Catholic Church's views and uses of digital media are largely informed by agendas established by responses to previous forms of mass media. Catholic response to the internet can be described as a willingness to adopt media that can serve church needs and support its structures.

The Catholic Church was arguably the first religious institution to embrace the internet, establish a web site, and develop an official policy regarding internet use for members of its community. The church's use of the internet began in the early 1990s as spurred on by Pope John Paul II's 1990 World Communication Day messages urging the church to embrace the opportunities offered by computers and telecommunication technology in order to fulfill its mission. As he stated:

> In the new "computer culture" the Church can more readily inform the world of her beliefs and explain the reasons for her stance on any given issue or event. She

can hear more clearly the voice of public opinion, and enter into a continuous discussion with the world around her, thus involving herself more immediately in the common search for solutions to humanity's many pressing problems. (PCSC, 1990)

Initially, the church underestimated the interest its presence online would garner. For example, the Vatican website crashed soon after it was launched when it was flooded with site traffic, and in 1995, a website commemorating the Pope's visit to New Jersey offered an "email the Pope" option that was soon overwhelmed by Catholic users (Italiano, 1996). These instances taught the Vatican valuable lessons regarding the need to filter and control this new technology, encouraging the establishment of a protocol whereby communication officers provide automated responses on the Pope's behalf when such emails are now received.

Even with these bumps, the Catholic Church continued to experiment with new ways to use the internet for religious education (*Catholic Distance University*, www.cdu.edu), spreading church news (*Catholic Online*, www.catholic.org), and missionary activities (*Catholic Internet Mission*, www.c-internet-mission.net). This take-up was based on the church's promotion of the internet as a valuable sphere of communication that could augment the mission of the church. Pope John Paul II spoke out publically about the church's relationship to the internet on a number of occasions, such as on World Communication Day, promoting the internet as a new sphere for evangelization (2002). This tradition was continued by Pope Benedict XVI's calls for the church to reflect carefully on the potential and shortcomings of social media for cultivating just communication (2009). Research has shown an extensive adoption of the internet at the Diocesan level (Arasa, 2007) and through church-related networks and organizations (Arasa, Cantoni, & Ruiz, 2010) to facilitate internal church communication and external church promotion.

However, it is important to note that Catholic adoption of internet technologies is consistent within a prescribed pattern of use in relation to set beliefs about media and structures of church governance. An example of Catholic Church negotiation with Web 2.0 technologies that supports this constrained appropriation is seen in its response to YouTube. YouTube was created in 2005, and by 2006 was established online as the premier video-sharing web site. Many religious groups quickly became concerned about the unregulated content being posted online, resulting in the creation of many alternative sites such as *GodTube* (www.godtube.com) and *Catholic Tube* (www.catholic-tube.com). Yet, Vatican officials recognized the influence of YouTube within popular culture, as well as how it was being used by individual Catholics to present their ideas about Catholicism. So it was decided to create an official presence on the site, and in early 2009, the Vatican launched a special YouTube channel (www.youtube.com/user/vatican) that is updated daily and offers news coverage of the main activities of the Holy Father Pope Benedict XVI and other Vatican events (Sweney, 2009). This adoption mirrors the Catholic Church's tradition of embracing new forms of media for religious purposes, though not without concern and thoughtful reflection about its potential impact on society. Unlike other YouTube channels, the Vatican negotiated with YouTube to have its ranking function and comment mode disabled, thus viewers are not allowed to leave comments on videos posted or give them a star ranking. In this way, the Vatican attempts to control its image on YouTube by eliminating features that could be problematic for an organization that seeks to maintain strong hierarchical control in the fluid, bottom-up culture of Web 2.0. This particular instance of media negotiation demonstrates a consistency between new and previous forms. Researchers must not overlook how novel aspects of digital media are dealt with in relation to traditional media strategies, seeing as religious communities often shape media so that it supports established institutional protocols and core values.

Official Catholic discourse on digital media

The negotiation of a new technology often requires religious communities to create a communal discourse that validates their technology choices so that its use fits more easily within the boundaries of the community. Official discourse serves to both reaffirm communal traditions, values, and practices of the community amongst its members and to serve as a form of external PR to affirm their beliefs and identity to those outside. While the Pontifical Council on Social Communication has traditionally guided church responses to new forms of media, it was the United States Conference of Catholic Bishops that issued the church's first statement on the internet. "Your Family and Cyberspace" (2000) sought to provide an introduction to the concept of cyberspace, how the church might benefit from the "proper use of Cyberspace" and what parents can do to protect against its misuse. It stated, "Internet use, then, can be a little like visiting the best theme park in the world and coming across a toxic waste dump" (United States Conference of Catholic Bishops, 2000). It emphasized the shared responsibility between parents, industry, government, and the church to ensure it maintains a safe place for young people and families.

Thus, it is no surprise that in 2002 the Vatican, via the Council, issued official statements on the Catholic view of the internet and ethics. The Pontifical Council for Social Communications described *Ethics in Internet* (PCSC, 2002b) as a starting point for the church's participation in a "dialogue with other sectors of society" on the proper and improper uses of the internet.

In this statement, the council, on behalf of the church, lays out areas of general concern related to the effects of the internet in society, including increased social inequity through the digital divide, the internet's connection to globalization and intercultural dialogue, complexity of freedom of expression online, and the effect of the internet on journalism. Drawing on *Communion et Progressio*, they emphasize that the media has "the ability to make persons everywhere a partner in the business of the human race." Through the internet, this vision can be made real, but only if it is used in light of "sound ethical principles, especially the virtue of solidarity" (PCSC, 2002b).

The Church and the Internet (PCSC, 2002a) served as a companion document, providing guidelines on how the internet should be employed for church ministry. It frames the internet as a space for the church to become involved in, in order to increase the church's ability for internal and external communication of the "Good News," as well as to be present as a witness to challenge the problematic "consumer approach to matters of faith." The document calls church leaders to the need for greater understanding of the "full potential of the computer age to serve the human and transcendent vocation." For Catholic educators and catechists, it urges more advanced training and fluency with new communication technologies. Parents, "for the sake of their children," are also encouraged to learn about the internet in order to model critical discernment and "prudent use of media in the home." Young people are charged to "use the internet well," not just as a "medium of entertainment and consumer gratification" but to see it as a space or "tool for accomplishing useful work" in the service of God and the church. And finally, to "all persons of good will" the internet requires us to recommit "to the international common good" in our use of this "remarkable technological instrument." These statements demonstrate how official documents play an important role for the Catholic Church in that they clearly spell out a distinct theology of communication related to the internet for the institution, and set out directives for its members as to how they should engage with the internet.

Studying Religious Use of Digital Media

These four stages of investigation highlight Catholic use of digital media at the official level, which requires the consideration of how traditions and beliefs inform this community's negotiations and discourse strategies related to new forms of media. The issues explored above demonstrate how religious groups justify their use and framings of the media in light of previously established community structures. It should be noted that the official response to a new form of media may not be adopted or sanctioned by all members of the community. Therefore, paying attention to the sources of media policies and responses within different sectors of a given community becomes an important part of studying the negotiation process. Media negotiation becomes a sphere to reestablish the identity and values of the religious community. Hoover argued that decisions made by religious communities regarding how they feel about how media should be used are often based on a struggle over validation. In other words, media use becomes a way to assert a certain "presence" in the media in order to be recognized as part of the religious establishment and public sphere (1993, p. 103). Media decision-making becomes a way for a community to internally authenticate itself and externally advocate or justify its practices. So a religious group's media adoption and innovation strategies can be as much about affirming its ideological convictions and the community's identity as they are an attempt to make functional choices about technology.

The religious-social shaping of technology offers a useful theoretical and methodological approach to reveal the factors and strategies that inform religious communities' and organizations' responses to new forms of media. Starting with a study of the history and tradition of the religious community provides insights on key issues that ground their approach to media forms. Highlighting the core values and priorities of the community provides guides to these groups' responses to decision-making regarding media. Considering the conditions and factors influencing the negotiation process religious communities undergo provides pointers to how they will respond to specific media. Also, examining the communal discourses that emerge about media indicates not only their base strategy, but points to an established trajectory of values and boundaries underlying the religious tradition. I suggest this method allows both researchers and practitioners to explore in a more nuanced way the motivations and processes underlying the decision-making at work in religious groups' negotiations with digital culture.

References

Arasa, D. (2007). *Church communications through diocesan websites: A model of analysis.* Rome, Italy: EDUSC.

Arasa, D., Cantoni, L., & Ruiz, L. (2010). *Religious internet communication. Facts, trends and experiences in the Catholic Church.* Rome, Italy: EDUSC.

Campbell, H. (2010). *When religion meets new media.* London, England: Routledge.

Careaga, A. (1999). *E-vangelism: Sharing the gospel in cyberspace.* Lafayette, LA: Huntington House.

Christians, C. (2002). Religious perspectives on communication technology. *Journal of Media and Religion, 1*(1), 37–47.

Clark, L. (2007). *Religion, media, and the marketplace.* New Brunswick, NJ: Rutgers University Press.

Cotter, T. F. (2003). Gutenberg's legacy: Copyright, censorship, and religious pluralism. *California Law Review, 91*(2), 323–392.

Eisenstein, E. L. (1980). The emergence of print culture in the West. *Journal of Communication, 30*(1), 99–106.

Ellul, J. (1964). *The technological society*. New York, NY: Vintage Books.

Evans, I. (1954). Television and the Catholic world. *New Blackfriars, 35*(409), 166–172.

Ferre, J. (2003). Popular piety, media and religion. The media of popular piety. In J. Mitchell & S. Marriage (Eds.), *Mediating religion. Conversations in media, religion and culture* (pp. 83–92). London, England: T & T Clark; New York NY: Continuum.

Hoover, S. (1993). What do we do about the media? *The Conrad Grebel Review, 11*(2: Spring), 97–108.

Italiano, L. (1996). Gimme that online religion. *Columbia Journalism Review, 34*(5: Jan/Feb), 36.

Loach, J. (1986). The Marian establishment and the printing press. *The English Historical Review, 101*(398), 135–148.

MacKenzie, D., & Wajcman, J. (2001). *The social shaping of technology: How the refrigerator got its hum* (2nd ed.). Milton Keynes, England: Open University Press.

McLuhan, M. (1964). *Understanding media*. New York, NY: Signet Books.

Niebuhr, H.R. (1951). *Christ and culture*. New York, NY: Harper Torchbooks.

Pontifical Council for Social Communications [PCSC]. (1971). *Communio et progressio*. Retrieved from http://www.vatican.va/roman_curia/pontifical_councils/pccs/documents/rc_pc_pccs_doc_23051971_communio_en.html

Pontifical Council for Social Communications [PCSC]. (1990). *Message of the Holy Father for the XXIV World Communications Day: The Christian message in a computer culture*. Retrieved from http://www.vatican.va/holy_father/john_paul_ii/messages/communications/documents/hf_jp-ii_mes_24011990_world-communications-day_en.html

Pontifical Council for Social Communications [PCSC]. (2002a). *Church and the Internet*. Retrieved from http://www.vatican.va/roman_curia/pontifical_councils/pccs/documents/rc_pccs_doc_20020228_church-internet_en.html

Pontifical Council for Social Communications [PCSC)]. (2002b). *Ethics in Internet*. Retrieved from http://www.vatican.va/roman_curia/pontifical_councils/pccs/documents/rc_pccs_doc_20020228_ethics-internet_en.html

Pope Benedict XVI (2009). *Message of the Holy Father for the XVI World Communications Day: "New technologies, new relationships. Promoting a culture of respect, dialogue and friendship."* Retrieved from http://www.vatican.va/holy_father/benedict_xvi/messages/communications/documents/hf_ben-xvi_mes_20090124_43rd-world-communications-day_en.html

Pope John Paul II (2002). *Message of the Holy Father for the 36th World Communications Day: "Internet: A new forum for proclaiming the gospel."* Retrieved from http://www.vatican.va/holy_father/john_paul_ii/messages/communications/documents/hf_jp-ii_mes_20020122_world-communications-day_en.html

Postman, N. (1993). *Technopoly: The surrender of culture to technology*. New York, NY: Vintage Books.

Schement, J., & Stephenson, H. C. (1996). Religion and the information society. In D. A. Stout & J. M. Buddenbaum (Eds.), *Religion and mass media: Audiences and Adaptations* (pp. 261–289). Thousand Oaks, CA: Sage.

Schultze, Q. (2002). *Habits of the high-tech heart: Living virtuously in the information age.* Grand Rapids, MI: Baker Academic.

Smith, M., Funkenstein, A., & Marty, M. E. (1972). Review: *The Cambridge history of the Bible. The American Historical Review, 77*(1), 94–109.

Strom, B. (2008). *More than talk: Communication studies and the Christian faith* (3rd ed.). Dubuque, IA: Kendall Hunt.

Sweney, M. (2009, January 23). Pope launches YouTube channel. *Guardian.co.uk.* Retrieved from http://www.guardian.co.uk/technology/2009/jan/23/pope-youtube-channel

United States Conference of Catholic Bishops (2000). *Your family and cyberspace.* Retrieved from http://www.usccb.org/comm/cyberspace.shtml

Walsham, A. (2000). "Domme preachers?" Post-reformation English Catholicism and the culture of print. *Past and Present, 168,* 72–123.

Wilson, W. (2000). *The Internet church.* Nashville, TN: Word Publishing.

6. *When Pinocchio Goes to Church: Exploring an Avatar Religion*

Jørgen Straarup

Introduction

Once hanging from Geppetto's threads, Pinocchio ultimately freed himself from his dependency on his former master. One century later, his contemporary comrades, the avatars of virtual worlds, are far behind the wooden fellow, still steered by their puppeteers' commands, dependent upon their masters' mouse clicks.

In computerized virtual worlds, avatars act as social beings. They interact, socialize, flirt, and go to church. Some even build their own churches. In a virtual community without geographical and temporal borders, a prayer meeting gathers participants, without concern for limitations imposed by geography or time zone.

Among avatars in virtual worlds there is a turn towards community; Pinocchio seems to be looking for a religious community. He and his comrades gather in religious groups, they participate in prayer meetings and services, and show a willingness to accept and participate in activities belonging to a certain pre-defined tradition, along with its predominant form of spirituality.

For technological reasons, one might see avatar religion as avant-garde. In those parts of the world where access to personal computers is the norm, however, the technological problems with virtual worlds are minor. This article addresses the question of whether the avant-garde stamp applies to the content of avatar religion or not. Is avatar religion "subjective," "anti-organization," "anti-traditionalist"? Although it is difficult to establish significance and probability levels in virtual worlds, and thus to prove the validity of these claims, this article will contest the idea that avatar religiosity is a kind of avant-garde.

The work of Linda Woodhead and Paul Heelas (2000, 2005) is a starting point for the analysis of avatar religion. They suggested a subjective turn of religion in the West, from "life-as" to "subjective-life" forms of the sacred, i.e., religion giving way to spirituality. Forms of religion defined by a confessional norm mark an earlier stage of development. In religious traditions and organizations the individual is able to find answers to important questions, be they Presbyterian, Lutheran, or Muslim, which set the borders for an individual's life as a Presbyterian, Lutheran, or Moslem, hence their term "life-as." In later "subjective-life" forms, the individual tends not to be defining herself or himself in terms of a religious tradition or body, but in consonance with that which flows from her or his inner self.

What is avatar religion? Is it to be seen as a culmination of the subjective turn? If so, why is it turning back to its origins, life-as, and religion-as?

Avatars and Virtual Worlds

Pinocchio is a marionette, a puppet made of pine (hence his name), carved by carpenter Geppetto. Miraculously, he manages to escape the control of his maker and master, taking on a life of his own. The story about the little fellow was written by Carlo Collodi (1905) and has been presented in books and films (Disney, 1940; Cotone, 2003), and in an opera by Jonathan Dove (2007). Collodi's story stresses the fact that Pinocchio—in his liberated life— is tempted to tell lies, but as a consequence of telling lies he develops a long nose. The importance of mentioning Pinocchio in this context lies not in him being more or less trustworthy, but in the fact that he has escaped the direct control of his puppeteer.

In the original sense of the word, avatars (*avatara*, which means "descending") are representations of the god Vishnu (Schalk, 1996, p. 366; Smart, 1989, p. 85). The recent James Cameron film, *Avatar* (2009), exploited the theme in its own way, with avatars depicted as carefully groomed carriers of an outsider's identity in a different—and to some extent hostile—planet environment. In the internet age, the term is used much more generally than previously. To quote Philip Rosedale, creator of the virtual world *Second Life*, an avatar is "the representation of your chosen embodied appearance to other people in a virtual world" (Britt, 2008, p. MM12). These representations are often shaped like humans, probably because they mostly represent humans. Somewhere, a non-visible agent, a puppeteer, is pulling the strings or tapping the keyboard, commanding the avatar to move, dance, talk, fall in love, and—go to church.

Religion and Religious Organizations

In the physical world, one finds *religion*, which, according to sociologist of religion Richard K. Fenn (2001), can be defined as "a way of tying together multiple experiences and memories of the sacred into a single system of belief and practice" (p. 6). One also finds *religious organizations*, which mediate and structure individuals' experiences of encounters with the sacred. Here, the words *sacred* and *holy* are used synonymously. Such structures are defined by Fenn (2001) as "the institution by which individuals and groups, communities and societies attempt to transcend the passage of time" (p. 4). Empirically, it is easier to see organizations' attempts at tying together experiences and memories of the sacred than it is to see people's attempts. But since the organizations, their hierarchy, buildings, and events are there, and since people take part in the events, one can conclude that somewhere there is religion (in Fenn's definition of the term) too.

In virtual worlds, one finds arrangements aimed at transcending time and space in order to give the participant an experience of sacredness or holiness. And in virtual worlds, avatars (Pinocchios) seek experiences of the sacred, while constructors with various kinds of entrepreneurial activity attempt to create environments in which avatars' (people's) experiences of the sacred may be made interpretable in a particular system of meaning or belonging. Again, due to the fact that "physical" construction is taking place in virtual worlds, and that avatars use the constructions, be they artifacts, churches, congregations, or networks, it is probable that avatars (people) actually experience encounters with the sacred in virtual environments.

When investigating sacredness in virtual worlds, the motives, experiences, and behaviors of both these groups need to be described: the avatars (and their agents) seeking meaning, and the entrepreneurs (and their avatars) constructing systems and artifacts. For both groups, it is necessary to try to go behind the avatars to their agents in order to find out whether or not the activity of the avatar is mere pastime. There is, on the one hand, a distinct possibility that avatar activity in virtual worlds for some avatar agents is for fun, and fun only. Some avatar behavior in virtual worlds points in that direction. On the other hand, other kinds of avatar behavior point in the direction that, to the avatar agents, the avatar's experiences are important. It is reasonable to hypothesize that the seekers of the sacred who are coming back to organized activities in virtual environments have good reasons to do so. There are reasons to believe that they seek, and get experience of, the sacred through their participation. Similarly, the entrepreneurs may be hypothesized to have motives for investing their time, ingenuity, and money in the construction of virtual systems, environments, and artifacts. Their motivation may be experiences of the sacred: a builder of a cathedral may participate in services in his/her own cathedral, or he/she may have done something that pleases his/her God. An element of entrepreneurial satisfaction may be present as well: when other avatars use one's system/construction/building, it, and oneself, cannot be altogether worthless.

Helland (2005) distinguished between *religion online* (RO) and *online religion* (OR). RO denotes a situation in which organized religions (churches, congregations, etc.) establish a presence on the web, whereas the term OR refers to religious practices that take place only on the web. From the point of view of the individual avatar and its master, the difference between RO and OR is not necessarily important. Both RO and OR offer places of worship in the virtual worlds. Similarly, constructors of places of worship operate from both points of departure. Some try to build structures which allow the avatars to recognize known forms of encounters with the holy in the physical world. Others try to liberate themselves from such associations.

Avatar and Agent

A basic complication to the investigation is the uncertainty about the relation between an agent and his/her avatar. When meeting an avatar, you have no idea to what degree it mirrors its agent, i.e., expresses his/her identity. In some respects it is reasonable to assume that the avatar is a copy of its agent: when it comes to *experience* it makes no sense to talk about the avatar repre- senting something which differs from the agent's experience. An avatar taking part in a religious service, experiencing something there, is a direct line to the experience of the agent. In other respects one might expect the opposite: the exterior design of an avatar is not necessarily mirroring the looks of its agent, and the *behavior* of an avatar is not necessarily similar to what the agent would normally do. In Figure 6.1 I attempt to illustrate the mixture of mirroring and difference between agent and avatar.

The proportion of difference or life-of-its-own in the avatar's *experience* is expectedly small. At the other end of the spectrum, i.e., the bottom of Figure 6.1, one finds the avatar's *behavior*; here, a substantial degree of dif- ference and independence from the agent may be expected. Between these extremes *emotion* (predominantly mirroring the agent) and *cognition* (pre- dominantly differing from the agent) are situated. Uncertainty as to the degree of overlapping between the two is systematic in the study of virtual worlds. One may never know to what degree an avatar represents its pup- peteer. In this respect, avatar research resembles ordinary research of human behavior. When human behavior is studied, a researcher must always realize that he/she can never totally distinguish a façade (~the avatar) from the true content (~the agent). In ordinary research of human behavior, however, it is seldom necessary to incorporate this insight into a methodological plan. In avatar research, this is a necessity.

Based on this complication, an important line of investigation revolves around the differences and similarities in the experience of the sacred between avatars and their agents in the virtual and the physical worlds, respectively.

Figure 6.1. The mixture of mirroring and difference between the avatar and its agent.

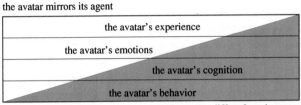

the avatar mirrors its agent

the avatar's experience

the avatar's emotions

the avatar's cognition

the avatar's behavior

the avatar differs from its agent

Furthermore, the entrepreneurs' inspiration and motivation to build structures (houses and congregations), as well as their methods for evaluation of these structures, needs to be analyzed.

Theoretical Tests

In undertaking this analysis, two goals may be achieved. *Firstly*, it becomes possible to test if the theoretical developments outlined by secularization theory (Bruce, 2002) and by the theory about the subjective turn (Heelas & Woodhead, 2005) are substantiated by the empirical study of virtual religion. *Secondly*, one can arrive at preliminary coordinates for tomorrow's presumed creativity and spirituality, in other words, if and how Pinocchio is going to visit church and build community and congregation in the future. It is indeed uncertain if the virtual worlds known today will exist in 10 years time, but probably similar meeting places will arise, worlds where virtual representations of physically existing human beings socialize, and in each other's company find ways to creativity, spirituality, and experiences of the holy, which transcend the irrevocable passage of time (Fenn, 2001, p. 4).

Two Discussions

Virtual rooms with a claim for holiness or sacredness actualize two theoretical discussions in the field of sociology of religion. One is about basic understanding of what constitutes religion, in other words what is expressed with the notions "the holy" or "the sacred." The other is about the development of religion in late modern society.

The holy

In virtual worlds, the *holy* or *sacred* is a functional characteristic. That which is experienced as holy or sacred is regarded in that way. Attempts at describing or defining holiness or sacredness in ways other than through individual experience are rare. In the mixture of psychology and sociology of religion that in the North American context is called *the scientific study of religion*, however, there is an ongoing discussion about these central concepts, i.e., *the sacred/holy* and *religion*, based on classical *œuvres* in these main areas, such as James (1902/1952), Durkheim (1912/1965), Otto (1917/2004) and Weber (1904–1905/1934). Apart from the mere fact that the holy or sacred is experienced by people, in the European tradition the holy or sacred is described as something dangerous (which is also a functional characteristic). The holy must be exempt from everyday contact; only specially qualified persons may be allowed to come near it. This understanding resounds in the definition of religion formulated by Durkheim (1912/1965):

> A religion is a unified system of beliefs and practices relative to sacred things, that is to say, things set apart and forbidden—beliefs and practices which unite into one single moral community called a church, all those who adhere to them. (p. 62)

The world is separated into two spheres, one sacred and one profane. They belong to different basic categories, which is why they do, and should, have limited contact with one another. The scientific tradition, building on this continental, philosophical-sociological tradition, is characterized by discussions about the possibility of pointing out substantial or functional qualities in a religion thatis conceived as fundamentally essentialist (Robertson, 1970). In Durkheim, this is expressed in his claim that religion is in a category of its own kind, *sui generis*.

Five years later, strangely silent about his contemporary colleague Émile Durkheim, Rudolf Otto (1917/2004) developed the idea that the holy is a category *sui generis*. He constructed his own term, *das Numinöse*, from the Latin *numen*, which means the power of a deity or a spirit in places and objects (originally "nodding"). The term has been translated into English as *the numinous*. Otto gave the new term qualifying descriptors such as "dependency," "fear," "majesty," "energy," "mystery," "fascination," and "wonder" (Otto, 1917/2004, pp. 8–52)—reactions in a human being when encountering the numinous. Again, the European tradition from the beginning of the 20th century sees the holy/sacred as something to be feared and avoided, since it might be dangerous, striking you with awe.

William James (1902/1952) inspired another research tradition, an understanding of the sacred/holy based on experience. What people experience as holy is the point of departure for James and the phenomenological tradition, which has become represented in North America as well as in Europe by proponents such as Alfred Schütz (1932/1974) and Peter L.

Berger and Thomas Luckmann (1966/1991). In this research tradition, Demerath (2000, pp. 1–3) suggested a new *sociology of the sacred*, i.e., an analysis of how people experience their encounter with something holy or—to use the William James book title—the varieties of religious experience. In this tradition, nothing is said about essence or "inner nucleus" of the sacred and the holy, or even its representations in everyday life. The problem of defining the sacred or holy has been passed on to the individuals themselves. Their narratives tell how they have met the holy, and their stories are not to be evaluated against some model of the holy and the sacred defined in advance. Demerath suggested that religion and the holy should be defined in separate ways: religion substantially and the holy functionally, a suggestion leading Toplean (2009, p. 34f.) to question if the holy can onlybe defined functionally.

The Development of Religion in Late Modern Society

During the latter part of the 20th century, the sociology of religion has been characterized by three major discussions. The *first* of these discussions concerns economic models for religious organizational development and the development of popular demand, also called supply side or rational choice reasoning (Warner, 1993). In this discussion proponents of rational choice theory have claimed that the kind of models used in the analysis of the popular demand of commodities applies to religious activities as well. This discussion will not be taken further here.

The *second* discussion is about secularization (Dobbelaere, 1981, 2002). Based on evidence from Asian, African, and South American scholars such as José Casanova (1994), who have refuted earlier claims from European secularization theorists such as Bryan Wilson (2001), a process of secularization is to be expected globally as a response to global modernization. However, a European exception has been described and acknowledged by sociologists earlier convinced about the soundness of the global secularization thesis, such as Peter L. Berger (1999) and Berger, Davie, and Fokas (2008). We will return to this discussion.

The *third* broadly defined discussion is about religiosity not fitting into religious organizations' ideas of true doctrine, i.e., such phenomena that, from the churches' point of view, appear as proof of a *de facto* secularization. There have been a large number of attempts to identify, both conceptually and terminologically, those kinds of people's religious thoughts and behavior that have no direct parallel in the doctrinal systems of the religious organizations. Demerath (2000) listed "invisible religion," "folk religion," "implicit religion," "quasi-religion," and "para-religion." His list can be supplemented with "popular religion" (Maître, 1975; Schneider & Dornbusch,

1973), "*Leuterelijion* [people's religion]" (Zulehner, 1982), "*Vorhofrelijion* [courtyard religion]" (Mensching, 1959, p. 65), and "spirituality" (Heelas & Woodhead, 2005), or for Sweden, "folk church religion" (Straarup, 1985, pp. 33–36, 91–110) and "church service Christianity" (Gustafsson, 1969, pp. 55–71; 1972).

The increasing multiplicity of religious beliefs and thoughts signaling an increasing difference between teachings of religious organizations (churches) and religious followers have been seen as some of the most important signs that a process of secularization is taking place. The interest on behalf of many sociologists of religion such as Eileen Barker (1982, 1984), J. Gordon Melton (1996), and Liselotte Frisk (2007) in studying new religious movements (NRMs), groups, and sects, has fed into the secularization discussion, providing secularization theorists with fresh empirical evidence of a clash between modernity and traditional religious bodies.

The free religious life of avatars represents a late phase in alternative religious expression. At first sight, avatar religiosity is far away from traditional religion, lacking institutional constraints and markers. Every avatar can do what his/her agent pleases. And so, the sociological analysis of avatar religiosity may be seen as yet another kind of NRM study.

At second glance, it becomes obvious that avatar religiosity is not necessarily of a "new religious movement" kind. Pilot studies carried out in virtual reality environments show that the religiosity of the avatars is particularly intense around the sites (places and activities) where the link to church organizations' traditional symbols and forms of activity is strong: virtual cathedrals, traditional religious symbols, and traditional services or prayer meetings (Schroeder, Heather, & Lee, 1998; Hutchings, 2007; Brasher, 2004). In their search for the sacred, a number of avatars look into the virtual field of traditional religion. Thus, that which may be seen as the utmost expression of secularization bends back towards the symbol system it is said to have left behind.

A Turn Towards Spirituality?

In recent sociology of religion, the sociologists of religion Linda Woodhead and Paul Heelas argued that a profound change is taking place, from "life-as"-religiosity and religion, to "subjective-life"-religiosity. Their theoretical discussion may be seen as one of the latest attempts at explaining a religiosity that is not conforming to traditional religion. Using mainly British material they (Heelas & Woodhead, 2005; Woodhead & Heelas, 2000) argue that religiosity and people's experience of the sacred in late modern Western society is changing radically. If, in an earlier epoch, one might say that God tended to be an external entity in relation to people, keeping control from the outside, the present Western society is characterized by the fact that the utmost authority has moved to within the individual him- or herself. In this respect, Heelas and Woodhead take a similar position to that of Taylor (2007), namely that the subjectivization of Western religious thought has lead to the conclusion that "religion is giving way to spirituality" (the subtitle of Heelas & Woodhead's book from 2005, see Repstad, 2009, p. 73).

Woodhead and Heelas' argument has been widely discussed and critiqued among sociologists of religion. Parts of the criticism of their propositions have centered on methodological problems. Woodhead and Heelas rely heavily on empirical results from just one investigation, in Kendal, a minor town in northern England, a fact which has been criticized because of that particular study's possible lack of wider representativity. Some of the criticism has come from Sweden. In a project with a rather grand design, *God's Nearest Town* (Ahlstrand & Gunner, 2008), a number of Swedish researchers have tried to reduplicate parts of Heelas and Woodhead's study of Kendal. The Swedish researchers, however, gleaned meager confirmation of the results from Kendal from their efforts. It has not proven easy to find similarities to the Kendal results from Enköping, which is called "Sweden's nearest town" by the local tourist office, inspiring the book title *God's Nearest Town* (Willander, 2008, pp. 241–276). A shift from "life-as"-religiosity and religion to "subjective-life"-religiosity was not an obvious interpretation of the outcomes of the investigation in Enköping.

Heelas and Woodhead (2005, p. 6) argue that "subjective-life forms of the sacred" are increasing, while "life-as forms of the sacred" are decreasing. At first glance, this conclusion seems to be underpinned by the picture of the lonely avatar in the vast cyberspace seeking an individual experience of the sacred in order to be carried home to the agent or puppeteer. The agent does not go to the local congregation in order to discuss his/her existential problems. Instead, he/she sends his/her avatar on a spiritual journey outwards—and inwards. Religious answers in a specific tradition, with specific presuppositions, norms, and conclusions, i.e., "religious-as"-answers, are not satisfying to the puppeteer. He/she enters into his/her own subjective life frame looking for answers there.

De facto, the situation in the virtual worlds is more complex. The virtual world into which the agent sends his/her avatar may be vast, but it is populated. Unlike space, cyberspace is fully equipped with signposts. An avatar is subjected to numerous suggestions as to both the content and direction of its journey. And so, in the virtual worlds, communities are being formed, meeting places constructed, prayer circle norms worked out, and dress codes specified. The avatar is not alone in its search for encounters with the sacred. In virtual worlds, the urge to develop "subjective-life" forms of the sacred are—broadly speaking—less pronounced than the urge to enter into a community where a "life-as" form of the sacred predominates. One might say that the isolated avatar finds verification of its experience in its own subjectivity, but along the way it meets others; it meets communities.

Avatar religion is one of the most recent ways of practicing religion. One may ask whether it points in one of the two basic directions outlined by the theoretical discussants of sociology of religion: secularization or sacralisation. Is avatar religion yet another way of substituting individual quest for collective action in an age of modernization, thus paving the way for new levels of secularization? Or is avatar religion a set of new ways of expressing collective concern over basic human problems, heralding an era of (re)sacralisation?

At this point it is too early to say whether the analysis of Pinocchio's church-going may be seen as a secularizing component, i.e., as part of a development in which traditional religious organizations lose their potential to form peoples' experiences of encounters with the sacred (Bruce, 2002), or as a sacralising component, i.e., as part of a development in which people's interest in encounters with the sacred are being redirected towards traditional religious organizations (Casanova, 1994). Virtual religion contains both these possible outcomes.

Tentatively the virtual worlds have been characterized as laboratories of the future, for instance by Rymaszewski et al. (2008). As such, the virtual worlds do not one-sidedly point out a road of subjectivity and isolation for members of "the lonely crowd" (Riesman, 1950). Even for isolated subjects such as avatars, one may identify a road or path back to community. Pinocchio's going to church, the religious life of avatars, opens up the possibility to describe individual religiosity of the future. In a strict sense of the word, it's not possible to test Heelas and Woodhead's claim, but since their central hypothesis is one of development (from "life-as forms of the sacred" to "subjective-life forms of the sacred"), an analysis of virtual worlds may become a corrective. Avatar analysis points out a probable development, partly for avatars and their agents, partly for entrepreneurs catching up on what the virtual population demands.

Explaining Social Action

In sociological theory, one of the most difficult tasks is to *explain* social action, which in a strict sense means to clarify its causes. When it comes to individual (and avatar) behavior the difficulties are identical. It is seldom possible to identify the causes or motives for individual action. Inspired by two British sociologists of religion, I will nevertheless suggest an argument that points to a possible individual *motivation* for engaging in religion in virtual worlds, where realizing that "motivation" does not satisfy normal scientific criteria for causes.

David Martin (1990, 2002) and Bernice Martin (1998, 2001) analyzed the development of Pentecostalism in Latin America. Bernice Martin investigated the factors leading to increasing numbers of members for Latin American Pentecostal congregations. Her analysis may be summarized in an almost classical way, in terms echoing the writings of Max Weber (1993) or even Karl Marx (Marx & Engels, 1972). The congregations or churches which, with their rules of behavior, make it easier for people to live decent lives, at the same time as they are responsive to peoples' need for active religious and emotional expression, i.e., keep a sufficiently high "temperature" of experience; those are the congregations or churches with growing numbers of motivated members.

According to Bernice Martin, life is hard for the Latin American urban middle class, and for those who aspire to enter it from below. A number of traps may stop the ambition of a family to achieve basic security and safety. The wages are low, and so one must keep a tight budget. Temptations supported by a traditional macho culture lure men, especially, to ruin their families through drinking, gambling, and prostitution. Cultural liberalization and individualization undermine stable families.

In a situation such as this, the Pentecostal congregations' message and demand for a specific way of life becomes a path for threatened families to make their situation safer. For the members of a Pentecostal congregation, the family income does not end up in the wrong pockets, fidelity in marital life is supported, and the families are stabilized with husbands at home when they are not working.

In Bernice Martin's interpretation, the form of religion that provides answers for the most important problems of everyday life, and that has the ability to support human dignity around the solution of these everyday problems, is the form of a successful religion. This interpretation has similarities with Friedrich Engels' (1894) description of early Christianity. A religion giving meaning to a life in hardship, and a path to a better life, and facilitating human dignity around the solution of everyday problems, can expected to attract a large following.

When we turn towards Pinocchio's religious life, applying Bernice Martin's conclusions, we inevitably come back to Geppetto, the puppeteer, or, in more contemporary terms, we come back to two questions: (a) what do anonymous avatar agents look for when they let their avatars roam in virtual worlds? And (b) what is sought by entrepreneurs building castles in the air? Following Bernice Martin, a preliminary answer to both questions can be given: agents—as well as avatars—seek the form of encounter with the sacred that helps them to solve their life problems with preserved, or even enhanced, human dignity.

In the epoch of "late modernity" individualization is a basic structural characteristic, pertaining to every aspect of human life. Technology opens up a possibility for individualized women and men to perceive a smaller demand for physical contact, communicating with the exterior world increasingly by means of computers and smartphones. Behind their screens, however, they are not lonely. In virtual worlds there are others to spend time with, simultaneously make-believe and real.

For some, time and attention is given to pluralist world-view supermarkets where all religious themes and ingredients are present, along with a number of confessional blends. For others, the avatar is steered away from plurality and into specific, known, contexts. Instead of going to Norwich Cathedral, the individual's avatar enters a virtual copy of an Anglican Cathedral. Instead of the agent sitting in on a prayer meeting in Québec, his/her avatar joins a virtual session lead by a woman from the small Danish town of Kibæk. The crucial motivation—as in the Latin American case—seems to be that a social community based around an encounter with the sacred strengthens the possibilities of the agent and his/her avatar to solve everyday life problems.

References

Ahlstrand, K., & Gunner, G. (Eds.). (2008). *Guds närmaste stad? En studie om religion-ernasbetydelse i ettsvensktsamhälle i början av 2000-talet [God's nearest town? A study of the significance of religions in a Swedish town in the beginning of the 21st century].* Forskningförkyrkan. Stockholm, Sweden: Verbum.

Barker, E. (Ed.). (1982). *New religious movements: A perspective for understanding society.* New York, NY: Edwin Mellen Press.

Barker, E. (1984). *The making of a Moonie: Choice or brainwashing?* Oxford, England: Blackwell.

Berger, P. L. (1999). The desecularization of the world: A global overview. In P. L. Berger (Ed.), *The desecularization of the world: Resurgent religion and world politics* (pp. 1–18). Grand Rapids, MI: W.B. Eerdmans.

Berger, P., Davie, G., & Fokas, E. (2008). *Religious America, secular Europe? A theme and variations.* Aldershot, England: Ashgate Publishing.

Berger, P. L., & Luckmann, T. (1991). *The social construction of reality: A treatise in the sociology of knowledge.* Harmondsworth, England: Penguin Books. (Original work published 1966)

Brasher, B. E. (2004). *Give me that online religion.* Piscataway, NJ: Rutgers University Press.

Britt, A. (2008, August 10). On language; Avatar.*The New York Times*, p. MM12.

Bruce, S. (2002). *God is dead: Secularization in the West.* Oxford, England: Blackwell.

Cameron, J. (Producer, Director). (2009). *Avatar* [Motion picture]. USA: Twentieth Century Fox.

Casanova, J. (1994). *Public religions in the modern world.* Chicago, IL: University of Chicago Press.

Collodi, C. (1905). *Le avventure di Pinocchio: Storia di unburattino; illustrata da Carlo Chiostri.* Florence, Italy: R. Bemporad.

Cotone, M. (Executive producer), & Benigni, R. (Director). (2003). *Roberto Benigni's Pinocchio* [Motion picture]. United States: Miramax Home Entertainment.

Demerath, N. J. (2000). The varieties of sacred experience: Finding the sacred in a secular grove. *Journal for the Scientific Study of Religion, 39*(1), 1–11.

Disney, W. (Producer), & Luske, H., & Sharpsteen, B. (Directors) (1999). *Pinocchio* [Video]. United States: Walt Disney Video.

Dobbelaere, K. (1981). *Current Sociology Series: Vol. 29. Secularization: A multi-dimensional concept.* London, England: Sage.

Dobbelaere, K. (2002). *Gods, Humans, and Religions Series: Vol. 1. Secularization: An analysis at three levels.* Brussels, Belgium: P.I.E.-Peter Lang.

Dove, J. (Writer). (2009). *The adventures of Pinocchio* [Opera DVD]. London, England: Opus Arte.

Durkheim, É. (1965). *The elementary forms of the religious life.* (J. W. Swain, Trans.). New York, NY: The Free Press. (Original work published 1912)

Engels, F. (1894). On the history of early Christianity. *Die NeueZeit, 1*, 4–13, 36–43.

Fenn, R. K. (2001). Editorial commentary: Religion and the secular; the sacred and the profane: The scope of the argument. In R. K. Fenn (Ed.), *The Blackwell companion to sociology of religion* (pp. 3–22). Oxford, England: Blackwell.

Frisk, L. (2007). *De nyareligiösarörelserna—Vart tog de vägen? En studie av Scientologi-kyrkan, Guds Barn, Hare Krishna-rörelsen, Moon-rörelsenoch Bhagwan-rörelsenoch-derasutvecklingöver tid [The new religious movements—where did they go? A study of the Church of Scientology, Children of God, The Hare Krishna movement, Moonies, and the Bhagwan movement and their development over time].* Nora, Sweden: NyaDoxa.

Gustafsson, B. (1969). *Svenskafolkets religion: Någraord till dessföraktare [The religion of the Swedish people: Some words to those who despise it].* Stockholm, Sweden: Gummesson.

Gustafsson, B. (1972). *Guds lilla barnaskara: Rapport om en samhällskonflikt [God'slittle flock ofchildren: Reportabout a social conflict].* Stockholm, Sweden: Gummesson.

Heelas, P., & Woodhead, L. (2005). *The spiritual revolution: Why religion is giving way to spirituality.* Religion and spirituality in the modern world. Malden, MA: Blackwell.

Helland, C. (2005). Online religion as lived religion: Methodological issues in the study of religious participation on the internet [Special issue]. *Online—Heidelberg Journal of Religions on the Internet, 1.1.* Retrieved from http://archiv.ub.uni-heidelberg.de/volltextserver/frontdoor.php?source_opus=5823

Hutchings, T. (2007). Creating church online: A case-study approach to religious experience. *Studies in World Christianity, 13*(3), 243–260.

James, W. (1952). *The varieties of religious experience: A study in human nature; being the Gifford lectures on natural religion delivered at Edinburgh 1901–1902.* London, England: Longmans, Green and Co. (Original work published 1902)

Kjærstad, J. (1995). *Forføreren: Roman [The seducer: Novel].* Oslo, Norway: Aschehoug.

Kjærstad, J. (1996). *Erobreren: Roman [The conquerer: Novel].* Oslo, Norway: Aschehoug.

Kjærstad, J. (1999). *Oppdageren: Roman [The discoverer: Novel].* Oslo, Norway: Aschehoug.

Maître, J. (1969). La religion populaire. In *Encyclopædiauniversalis* (Vol. 14, pp. 35–36). Paris, France: Encyclopædia Britannica.

Martin, B. (1998). From pre- to postmodernity in Latin America: The case of Pentecostalism. In P. Heelas (Ed.), *Religion, modernity, and postmodernity* (pp. 102–146). Oxford, England: Blackwell.

Martin, B. (2001). The Pentecostal gender paradox: A cautionary tale for the sociology of religion. In R. K. Fenn (Ed.), *The Blackwell companion to sociology of religion*, (pp. 52–66). Oxford, England: Blackwell.

Martin, D. (1990). *Tongues of fire: The explosion of Protestantism in Latin America.* Oxford, England: Blackwell.

Martin, D. (2002). *Pentecostalism: The world their parish.* Oxford, England: Blackwell.

Marx, K., & Engels, F. (1972). *On religion.* Moscow, Russia: Progress.

Melton, J. G. (1996). *Encyclopedia of American religions.* Detroit, MI: Gale.

Mensching, G. (1959). *Die Religion: Erscheinungsformen, Strukturtypen und Lebensgesetze.* Stuttgart, Germany: Schwab.

Otto, R. (2004). *Das Heilige: Über das Irrationale in der Idee des Göttlichen und seinV erhältniszumRationalen.* Munich, Germany: C. H. Beck. (Original work published 1917)

Repstad, P. (2009). Charles Taylor ogreligionssociologien [Charles Taylor and sociology of religion]. In A. Davidsson-Bremborg, G. Gustafsson, & G. Karlsson Hallonsten (Eds.), *Religionssociologiibrytningstider: En vänbok till Curt Dahlgren [Sociology of religion in transition: Festschrift for Curt Dahlgren]*, Lund Studies in Sociology of Religion (p. 66–80). Lund, Sweden: Centrum för teologi ochreligionsvetenskap, Lunds universitet.

Riesman, D. (1950). *The lonely crowd: A study of the changing American character.* New Haven, CT: Yale University Press.

Robertson, R. (1970). *The sociological interpretation of religion.* Oxford, England: Blackwell.

Rymaszewski, M., Au, W. J., Ondrejka, C., Platel, R., Gorden, S. V., Cézanne, J., & Cézanne, P. (2008). *Second Life: The official guide* (2nd ed.). Indianapolis, IN: Wiley.

Schalk, P. (1996). 13. Hinduismen [Hinduism]. In T. Jensen, M. Rothstein, & J. PodemannSørensen (Eds.), U. Kristiansson (Trans.), *Religionshistoria: Ritualer, mytologi, ikonografi [History of religions: Rituals, mythology, iconography]* (pp. 363–391). Nora, Sweden: NyaDoxa.

Schneider, L., & Dornbusch, S. M. (1973). *Popular religion: Inspirational books in America.* Chicago, IL: University of Chicago Press.

Schroeder, R., Heather, N., & Lee, R. M. (1998). The sacred and the virtual: Religion in multi-user virtual reality. *Journal of Computer-Mediated Communication, 4*(2).

Schütz, A. (1974). *Der sinnhafte Aufbau der sozialen Welt: Eine Einleitung in die verstehende Soziologie.* Frankfurt am Main, Germany: Suhrkamp. (Original work published 1932)

Smart, N. (1989). *The world's religions.* Cambridge, England: Cambridge University Press.

Straarup, J. (1985). *Kyrkaniförorten: Folkligreligiositetochåsikteromnybyggdakyrkor [Church in the suburb: Popular religiosity and views on newly built churches].* Uppsala, Sweden: Förortskyrkan.

Taylor, C. (2007). *A secular age*. Cambridge, MA: Belknap Press of Harvard University Press.

Toplean, A. (2009). Crossroads between modern death and the secular sacred. In A. Davidsson Bremborg, G. Gustafsson, & G. Karlsson Hallonsten (Eds.), *Religionssociologiibrytningstider: En vänbok till Curt Dahlgren [Sociology of religion in transition: Festschrift for Curt Dahlgren]*, Lund Studies in Sociology of Religion (pp. 29–49). Lund, Sweden: Centrum för teologi ochreligionsvetenskap, Lunds universitet.

Warner, R. S. (1993). Work in progress: Toward a new paradigm for the sociological study of religion in the United States. *The American Journal of Sociology, 98*(5), 1044–1093.

Weber, M. (1934). *Die protestantische Ethik und der Geist des Kapitalismus*. Tübingen, Germany: Mohr. (Original work published 1904–1905)

Weber, M. (1993). *The sociology of religion* (E. Fischoff, Trans.). Boston, MA: Beacon Press.

Willander, E. (2008). Avslappnad och berörd: Synen på hälsa och and lighet bland hälsofrämjande företag i Enköping [Relaxed and touched: Views on health and spirituality among health businesses in Enköping]. In K. Ahlstrand & G. Gunner (Eds.), *Guds närmaste stad? En studie om religionernasbetydelse i ettsvensktsamhälle i början av 2000-talet [God's nearest town? A study of the significance of religions in a Swedish town in the beginning of the 21st century]*, Forskningförkyrkan (pp. 241–276). Stockholm, Sweden: Verbum.

Wilson, B. (2001). Salvation, secularization, and de-moralization. In R. K. Fenn (Ed.), *The Blackwell companion to sociology of religion* (pp. 39–51). Oxford, England: Blackwell.

Woodhead, L., &Heelas, P. (Eds.). (2000). *Religion in modern times: An interpretive anthology*. Malden, MA: Blackwell.

Zulehner, P. M. (1982). *"Leutereligion": Eineneue Gestalt des Christentums auf dem Weg durch die 80er Jahre?* Vienna, Austria: Herder.

Part II: Empirical Investigations

7. Pastors on the Internet: Online Responses to Secularization

PETER FISCHER-NIELSEN

The interrelationship between the media and the process of secularization is ambiguous. While the new media of the last century, especially radio and television, are enthusiastically being used by many religious groups for missionary and proselytizing purposes, mediatization theory suggests that the interests and the logic of the increasingly powerful media institutions more often than not run counter to the goals of churches and other established religious institutions. This article investigates what new dimensions the latest developments on the internet add to these conflicting understandings of the interrelationship between the media and secularization. The empirical basis for the analysis is the pastors of the Evangelical Lutheran Church in Denmark.[1] While the official bodies of this church, as is the case for many other large state churches, have been slow to adopt the new tools and trends of the internet, and have so far approached them with caution, this study shows that for the individual pastor, Google, Facebook, and YouTube have indeed become integrated elements of the daily working life.

Whether an active church use of the new possibilities on the internet will lead to more or less secularization is a difficult question that has yet to be answered empirically, and that also depends on the understanding of secularization. The suggestion in this article, as it will be presented in the concluding discussion, is that different strategic approaches to the internet will entail different consequences for the church with regard to secularization. First, a monological strategy could help the church to maintain control of its teachings and traditions, but possibly at the cost of appearing countercultural and irrelevant to the majority of the people. Second, a dialogical approach, where the contribution of common people is appreciated, could stimulate the continuing circulation of religion in society, but at the risk of blurring the central dogmas of the church. Third, a more spiritualizing approach to the internet could, if successfully carried out, engage more people in church activities online, but at the price of possibly downplaying the importance of the local congregational life. Since one of the key points of the argumentation throughout this article will be the concept of secularization, this will also be the point of departure.

Understandings of Secularization

Secularization is a contested term, used in many different ways, and therefore it is important to be careful when applying it. This study is inspired by the understanding of secularization that was proposed by the philosopher Charles Taylor in his voluminous book, *A Secular Age* (2007). He gave a threefold definition of the concept, and distinguished between (a) secularization as separation of religion from political structures and institutions; (b) secularization as people turning away from God, church, and traditional religious belief and practice; and (c) secularization as "a move from a society where belief in God is unchallenged and indeed, unproblematic, to one in which it is understood to be one option among others, and frequently not the easiest to embrace" (p. 3). This definition enables us to look at the secularization processes in more nuanced ways, as more than just the continuous decline of religion. A society can, for instance, be relatively non-secularized in the second sense of Taylor's definition, while being highly secularized in the third sense of the word, as the American case shows: People still attend church frequently, but what it means to be an American Christian today is an open question, just as the Christian position increasingly is being challenged by atheist and secularist voices.

If we look at Denmark under this approach to secularization, we can make the following observations, which are also to a high degree applicable for other European countries with a similar state-church relation. With regard to the first sense of the word, the weakening of the state-church relation, Denmark must generally be perceived as a secularized society, since the church no longer has a direct influence on law, education, health care, or other sectors of society. Due to the gradual differentiation of society, these sectors have gained autonomy, and the power of the church has been much reduced. Still, the Danish National Church holds a privileged position in the Danish Constitution, and can also be said to have a certain indirect influence on a societal level, primarily as the carrier of a collective cultural identity (Taylor, 2007, p. 514), as the source of collective meaning or comfort (Bruce, 2002, p. 30), and as the supplier of welfare benefits (Davie, 2002, p. 18). Still, the strength of this indirect church influence is hard to measure, and may diminish as people's church affiliation weakens further.

Often the concept of secularization is only used in the second of Taylor's three understandings, which formulates secularization as a general drop in religious belief and practice. Whether this applies to the Danish situation depends very much on one's definition of religion. If we take an inclusive approach to religion that encompasses not only the institutionalized religious rituals and dogmas, but also the personal more or less coherent beliefs and spiritual practices, we will find that the Danish population has not become much less religious over recent decades. In the European Values Study surveys that were carried out four times between 1981 and 2008, the level of religiosity in Denmark appeared relatively stable: In the 2008 survey, 72 percent described themselves as religious (75 percent in 1981), 64 percent believed in God (69 percent in 1981), and 49 percent prayed or meditated occasionally (the same in 1981).[2] The fact that people, by and large, stay religious in the broad sense of the word does not mean, however, that the ways this religiosity is carried out remains unchanged. The tendency, as has been shown in different studies, seems to be that people's religiosity is rather lived out in individual and loose ways than practiced within the firm teachings of a church (Rosen, 2009). In addition, statistics for the Danish National Church show that from 1990 to 2011, the membership figure decreased from 89 percent to 80 percent, the baptism figure dropped from 81 percent in 1990 to 70 percent in 2009, and similarly, the confirmation figure fell from 80 percent in 1998 to 70 percent in 2010. Likewise, the number of church weddings and funerals is decreasing, just as the yearly number of church leavers by far exceeds the number of new members.[3] There is no evidence for a decrease in the level of church attendance, but, on the other hand, this has always been low in Denmark. Over the last 30 years, the figure for regular (at least once a month) churchgoers has stabilised between 10 and 13 percent, according to the European Values Study. Though the church still engages a majority of the population on at least some occasions during a lifetime, a gradual decline in the influence of the Danish National Church must be recognized from the above mentioned developments.

Secularization in the third sense of the word, as a general condition of religious choice, is more difficult to show empirically. Taylor (2007) described how the historical development in Western societies since the Reformation has led to a situation where religion—and certainly not any specific kind of religion—can no longer be taken for granted. This does not mean that people stop being religious in a broad sense (as shown above), but that religion becomes more of a personal choice, which also entails an acknowledgement of other religious and non-religious alternatives. Scientific discoveries, theological developments, the increased level of education, immigration, the expanded media networks, and the improved mobility of people are all factors that have increased the number of choices for the individual Dane, especially over the last century. Still, Denmark is a fairly homogenous society compared with most other Western countries, and for many Danes, choosing the national church will therefore tend to be more natural than choosing Islam or Judaism, for instance. But under this broad church identification, a number of personal religious variants are lived out that are more inspired by daily experiences and media images than by occasional visits to a church.[4]

To sum up, it is reasonable to state that Danish society is undergoing a secularization process when it comes to the interrelationship between the state and the church and between the individual and the church. The Danish National Church possesses a limited power in society, and though there is still a majority of Danes who keep their membership, only a few visit the church regularly, and their religious imagination is inspired by many other sources than just the church. Thus, people are not secularized in the sense of losing religion, as shown in the statistics above, but only in the sense of losing touch with the church and its teachings. The aim of this article is to investigate how the pastors can challenge this development through their use of the internet. Does the internet, to some degree, enable pastors to re-connect with the people and re-Christianize their beliefs, or is the process of secularization only strengthened through such efforts?

The Internet as a New Arena for Religion

Mediatization theory provides an appropriate framework for further discussing the ambivalent interrelationship between the church and the media. At the core of the theory is the thesis that the modern mass media today have reached such a position in society that all other institutions have become dependent on them. This is expressed in two ways: First, the media have become an integrated element of the communication of all other institutions, and second, the media have become social institutions "in their own right," no longer serving either the state-political interests or the church as their first priority (Hjarvard, 2008a, p. 109). This situation has emerged in Denmark, as in the rest of the Western world, at the same time as these societies have undergone a process of secularization.

The dual development poses a dilemma for the church: On the one hand the church must use the media to get access to their members and to the people in general, who are increasingly alienated from the church. On the other hand, by doing so, it also, to some extent, submits to the logic of the media and the will of the media agents, who, typically, will use religious symbols only as "raw material" that they can edit and transform to serve their own ends. This mediatization will often result in a kind of *banal religion*, which is an incoherent use of religious or quasi-religious fragments such as [a] elements usually associated with folk religion, like trolls, vampires and black cats crossing the street; [b] items taken from institutionalized religion, like crosses, prayers, and cowls; and [c] representations that have no necessary religious connotations, like upturned faces, thunder and lightning; and highly emotional music (Hjarvard, 2008c, p. 15).

Sometimes, however, the interests of the media and the church coincide, such as when the media broadcast royal weddings, and the pure, unadorned church ceremony is made the climax of the transmission (Hjarvard, 2008c, p. 19), or in times of crisis, where the media often help to affirm the church as an important centre of society (Pantti & Sumiala, 2009, p. 131). Still, no matter how well the media treat the church, the terms will always be set by the media unless a strategic effort is made by the church to put forward its agenda.

The question is, of course, whether the theoretical concept of mediatization makes sense at all when it comes to the internet. The theory, as presented by Stig Hjarvard (2008), focused on the traditional mass media, such as television, radio, and newspapers, which are all characterized by large media institutions and economies, firm gate keeping procedures, and strict publishing criteria. Hjarvard claimed a certain media logic behind all of these. Knut Lundby (2009) was on the whole critical of the concept of a media logic, and found it especially difficult to apply such an idea to the internet: "Web designers as well as web users interact with the Web and its multimodal texts in such complex and varied ways that it cannot easily be subsumed under an overall media logic" (p. 116). Likewise, Friedrich Krotz (2009) argued that a media logic cannot be separated from the cultural and social contexts, just as the historical circumstances must be taken into account (p. 26). Mediatization, however, can still function without the idea of a firm media logic. When the internet becomes an integrated and inescapable part of the communication of the different sectors of society, and when a societal dependency emerges on the internet medium as a whole, or on the different specific new online media, we can speak of mediatization. How this process appears in different contexts can only be determined through empirical investigation. The following analysis is one such attempt at looking specifically at how the pastors in the Evangelical Lutheran Church in Denmark use the internet in their work, and what consequences different uses might have for a church faced with the challenge of secularization.

The Study

The analysis builds on the results of an electronic survey among all the pastors of the Evangelical Lutheran Church in Denmark. The questionnaire was sent out to the 2,007 e-mail addresses found in the directory http://www.sogn. dk in June 2009, and during the following month, 1,040 pastors (52 percent) chose to complete the questionnaire, which had 23 main questions (136 variables).[5] Some of the questions were aimed at mapping how the pastors use the internet. Other questions asked the pastors to evaluate the presence of the internet in their work, and others again invited the pastors to comment on how the church in general should make use of the internet. For reasons of space, this article can only present a few of the survey results. First, it will show how the internet has become an important medium for the pastors' daily communication, and point to a few consequences of this development. Second, it will investigate how the pastors evaluate three different kinds of church uses of the internet, and discuss the possible consequences of these uses for the church in the light of both mediatization and secularization theoretical insights.

The Influence of the Internet on Pastors

Just two decades ago, the internet was not an issue for many people other than developers, but since the popular breakthrough of the internet in the mid 1990s, it has permeated all sectors of society to such an extent that many work and social routines today are dependent upon a fast and stable internet connection. We expect this development to have influenced the church as well, even though we lack a thorough description of this. Over the next few pages, I will attempt to clarify the influence of the internet on the Danish pastors by answering the following questions: How much do the pastors use the internet, and for what ends? What consequences will this increased mediatization of the pastors' work life have for the church?

Table 7.1 indicates that the internet has in many ways become an integrated part of most pastors' daily work life. Ninety-five percent of the pastors are online daily, which is considerably more than average (72 percent) for the Danish population, and a little more than average for persons with a higher education (91 percent) (Danmarks Statistik, 2009, pp. 15, 48). Eighty-one percent of the pastors use the internet daily in relation to work. Much of this use is focused on searching for information or inspiration, with 96 percent searching regularly for information, and 93 percent visiting online churches or religious websites within the last three months. Also, when it comes to preparation of the service, there seems to be a great dependency on the internet. Many pastors go online to find inspiration for a sermon (86 percent), or to find hymns or songs (61 percent), and some also search online for prayers (35 percent). Some pastors take a more active role on the internet: Forty-six percent have recently shared a sermon, 34 percent have edited a home page, and 23 percent have participated in online debate. Facebook engages 17 percent of the pastors, and not less than 29 percent of those pastors who are under 40 years of age. Chatting and blogging are, on the contrary, activities that are still only used by a minority of the pastors. Only 4 percent have written a work-related blog within a three-month period, and only 5 percent have participated in an online chat.

The figures show that the internet is widely used by the pastors to communicate with different target groups. A majority of the pastors have recently had online contact, primarily through e-mail, with bridal couples (87 percent), parents of infants for baptism (80 percent), candidates for confirmation

Table 7.1 The Pastors' Online Activities within the Last Three Months

	Percent
Time consumption:	
Used the internet every day/almost every day	95
Used the internet every day/almost every day—for work	81
Purposes related to work:	
Sent/received e-mails	99
Searched for information	96
Visited church/religious websites	93
Found inspiration for a sermon	86
Searched for pictures/video clips	68
Looked up passages in the Bible	66
Found hymns or songs for a service	61
Shared a sermon	46
Found prayers for use in the church	35
Edited home page	34
Participated in online debate	23
Been on Facebook	17
Participated in chat	5
Written on a blog	4
Work-related contacts with:	
– other employees in the parish church	98
– pastors in other parishes	97
– bridal couples	87
– parents of infants for baptism	80
– candidates for confirmation	63
– volunteers in the parish	59
– relatives before a funeral	53
– the elderly in the parish	10
– the sick in the parish	8

Note. N = 1,040. The percentage column indicates how many pastors responding to the survey gave a positive answer to the different choices mentioned in the left column.

(63 percent), volunteers in the parish (59 percent), and relatives before a funeral (53 percent). The most frequent contact, however, is with colleagues in the parish (98 percent), and other pastors (97 percent). The least frequent online contact is with the elderly (10 percent), and the sick in the parish (8 percent).[6]

On the basis of the frequencies shown in Table 7.1, it is fair to conclude that the internet plays a significant role in the pastors' work-related communication when it comes to central pastoral activities such as preparation of the Sunday service and daily contact with parishioners. Some of the consequences of this widespread internet use—as experienced by the pastors themselves—are shown in Table 7.2. In general, there is a positive evaluation of the influence of the internet, especially among the youngest pastors, who have been used to using the internet throughout most of their career. Thus, 94 percent of the pastors aged between 25 and 39 years think that the internet has had a positive influence on their work. The table points to increased reach as an important consequence of the integration of the internet in the pastors' work life. Sixty percent think that the internet has enabled them to get in touch with more parishioners, and 39 percent experience a more frequent communication with persons outside the parish thanks to the internet. Where increased reach might be seen as mainly a positive consequence, it is worth noting that 27 percent find that the communication that they have on the internet is often superficial.[7] Finally, the internet seems to have the deepest influence on the youngest pastors, with only 19 percent of them thinking that the internet does not much change the way they work as a pastor, as opposed to 42 percent in the oldest age group having the same view.

As this brief overview of the pastors' online engagement shows, the internet has become a central component of the church. It is widely used by the pastors, especially for their work, and the fact that the youngest pastors are also the most frequent users shows that the importance of the internet in this particular context continues to grow. It is, therefore, also relevant to consider a more conscious and strategic use of the internet within the church. The following section will look at three different forms of internet use, showing how

Table 7.2 Consequences of the Pastors' Use of the Internet

	Total percent	Age 26–39	Age 40–59	Age 60+
"The internet has had a positive influence on my work"[a]	88	94	88	77
"I am in contact with more parishioners"	60	75	58	41
"I am more often in contact with persons outside of the parish"	39	41	40	29
"The internet does not change much the way I work as a pastor"	30	19	32	42
"The communication I have on the internet is often superficial"	27	27	28	26

Note. N = 1,040. The percentage column indicates how many pastors responding to the survey gave a positive answer (fully agree/partially agree) to the different choices mentioned in the left column. There are statistically significant differences between the answers given within the different age groups ($p \leq 0.05$).

[a] This question was formulated slightly differently. The pastors were asked to indicate whether the internet had a positive or negative influence on their work. The figure includes those who answered very positive or mainly positive.

each of these is evaluated by the pastors, and discussing the possible consequences of each of the uses.

Three Forms of Internet Use

When a church goes online, there are several ways to approach the communication. Here, I will consider three different kinds of use that appear in the survey,
namely (a) one-way information sharing, (b) user-involving dialogue, and (c)
cyberchurch. The first of these reflects a classic view on communication, focusing
on the distribution of information from an active sender to a passive receiver. The
second use acknowledges that the receiver is an active part of the communication
process and invites her or him to take part in it. Finally, the third use is a more
narrow religious use that aims at creating a sacred space online, where people—
just as in a physical church—can participate in ritual activities such as prayer or a
church service. The ensuing observations about each of the three types are based
on the pastors' answers to the following two open-ended questions in the survey:
"For what purposes should the church use the internet?" and "Is there anything
that the church should *not* do on the internet?" These individually formulated
comments are supplemented by the answers to a question on required content
on the official church website www.folkekirken.dk (Table 7.3).

One-way information sharing

The informational use of the internet is the one that the pastors have most
embraced. Besides the word *information*, the pastors describe this activity
with terms such as *education, enlightenment, dissemination,* and *presentation.*
Some defend a *solid, nuanced,* and *objective* kind of information, while others
find it important that it is *simple* and *accessible.* Others again think that the
church should provide a *professional* kind of information, and businesslike
terms such as *branding* and *profiling* are used in that context. The answers
in Table 7.3 underline this focus on information. The pastors' most required
content on an official church website is practical information about baptism,
confirmation, weddings, and funerals (94 percent) and articles about the
Christian faith (86 percent). Articles about the theology of the church (78
percent), the activities of the local churches (76 percent), church membership and withdrawal (74 percent), and the history of the church (70 percent)
also rank high on the list.

The focus on information can be interpreted as one way of responding
to secularization. In a situation where people have lost touch with the church
and its teachings, it seems like an obvious communicative strategy to use the
internet "to give precise information about faith and Christianity," as one pastor formulates it. Additionally, many pastors hope that the online information

Table 7.3 Content Required on www.folkekirken.dk or Another Official Church Website

	Pastors percent	Danes percent
One-way information sharing:		
Practical information about baptism, confirmation, weddings, and funerals	94	43
Articles about the Christian faith	86	19
Articles about the theology of the church	78	16
Articles about the services and activities of the local parish churches	76	16
Information about church membership and withdrawal	74	20
Articles about the history of the church	70	23
Information about church tax	56	15
User-involving dialogue:		
Online pastor that can be consulted with questions about faith and religion	82	29
Debate on faith and religion	75	21
Blogs written by pastors and bishops	56	12
Ways to get in contact with other Christians	49	5
Cyberchurch:		
Bible search	84	28
A place to read and write prayers	56	5
Video-transmitted church services	39	3
Web-based services (participation online)	26	3
Other religious rituals online	13	2

Note: N (pastors) = 1,040. N (Danes) = 1,015. The percentage column indicates how many pastors and Danes responding to the surveys ticked off the choices mentioned in the left column. The survey among the Danes is presented in Fischer-Nielsen (2010).

could even serve the purpose of motivating people to visit the church. Table 7.3 shows that the informational aspect has some support among ordinary Danes. Thus, almost half of them (43 percent) would find information about baptism, confirmation, weddings, and funerals interesting on a church website. This is not surprising, since it is at these occasions that most Danes experience the church as a relevant context for their lives. Considerably fewer Danes are interested in the other informational possibilities, such as articles about the Christian faith (19 percent) and articles about theology (16 percent).

Though important for many pastors, the informational communication does not necessarily guarantee success online. If the church presence on the internet (and in general) is nothing but information, there is a possibility that, in the long run, people will feel further distanced from the church.

Given what we have seen above regarding secularization, a one-sided focus on information as monologue conflicts with the way religion is experienced in a secular and individualized age, where choice and personal influence are important elements. And, in a sense, it also runs counter to the way the internet works. The Web 2.0 development suggests that the internet user wants to be involved, or at least to have the option of involvement. If this is not possible on a church website, people might lose interest. In the language of mediatization theory we could say that a monological approach clashes with the overall logic that dominates the internet, which could be described in terms such as "decentralized, networked, dynamic and global" (Fuchs, 2008, p. 278). Where a counter logical approach to the old media often meant not being represented at all, on the internet, where anybody can publish and thus be represented, the consequence is more likely not being seen.

Another objection against a narrow focus on information is raised by the pastors themselves. Some fear that this approach might lead to a too centralized and uniform picture of the church, which goes against the understanding of the Danish National Church as a broad and open church with lots of different theological points of view. One pastor puts it this way: "Since the Danish National Church is not a unit, but a church consisting of several congregations with very different situations, the church must never appear as one 'company'." This leaves us with the central dilemma of today's church at a time of secularization and religious competition: How to appear publicly with a clear and convincing voice without compromising the identity of the church as a broad and open organization?

User-involving dialogue

The second use, which stresses a dialogical approach to internet communication, has some support among the pastors, though it is not mentioned as often as the informational use. In this approach, the communication is seen as a two-way interaction between church representatives and the people. Words such as *contact, debate, conversation, network, openness, democracy, co-influence,* and *interactivity* are offered by the pastors to describe the use. Here, it is not so much the communicated message that is important, but more the relational presence of the church. In other words, the purpose is to show that the church is relevant and present in society, but also to give people a reason to visit the local church. Table 7.3 shows some of these dialogical purposes, for example the pastors' support of web content such as online pastors (82 percent), debate on faith and religion (75 percent), and blogs written by pastors and bishops (56 percent).

A focus on a dialogical presence could be seen as very much on par with the present condition of religion in a secular age. Though most of the Danes describe themselves as religious, only a few have a regular connection to the church, and the church has, to a high degree, lost its daily relevance for people's lives. A dialogical church presence on the internet might in this regard enable the church to re-establish a bond to people's everyday lives and beliefs. This is not easily done, however. Previous studies from both the United States and Europe show that religious websites don't attract many of the non-committed, but rather tend to engage those who are already actively involved in a religious group, for instance regular churchgoers (Larsen, 2004, p. 18; Hjarvard, 2008b, p. 203; Fischer-Nielsen, 2010, p. 79). Still, religion is presented and discussed on many other websites than just on the strictly religious ones. Online newspapers and websites for TV stations are the places where Danes are most often faced with religious issues, and the youngest Danes (18–29 years of age) more often encounter religion on social networking sites such as Facebook, and on discussion boards, than on the religious websites (Fischer-Nielsen, 2010, p. 86). In other words, if the church wants to establish a dialogue on the internet in a Web 2.0 era, it requires more than simply a website. It needs a broad and varied online presence, where the website is supplemented with other online products, as well as an active presence on media sites and social networking sites.

While a dialogical presence can be seen as a suitable strategy in the religious landscape of today, some objections, however, are raised by the pastors. Firstly—and most importantly—some pastors fear that this approach will lead to more individualized ways of believing, and more blurred dogmas, whereas what is needed (in their view) is a firm and clear presentation of the Christian faith. One pastor gives voice to that opinion by saying: "The church should not fall too much for the internet and the blog mania of our time, for the proclamation of the words of God disappears in peoples' own many words." Another more pragmatic objection focuses on the difficulty of achieving a fruitful internet dialogue that does not drown in negative speech and criticism of the type that would undermine the positive message of the church. Different studies support this fear: A genuine dialogue leading to some kind of understanding is hard to achieve (Bunt, 2000, p. 124; Introvigne, 2005, p. 113; Lövheim & Linderman, 2005, pp. 133–134). From the perspective of secularization theory we can say that while the dialogical presence in some ways can counteract secularization in the first and second of Charles Taylor's three meanings, it is less likely to change the fact that the church and its message is subjected to individual choice and religious competition that is characteristic of secularization in the third meaning of the word.

Cyberchurch

The term *cyberchurch* is applied here to describe the elements that enable visitors to use a website as they use a physical church building: It includes the collective elements of a service: rituals, sacraments, prayers, and hymns, but also individual activities such as devotion, candle lighting, personal prayer, etc.[8] In other words, we are talking about the *doing* of religion in a narrow sense. Table 7.3 shows that besides Bible search, which is not the clearest example of a spiritual or ritual online exercise, most other possibilities are met with a fair amount of scepticism. About half of the pastors think that the church should offer a place online where people can read and write prayers (56 percent). Fewer still defend video-transmitted church services (39 percent), web-based services (26 percent), and other religious rituals online (13 percent).

Where information and dialogue are fairly accepted purposes for a church website, the ritual use is more debatable, and it raises the overall question as to whether it makes sense to perform a ritual online. On the one hand, it is possible within a Protestant tradition to claim that it is not the physical space of the church that is sacred, but the rituals that are performed in it. Therefore, it makes sense to perform the church rituals wherever people are. On the other hand, it can be argued that ritual practice requires certain spatial and bodily qualities that cannot be attained online (Højsgaard, 2001, p. 99; Dawson, 2005, p. 16). This point of view is supported by many pastors, who voice the understanding that a real church practice is grounded in a community of *flesh and blood*, and thereby the internet is excluded as a genuine ritual space. A cyberchurch is therefore, at the most—to use some of the pastors' own words—an *artificial, casual,* and *superficial pseudo-community* or a *replacement church* with *surrogate services*.

In relation to secularization, cyberchurch poses both threats and possibilities to the established church. For one thing, the very structure of the Danish National Church, with its narrow focus on the parish, is challenged if the physical building and the local community can no longer uphold a privileged position. For another, it can be argued that this structure was outdated long before the internet occurred, and that cyberchurch and other kinds of new church types will help the church to remain relevant in the population after the natural bond to the parish church has been lifted. However, data presented in the far right column in Table 7.3 indicate that the church should not expect cyberchurch developments to cause a massive renewal of church engagement. Only a very small percentage of the ordinary Danes find the more ritualistic activities on a website appealing.

Conclusion

In this article, I have touched on a dilemma faced today by the Evangelical Lutheran Church in Denmark: Being church in a society coined with secularization requires an active presence in the media if the church wants to keep in touch with the people. By entering the media, however, the church also loses control of its message, as it is used according to the interests of the media agents. This mediatization effect has convincingly been presented by Stig Hjarvard (2008) and other media scholars primarily with regard to the traditional mass media. The solution to the dilemma could be a more strategic approach to the media, where the Danish National Church actively uses the media without limiting itself to a mere supplier of raw materials, but instead insists on carrying its own agendas through. It could be argued that the internet, which is more accessible and less institutionalized than the traditional mass media indeed offers such possibilities for the church.

Throughout this article I have focused on the Danish pastors' use of the internet. First, I showed how the pastors' work life today has been greatly affected by the internet. Pastors prepare services with the help of the internet, and much of their daily contact with parishioners and colleagues is now carried out online. Since we presume that the use of a medium affects the message, it is important to enter into a deeper investigation of how the use of the internet changes the pastors' work life. Here I have only pointed to a few of the consequences, but more thorough investigations are indeed needed. Still, we can conclude that the internet has become an important element of the daily life of today's church.

Therefore, the church must also consider its use of the medium. In the last part of each subsection of the above paragraph, I have analyzed three different communicative strategies and shown how, in a secularized world, all three offer both challenges and possibilities for the church. First, the use of *one-way information sharing* may serve as a strong voice in the flow of information, but it can also uphold stereotypes of a distant and elitist church, which is not likely to appeal to the ordinary Dane. Second, *the user-involving dialogue* satisfies the expectations of the internet surfers ("the internet logic") and fits with contemporary religious tendencies, but carries a risk of blurring and individualizing the Christian message. Finally, *cyberchurch* expands the sacred space of the church, and might engage more people in religious practice, but, on the other hand, will also lead to an increased denigration of the importance of the parish church and the bodily community.

These pros and cons indicate that there is no simple or obvious way for a church to respond to secularization online. Therefore, the main conclusion must be that a fruitful online engagement can be achieved only through a conscious awareness of the positive as well as negative consequences of different internet uses. The church cannot do without the media, and the internet is one of the most important media in today's world. But the church can decide whether the communication should be formed by coincidences, or whether it should be intentionally guided by the church towards the best possible gains.

Notes

1. The names The Evangelical Lutheran Church in Denmark and the Danish National Church are used synonymously in the article.
2. The survey data can be studied on the website http://www.europeanvaluesstudy.eu
3. See church statistics on http://www.km.dk/folkekirken/statistik-og-oekonomi/kirkestatistik.html
4. A more thorough overview of the historical religious developments in Denmark since the Reformation and an introduction to the present situation of the Danish National Church can be found in Mortensen (2005).
5. Thanks to information put at my disposal by the Danish Pastors Association, it has been possible to compare the answers to the background questions with the actual distribution. Through this comparison, the survey respondents proved to be representative with regard to age, sex, and geography.
6. Since the aim here is only is to give an impression of the pastors' overall use of the internet, I have not dealt with differences due to sex and age. There are some uses that are significantly more widespread among men than women, for instance editing websites. The female pastors, however, are most active when it comes to finding inspiration for a sermon, finding hymns or songs for a service, sharing a sermon, and finding prayers for use in the church. Generally, the younger pastors are more active on the internet than their older colleagues.
7. It is difficult to judge whether this is a high or a low figure, since the pastors were not asked to compare the degree of superficiality in their internet communication with that of face-to-face conversation, which is probably also experienced as superficial from time to time.
8. The concept is used here in a more narrow sense than in Timothy Hutchings' (2010) definition, for instance. He referred to online churches as "internet-based Christian communities, seeking to pursue worship, discussion, friendship, teaching, support, proselytization and other key religious goals through computer-mediated communication" (p. 2).

References

Bruce, S. (2002). *God is dead: Secularization in the West.* Oxford, England: Blackwell.

Bunt, G. R. (2000). *Virtually Islamic: Computer-mediated communication and cyber Islamic environments.* Cardiff, Wales: University of Wales Press.

Danmarks Statistik. (2009). *Befolkningens brug af internet 2009 [The Danes' use of the internet 2009].* Copenhagen, Denmark: Statistics Denmark.

Davie, G. (2002). *Europe, the exceptional case: Parameters of faith in the modern world.* London, England: Darton, Longman, & Todd.

Dawson, L. L. (2005). The mediation of religious experience in cyberspace. In M. T. Højsgaard & M. Warburg (Eds.), *Religion and cyberspace* (pp. 15–37). London, England; New York, NY: Routledge.

Fischer-Nielsen, P. (2010). *Mellem sogne-og cyberkirke: En analyse af folkekirkens kommunikation på internettet [Between parish church and cyberchurch: An analysis of the internet communication of the evangelical Lutheran Church in Denmark].* (PhD dissertation). Aarhus University, Denmark.

Fuchs, C. (2008). *Internet and society: Social theory in the internet age.* New York, NY: Routledge.

Hjarvard, S. (2008a). The mediatization of society: A theory of the media as agents of social and cultural change. *Nordicom Review, 29*(2), 105–134 .

Hjarvard, S. (2008b). *En verden af medier: Medialiseringen af politik, sprog, religion og leg [A world of media: The mediatization of politics, language, religion and play].* Frederiksberg, Denmark: Samfundslitteratur.

Hjarvard, S. (2008c). The mediatization of religion: A theory of the media as agents of religious change. *Northern Lights, 6*(1), 9–26.

Højsgaard, M. T. (2001). Virtuelle lokaliteter: Dansk kristendom på internettet [Virtual localities: Danish Christianity on the internet]. *Chaos, 35*(1), 99–115.

Hutchings, T. (2010). *Creating church online: An ethnographic study of five internet-based Christian communities.* (PhD dissertation). Durham University, England.

Introvigne, M. (2005). A symbolic universe: Information terrorism and new religions in cyberspace. In M. T. Højsgaard & M. Warburg (Eds.), *Religion and cyberspace* (pp. 102–118). London, England; New York, NY: Routledge.

Krotz, F. (2009). Mediatization: A concept with which to grasp media and societal change. In K. Lundby (Ed.), *Mediatization: Concept, changes, consequences* (pp. 21–40). New York, NY: Peter Lang.

Larsen, E. (2004). Cyberfaith: How Americans pursue religion online. In L. L. Dawson & D. E. Cowan (Eds.), *Religion online: Finding faith on the internet* (pp. 17–22). New York, NY: Routledge.

Lövheim, M., & Linderman, A. G. (2005). Constructing religious identity on the internet. In M. T. Højsgaard & M. Warburg (Eds.), *Religion and cyberspace* (pp. 121–137). London, England; New York, NY: Routledge.

Lundby, K. (2009). Media logic: Looking for social interaction changes. In K. Lundby (Ed.), *Mediatization: Concept, changes, consequences* (pp. 101–122). New York, NY: Peter Lang.

Mortensen, V. (2005). *Kristendommen under forvandling: Pluralismen som udfordring til teologi og kirke i Danmark [Christianity under transformation: Pluralism as challenge to theology and church in Denmark].* Aarhus, Denmark: Univers.

Pantti, M., & Sumiala, J. (2009). Till death do us join: Media, mourning rituals and the sacred centre of the society. *Media, Culture and Society, 31*(1), 119–135.

Rosen, I. (2009). *I'm a believer—But I'll be damned if I'm religious: Belief and religion in the greater Copenhagen area: A focus group study.* (PhD dissertation). Lund University, Sweden.

Taylor, C. (2007). *A secular age.* Cambridge, MA: Belknap Press of Harvard University Press.

8. PICTURE: The Adoption of ICT by Catholic Priests

Lorenzo Cantoni, Emanuele Rapetti, Stefano Tardini, Sara Vannini, and Daniel Arasa

Introduction: New Media and the Catholic Church

In this chapter, we discuss the origins, operations, and newly emerging results of a multi-country investigation of the ways in which priests are interacting with new media. We regard this study on internet use by the members of the Church, and, in particular, its ministrants (priests), as an investigation of one stage in the history of developments in the Church's activities (Cantoni & Zyga, 2007; Arasa, 2008; Arasa, Cantoni, & Ruiz, 2010). The Roman Catholic Church is one of the few worldwide institutional religions that have lasted for more than 20 centuries. Many reasons may be attributed to its longevity. Beyond its supernatural origin, considered by its followers as the main reason, is the beauty and universality of its message and its capacity to adapt to all times, as well as its ability to incorporate the media of each period in order to carry on its mission, i.e., spreading the gospel.

The originality of this analysis stands in the investigation of the hierarchical structure of this religious institution and the particularly important role that bishops and priests play in the guidance (and service) of the one billion Catholics around the globe. The implications of this study also bear upon the larger Catholic congregations around the world. As the diffusion of innovation literature suggests, the more the leadership uses, and fosters the use of, the new technologies, the more their use among members of the Church will spread (Rogers, 1995).

The expansion and penetration of Information and Communication Technologies (ICTs) in society during the last few decades is a reality that cannot be ignored (Cantoni & Tardini, 2006). ICTs deeply influence the things we learn and how we learn them. Almost any sector, institution, or person is somehow touched by ICTs. The Catholic Church and its members are not alien to that influence. Analyzing how Catholic priests use, and have incorporated, ICTs in their ministry activities is, thus, an interesting exercise not only for the Church itself—which can see the effects that their influence has—but also for the academic research—which may discover the importance of knowing how such an influential group as Catholic priests see and use ICTs (Christians, 2002).

With regard to the Church, the results of the present study suggest that future educational initiatives need to consider the importance of new media. Understanding how new media facilitate or impair priestly activities will somehow influence traditional methods of teaching and education of candidates for the priesthood as well as the continuous education programs of ordained members.

To our knowledge, no in-depth and comprehensive study on this subject (Catholic priests and the internet) exists prior to our efforts, in part because of the difficulties of reaching such a widely dispersed universe (there are more than 400,000 Catholic priests worldwide, according to the data of the Congregation for the Clergy—see: http://www.clerus.org/clerus/dati/2008-12/08-6/totalclerge08.htm). Yet it is precisely through the use of new media (online questionnaires) that this research was carried out.

The Project PICTURE: An Overview

Research description and background

The international research project named "PICTURE" (Priests' Information and Communication Technologies Usages in their Religious Experiences, www.pictureproject.info) was developed according to the scientific objective as mentioned above. The acronym itself illustrates the aim of the project: PICTURE studies the usages of ICTs and of the internet in particular, by the priests of the Catholic Church all over the world. It is worth specifying that PICTURE does not intend to answer the question: how many priests use ICTs? The research aims instead to offer a picture of what kinds of activities priests perform online, and what attitudes they hold about digital technologies. In this study, priests who access the internet are called *ePriests*.

Such an ambitious research project as PICTURE was made possible thanks to the fruitful collaboration between the two institutes that built the entire investigation process and protocol: the New Media in Education Laboratory (NewMinE Lab) of the Università della Svizzera italiana (USI, Lugano, Switzerland), and the School of Church Communications of the Pontifical University of the Holy Cross (PUSC, Rome, Italy). Some researchers in the two institutions had already initiated a path of study about the role ICTs play within the Catholic Church (Arasa, Cantoni, & Ruiz, 2010): our research can be seen as a second step in this path. The research project was supported by the Congregation for the Clergy. It is worth noting that the approval of the Catholic Church hierarchies was needed for the reliance of PICTURE within the sample, but as a sign of autonomy in the scientific process of analysis, no funding was received from the organization.

Methodology.

Data have been collected through a questionnaire, which was made available, both online and on paper, in seven languages: English, French, German, Italian, Polish, Portuguese, and Spanish. As there were no prior models of a comprehensive survey on Catholic priests that we could find, the research architecture was built by our team. The questionnaire was composed of 12 multiple-choice questions (plus personal data and the opportunity to add comments) and organized in eight sections: personal data, owned digital technologies, technological competences and internet use, perception of the usefulness of digital technologies, frequency of online activities, preferred tools for learning, attitude towards technology, and digital communication.

Due to the vast sample under consideration, the research was intended to collect the answers of 1% of Catholic priests worldwide, proportionately to the countries where they perform their activity. According to the data of the Congregation for the Clergy, updated in 2007, the total number of Catholic priests in the world is about 408,000 (see the distribution in Fig. 8.1).

In terms of sampling, the first intention was to have a two-level sampling in which we expected to collect from every country a number of questionnaires

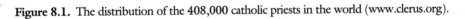

Figure 8.1. The distribution of the 408,000 catholic priests in the world (www.clerus.org).

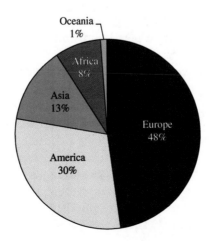

proportional to the number of priests in that country for the first level, and, within the national context, a random sample for the second level. Unfortunately, it was not possible to follow these criteria, mainly because of the low number of answers received from some developing countries. So, it was finally decided to have a self-selected sample on an international basis, with some implications that will be explained in the next paragraphs.

The empirical research started in autumn 2009 with the intention of exploiting the incoming Priestly Year (which was promoted within the Catholic Church), as a suitable occasion to publicize the research project. The questionnaires were collected over more than three months, from November 15th, 2009 to February 28th, 2010. In order to ensure the widest possible distribution, the questionnaire was diffused in several ways: all the Bishop's Conferences of the world were contacted, both via e-mail and ordinary mail; all the dioceses of the 50 countries with the largest number of priests and the largest religious orders were contacted via e-mail as well. The questionnaire was also advertised through several Catholic news agencies. To prevent errors and fraud, the research was publicized only through Catholic agencies, and the incoming traffic to the research web page was constantly monitored; in addition, although the questionnaire was anonymous, many priests left their names and contact data.

In total, 5,189 questionnaires were collected. From them, all the priests who declared that they did not access the internet were excluded, as they did not match the research purposes. The number of valid respondents was 4,992 priests, accounting for 1.2% of the total number of priests in the world. 93.4% of questionnaires (4,664 units) were filled in online, 6.6% (328 units) were returned on paper.

The data treatment followed four sequential steps:

1. Because of the novelty of the investigation addressed by PICTURE, the major point was to describe the observed population. To do that, the database was first cleaned and uniformed: paper questionnaires were digitized, all data were re-coded in English, and some problems in the database were solved (e.g., one blind item was added to the Portuguese questionnaire, and the order of possible answers of one question in the Polish questionnaire was inverted).
2. A statistically founded weighting of responses was made, in order to balance between the overrepresented continents (Europe, Latin and North America, Oceania) and the underrepresented ones (Africa, Asia).
3. Cross-tabulations and tree-analyses were performed in order to infer the impact of personal data on respondents' behavior (e.g., it emerged that the priests who were more confident in the effectiveness of ICTs in their pastoral activities were, on average, the ones from Africa).

4. In order to delineate profiles of priests and to verify hypotheses, cluster-analyses and factor-analyses were run. This point is still under development, because of the vastness of the database.

Promotion and dissemination of results

Some findings of the descriptive statistics have been published on the project's website, including the general results (worldwide), the main results for each continent, and the results of the major countries, i.e., those for which the number of received answers is statistically relevant.[1] The reports are available as a free download under a Creative Commons License (Noncommercial-No Derivative Works 3.0 Unported License[2]). All the reports are published in English, then, when possible, they are translated into other languages. All reports have the same structure: introduction to the research, demographic data, ownership and frequency of ICTs use, key activities in the priestly mission, formation, enculturation of faith, communication and socialization in the "digital continent," conclusion.

For PICTURE to become relevant in different fields (for example, within the Catholic Church, among the scholars reflecting on Knowledge Society issues, in the field of Media and Religion, and so on), a remarkable effort has been devoted to guaranteeing the widest possible publicity for the study: Once the first results were made available and published on the website, an e-mail message was sent to all the people who had registered on the project's mailing list, to all the worldwide Bishop's conferences, to all the involved congregations, and to a number of colleagues and associations or institutions that might be interested. Moreover, two press conferences were organized to present the data from Italy, and the worldwide data, respectively. Press releases were sent to several news agencies and to a number of national newspapers. Also, the PICTURE results have been presented in different countries (Spain, Portugal, Switzerland) through public presentations and media interviews. Most of the promotion and spreading of the results takes place via the project website, from where it is possible to freely download all the reports, have an in-depth look at the press hype, learn about the research project, retrieve information about the team, and ask for more data or info.

PICTURE: Main Findings

The results of the research do not offer a black and white, one-dimensional image of the use of ICTs by the ePriests of the Catholic Church. On the contrary, they offer a multifaceted and differentiated reality, depending on the context of use, accessibility, and, often, the geographical region they operate in. It is possible, however, to identify some specific lines in their practices of use; although they don't return a complete "picture" of the phenomena, they draw a useful identikit of ePriests in the world. In the next section, several general aspects of the respondents' profiles will be presented.

Demographics

The average age (mean) of the respondents is 48 years old: They range from a minimum age of 25 to a maximum of 96. Respondents have been ordained for a mean of 20 years, with a slight difference between ordained religious (20 years) and secular or diocesan priests (19 years).[3] 22.9% of the respondents[4] belong to religious congregations, while 77.1% are secular priests. Comparing it to the official statistics (Congregation for the Clergy, 2007), this datum is a little biased towards the secular priests. This is probably because the dioceses have been one of the main means of promoting the questionnaire, as they constitute the administrative territorial unit of the Church, and they were the most consistent way to spread the questionnaire among the regions of the world.

Respondents operate in 117 countries; 94 of them, however, did not indicate their nationality, and the nation where they are carrying out their pastoral activities, so it was not possible to deduce the geographical region they belonged to. Of the 4,898 respondents who indicated the country where they are operating, 54.6% come from Europe, 25.0% from Latin America (including all the countries of Central and South America plus Mexico), 11.5% from North America, 3.9% from Asia, 2.6% from Africa and 1.6% from Oceania.

Hereafter, the countries are summarized per number of respondents (Table 8.1). We have considered the country where the ePriests are working, because this datum is more meaningful in order to study their use of ICTs than their country of birth.

As for the languages of the questionnaires, 31.9% (1,593 units) have been filled in in Spanish, 21.9% (1,072) in English, 18.0% (897) in Italian, 9.6% (478) in Polish, 5.8% (291) in German, and 4.9% (246) in Portuguese.

Access to ICTs and to the Internet

ePriests seem to have a good number of technologies at their disposal: on average, 90.6% of them have a mobile phone, 82.8% a laptop, 81.2% a desktop computer, 73.1% a digital camera, and 44.0% an MP3 player. In terms of access to the internet, 94.7% of ePriests report that they access the Internet daily, 4.6% on a weekly basis and 0.7% only access the Internet once per month.

Table 8.1 Respondents per Country (Descending Order)

Country	Freq.	Country	Freq.	Country	Freq.
Not indicated	94	Pakistan	18	Haiti	2
Italy	834	Congo, Democratic Republic of the (Congo-Kinshasa)	15	Jamaica	2
USA	485			Liberia	2
Spain	427			Morocco	2
Poland	425			Norway	2
Mexico	362			Rwanda	2
Brazil	201	Uruguay	15	Sri Lanka	2
France	191	Burkina Faso	14	Taiwan	2
Argentina	139	South Africa	13	Thailand	2
Switzerland	131	Dominican Republic	11	Algeria	1
Colombia	122			Angola	1
Germany	110	Ivory Coast	11	Azerbaijan	1
Chile	109	Netherlands	11	Bahrain	1
Canada	91	Kenya	10	Bangladesh	1
Slovakia	62	Lebanon	10	Belarus	1
UK	62	Russia	10	Central African Republic	1
Belgium	58	China	9		
Romania	54	Honduras	9	Cuba	1
Peru	52	Indonesia	9	Denmark	1
Czech Republic	46	Iraq	8	Egypt	1
		Paraguay	8	Fiji	1
Portugal	44	Japan	7	Lithuania	1
Australia	43	Bosnia and Herzegovina	6	Luxembourg	1
Hungary	41			Malaysia	1
Venezuela	41	Tanzania	6	Mali	1
India	40	Zimbabwe	6	Mauritius	1
Ecuador	38	Nicaragua	5	Mozambique	1
Philippines	37	Uganda	5	Namibia	1
Austria	33	Holy Land	4	Palau	1
New Zealand	33	Kazakhstan	4	Sierra Leone	1
		Madagascar	4	Sudan	1
Costa Rica	32	Cameroon	3	Swaziland	1
Croatia	28	Gabon	3	Syria	1
Ireland	28	Ghana	3	Tajikistan	1
Puerto Rico	28	Moldova	3	Togo	1
		Serbia	3	Trinidad & Tobago	1
Ukraine	27	Sweden	3		
Bolivia	24	Albania	2	Turkey	1
Guatemala	23	Benin	2	Vatican City	1
South Korea	23	Cambodia	2		
		Cape Verde	2	Zambia	1
Slovenia	23	Chad	2		
El Salvador	18	Congo	2		

Figure 8.2. "How often do you access the internet?" (The horizontal axis in this chart starts at 75%).

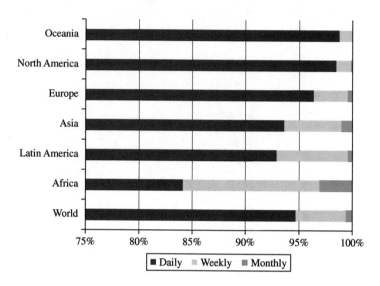

These data vary significantly if we compare the continents to one another and to the world average. As shown in Figure 8.2, more than 90% of ePriests in all the continents declare that they access the internet on a daily basis, except for Africa, where this percentage drops to 84.1%; however, the percentage of African ePriests accessing the internet on a weekly basis increases (12.7% compared to a maximum of 6.6% in the other continents). This can probably be explained by a lack of facilities in Africa, rather than by a lower interest in ICTs by ePriests operating there. The chart suggests, as a matter of fact, that ePriests operating in richer continents can more easily access the internet, while the chances to do so decrease more and more as we consider the emerging ones. If we order the continents by frequency of access, Oceania is first in the list (with 98.7% of the respondents accessing on a daily basis and no one accessing less than once per week); North America (98.4%) and Europe (96.4%) follow close behind; Asia and Latin America are slightly below that, with 93.7% and 92.9% of ePriests accessing every day, and 5.3% and 6.6% accessing once per week, respectively.

The same difference is not reflected, however, in the support used to participate in the questionnaire: the percentage of ePriests from Africa answering online was 91.3%, very similar to the European one (92.0%), while in Latin America it was 95.4% (closer to Oceania—98.7%—and North America—97.4%). Asia had the highest percentage of questionnaires filled in on paper (15.7%), while only 84.3% were filled in online.

Websites

Each respondent was asked to list up to five websites that he found useful in his experience as a priest. The total of records received was 17,072; among them, 22 websites were indicated more than 100 times. The most cited site (1,854 times) was *The Vatican*, followed by the Catholic news agency *Zenit* (1,124 times) and *Google* (678 times).

Other important websites cited were the following:

- Appearing more than 300 times: *Catholic.net* and *Qumran* (366 and 360, respectively);
- Appearing more than 200 times: *ACI Prensa, Maranatha, Encuentra* and *La Chiesa* (295, 234, 230, 221, respectively);
- Appearing 100 times or more: *Opoka* (193), *USCCB* (182), *Yahoo!* (182), *CEI* (162), *Mercaba* (161), *Mateusz* (147), *Wiara* (145), *Betania* (136), *Wikipedia* (133), *Clerus* (128), *Opus Dei* (114), *CEF* (113), *Facebook* (100).

The above-mentioned results are presented in Figure 8.3.

Figure 8.3. Websites indicated more than 100 times.

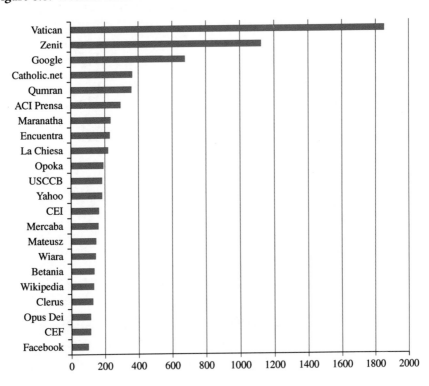

Communication and social networks

Most ePriests (79.1%) consider the internet "useful or very useful" for communication with others. Nonetheless, the use of social networks is still not pervasive. 26.4% of respondents affirm that they access them daily, and 17.6% once per week, but 35.3% have never accessed them. Furthermore, most of those who use social networks do not seem to use them to stay in touch with other priests: 41.0% of ePriests are not in contact with any other colleagues through social networks, while 29.8% of respondents have from 1 to 10 other priests among their contacts, and 2.8% report that they have more than 100 priests.

Also in this case, there are big differences in the use of social networks depending on geographical conditions: In Latin America and Asia, ePriests are in contact with other priests through social networks much more than in other continents: only 32.7% of Latin American respondents and 27.9% of Asian ones report that they have no priests among their contacts (world average: 41.0%).

In Figure 8.4 the worldwide results are compared with the Latin American and Asian ones.

Finally, 36.3% of respondents report that they are in contact with 1 to 10 other priests through Instant Messaging or VoIP services (MSN, Yahoo! Messenger, Skype, etc.), while 26.4% of them have no other priests among their contacts.

Figure 8.4. Number of contacts with other priests in social networks.

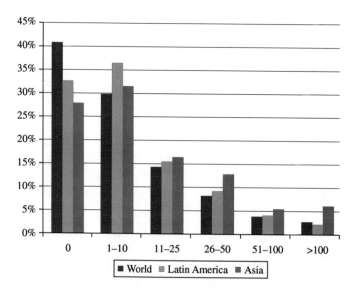

PICTURE: In-Depth Analyses

Priestly activities at the time of the Internet

In this section, the most relevant results concerning the use of the internet for some activities that are specific to the priestly mission (e.g., preparing homilies, praying, offering spiritual advice, and so on) will first be presented; then, they will be analyzed according to the priests' age, in order to assess whether being a "digital native" (Prensky, 2001) influences the way ICTs are used by Catholic priests.

With regard to the perceived usefulness of the internet for accomplishing priestly activities, it is considered useful to facilitate parish activities, for preparing homilies, and for spreading the Christian message. Less positive is the perception of its usefulness for offering spiritual advice, and even lower than that is the perceived usefulness of the Net for praying. In Table 8.2, the figures for these activities are presented.[5]

When it comes to the actual practices of priests (Table 8.3), not surprisingly the situation reflects the perceived usefulness of the internet. 61.4% of respondents search for homily materials online at least once per week (14.7% do it on a daily basis), while only 22.9% of them do it less than once per month (8.7% have never searched online for homily materials). Conversely, only 35.9% of respondents pray online[6] at least once per week (17.5% do it every day), and 35.7% of ePriests report never having used the internet for praying online.

Comparing the results for the same questions among the continents, some relevant differences emerge. For instance, in Asia, Africa, and Latin

Table 8.2 Perceived Usefulness of the Internet for Priestly Activities

Activity	Very useful/useful	Not at all/almost not useful
Facilitating parish activities	60.6%	9.6%
Spreading the Christian message	52.5%	17.5%
Preparing homilies	50.6%	17.8%
Offering spiritual advice	26.7%	38.6%
Praying	17.7%	53.6%

Table 8.3 Frequency of Online Activities

Activity	Never	A few times a year	Once a month	Once a week	Every day
Online search for homily materials	8.7%	14.2%	15.6%	46.7%	14.7%
Online praying	35.7%	17.4%	11.1%	18.4%	17.5%

America, the perceived usefulness of the internet for offering spiritual advice is higher than the world average (30.7%, 28.5%, and 38.8%, respectively, consider the internet as useful or very useful for this purpose, while the world average is 26.7%). In North America and Oceania the internet is perceived as particularly useful for preparing homilies: 61.9% of ePriests in North America and 58.7% in Oceania consider it useful or very useful for this purpose (world average: 50.6%). Also, 69.0% of ePriests in North America search online for homily materials at least once per week (worldwide: 61.4%).

Moreover, ePriests in Latin America have a much higher regard for the usefulness of the internet for all priestly activities: 74.7% of them consider it useful or very useful for facilitating parish activities, 70.2% for preparing homilies, 66.4% for spreading the Christian message, 22.4% for praying. Correspondingly, the actual practices of use of the internet are also considerably higher than the world average: 77.8% of Latin American ePriests search for homily materials online at least once per week (29.3% every day), and 42.3% pray online at least once per week (24.7% every day). On the contrary, in Europe, the consideration of the usefulness of the internet for these activities is lower than the world average: For instance, only 41.7% of European respondents consider the internet useful or very useful for preparing homilies, and 23.0% consider it almost not or not at all useful for that same purpose.

To sum up, the ePriests' general perception of the usefulness of ICTs for their priestly mission is positive (Figure 8.5): 41.6% of them think that ICTs have significantly improved the way they perform their priestly mission to a certain or great extent (values 4 and 5 in a scale from 0 (= not at all) to 5 (= a lot).

Figure 8.5. "How much has the use of digital technologies improved the way you perform your priestly mission?"

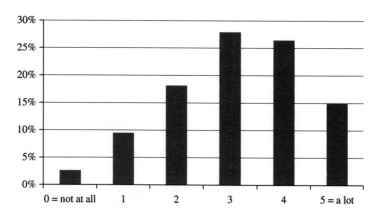

Again, when comparing the results of the single continents, the perception differs from one continent to another. In Europe, the perception is relatively more negative, since only 34.8% of ePriests consider that ICTs have improved their priestly mission much or very much, and 14.1% have noticed no or very few improvements. In all other continents, the general perception is more positive, in particular in Africa and Latin America, where the percentage of ePriests who perceive large improvements is higher than the world's average (52.1% and 51.6%, respectively; world's average: 41.6%), and that of those who see no improvements is lower (11.1% and 7.3%, respectively; world's average: 12.2%).

The age factor

In the last few decades a big debate (see, for example, Schulmeister, 2008, 2010; Bennet, Maton, & Kervin, 2008; Cantoni & Tardini, 2010) has grown up around the awareness of the penetration and deep impact of ICTs in people's everyday lives, especially concerning the youngest, i.e., those who were born in a "digital" environment. Some popular expressions—e.g., Generation Y, Digital Natives, NetGeneration, New Millennium Learners (for a detailed review, see Cantoni, Rapetti, & Tardini, 2010; Cantoni & Tardini, 2010)—have been proposed in order to highlight important behavioral shifts in tandem with age differences in the field of education. Although there is not yet agreement as to whether a generation of digital learners exists or not, some scholars have suggested that youths learn and think in a different way, in part related to their exposure to digital devices since their childhood.

Although the debate is still ongoing, it offers an interesting path of analysis for our PICTURE data. Accordingly, this section is devoted to addressing the question of whether younger ePriests demonstrate different behaviors in their ICTs use when compared to their older colleagues. Data emerging from cross-tabulations between the perceived usefulness of the internet when doing priestly activities and age of respondents will be discussed. For this analysis, all respondents have been grouped in five classes: from 25 to 34 years old, from 35 to 44, from 45 to 54, from 55 to 64, and older than 65 (in the following text, the term "the youngest" is also used to refer to the first class).

As we have seen, ePriests as a whole declare a high level of appreciation about the usefulness of the internet for parish activities. In light of the digital natives hypothesis, it may be expected that the more enthusiastic internet users are the youngest ministrants. On the contrary, findings indicate that it was the 35–44-year-old group that report that they find the internet much more useful for parish activities, while people under 35 seem to be less favorably disposed. 62.4% of the 35–44-year-old group of ePriests find the internet useful or very useful to facilitate parish activities, compared to 58.5% of the 25–34-year-old

Figure 8.6. Age distribution of ePriests who consider the internet very useful for offering spiritual advice (573 units, corresponding to 13.3% of all respondents).

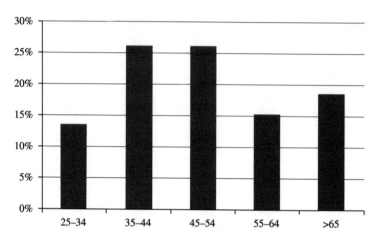

group. Again, 10.1% of the youngest find the internet not at all or almost not useful for the same purpose, compared to 7.9% of the 35–44-year-old group.[7]

Thus, younger ePriests express a lower perception of usefulness, and the age variable is not able to significantly explain the preferences for using ICTs for their priestly mission. In any case, there is a worthy point to observe: among the 13.3% of respondents who consider the internet very useful for offering spiritual advice, the youngest cohort—astonishingly—scores less than the oldest (as shown in Figure 8.6).

Similar conclusions can also be drawn for those who consider the internet very useful for spreading the Christian message (Figure 8.7), representing an

Figure 8.7. Age distribution of ePriests who consider the internet very useful for spreading the Christian message (count 1,330, corresponding to 30.7% of all respondents).

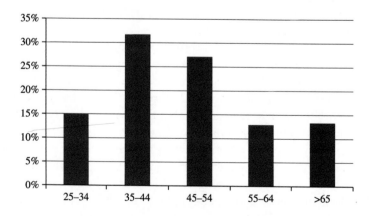

important portion of the sample (30.7%). In this data, again, what does not fit the idea of a "digital generation" is the fact that 25–34-year-old ePriests, who would be expected to be the most confident about new devices for the needs of evangelization are, on the contrary, appearing to only tepidly support this option in their priestly mission.

Moreover, it must be noted that ePriests between 25–34 years old are not significantly different from those over 65 years old in terms of their response to the perceived usefulness of the internet for preparing homilies and for praying.

Finally, there is no direct statistical relationship between age and the perception of how much the usages of ICTs have improved the way ePriests perform their mission. Coherent with the profiles outlined so far, ePriests, on average, seem to be aware of the potentialities of the internet, but not in a naïve way. In short, data tell us that the youngest ePriests are unlikely to behave according to some distinguishing traits that are commonly attributed to digital natives. A possible reading of this could be that the mission of priests—not unique to the youngest ones—is locationally positioned and locally committed, i.e., highly related to the needs of their local community, where meetings happen mostly face-to-face, and even if ICTs do play a significant role in their private activities, they do not essentially impact the ways that some of them perform their pastoral duties.

PICTURE: A Portrait of ePriests with a Negative Attitude towards ICTs

In this section, we sketch a brief portrait of the ePriests who have a negative attitude towards ICTs. This analysis can help further understanding as to why priests are less favorably disposed to technologies because of specific reasons related to their religious role, or because they are responding to the cultural conditions in their societies, which vary in technology adoption.

These ePriests have been individuated according to two parameters:

1. Those who—when asked to choose one statement out of five that best represented their attitude towards ICTs—chose the option: "new technologies are a nuisance, but I'm forced to use them" (141 ePriests). We will refer to this sample as the "annoyed ePriests."
2. Those who assigned the lowest scores to the questions related to the priestly activities in the group of questions "How useful do you consider using the internet for...." According to the scores they assigned to these questions, all the respondents have been divided into five categories, from the most skeptical to the most enthusiastic. We will refer to the ePriests in the two lowest categories, which include 1,379 ePriests in all, as the "skeptical ePriests."

As could be expected, ePriests with a more negative attitude towards technologies returned more of their responses via paper questionnaires than the general average (10.6% of annoyed ePriests and 7.8% of skeptical ones, against 6.6% general average). Interestingly, 24.1% of the "annoyed ePriests" filled in the questionnaire in German. Among the "skeptical ePriests," Italian, German, and English questionnaires were filled in more frequently than average, while Spanish questionnaires much less frequently, thus showing that Spanish-speaking ePriests are the most enthusiastic about ICTs.

With regard to geographic location, the most skeptical ePriests come from the countries with a high IDI (ICT Development Index, as established by the International Telecommunication Union; see ITU, 2010), i.e., from the most advanced ones, such as Canada, USA, Switzerland, Germany, France, and Italy. Skeptical ePriests are not bereft of technology, they tend to have a desktop computer, but their possession of technological gadgets such as laptop computers, MP3 players, handheld devices, and cameras is relatively lower than the world's average.

Annoyed and skeptical ePriests access the internet on a daily basis less than average: only 39.7% of annoyed ePriests access the internet several times a day, compared to the general average of 57.8%. Unsurprisingly, annoyed ePriests have a much lower consideration of the usefulness of the internet for priestly activities, and correspondingly perform these activities online less frequently than average. Also, skeptical ePriests, consistent with their views, perform activities related to their priestly mission less frequently than average: for instance, 52.8% of the most skeptical ePriests never pray online, compared to a world average of 35.7%.

Annoyed ePriests agree with the statement that the dangers of digital technologies are greater than the opportunities they offer: 16.5% of them strongly agree with this statement (world average: 5.5%), and only 11.8% disagree (world average: 37.1%). Furthermore, they feel overloaded with information much more than the average ePriest: 44.1% agree or somewhat agree with this statement, against a world average of 20.9%. The same attitudes can be observed in skeptical ePriests. Furthermore, the perception of how much ICTs have improved the way they perform different activities, such as learning, interacting with friends and family, and exchanging ideas, is in both annoyed and skeptical ePriests much lower than the average. In particular, as regards the priestly mission, only 15.4% of skeptical ePriests and 28.2% of annoyed ones think that ICTs have improved it much or very much (world average: 41.1%), while 36.1% of skeptical ePriests and 26.7% of annoyed ones consider that ICTs have not improved their mission at all, or have improved it very little (world average: 12.2%).

Conclusions and Further Developments

How Catholics use the internet and the new technologies will necessarily influence the spread and usage of ICTs worldwide, considering that Christians represent a substantial portion of religious followers, and constitute the religious majority in the world, with Catholics as the biggest sub-group within them. In this sense, PICTURE is an important step forward in the analysis and study of ICTs development. The PICTURE study allows us to extract a few interesting conclusions for religious leaders as well as for academic researchers.

Regarding religious leaders, three important aspects may be pinpointed:

1. The use of the internet and ICTs is now widespread and in a continuous growing tendency among Catholic ministrants. Therefore, Church leaders need to take into consideration the ownership and use of these technologies in order to facilitate the responsibilities and activities of their ministers.
2. Church ministers get much of their information and material from the internet. Church leaders must cope with the fact that a significant portion of that material may be in direct conflict with Catholic doctrines. This objective difficulty may be seen as an opportunity to improve the education regarding new technologies that priests and candidates to priesthood receive in Church structures. How do they select and choose adequate content? How do they develop critical and theologically informed viewpoints? What criteria should be followed to evaluate the quality on the Net?
3. The centrality that the Vatican website occupies in the minds of Catholic ministers is significant. Therefore, if this site is well managed in terms of its content and social interaction opportunities, the official website of the Catholic Church hierarchy may potentially influence the masses that are not reached by any other website worldwide.

With regard to academic research, two other points may be highlighted:

1. Religious faith and religiosity are not aside and apart from developments and innovations in society. Indeed, as this chapter shows, religious activities, and particularly priestly activities, seem to integrate very well with the advancement of communication technologies.
2. More skeptical attitudes towards ICTs use and usefulness happen in countries with higher IDI (ICT Development Index). Although

further studies need to be carried out, some hypotheses may be advanced in this regard, starting from acknowledging the complexity of the adoption path of innovations in given communities. As a matter of fact, in the poorest countries, where the adoption path of new technologies is at an earlier stage, ICTs are used mainly by early adopters, i.e., by motivated and enthusiastic persons, who have a higher perception of their usefulness; in contrast, in more technologically developed countries, ICTs are widespread, thus being used by the majority and also by late adopters, i.e., plausibly by persons with a less positive attitude towards them.

Further research can be conducted along the same lines as PICTURE. Firstly, specificities by continents and countries can be studied in more detail to explain the differences among diverse geographical, cultural, and economical environments. In this sense, interdisciplinary studies may be helpful to advance more in-depth inquiries on some of the questions raised by our research. For example, it might be interesting to explore why the internet is not seen as useful for praying or for offering spiritual advice, yet it is seen as useful for improving parish activities or spreading the Christian message. Secondly, our study points to interesting patterns of social media use among priests. Further research may be implemented about the use of social networks by ministrants of the Catholic Church, which could be used not only to relate to other ministers, but also to relate to other congregational members and seekers as well.

Notes

1. The reports for the following countries have been, or will be, published: Argentina, Brazil, Canada, Colombia, France, Germany, Italy, Mexico, Peru, Poland, Portugal, Spain, Switzerland, and the USA.
2. See: http://creativecommons.org/licenses/by-nc-nd/3.0/ for details.
3. According to ecclesiastical law, secular or diocesan priests are those who live among laypeople and are directly dependant on a bishop, while religious or regular priests belong to a religious institute (such as the Dominicans or the Franciscans), take vows, and follow the spirituality of their founders (see Code of Canon Law, canon 206).
4. All percentages are calculated only from the effective answers and do not take into consideration those who did not respond.
5. The questionnaire items presented a scale from 0 (not at all useful) to 5 (very useful). In Table 2, only the answers for the values 4/5 (very useful/useful) and 0/1 (not at all/almost not useful) are presented.
6. This refers mainly to the Liturgy of the Hours (book of priest's daily prayers) loaded and accessed through a portable device.

7. However, it must be remarked that, although the two variables are somehow related, the Cramer's V value of significance is low (0.048). Cramer's V value is the indicator used to verify the statistical significance of the relationship between variables.
8. Through a factor analysis, a new variable out of the priestly activities that are closer to each other was created. As a result, respondents could be clustered into groups according to their answers to these questions.

References

Arasa, D. (2008). *Church communications through diocesan websites. A model of analysis.* Rome, Italy: EDUSC.

Arasa, D., Cantoni, L., & Ruiz, L. (Eds.). (2010). *Religious internet communication. Facts, trends and experiences in the Catholic Church.* Rome, Italy: EDUSC.

Bennet, S., Maton, K., & Kervin, L. (2008). The "digital natives" debate: A critical review of the evidence. *British Journal of Educational Technology, 39*(5), 775–786.

Cantoni, L., Rapetti, E., & Tardini, S. (2010). Generation Y and "glocal" working. In B. Bertagni, M. La Rosa, & F. Salvetti (Eds.), *"Glocal" working. Living and working across the world with cultural intelligence* (pp. 252–272). Milan, Italy: FrancoAngeli.

Cantoni, L., & Tardini, S. (2006). *Internet (Routledge introductions to media and communication).* London, England; New York, NY: Routledge.

Cantoni, L., & Tardini, S. (2010). Generation Y, digital learners, and other dangerous things. *QWERTY—Interdisciplinary Journal of Technology, Culture and Education: Generation Y, Digital Learners, and Other Dangerous Things* [Special issue], *5*(2), 11–25.

Cantoni, L., & Zyga, S. (2007). The use of internet communication by Catholic congregations: A quantitative study. *Journal of Media and Religion, 6*(4), 291–309.

Christians, C. G. (2002). Religious perspectives on communication technology. *Journal of Media and Religion, 1*(1), 37–47.

Code of Canon Law. (1983). Vatican City, Vatican City: Libreria Editrice Vaticana.

Congregation of the Clergy (2008). *Clergy- Total number 2006.* Retrieved from http://www.clerus.org/clerus/dati/2008-12/08-6/totalclerge08.htm

ITU—International Telecommunication Union. (2010). *Measuring the information society 2010.* Geneva, Switzerland: ITU.

Prensky, M. (2001). Digital natives, digital immigrants, part II: Do they really *think* differently? *On the Horizon, 9*(6), 15–24.

Rogers, E. M. (1995). *Diffusion of innovations* (4th ed.). New York, NY: The Free Press.

Schulmeister, R. (2008). *Gibt es eine "Net Generation"?* (Version 2.0), (University of Hamburg). Retrieved from http://www.zhw.uni-hamburg.de/uploads/schulmeister-net-generation_v2.pdf

Schulmeister, R. (2010). Deconstructing the media use of the Net generation. *QWERTY—Interdisciplinary Journal of Technology, Culture and Education: Generation Y, Digital Learners, and Other Dangerous Things* [Special issue], *5*(2), 26–60.

9. Voting "Present": Religious Organizational Groups on Facebook

MARK D. JOHNS

Religious expressions have been evident on the internet from very early in the history of computer-mediated communication. Religious bulletin boards and newsgroup discussion lists emerged in the early days, followed by the appearance of informational websites (Brasher, 2001; Zaleski, 1997). Researchers have identified communities formed by way of chat, discussion lists, and blogs (Campbell, 2004, 2005a), and even actual religious rituals conducted online (Davis, 1998). These online communities spanned a vast array of religious expressions, from traditional Judaism, to evangelical Christian, to neopagan (Zaleski, 1997).

Religion has continued to be a significant focus of online activity. Studies associated with the Pew Internet and American Life project show that at least a quarter of all adult internet users in the U.S. have searched for religious material of some sort online (Larson, 2004). Creation of websites by religious groups has become a common activity, blogs by religious leaders and would-be leaders have flourished, and religious portal sites, such as BeliefNet.com, have become immensely popular. By some measures, religion is second only to pornography as the most popular activity on the internet (Last, 2005).

Early in the last decade, college and university students on campuses around the globe became enthralled with social networking web sites, most notably Facebook. Designed originally for students, with networks localized to specific campuses (Applebome, 2004), Facebook grew to enable users to create a personal profile page, providing biographical and contact information, to exchange both public and private messages with other users, to share photos, and to broadcast "status" reports of their daily activities to others within their array of "friends." Late in 2006, Facebook opened to the general public and created "global" networks in addition to campus networks. This move almost immediately led to a large influx of high school students and younger teens, as well as adult users of the site. In April of 2008 Facebook surpassed MySpace to become the largest social networking site on the web (Deleon, 2008), and in July of 2010, it surpassed half a billion users (Arthur & Kiss, 2010). Mehlhaff (2008) suggested that the ubiquity of Facebook participation among teens and young adults has made the site a natural tool for youth ministers and religious organizations, enabling them to maintain contact with their younger members.

In addition to individual profiles, participants on Facebook are able to form "groups" for all sorts of purposes. A quick search showed more than 500 global groups on Facebook registered in the category of "religious organizations." These ranged from groups affiliated with mainline Protestant denominations, to evangelical religio-political groups, to those dedicated to the Prophet Mohammed posted in Arabic, to a number proclaiming god-like devotion to a particular movie or TV star, or other celebrity. Some of these groups had only a few members, while others had more than a quarter of a million users who had signed on by clicking the "join" button on the group's page.

Given the high interest in religion on the internet in general, and the popularity of Facebook among teens and young adults, these Facebook groups devoted to religion offer an intriguing arena for the examination of the formation of religious community and the construction of religious identity online by adolescents and young adults.

Religions Online

Despite the high level of online religious activity, religious expression has been largely ignored as an area of research in internet studies, and by the social sciences generally (Asthana, 2008; Campbell, 2005b). Heidi Campbell (2006) summarized most of the scholarship through 2005 in a review article. Campbell pointed out that researchers have identified four categories of religious activity online: The most common, characterized by the findings of the Pew Foundation studies (Hoover, Clark, & Rainie, 2004; Larsen, 2004), is information gathering and/or the exchange of advice among individual internet users. A second common religious activity online is participation in online rituals, as documented by Brasher (2001). A third activity is "e-vangelism" or missionary activity online—an activity not limited to evangelical Christian groups, despite the terminology. While Campbell was able to cite several examples of this activity, additional examples are provided by Last (2005). Finally, a fourth category of religious activity online is the formation of online religious communities. Again, Campbell was able to cite examples, but these are superseded by Campbell's own work on this subject (2005a).

More helpful, perhaps, than a categorizing of activities, Mia Lövheim (in Campbell, 2006) suggested a taxonomy of religious discourses online.

Among these is the discourse of "religious identity." Lövheim noted that "religious beliefs and practices are salient examples of the meanings and practices that have provided a basis for the construction of personal as well as social identities throughout history" (p. 60). Lövheim also noted that identity construction is a reflexive activity involving communicative gestures (words, actions, symbols, images, etc.) and apprehension of the responses of others to these gestures. Early research suggested that identity formation online would occur in unique ways (Turkle, 1995), while later studies (Baym, 2000; Kendall, 2002) pointed to close parallels between identity construction online and one's real life situation. The implications of this more contextual understanding of identity construction for the construction of religious identity, more specifically, remain unexplored. However, one might speculate that these findings suggest religious identity online would be developed very much in the context of one's family, community, and culture. That is, online religious identity would arise from one's religious traditions rather than in opposition to these traditions. If online and offline identities are closely tied, teens and young adults will tend to experiment online with variations on the religious tradition in which they have been raised, while online experimentation with, or conversions to, radically different religious traditions would be the exception rather than the rule, just as is the case in offline communities.

Social networking sites have become the primary venues of online activity in recent years, particularly for teens and young adults (Applebome, 2004; Arrington, 2008). Previous research has pointed to social networking sites as loci for identity construction for persons in this age group (boyd, 2007; boyd & Ellison, 2007) and Facebook has been explored specifically as a locus for identity construction online (Johns, Boettner, Powers, & Lindsay, 2007). Religious groups on Facebook have been noted as features growing in popularity (Eldon, 2007; Fischer-Nielsen, 2008). Further, religiosity has been identified as a factor in predicting how users participate in Facebook (Nyland & Near, 2007). However, there has been no investigation as to the way in which social networks generally, or Facebook in particular, may be functionally employed by teens and young adults for information seeking, ritual practice, e-vangelism, or community building, or in the construction of religious identity. The present research, thus, seeks to examine and describe the religious activities taking place on Facebook, and specifically to look for evidence of the various functions suggested by Campbell (2006) and/or the discourse of religious identity construction suggested by Lövheim.

Method

Religion has been part of Facebook from the beginning as a category available to be supplied in constructing a personal profile page. The free-form nature of these categories makes it possible for users of Facebook to describe their "Religious Views" in any way they might wish. A cursory look at several personal profiles shows that some users choose to type in a general category, such as "Christian" or "Jewish," while others provide the name of a particular denomination or group. Others have completed the category with non-committal, nonsensical, or derogatory terms, while still others have left the category blank entirely. A study of religious self-identity on Facebook profile pages could be revealing, however the security features of the site severely limit access to personal profile pages, making sampling difficult.

Fan pages were established on Facebook in response to the growing number of celebrities, politicians, and organizations that created Facebook identities for purposes of publicity and promotion. These entities began to set up profiles and to seek "friends" so that status updates and personal information spaces could be employed to inform Facebook users about events, products, and services. Because these entities taxed the capacity of the system, Facebook created the category of fan page and allowed any user to establish such a page devoted to things, concepts, brands, ideas, or other non-personal subjects. In appearance, a fan page is very similar to a personal profile or group page, except that it is more compact, with a much abbreviated information area, a smaller wall (a space for posting brief notes visible to all) for short posts from fans, and spaces for posting photos and videos (with separate fan content areas away from that posted "officially" by the entity). Also, most fan pages do not include areas for discussion topics, other than the wall. However, some fan pages enable the topics function, while others disable the wall. In 2009 Facebook added the "like" feature, and in 2010 streamlined fan pages to simply "pages."

The fan relationship is somewhat more passive than a friendship between users. When a user declares that she or he "likes" a page, this appears in a different area on the user's profile and the system does not establish the same type of two-way relationship between the user and the entity that is created when two users mutually agree to befriend one another. The user declares fandom and there is no requirement that the page entity approves, acknowledges, or accepts this declaration. The user's declaration establishes the fan status unilaterally. Because the initial data collected on religious groups on Facebook suggested that the groups were being used in ways indistinguishable from fan pages, fan pages parallel to the selected groups were sought for comparison. However, because very few religious organizations seemed to be promoting themselves actively to a fan base through pages, other than certain brands such as Christian rock bands, detailed study of activity there was abandoned as too broad for the present project.

As Facebook has evolved, additional features continue to be added by Facebook itself, as well as by others through Facebook's open application programming interface (API). Third-party developers have created applications, such as *My Church*, that users may choose to add to their profile pages, allowing more formal and detailed religious self-identification (Eldon, 2007). However, the multiplicity of these available third-party applications creates a diverse selection by users. For example, one Facebook user might choose to install the third-party application called *Daily Bible Verse*, while another user might choose to install a similar application by a different developer, called *Daily Bible Scripture*. If a researcher were to attempt to study users of either application as a means of determining how Facebook users participate in devotional reading on the site, he or she would only be getting a partial picture. Not all, or even most, users choose to add the same applications, and applications often duplicate or overlap in functions, making them interesting, but unsuitable as a common unit of analysis for study.

Facebook itself, however, very early in its history created the facility for users to create and join "groups" for the purpose of having discussions on any topic. Because groups allow users to join across network and privacy barriers, the activities on these group pages are openly available. Any user may create a group for almost any purpose, or elect to join any existing group that is open. When a group is created, the creator is asked to specify a category and sub-type for the group, with "religious organizations" one available sub-type under the category of "organizations." Other possibilities would be the sub-type "religion and spirituality" under the category of "common interest." Once established, the group's creator becomes its "administrator," with control over what features may be opened to group members, and what features are closed or turned off. The creator may invite others to become co-administrators, or even abandon the group completely, leaving any member to take over administrative duties. Because of the open nature and wide variety of groups, they make an ideal unit of analysis for getting a sense of how religious beliefs and practices are expressed on Facebook.

In 2008 Facebook introduced "causes"—another type of page allowing a category for religious organizations. Cause pages are often used by non-profit organizations to attract supporters and raise funds. However, causes will be explored separately in a later project. Also, as noted above, in 2010 "fan pages" were streamlined into "pages." As a result, behavior may now be changing for some religious groups and organizations, as they choose to use pages rather than groups. Nevertheless, this study restricts itself to studying groups.

In consultation with my Institutional Review Board (IRB) and with reference to the Ethics Guidelines of the Association of Internet Researchers (Ess, 2002), it was determined that data collection would be limited to passive observation. I would join a number of open public groups, but would neither post to them nor engage members in conversation or interview them. My Facebook profile clearly identifies me as a person engaged in internet research, but I would not announce my presence or seek consent. The IRB saw the impossibility of securing consent from more than 300,000 group members. The open nature of groups was judged by the IRB to be similar to passive observation of persons in a public place, for which informed consent would normally be neither necessary nor possible.

Selections for study

For the present study, I browsed the globally available groups in the type "religious organizations," to identify a manageable number for tracking, guessed to be about half a dozen. The types and categories are self-selected by the group creators, so not all groups in the type would necessarily conform to what others might usually consider a religious organization. I sought groups representative of the major religious traditions, as well as at least one that might be somewhat unusual. Additionally, I sought a variety of group sizes, looking first for the largest group I could find in the type, as well as at least one that had very few members. The selection was based primarily on how the pages presented themselves in the browsing window, and could be considered a convenience sample, except that some additional Christian groups immediately presented to me by Facebook were passed over in order to go down the list to select Hindu, Muslim, or Jewish groups for variety of traditions. Seven groups were selected for observation: "I'M A CHRISTIAN. . . . AND I'M PROUD TO SAY IT!!," "Hindu Dharma," "The Church of Jesus Christ of Latter-day Saints," "The Quran, the most Perfect Book known on this Earth," "you know you're a jew when . . . ," "ELCA Lutherans," and "If I Weren't an Atheist I'd Think Richard Dawkins Was God." The primary observations were conducted through March and April of 2008, and have been revisited occasionally, though less systematically, throughout 2009 and 2010, to look for any major changes in group behavior.

Observations

Large, Christian, and out of control

"I'M A CHRISTIAN . . . AND I'M PROUD TO SAY IT!!," is one of the largest groups on Facebook with more than 287,000 members at the beginning of the observation period. It also grew very rapidly during those two months, often adding more than 500 new members in a single day, and exceeding 300,000 members before initial observations were complete in 2008. By the end of 2010 the group was approaching 700,000 members. The group is administered by nearly a dozen users, most of whom appear to be high school students from Southern states in the U.S. The title of the group in all upper case letters, and with two exclamation points, is considered in the norms of online text to be "shouting." The graphic is artwork depicting a mountain sunset with three crosses in the foreground. The purpose of the group appears to be entirely to collect as many members as possible. The group description is a quote from the New Testament followed by an appeal to "invite all your friends." The description also contains an admonition to avoid use of profanity, accompanied by two more verses from the New Testament. However, there is no longer much opportunity to use profane language, or any type of language on the page. In the "news" segment, a posting from October 2007 reads,

> As the creator of this group, I have decided to turn off the wall and board on this group. There were too many negative comments/topics being discussed and since it is hard to please all 150,000 members, that is the only course of action that is fair to everyone. i appreciate the messages and emails regarding this but this was the only reasonable course of action.[1]

Other news posts simply note milestones in the group's growth, such as, "REACHED 10,000 MEMBERS on . . . 10/1/2006 at 5:04 PM. . . ." More than 700 photos were posted to the group, most very stylized (some might say kitsch) contemporary Christian artwork. Two videos of "Christian bands" had been posted by the creator. Otherwise, there was no opportunity for discussion or interaction of any kind. Hundreds were joining this group daily, simply to declare that, "I'M A CHRISTIAN . . ." The various features for conversation have been turned on and off at intervals over the years, with the administrators now stating that, "THE WALL WILL BE AVAILABLE INTERMITTENTLY TO ALLOW FOR SUPERVISION."

When the wall is open, many of the comments posted were what I came to call (in all of the group pages) "praise posts." These are merely statements glorifying God or gods, the religion, the believers, or the group itself. These "praise posts" were addressed to no one in particular and did not appear to be in response to any previous posts. In the case of this group, these were posts simply declaring things like, "I love Jesus" or "FEAR only GOD, HATE only SIN." Many wall posts were Bible verses, again apropos of nothing and requiring no response. Relatively few posts were clearly the sort of harassment that had caused the wall to be closed—derogatory remarks about Christianity or Christians, or regarding religious belief in general. Some drew a response from group members, while others were ignored.

Lively Hindu conversation

"Hindu Dharma," in contrast to "I'M A CHRISTIAN . . . ," was a much smaller group, comprising just over 7,400 members and growing much more slowly, to approximately 7,600 at the end of the initial two month observation period. However, by the end of 2010 it had grown to more than 11,000 members. This group had two administrators, but listed over 30 "officers," many with formal titles such as "President," "Vice President," etc., all with names that might have origins on the Indian sub-continent, and most from university networks associated with campuses in the U.S., Canada, and the U.K. There was no reference to any off-line organization related to these offices and titles. The group description provides a brief, five paragraph introduction to the Hindu religion, including a number of Sanskrit terms and references to the religion's roots in what is now the nation of India. The "news" section also included some facts about Hinduism, as well as a somewhat outdated calendar of "upcoming" (but now past) Hindu feast and fast days. Also posted was a "Code of Conduct" forbidding profanity, "ad hominem attacks," and the insulting of any religion, nation, or ethnicity.

"Hindu Dharma" was a page of lively interaction, with more than 1,000 posted photos, a dozen videos, more than 30 posted links, a discussion board with more than 700 topics, and more than 2,700 posts to the group's public "wall." A unique feature of "Dharma" was that the administrators edited the group's descriptive profile almost daily during the observation period. Most days, there were no visible changes (even to the outdated calendar items), but the act of editing flagged the group in the Facebook news feeds of all the members (the news feed is the first page users encounter upon logging into Facebook and it is customized to show activity among that user's friends or other affiliations), thus reminding members daily of the group's existence and their membership in it. Several weeks into the initial observation period these edits yielded actual, noticeable changes, such as an updated calendar of religious festivals (though this, too, was allowed to remain unchanged months after it was out of date), but most days there were no apparent alterations, only the feigning of an edit in order to cause Facebook to flag the group to members—a rather effective strategy, I suspect, for gaining repeat visits to the page.

The "wall" discussion in this group was dominated by posts from a young woman, whom I shall simply identify only as Ms. S, who posted to the wall several times daily, often posting comments or open-ended questions designed to generate discussion. These were sometimes related to Hinduism, including a number of "praise posts." Just as often, Ms. S posted comments about dating, clothing fashions, favorite foods, or other trivia. At one point, several weeks into the initial observation period, other group members began responding to these trivia posts somewhat angrily, asking what they had to do with Hinduism. Ms. S said she was just trying to keep the group discussion active, and persisted for a time, until the negative responses grew. At this point, a new member appeared in the wall discussions, identifying himself as Mr. S, and claiming to be the father of Ms. S. He commended the other members on their religious devotion, and began frequent praise posts as well as daily quotes from Hindu scriptures and messages that had a didactic tone, focused on Hindu teachings. All posts from Ms. S ceased at the same time that Mr. S appeared. My guess is that Ms. S and Mr. S are the same person, using different personas, but this is not verifiable without attempting a contact, which would be outside the parameters established with my IRB. Clearly this individual was seeking interaction with the group at any available level of discussion, but others were not cooperating.

The Mormons

"The Church of Jesus Christ of Latter-day Saints" group had a few more than 24,100 members and grew to just a bit less than 26,400 members during the initial observation period. This group has since swelled to more than 60,000 members as of the end of 2010. Its half-dozen administrators and officers were affiliated with the networks of universities in the Western U.S. and Canada. The profile noted that "The members of this group are simply members (or friends) of the Church. . . . There is no official affiliation with the Church itself." The usual caveats against abusive or harassing posts were also included, but an additional rule is that "discussing sacred ordinances is strictly prohibited, and will result in an immediate ban." Despite these rules, the group's wall was the frequent venue for spam, obscenities, and name-calling. Even though it received no more than three or four posts per day on average, many of these were abusive. Since only group members may post to the wall, clearly some were joining the group for the sole purpose of harassing Mormons. Some of the posted news items appeared to have come from official news releases of the LDS Church, and a number of posted links were led directly to the Church's official website. Many of the posted videos and photos appeared to have come from official sources as well. By the end of 2010, wall posts had slowed to only one or two per week.

This group appeared to have some lively discussion topics, but Facebook's statistics indicated that, while the number of topics and postings was impressive, the number of actual participants was less so. For example, a discussion of Mormon presidential candidate Mitt Romney garnered 39 posts in a short time, but all of these came from only six individual members. Even more striking, a discussion topic on the role of women as wives and mothers had drawn 126 posts, but all came from only 17 unique users. Another discussion had 155 posts, but only 38 members had posted. Several new topics were begun with a single post by one member, drawing no further response. While no attempt was made to determine the total number of group members actually using the discussion boards overall, it was noted that many of the same users were showing up in several discussions, so the total number taking part was a tiny fraction of the group's membership. While activity increased with the growth in membership, this general pattern did not change for many months, but by the end of 2010, discussion posts had dwindled to only a few per week on all topics combined.

The Quran disappears

"The Quran, the most Perfect Book known on this Earth," was a group of almost 60,500 members at the outset, growing to more than 65,600 by the end of the initial observations. By the fall of 2010 the name and administration of the group had changed, but it had grown to more than 100,000 members. The half-dozen administrators and officers were from university domains in New York City or Toronto, and three of them had variations of "Muhammad" in their names (a very common name in Muslim communities). Over the longer period of revisiting the page, it appears that the originators of the group either abandoned it or turned it over to others who declared themselves to be from locations in the Middle East. The original profile description was long, with several substantial quotes from the Quran and the Hadeeth, and focused on using the internet as a means to unite the "Ummah," or worldwide Muslim community. The later profile of the renamed group was much shorter, but with many links to websites outside of Facebook. Many posts to both the wall and to the discussion boards were in Arabic script. One member, represented in his photo as a grey-haired older gentleman from the network of "Egypt" posted to the wall an identical 14 lines of Arabic each and every day of the observation period during which the wall was available. So many spam and harassment messages were posted that the administrators turned off the interactive features for several weeks, closing the wall and the discussion topics. Most discussion topics associated with this group were single posts by individual users with no replies. There was some interaction here, but when one subtracts the sex spam (it seems ironic that groups dedicated to religion would get so much of that) and the anti-Islamic rants, there were really just a tiny fraction of a percent of the group members posting among themselves. By summer of 2010, wall posts were almost entirely sex spam with no other activity for months. There were a few discussion posts, engaging a very limited number of group members, but several weeks elapsed between postings and many discussion threads still had only a single post with no response. While membership had grown, interaction had decreased markedly. By the end of 2010 the page had been removed—most likely by its administrators, but possibly by Facebook due to abuse of the terms of service. It is possible that the various sexual, advertising, or abusive wall posts drew complaints.

Jewish humor

"you know you're a jew when . . . ," is a group that appears to have begun largely for the sake of humor and an opportunity for Jewish teens and young adults to poke fun at themselves and their tradition. The youthful nature of the page is suggested by the many comments about Bar or Bat Mitzvah celebrations, parents, summer camps, and other youth-oriented topics. There were slightly fewer than 3,800 members of this group at the outset of the initial observation period, and it hadn't yet achieved 4,000 members by the end. Two years later it had grown only to 6,700 members, and actually declined by a couple of hundred members by the end of 2010. The administrator was represented as a female high school student from the Northeastern U.S., but the 25 "officers" appeared to represent high school and university networks from across the U.S., and to include a few somewhat older adults, as well. The group profile contains a long list of humorous lines completing the sentence "you know you're a jew when . . . ," such as, "You know the only reason Chanukah is a big deal is so we can have a holiday to throw into Christian's faces," and "Bar/bat mitzvahs gave you a social life in 7th grade." Many wall posts and discussion boards continued in this vein. This group also received a number of harassment posts to its wall. Early on, the administrator was fairly quick in deleting them, showing a greater level of attention than some groups. Over the years the number of wall posts diminished further, and were dominated by sex spam and sexually provocative photo uploads, or links to sites apparently unrelated to the topic of the group—all of which were apparently being ignored by the administrators. There were, however, even on this humor page, occasional "praise posts" such as "its so true, . . . least like half of that list [of jokes applies to me]." Discussion topics were fewer in this group, but drew more participants. One topic, for example, had 50 posts by 46 different individuals. Still, the number of active participants was a small percentage of the members. Discussions dwindled over the years. By the end of 2010 it was not uncommon for several months to pass between posts to any discussion, and many discussion threads were begun with a single post, to which no one had responded.

A very few Lutherans

"ELCA Lutherans," was the smallest group observed, with only slightly more than 3,300 members, growing only to about 3,500 members during the initial observation period. The group is intended for members of the Evangelical Lutheran Church in America, a large, mainline denomination in the U.S. Administrators of the group are represented as four U.S. high school students. Aside from a few people becoming members, activity in this group was almost non-existent, with only a few wall or discussion topic posts through the entire observation period. By the summer of 2010 the membership of this group had grown to 8,000, but there was absolutely no activity. The most recent wall post was in the previous year, and the discussions had been shut down. By the end of 2010, the most recent activity of any type was more than a year old, and membership had fallen back to just under 7,900.

Is Atheism a Religion?

The "If I Weren't an Atheist I'd Think Richard Dawkins Was God" group, as may be surmised from the title, is not associated with any traditional religious group or denomination. This group, dedicated to British biologist Richard Dawkins and his 2006 book *The God Delusion*, has one administrator represented as a university student from the U.K. The group had about 5,500 members at the outset, and grew to a few more than 6,000 members by the end of the initial observations. By the end of 2010 there were about 8,400 members, down from a high of around 8,600. This group featured an active wall discussion, characterized by comments critical of persons adhering to religious faith, and harassing counter-attacks by the faithful (who, again, must actually join the group in order to post, even if the group is contrary to their beliefs). One wall post read, "Bear in mind, also, that the most arrogant atheist is still far less arrogant than the least arrogant Christian. Christianity is, at its core, the belief that the entire universe is all about you." Another member posted:

> There is still time to be saved non-believers! god is everywhere just turn to him and accept his word! i know u are all lost and confused, thats y u r part of this group but dont worry salvation is here! dont choose the path to eternal damnation, u will burn in the fires of hell!!

These quotes reflect the character of many similar postings. Over the years members seemed to grow weary of this sort of wall warfare, with most wall posts becoming only the posting of a link to some news story or a website a member found interesting. There were also an increasing number of sex spam and advertising posts that the administrators tended to ignore. At the end of 2010 there were still a few legitimate wall posts each month, amid the spam.

Even in the heyday of this group, discussion topics were carried by small numbers, such as the topic titled, "The Real holy Trinity!!!" containing 42 postings, but all by only nine contributors. Arguing with Christians and Muslims was great sport in the public forums of this group, but only for a tiny fraction of the group's thousands of members. Interestingly, there appeared—on both the wall and in discussion topics associated with this group of presumed atheists—a number of what would be termed in the other religious groups as "praise posts." As described earlier, these appear not to be addressed to anyone in particular or to demand any sort of response, but merely to affirm the "faith." In this case, these posts came in the form of praise of Dawkins or of atheism in general, or of the group itself, such as, "This group has cheered me up, not only with its name but to think that there are over 5,000 rational people in it. Thanks!" Or, "Looking at this site always cheers me up after a long hard day fending off others irrationalities." By mid-2009, discussion activity had dwindled considerably. At the end of 2010 there was only about one discussion post per month for this group.

Discussion

Based on these examples, religious groups appear to have been very popular on Facebook, with several such groups attracting many thousands of members, and even the smallest of such groups showing steady growth in membership through the initial observation period. Observations suggest that most members joined as a way of voting affirmation for the group, its goals, and/or its creator—rather than for the purpose of encountering or engaging with like-minded others—because almost no activity was apparent after joining. Very little interaction took place within the observed groups, with only a tiny fraction of group members participating in any way, and even fewer engaged in any dialog. Because hundreds or even thousands joined, but mere dozens actively engaged in conversation, one must assume that Facebook users, at least in these groups, became group members as a way of affirming the person or organization—or occasionally affirming a mere concept or ideal. In many cases the pages either have no facility for interaction among members (that is, the wall and/or discussion tropics are disabled) or only a fraction of the members actually post to these. Many of the posts that do appear fall into the category of "praise posts," which declare and celebrate the user's religious affiliation, faith, or identity, but are directed at no other user and expect no response from others.

Thus, it might be concluded that there is little or no interaction among Facebook users taking place as a result of the formation of these groups. However, I speculate that symbolic communicative acts are, in fact, taking place. It is simply the case that these communicative acts are not being directed at other group members. Instead, these communications are directed externally, to those outside the group. When Facebook users join a group of any sort, the group appears on their personal profile, and the act of joining may be broadcast to their friends through the news feed that updates users about their friends' activities whenever they log onto the site.[2] The symbolic act of joining a group is thus directed toward those who may read the user's personal profile or to "friends" who see this activity their news feed. These communicative actions say, "this is who I am, this is what I believe," to other believers, perhaps, but primarily to "friends" of the user. They become data by which friends may measure the fervor of the user. Thus, there is a "discourse of religious identity" taking place (Lövheim, 2004), but this discourse is not occurring within the religious group. It takes place among the individual group members and their unique circles of friends. The reflexive process of identity construction is not evident within the group pages on Facebook, but is evident to those who view the group member's profile or read his or her news feed entries.

As noted above, Campbell (2006) posited four religious functions being carried out online: information, ritual, e-vangelism, and community. Yet it is apparent that none of these are taking place within these religious groups observed on Facebook. Rather, a different function is taking place—one to which the religious group on Facebook plays only an ancillary role. This function might be termed "confession of faith," or more directly, "declaration of belief." By joining a particular religious group on Facebook (and then, in most cases, ignoring it and avoiding interactive participation within it) these individuals are declaring who they are and what they believe. But there is no dialog, no reflexive process within the group. There is only the statement or confession.

Research has questioned the definition of "friend" on Facebook (boyd & Ellison, 2007), demonstrating that this term carries a broad range of meanings, from passing acquaintance to "Best Friends Forever." The present research calls into question the definition of "group" on Facebook. For most users in the observed groups, it would appear that this term does not imply a community of social interaction, much less a community of spiritual formation, but merely a label to be worn for the sake of friends, and perhaps a source of affirmation that there are others who wear this label also. Although some choose to join a group contrary to their self-identity—such as those who join merely so that they may post harassing comments on the group's wall or engage in argumentative discussion topics—there is little evidence that most users choose to join groups with which they do not already identify. For most in these groups, it appears that "group" is simply a label to be displayed on one's profile.

Thus, many thousands of users of Facebook are eager to proclaim their religious identity as they construct a profile that will represent their life, beliefs, values, and interests to others who are their "friends." Filling in the "Religious Views" box on a profile page provides one means of presenting a religious identity, but a collection of groups, fan pages, and/or causes related to religious organizations flesh out the picture and provide additional details about one's beliefs. By declaring oneself a "proud Christian" and/or an "ELCA Lutheran" one selects from an array of symbolic associations that can be presented as part of a fuller identity.

Conclusion

Of the four most common religious activities taking place online (Campbell, 2006; Hoover, Clark, & Rainie, 2004; Larsen, 2001) the present research suggests that most may be absent from Facebook. The severely limited nature of interaction among members of observed religious groups excludes the formation of online religious communities in the sense described by Campbell (2005a). Further, no evidence was found of any sort of online rituals, unless one could make a case to establish the creation of "praise posts" as some sort of ritual behavior. In any case, the usual response appears to be to ignore them— hardly a ritualistic pattern. A certain amount of information sharing takes place in the descriptions and outside links, although from this study it is impossible to measure the extent to which users of Facebook explore or seek such information from these pages. This might be an opportunity for further research. One might conclude that the harassment, attacks, and arguments observed in the very limited discussions constitutes a form of e-vangelism, however these confrontations do not appear to be intended as persuasive. It is more likely that these are primarily means of aggressively solidifying boundaries of religious identity, and establishing distinctions between "us" versus "them." In any case, few group members were observed to be engaged in these debates. If what was observed in these groups is typical, group membership serves for most as merely an online religious bumper sticker. The symbolic interaction is directed outward towards those who view the individual user's profile or news feed.

While these groups might offer the opportunity for young users to experiment with alternative religious identities, there appears to be little evidence in these observations that such exploration is widespread. Christian pages tend to be populated with teens from the Bible belt, Muslim pages are run by persons presenting themselves as being of Middle Eastern or Asian descent, Hindu pages are frequented by those of South Asian heritage, Mormon pages are dominated by students from the American West, and so forth. Although these representations, themselves, could be experiments in some cases (such as the fluid identity of Ms./Mr. S), there is little overt suggestion in these observations that such identity play is widespread on Facebook.

Declaration of belief as a religious activity may be related to identity formation; however, Lövheim (2004) correctly termed identity formation as a discourse. That is, in observing the statement of faith, we see only one isolated step in a discursive process. Identity formation only occurs as others react or respond to that declaration. When friends or family members affirm this declaration, or react negatively to it, in ways that are either overt or subtle, a discursive process is taking place. The present study offers only a snapshot of this process, and not the moving picture necessary to observe whether a true discourse of identity is taking place.

Future research should be directed at accessing self-reports of Facebook religious group members, fans, and cause members through surveys or interviews. The lack of such reports is a limitation of the present study. But the evidence gathered here tends to confirm the suggestion that a function of religious declaration is taking place on Facebook, and that religious community, ritual, or other group interaction is essentially non-existent on some faith-oriented Facebook public group pages.

Notes

1. All quotations are shown as they appeared online without corrections in grammar, spelling, capitalization, etc.
2. The function of the news feed is somewhat random, in that it is custom-generated for each Facebook user, gathering as many status updates or other activities as will fit on the web page. Thus, a posting regarding a particular group page may not be shown in the news feed of all of the member's "friends," especially if a user has a great many other "friends," group, fan, and cause links. If there is too much activity, some items will be left out.

References

Applebome, P. (2004, December 1). Our towns: On campus, hanging out by logging on. *The New York Times*, Metro section, p. B1. Retrieved from http://www.nytimes.com/2004/12/01/nyregion/01towns.html

Arthur, C., & Kiss, J. (2010, July 22). Facebook reaches 500 million users. *The Guardian*, Main section, p. 5. Retrieved from http://www.guardian.co.uk/technology/2010/jul/21/facebook-500-million-users

Asthana, S. (2008). Religion and secularism as embedded imaginaries: A study of Indian television narratives. *Critical Studies in Media Communication, 25*(3), 304–323.

Baym, N. K. (2000). *Tune in, log on: Soaps, fandom, and online community*. Thousand Oaks, CA: Sage.

boyd, d. (2007). Why youth (heart) social network sites: The role of networked publics in teenage social life. In D. Buckingham (Ed.), *MacArthur Foundation Series on Digital Learning—Youth, identity, and digital media* (pp. 119–142). Cambridge, MA: MIT Press.

boyd, d. (2008). None of this is real. In J. Karaganis (Ed.), *Structures of participation in digital culture* (pp. 132–157). New York, NY: Social Science Research Council.

boyd, d., & Ellison, N. (2007). Social network sites: Definition, history, and scholarship. *Journal of Computer-Mediated Communication, 13*(1), article 11. Retrieved from http://jcmc.indiana.edu/vol13/issue1/boyd.ellison.html

Brasher, B. (2001). *Give me that online religion.* San Francisco, CA: Jossey-Bass.

Campbell, H. (2004). Challenges created by online religious networks. *Journal of Media and Religion, 3*(2), 81–99.

Campbell, H. (2005a). *Exploring religious community online: We are one in the network.* New York, NY: Peter Lang.

Campbell, H. (2005b). Making space for religion in internet studies. *The Information Society, 21*(4), 309–315.

Campbell, H. (2006). Religion and the internet. *Communication Research Trends, 25*(1), 3–24.

Davis, E. (1998). *TechGnosis: Myth, magic and mysticism in the age of information.* New York, NY: Random House.

Deleon, N. (2008, June 12). Facebook no longer the second largest social network [Web log post]. Retrieved from http://techcrunch.com/2008/06/12/facebook-no-longer-the-second-largest-social-network/

Eldon, E. (2007, August 24). Religious social networks gain faith in Facebook. *Venture-Beat.* Retrieved from http://venturebeat.com/2007/08/24/religious-social-networks-gain-faith-in-Facebook/

Ess, C. (2002). *Ethical decision-making and Internet research.* Retrieved from Association of Internet Researchers website: http://www.aoir.org/reports/ethics.pdf

Fischer-Nielsen, P. (2008, July 11). Tro på Facebook. Retrieved from http://e-religion.religionblog.dk/k

Hoover, S., Clark, L. S., & Rainie, L. (2004). Faith online: 64% of wired Americans have used the internet for spiritual or religious purposes. *Pew Internet and American Life Project.* Retrieved from http://www.pewinternet.org/~/media/Files/Reports/2004/PIP_Faith_Online_2004.pdf.pdf

Johns, M. D., Boettner, K., Powers, E., & Lindsay, M. (2007). Profile updated: The presentation of identity on Facebook.com. *Iowa Journal of Communication, 39*(1), 46–62.

Kendall, L. (2002). *Hanging out in the virtual pub: Masculinities and relationships online.* Berkeley, CA: University of California Press.

Larsen, E. (2004). Deeper understanding, deeper ties: Taking faith online. In P. N. & S. Jones (Eds.), *Society online: The internet in context* (pp. 43–56). Thousand Oaks, CA: Sage.

Last, J. V. (2005). God on the internet. *First Things: A Monthly Journal of Religion and Public Life, 158,* 34–40.

Lövheim, M. (2004). Young people, religious identity, and the internet. In L. L. Dawson & D. E. Cowan (Eds.), *Religion online: Finding faith on the internet* (pp. 59–73). New York, NY: Routledge.

Mehlhaff, R. (2008). Churches using internet for social networking. *Christian Century, 125*(16), 13–14.

Nyland, R., & Near, C. (2007, February). Jesus is my friend: Religiosity as a mediating factor in internet social networking use. Paper presented at the AEJMC Midwinter Conference, Reno, NV.

Turkle, S. (1995). *Life on the Screen: Identity in the Age of the Internet*. New York, NY: Simon & Schuster.

Wertheim, M. (1999). *The pearly gates of cyberspace: A history of space from Dante to the internet*. New York, NY: W. W. Norton.

Zaleski, J. (1997). *The soul of cyberspace: How technology is changing our spiritual lives*. San Francisco, CA: HarperCollins.

10. *"Keeping the Line Open and Warm":* *An Activist Danish Church and Its* *Presence on Facebook*

STINE LOMBORG AND CHARLES ESS

Introduction

Much has been written regarding Web 2.0—a rubric that seeks to mark out a significant shift in the capacities and potentials of the World Wide Web from ca. 2005 on. In particular, proponents of the term characteristically highlight greater *interactivity* as a core feature—where this interactivity is immediately coupled with the "prosumer" or "produser" (cf. e.g., Bruns, 2008): that is, whether in the form of social networking sites, blogs, location-based services, microblogs, photo- and video sharing sites, or other so-called social media, the "user" is now increasingly the producer or author of much of the content posted in these venues. Web 2.0, as epitomized in social media, is thus supposed to herald a new age in the use of the internet and the web, one in which the user is increasingly empowered and at the center—with the institutional and political result that traditional hierarchies and hierarchical institutions will be increasingly flattened and democratized, if not simply made irrelevant and left behind entirely (cf. Ess, 2011). Indeed, insofar as interactivity is thought to lead to a flattening of hierarchies, these contemporary claims directly echo some of the earliest techno-utopian hopes for the democratizing potentials of the internet (cf. Ess, 1996).

Partly in light of important criticisms of initial claims surrounding Web 2.0, more refined and better empirically informed views have begun to emerge, ones that recognize the continuity between earlier forms of internet-based communication and more recent digital media phenomena, including social media, in which ordinary users (and not only media professionals) can communicate with each other and create and share content to others online through their personal networked computers and mobile phones (e.g. Boyd, 2008, p. 92; Lüders, 2008; Baym, 2010).

In particular, social media, as often contrasted with mass media, are broadly characterised by *de-institutionalised communication processes*, in the sense that social media are not dependent upon media companies producing content to pre-determined audiences in a programmed, prescriptive, and controlled media production process. Rather, social media imply a reliance on *ordinary users as producers* contributing, filtering, and sharing content with audiences of their choice (Lüders, 2008). In short, social media represent communicative spaces in which the ordinary media user has greater potential to take control and responsibility in the communication process. Despite often being attributed specifically to *new* digital media phenomena, these characteristics can more broadly be associated with the internet and mobile phones as media (cf. Finnemann, 2005).

Nonetheless, user empowerment is, of course, not unlimited in social media. For instance, José van Dijck (2010) cited data suggesting that less than 20% of users indeed become "prosumers," i.e., so as to make the transition from consumer to active producer, say, of content on YouTube, etc. (p. 44), The power of the individual user remains limited in other ways as well. As Peter Fischer-Nielsen observes: "the communication must fit into a framework/logic set by Facebook, Twitter, Microsoft etc. The user does not have full control" (personal communication, February 11, 2011). Indeed, as we explore in both the Introduction and Conclusion to this volume, prominent researchers such as Sonja Livingstone (2011) warn against the dangers of self-commodification, as users are forced by these frameworks and logics— e.g., as exemplified in the limited range of choices a social networking site such as Facebook offers for presenting one's identity in an online profile—to thereby fit within a relatively narrow range of categories and taste preferences dictated primarily by commercial interests who are concerned with acquiring demographic data of value to advertisers (p. 354; cf. Baym 2011, pp. 399f.).

Given these developments, it is hardly surprising that social media have attracted considerable attention among researchers and scholars interested in the impacts and interactions of these media with religion—a category within which we include communities and organizations centered on distinctive practices, beliefs, and norms of diverse religious traditions (e.g., the Abrahamic traditions, Buddhism, Confucian traditions, Hinduism, etc.). Following upon the general claims made for Web 2.0—that greater interactivity and user control entail greater democratization and flattening of hierarchies—a particular theme in this research is how social media may facilitate challenges to, and (re)negotiations of, religious authority. Indeed, Heidi Campbell (2011) identifies this theme as definitive of what she characterizes as the (current) third wave of internet research in religion (p. 242; cf. Cheong, Huang, & Poon, 2011).

Against this background, we became curious as to how the characteristics and dynamics of social media and the alleged implications for religious community and authority would work themselves out in a Danish context of very high internet and social media penetration, a strong cultural commitment to equality, and, at least from a U.S. perspective, the generally liberal theology of the Evangelical Lutheran Church in Denmark (the *Folkekirken* or Danish National Church for short).

The Danish National Church: A Brief Introduction

The theology of the Danish National Church is centrally characterized by Enlightenment rationalism, individual autonomy, equality, and democratic process. The institutions and congregations constituting the Danish National Church in general reflect strong Danish traditions of egalitarianism, and what in the U.S. context would be called the highly progressive theological and social commitments affiliated with the dramatic transformations of the Danish National Church and broader society inaugurated by N.F.S. Grundtvig and his followers in the 19th century. Among other influences, Grundtvig and his cohorts were consciously following new paths and directions marked out by Enlightenment Rationalism: this seems to mean that the "mainstream" congregations of the Danish National Church are generally more likely to endorse theologies shaped by critical rationalism (e.g., religious claims must be submitted to the critical scrutiny of reason), in contrast with the more characteristic embrace of emotivism and fideism (briefly, supernatural revelation trumps reason) that mark, say, Evangelical, Pentecostal, and Fundamentalist movements in the U.S. (Ess, 2004). At the same time, these more emotivist-fideist movements consistently hold to what we would consider to be more traditional theological and doctrinal commitments (e.g., the Virgin Birth) as well as more hierarchical/authoritarian organizational structures (including traditional patriarchy). Reflecting these more conservative theological commitments—including the "Great Commission" that enjoins believers to spread the Gospel and brings others to what are taken to be its exclusive truths (Matt. 28: 19–20)—these traditions have consistently been at the vanguard of new media use, beginning with radio, movies, and TV, and then with the technologies of computer-mediated communication (e.g., Mullins, 2004). While within these traditions we can discern different patterns of use—most notably, the contrast between the official Vatican website as primarily a one-to-many broadcast and text repository, vis-à-vis much more interactive websites as developed by Evangelicals— nonetheless, what Martin Marty identified as the Protestant mainstream in the U.S., by contrast, as a whole has lagged behind Catholics and Evangelicals in media use and development (cf. Ess, 2007; Helland, 2007).

These fairly neat patterns from the U.S. context, however, are complicated and confounded in the Danish context. In his recent study, Peter Fischer-Nielsen (2010) found that only 5% of the ministers in his survey identified themselves as "liberal," while 7% self-identified as "conservative." By contrast, by far the largest category of theological commitment is "Grundt-vigian"—47% chose this category (among a total of 11) as their first category of identity. And while there is not a perfect congruity of categories between the U.S. and Denmark, we might, nonetheless, be able to fairly include some of Fischer-Nielsen's categories—e.g., "activist" (20%) and "low church" (14%)—within the category of "liberal," in contrast with his categories of "classic Christian" (24%), "high church" (4%), "charismatic" (4%), and "*Tidevhervsk*," a small (7%) movement within Denmark notorious for its affiliation with the far-right Danish Folk Party: these latter would certainly count as "conservative" in a U.S. context. Insofar as this mapping holds, attitudes towards media are just the reverse from the U.S. pattern. That is, the largest percentages of supporters of a central church strategy for media use are in the categories of activist (ca. 75%) and liberal (68%), in contrast with charismatics (ca. 65%), conservatives (53%) and *Tidehvervsk* (38%).

Against this complex background, it nonetheless seemed clear to us that, broadly speaking, there is already a clear match between the claims made regarding social media and the characteristics of the Danish National Church—thus suggesting the initial question: how would social media "work" in a religious environment already marked by greater equality and democratic processes?

Exploring Social Media Use in Danish Lutheran Waters: A Case Study

Specifically, we chose to study a congregation that we will call an Activist Danish Church (ADC). To begin with, our ADC exemplifies characteristic Danish National Church commitments to more egalitarian approaches. These commitments can be seen, for example, in the practice of a more informal liturgy and organizational initiatives that increase lay engagement with worship planning.[1] Our ADC is further marked by commitment to progressive social values, such as environmental activism, gender equality, and other commitments to what we can broadly call social justice issues, including interfaith dialogue. Further, in contrast with many other mainstream Danish National Church congregations, our ADC attracts the participation of an unusually large number of young people. This is in part because the activist missions of the church attract students from the nearby university, and in part because the church is located in a less-expensive area, making it a relatively desirable neighborhood for young people just starting out in their careers—as well as for retirees on fixed incomes. Finally, progressivity is also marked by the church's use of digital media. In addition to traditional communication channels such as *Kirkebladet* [Church Newsletter] and advertisements in local magazines and newspapers, the ADC was a fairly early adopter of the internet in communicating church-related activities. According to the church officials, the church established its online presence in 1999 with a church website primarily for announcements and contact information. Since 2004 the church officials have produced and distributed weekly online newsletters. The church's group on Facebook was established in mid-2008, in a period when Facebook was growing rapidly in Denmark. At the time of the study, the group had about 85 members and was fairly active in terms of postings from the church officials about upcoming events, resumes, and photos from recent events and so forth.

With these values, parish demographics, and media activities in mind, the church is a promising candidate for exploring the potentials of social media as interactive, fostering equality, and challenging traditional religious authorities. We took the ADC to constitute a critical case (Flyvbjerg, 2006) in the following sense: since the ADC is in many ways comparatively progressive vis-à-vis the Danish National Church, it is likely to more readily appropriate social media in the daily work of the church. That is, our ADC, as already committed to equality and dialogue in multiple ways, constitutes an environment in which the use of social media in church life is likely to be successful at facilitating dialogue among church officials and congregants. Our efforts to discern in empirical ways how far the ADC in fact succeeds (and/or fails) in its uses of social media should thus shed interesting new light on the usual claims made for social media. At the same time, however, while our study brings us forward in terms of providing empirically grounded ways of testing common claims made for social media— given the distinctive characteristics of our ADC vis-à-vis the complexities of the larger Danish religious landscape, we emphasize that our findings cannot be taken as representative for the Danish National Church as such.

In the present study, we approach the role of social media in the specific religious community from the perspective of ordinary usage patterns, rather than from the perspective of religious practices, exploring what happens when a de-institutionalized space (Lüders, 2008) is "invaded" by an official organization such as the church. Specifically, we ask:

1. How is an already popular and broadly used site, namely Facebook,[2] appropriated for religious and community purposes in a Danish Lutheran context?
2. How do religious leaders and congregation members negotiate roles in Facebook, and how can this inform current understandings of religion and social media?

To explore these questions, we undertook a case study in two stages. First, we conducted an initial pilot study that helped us develop a fairly detailed understanding of the general characteristics of our study church and its use of media, including social media. At this stage we collected data through interviews with church officials and through participant observation of the ADC (one of us has been active in the life of the ADC). This was then followed by a second stage, consisting of in-depth interviews with congregants who utilized the church's Facebook page. The case study was carried out over an extensive period in 2010: a researcher and a research assistant—neither having any personal engagement with the ADC—carried out all interviews. In the following pages, we describe the specific methodology and research questions of both stages of the study, present our analysis and findings, and conclude with remaining questions and suggestions for future study.

Church Officials and the Role of Facebook in the Life of the ADC

The initial study set out to explore the role of Facebook in the church's communication by (a) mapping the official communicative activities of the church, including which communicative channels are used and how often, and (b) uncovering the church authorities' intentions and strategies for establishing church presence on Facebook as well as their experiences with Facebook as a tool in the church's communication. To contextualize the organizational motivations for the Facebook presence, we further sought to locate the church's use of Facebook within the institution of the Danish National Church.

For this purpose we conducted an exploratory study, collecting empirical data primarily through extensive interviews with the two officials in charge of the Facebook group and the church's online communication, i.e., one of the pastors and the webmaster, both younger males. The interview data were supplemented by data from the Facebook group itself, including membership structure, demographics, and communication within the group, as well as reading of other communication material from the church, and informal observations by the participating researcher. The case study constituted a modest, initial attempt to explore empirically what Danish church authorities do with Facebook, and how they might see Facebook play a potential role in the larger context of church work and mission.

Social Media and the Danish National Church

According to the church officials, there is no systematic attention to, and discussion of, social media as part of the larger mission of the Danish National Church at an institutional level. That is, there is no official strategy or policy for using social media as part of the activities of the Danish National Church.

This gives the impression of a lack of awareness of, and interest in taking up, the opportunities of social media in church work, such as using the interactive potentials of social media to facilitate dialogue with church members and using social media to make connections with younger Danes. Such a lack of awareness would be surprising, insofar as a majority of younger Danes do not attend a church of any sort (other than for baptisms, confirmation services, weddings, and funerals, which still play a significant role in the "cultural Christianity" of otherwise highly secular Denmark), and so, as with "greying congregations" elsewhere throughout the world, there is considerable attention on both local and national levels as to how the Danish National Church can attract and retain young people who appear to be increasingly uninterested in "church" (e.g., Jensen, 2011).

This does not, however, mean that the Danish National Church does not allow for, or support, the use of social media as part of the mission at a grassroots level, i.e., the specific church as an organization within the Danish National Church. To the contrary, the decentralized structure of the Danish National Church implies individual freedom and flexibility for pastors and congregations to explore the potentials of social media such as Facebook. The Danish National Church's use of social media is thus organized *ad hoc,* and dependent upon the grassroots, and the ADC's use of Facebook is one such grassroots initiative. The officials whom we have interviewed consider the ADC's use of Facebook to be part of a strategic effort to build relationships within the church. This is useful both at an organizational level, and for the pastor and his profession in carrying out the daily work in the local community.

The Facebook Group of the ADC

If the Danish National Church's use of Facebook is organized *ad hoc,* the same is in a sense true for the church's appropriation of Facebook for work in the congregation at a grassroots level. The webmaster reports that the establishment of the ADC's Facebook group was done with no other explicit intention than a wish to be modern as a church. "We need to be where the people are—especially the young," he argues, indicating that Facebook is considered a potential platform for engaging young Danes in the church. The initiative on Facebook, however strategic, appears not to be an organizational decision, but rather based on individual effort from the younger pastor and the webmaster. The older pastor of the church, although on Facebook, is not even a member of the church's Facebook group.

The church officials we interviewed see Facebook as a useful supplementary communication channel, primarily for internal communication with the parish. Our observations of the Facebook group page confirm that Facebook is mainly used to broadcast information about church-related activities.

The announcements posted on Facebook are the same as on the website, and they are all posted by either the pastor or the webmaster. Thus, there is not much participatory engagement with the congregants, despite the interactive features that Facebook makes available. While it is clear to the officials that Facebook cannot stand alone in the church's communication with the parish, they emphasize it as a central communication channel because it reaches an important target group for the church: namely the young members of the congregation. Looking at the membership demographics within the church's Facebook group, the majority of the group members are young. About two-thirds of its 85 members at the time of the study were aged between 20 and 40. There was a majority of females (55%) and the members were primarily ethnic Danes.[3] This demographic group constitutes quite a large part of the parish, although those who attend church activities most consistently are older and more ethnically mixed. To judge from these characteristics, the Facebook group actually does establish a platform for communication with the younger congregants, while it is also clear that this use does not touch other important demographics of the church, primarily older Danes and international members of the church.

The webmaster frames the presence of the church on Facebook in terms of brand value, i.e., as a signal that the church is progressive, also in terms of attitudes towards new communication technology. Being on Facebook contributes to a sense of the church as a front-runner in the Danish National Church.[4] Along the same lines, the webmaster reports that the church's group page on Facebook is useful for marking to those outside the group that many support the church, thus, in a sense functioning as a form of PR for the church in members' personal Facebook networks. We stress here for non-Danish readers: many Danes view religion as an extremely private matter, one that is simply not broached in most social and work-related contexts. In this light, the fact that members voluntarily and publicly mark their affiliation to the church through the Facebook group could be seen as an indicator of a strong sense of connectedness to the church. This public expression of connectedness to the church through membership in the Facebook group further implies that church members become very visible to each other; by accessing the group page they can identify other members and put a name to faces they have possibly seen at church. This, the church officials hope, contributes to strengthening the attachment among the congregants and to crafting a more personalized relationship to the church as an organization. The Facebook group is thus used as a tool for building and reinforcing group identity within the congregation.

The Pastor on Facebook

The interviews revealed an interesting aspect of the church's use of Facebook, namely that it was not only centered on the church's group page, but also on the pastor's own personal profile and network of Facebook friends. Both pastors engage in friending practices with the congregation members, with the younger pastor we interviewed being the most active in this aspect of the church's use of Facebook. With this use of Facebook, the pastors, and thus indirectly the church, promote an individualization and personalization of the relationship between the pastor and their congregants.

The younger pastor considers his individual profile on Facebook a quite efficient tool for building and maintaining relationships to the congregation members. In the interview, the pastor described how his own Facebook profile has grown more and more into a strategic work tool that he uses to stay in touch with the church community. He systematically adds the people who sign up for the church's group page on Facebook as his personal friends if he has not already been friended by them. Furthermore, he accepts friend requests from members of the church who, for some reason, are not members of the group page.

The pastor does not distinguish between the people in his Facebook network, so personal friends, colleagues, and church attendants have equal access to his profile and his updates. This implies for the pastor that he has to actively manage his self-presentation on his Facebook profile with a view to both his professional and personal roles and relationships. For instance, in the interview the pastor notes his careful efforts to strike a balance that enables him to present himself as both a pastor and a private person in his status updates. He considers it professionally helpful to give the congregation members who are part of his Facebook audience glimpses into his private life. "Facebook provides a platform for direct contact between the congregants and me," the pastor further contends, and that way, he hopes congregants will feel like they know him and can relate to him more personally than would be possible simply through encounters at church. Given that congregants experience a closer relation with the pastor through Facebook, this might also make congregants more likely to approach the pastor for good advice and comfort in their daily lives. Along these lines, the pastor notes that young members of the congregation have approached him several times on Facebook with theological questions.

At the same time, however, the pastor is careful not to post status updates that could compromise his status as a leader or authority in the congregation, such as complaints over something at work or in his private life. While apparently finding a way to manage this "collapse" in roles by acting in a more strategic manner, the pastor acknowledges the potential concern that he suspects some of his pastoral colleagues might have regarding taking the pastor-congregant relationship to a more personal and friendly level. This concern is even more pertinent when considering that, however careful and strategic one may be in terms of self-presentation, it is not possible to fully control the personal information and impressions conveyed to one's network of friends on Facebook. Donath and boyd (2004), for instance, have vividly described how self-presentations on social network sites are collaboratively constructed, perhaps most notably in that the public display of connections of a given individual on Facebook, for example, gives the curious audience many hints regarding the personal identity of the profile holder. In addition, people in the friend network contribute directly to shaping the self-presentation of the profile holder by commenting on status updates and tagging the profile holder in the private photos they upload to Facebook, in what Walther and colleagues (2009) have termed "other-generated statements" about the profile holder (see also boyd & Heer, 2006). Taking this into consideration, engaging with congregants through Facebook friendships and thereby reducing the interpersonal distance may be rewarding for relationship building in the congregation, but it is a delicate balance to strike, as this strategic presentation of the pastor as an ordinary person also possibly entails a risk of jeopardizing the professional respect and authority so important for a pastor in his work and leadership within the community.

In addition to portraying and making himself available for conversation as a regular, private person, the pastor makes clear that he has other, perhaps still more pertinent, reasons for having friendships with members of the congregation on Facebook. Just as he hopes that his own presence and activities on Facebook will make congregants feel that they know him better, he feels closer and more in tune with them. Facebook enables him to monitor what is on people's minds, because the site establishes a hitherto non-existent platform for being with them in their daily lives. Facebook simply facilitates ambient or peripheral awareness of the congregants, their experiences, and their whereabouts. Through his Facebook news feed, the pastor follows the congregants on a daily basis and posts "likes" to their status updates if they are interesting. As the pastor argues, being personal friends with congregants "is a way for me to show engagement in their lives as well," and to manage to communicate somewhat personally with a larger number of congregants than would otherwise be possible. Along similar lines, the pastor considers being friends with congregants on Facebook a way to "keep the line open and warm," thereby making it easier to start a conversation when he meets the congregation face to face. For instance, the pastor amplifies in the interview, it is an advantage when meeting the community for Sunday service. "Meeting more than one hundred church attendants in church every Sunday, it is impossible to talk to everyone in person, but the Facebook interaction during the week can compensate for this," he explains. Being friends with congregants on Facebook thus enables him to sustain and reinforce the social contact with the congregation on a daily basis. Accordingly, the interpersonal connection on Facebook becomes a tool for more efficient interpersonal relationships between pastor and congregation. The pastor hopes that this relational maintenance will ultimately strengthen congregants' commitment to the church, because it creates mutual trust and a sense of togetherness between himself and the community, thereby performing a vital task in the church's work portfolio. "The work on reinforcing trust and mutual commitment through interpersonal relationships on Facebook is very much in line with [the ADC's] goal and mission towards creating community and relation-rich services," he notes. Said more sharply, the pastor argues that being friends with congregants on Facebook creates and sustains a mutual commitment that will spark greater involvement in the life of the church and encourage people to continue to attend the Sunday services.

The fact that the pastor uses Facebook in his daily work is interesting, because it reflects an expansion of his work sphere into a more de-institutionalized space (recall Lüders, 2008). Or, more precisely, by entering and participating in the interpersonal relationship dynamics on Facebook, the pastor steps beyond what is normally considered his professional sphere. Facebook represents a communicative space for interpersonal communication and management of relational presence that is seamlessly interwoven with other forms of communication in many Danes' lives, including the members of this specific congregation. This considered, what happens when institutionalized and clearly defined relationships such as the one between pastor and congregant, church and congregation, which normally plays out within the boundaries of official church-related activities, suddenly enters this everyday communicative space? Likely, this challenges and affects norms guiding the relationship between congregation and church officials.

The Congregants' Perspective

Having explored the visions, strategies, and uses of Facebook as a communication tool from the church authorities' perspective, the logical question to raise is how do the church congregation members experience the relationship and possibility for contact with the church and pastor on Facebook? To examine this, we set up a second explorative study asking the basic research question: How do congregation members' practices and experiences match the church officials' expectations and hopes of relationship-building in the church through the church's presence on Facebook and in the interpersonal connections between pastor and congregant as friends on the site? With this, we emphasize a research interest in the congregants who are members of the ADC Facebook group and use Facebook, rather than seeking to elicit responses from a representative sample of the congregation as such.

Following a first unsuccessful attempt to recruit participants to a qualitative survey and follow up interview through the ADC's Facebook group, we modified our study design to rely solely on in-depth interviews, starting with those two Facebook group members that had responded to our initial request for study participants. We contacted and interviewed them, and asked them to help put us in touch with other members that would agree to be interviewed. This snowball-sampling procedure proved quite useful in terms of getting data to work with, but of course it also meant that we were less able to get the broad picture on experiences with the church on Facebook that a more extensive survey could have enabled. To compensate for this, we asked interviewees to not only point us to their own closest relations within the community (with whom they are more likely to be similar), but also to try to recruit members of a different age, gender, and involvement in the church than themselves.

We ended up with six in-depth interviews with a demographically diverse sample of members matching the demographic profile of the Facebook group quite well. Four interviewees are women, two are men, and they were all aged between 24 and 61 at the time of the interview (two in their twenties, two in their thirties, one in his forties and one in her sixties). A diverse range of educational backgrounds and occupations were represented. All but one of the interviewees are Danes, and three of them volunteer to different degrees in the church. All but one of the informants are members of the church's Facebook group and friends with one or both of the pastors. The interviewee who is not a member of the Facebook group simply hasn't thought of joining, but indicates that she wouldn't mind being a member and would in fact consider joining the group to get information about church activities quicker than she does now. Hence, her non-membership is not an active deselection. All the interviews were recorded and carried out in spring and summer 2010.

Congregants' General Experience of the Church

When asked to describe how they experience the church, most of the interviewees stress its progressivity as a core characteristic and quality. Some emphasize progressivity in terms of the church's political engagement in interfaith dialogue and climate issues; some mention the willingness of the church to take up new communication technologies including Facebook, whereas others link their sense of the church's progressivity to religious openness and inclusivity, i.e., that there is room for individual theological differences. Another common characteristic stressed is that the church is considered very "down to earth," reflected in the fact that the pastors are Facebook friends with congregants and in the fact that a lot of congregation members meet outside the official Sunday services. Most of the interviewees have friends from the church with whom they hang out in their free time, e.g., for sports, dinner parties, and the like. The social relationships with fellow members of the congregation are a large part of the motivation in attending church activities, especially for the younger congregants.

The general description of the church by the members thus seems to fit quite well with both our initial impression of the church and the spirit of openness and informality that the church officials seek to promote.

The Facebook Group

Before going into detailed accounts of how the interviewed congregants experience the Facebook group as part of their relationship with the church, it is pertinent to shed a little general light on Facebook groups and their place within the daily use of Facebook.[5] For most of the interviewees, as well as for users of Facebook in general, Facebook is something that users check into, sometimes several times a day, for short visits, i.e., for breaks at work, procrastination, or brief exchanges with friends (see, e.g., Wagman, 2010; Ellison, Lampe, Steinfield, & Vitak, 2011; Joinson, 2008). Moreover, contrary to other social media (e.g., blogs, Twitter), Facebook is typically not centered upon shared interests, but fundamentally rests upon the articulation and maintenance of existing relationships. With an emphasis on short visits and relational management, Facebook appears to not be an ideal space for promoting in-depth dialogue, long, drawn-out debates, and political or religious engagement.

Concerning Facebook groups, all the interviewees use Facebook groups, but groups are not considered a core activity on Facebook. Groups are mostly something people join (e.g., upon invitation) and do not think too much about after that. This supports findings from Mark Johns' study of religious groups on Facebook (reported in this volume) that joining Facebook groups must largely be seen as an isolated act marking identity or fandom. The interviewees in our study report very minor use of Facebook groups: "to be honest, I rarely visit my groups," as one interviewee explains. Only two of them are members of Facebook groups in which actual interaction among members is taking place. These active groups are socio-political in orientation, thus inherently promoting debate.

When asked to reflect upon the function of the church's group on Facebook, all interviewees suggest that the group has no unique function in the communicative circuit in the church. It functions mainly as a broadcasting channel, and the members receive the same information from the group page as from *Kirkebladet*, the newsletter, and the website. The interviewees do not tend to visit the group page out of their own initiative, although some report visiting the group when they feel like going to church. However, for some of the interviewees the group page is a useful tool to create awareness about church-related activities. Whenever church officials post something to the group page, a message is sent to each member who is then reminded of the existence of the group page and may choose to check it out. Along those lines, one interviewee explicitly calls for more frequent updates because this would lead him to visit the group more often and thus perhaps lead to more activity on the group page.

Several informants voluntarily state (without our probing encouragement) that they would like a greater activation of Facebook's interactive potential on the church's group page. They call for more debate and interaction in the group, although it is a bit unclear who is supposed to initiate this interaction. For one of the interviewees, the lack of mobilization of the Facebook group for debate misses an important opportunity for the church. While debate seems to thrive well within the church (i.e., in the volunteer groups who organize church-related events and excursions), the debate should be less internal. The Facebook group, the interviewee suggests, could facilitate a broadening of the debate to include those regular members of the congregation who just attend church activities but are not otherwise actively involved with the church.

The Facebook group appears to be used as if it were a Facebook page—users mark social affiliation by joining the group, and it is useful as a broadcast channel for news, announcements, and so forth in the ADC. While the Facebook group administrators have enabled both the Facebook wall and a debate page, thus providing the space for congregants to start a debate, there are no posts on the debate site, and only activity announcements from church officials and volunteers on the group wall. This suggests that despite calling for more debate, congregants are not willing to take advantage of the dialogic features provided on the group page and initiate it themselves, indicating that the need for more debate is not actually very urgent to congregants.

Despite the reliance on traditional broadcast communication and the informational functions and potentials of the Facebook group not being explored by either officials or congregants, the Facebook group may serve other, more relational functions. Some interviewees report having used the group to find and "befriend" other church members, including former church members who have left the parish and moved elsewhere. The group page thus enables people related to the church to keep in touch with each other and with the church despite geographical dispersion.

Moreover, one interviewee considers the group valuable because it creates a common space for the congregation. This brings them closer together, he argues. In relation to this, some of the informants mention that the group can potentially enhance and broaden their contact with other members at church-related events, because they have their group membership in common as a point of departure for building a relationship in person. However, the interviewees have not made use of this opportunity themselves, and it is evident from the Facebook group page that it is not used as a forum for creating social contact among members, e.g., for coordinating social activities. Indeed, even for the interviewees who are very socially involved with other congregants, Facebook does not constitute an important communication channel. For personal relationships, texting and face-to-face interaction are more central.

To sum up, based on the absence of interaction on the Facebook group as well as comments from interviewees, the group is an inactive and impersonal space. There are, it appears, certain difficulties in exploiting the dialogic and interactive potentials to the benefit of the church, and neither church officials nor congregants are making any efforts at starting debate on the group page. This is surprising considering the church's apparent openness and dialogic core purpose. However, we suggest that it is not at all surprising from the perspective of general Facebook usage patterns in everyday life. For the most part, Facebook is used to maintain personal networks, for small talk, and to coordinate activities and entertainment with friends (see Quan-Haase & Young, 2010; Wagman, 2010). These activities and communicative practices so well-established on Facebook are far from those associated with debate in general, let alone theological discussion, especially in a Danish context, suggesting that Facebook may simply not be all that easy to appropriate for that kind of usage, because it demands a fundamentally different type of engagement on the site and thereby conflicts with users' common expectation of Facebook as a venue for sporadic and informal socializing. At the same time, however, it seems that the Facebook group functions to mark the identity of its users and the church more broadly—i.e., as progressive, as contemporary, etc. (cf. Mark Johns, this volume).

Being Friends With the Pastor

Consistent with findings on the church officials' expectations and experiences with the interpersonal features on Facebook, all but one of the informants confirm the positive effects of being friends with their pastors on Facebook. The interpersonal bond brings the pastor down to earth, and the congregants get to see the pastor as a regular guy. As one interviewee puts it, being Facebook-friends with the pastor enables her to see him as "a father and husband and somebody who goes home at night and does things that normal people do. Complete with pictures. Just seeing him at Sunday service does not give me a sense of what he does in his free time." Most congregants do not get to talk much with the pastor on Sunday services when the congregation is gathered, so without Facebook, their relationship with the pastor would be a lot more impersonal, they feel. Important here is that the interviewees in general do not consider the pastor to present himself particularly strategically. They experience him as a private person on Facebook, something they all value positively. Some say that being friends with and getting to know the pastor has great value, primarily because it would make it safer and more comfortable to seek the pastor's advice in a private situation, again confirming the hopes of the pastor.

By being part of the interviewees' friend networks, the pastor blends in with other relationships that the congregants keep on Facebook, most prominently visible in the informants' daily news feeds and streams of status updates. Informants appear not to be particularly aware of the pastor's updates compared to their other friends' updates, but the Facebook stream creates a sort of "awareness at a distance" as one interviewee puts it, that is, an ambient awareness that can be developed when needed, i.e., at face-to-face meetings. Reading (and sometimes commenting on) each other's status updates functions as an icebreaker when the members meet the pastor in church. Again, this is consistent with the experience of Facebook friendship from the pastor's point of view. While the ambient awareness does not add up to a deeply personal relationship, one of the interviewees argues, it is actually quite suitable for the congregant-pastor relationship. They can have an interpersonal connection, but still maintain a proper distance that might be useful for both parties. Useful for the congregants, because following each other only at a distance seems harmless and ensures that the pastor, and with him the church as an institution, does not appear intrusive to their private sphere on Facebook. Useful for the pastor, because this distance enables him to keep a professional authority in relation to the congregants. Along these lines, the relationship between pastor and congregant as experienced by both parties on Facebook may be characterized as a "weak tie," that is, a relationship that relies mainly on informational, professional exchange (e.g., acquaintances and distant colleagues), as opposed to a "strong tie" (personal relationships such as close friends and family) (cf. Granovetter, 1973; Haythornthwaite, 2005). Social network sites are often emphasized as being particularly useful for maintaining weak tie relationships, whereas strong ties typically rely on multiple forms of contact (e.g., face-to-face meetings, telephony, email, and so forth) (Ellison et al., 2011).

One of the interviewees is not friends with the pastor on Facebook. When asked for her reasons, she responds that she would feel uncomfortable and in a sense finds this kind of interpersonal relationship intrusive. Contrary to the other congregants, she considers the pastor not as a private person, but as a professional on Facebook whom she only knows from his professional role (similar to her colleagues or her doctor), and thus he does not appear to her as qualified for Facebook friendship. To her, the problem is that being Facebook-friends with someone entails that she becomes more "vulnerable" to that person, because it would allow the friend access to the personal information that she might share on Facebook. She may not wish the pastor to act upon her personal status updates. She contends: "if I wrote that I had had a bad day, I would not like to be addressed by the pastor, asking if there is a problem to which I need his help. This is not what Facebook is meant for.

In such a situation it would be more appropriate that actual friends contacted me, if at all. Facebook is the right forum for this." Her views complement the other informants by providing a take on the flip side of sharing personal information in the relationship with an authority figure in connection with the experience and protection of individual privacy on Facebook.

Acknowledging this possible disturbance of the congregant's sense of privacy, our analysis generally suggests that the church's appropriation of Facebook on an interpersonal level (i.e., being Facebook-friends with congregants) is more likely to succeed in aiding the church's work on continually establishing and developing a sense of cohesion and trust within the parish. In addition, interpersonal connections between pastor and congregants make the pastor more immediately available for the congregants. A likely explanation for this apparent success is that the activities implied in building closer relationships between pastor and congregation members fit nicely into already established core practices on Facebook, whether directly engaging in interpersonal conversation through status updates and commenting or through mere awareness of each other at a distance, i.e., appearing in each other's news feeds.

Privacy and the Negotiation of Authority

Our analyses point to two important implications when institutions such as the church enter a de-institutionalized space such as Facebook, where ordinary users share personal information and maintain personal relationships with their peers. For the congregants, the church's presence on Facebook raises questions to the issue of protection of personal privacy and the private sphere from intrusion of authorities and formal institutions. Specifically, it points to Facebook as an increasingly semi-public, rather than private, sphere of interaction.[6] From the pastor's perspective, the findings from the analysis speak to the issue of what happens to the pastor's authority when he enters an interpersonal relationship with members of the congregation on Facebook and thus becomes more like "one of them." As one of our congregant respondents reckons, the pastor's challenge is always to navigate and find a balance in his or her behavior so as not to offend or alienate anybody. This means that sometimes, personal opinions must be toned down for the pastor to be able to act as a unifying figure for the community. People of course know that their pastor is a regular person with personal opinions, political inclinations, and theological values, but the pastor is also the "god-person" for everybody on Sunday mornings. How frail can this god-person be? While Facebook presence might enhance this delicate balancing act, there is (and has always been) a continuous tension between the professional role as a pastor, and the person behind this most significant rôle.

When an institution such as the church enters a de-institutionalized, interpersonal space such as Facebook, it implies a renegotiation of the interactional role and relationship between congregants as church members on the one hand and the pastor as an authority and leadership figure in the parish on the other hand. Establishing relationships on Facebook reveals both parties as private persons with various interests and activities beyond the religious sphere. At the same time, however, both congregants and the minister are conscious of the risk of going too far in blurring the boundaries between the professional and the personal—a caution also underlined by our finding that the primary use of Facebook is to sustain weak-tie relationships.

Conclusions and Future Research

We can summarize our findings as follows. To begin with, while Facebook emerges as a very useful tool in the ADC's efforts at building relationships with congregants, it is predominantly used as a supplement to other forms of communication, and to maintain weak-tie relationships: strong-tie relationships are regularly maintained and fostered in the other components of church life—i.e., face-to-face, embodied co-presence in worship, social events, planning activities, etc. While the Facebook group plays a minor role in the official communicative circuits of the church—by contrast, being friends with the pastor creates a mutual ambient awareness that feeds into the communication (ice-breaking) at church-related events and thus contributes to relationship building. This dialogic use of Facebook by the pastor in relation to the congregants, moreover, is consistent with the general claim for social media, namely, that it facilitates a renegotiation of authority—at least in terms of the relationships between congregants and the pastors as authority figures. Broadly, it appears that Facebook use in our ADC indeed fosters a greater sense of equality—in keeping with both the egalitarian commitments of the church and the claims made for these media.

At the same time, however, the non-dialogical use of the Facebook group by the church contradicts our initial expectation—and, as it turned out, that of the church's webmaster (see p. 176)—that as an open, egalitarian, and activist institution, the church's use of Web 2.0 would be more "cutting edge," i.e., so as to exploit the interactivity and democratizing potentials of Web 2.0 as fully as possible. On the contrary, the church's use of Facebook, while crucial for establishing and sustaining contact with, especially, younger members who move away from the physical church, remains comparatively limited.

It is clear that our research is preliminary and not statistically representative (both for the congregation under study and for the Danish National Church at large). Hence, although our case is one of the first of its kind, and interesting, we think, as it appears to show distinctively mixed results regarding broader claims and initial expectations surrounding social media, clearly more exploration is needed.

First of all, we do not know how far the use of Facebook "works" better with younger people at this particular ADC because (a) they're younger, and/or (b) the church already has a strong group identity driven by its distinctive missions and goals as an activist church. A better understanding of these factors and their influence on Facebook use is crucial, however, if we are to hypothesize and examine, for example, whether or not Facebook would be useful in relation to other demographics and less committed and cohesive communities. However, given that this ADC, despite its commitment to dialogue and invitation for the active involvement of lay members of the congregation in church activities, is not particularly successful in generating a vibrant Facebook group, it seems unlikely that other more traditional and hierarchical congregations in the Danish National Church, would be able to.

More broadly, more research is required in terms of additional examples of other churches' presence on the web, i.e., home pages, use of mailing lists, etc., as well as use of Facebook and other social media, to explore the general applicability of such tools for the church. For example, Peter Fischer-Nielsen (2010) found similar practices of friending among pastor and congregants in his study, as based on qualitative interviews with eight Danish pastors about their media use. This suggests that rather than our ADC being unique, the patterns and reflections we found relating to the pastor using Facebook in daily church work might have broader resonance in the Danish National Church. But this is, at best, only a preliminary finding—one that points to a specific direction of future research within the Danish context. Perhaps most ambitiously, we would like to have a much better understanding of how far the use of social media by our ADC reflects upon larger patterns, both within the Danish religious landscape and those suggested more broadly by research on religion and CMC over the past decade or so.

In conclusion: Is there anything in the affordances and use of social media that make a difference in the life and work of a congregation? Our case seems to make clear that social media offer new opportunities for relational management and more personalized relationships between pastor and parish. Insofar as they do so, especially for a national church that is otherwise losing its already very small appeal to younger generations, social media would seem to promise important new ways of sustaining at least weak-tie, if not strong-tie relationships among younger people. In this direction, the younger pastor at ADC is optimistic that at least some of his colleagues—if not the larger church in a more programmatic way—might pick up on one or more of his church's successful practices over time. He may well be right: but in light of our larger questions about the complex theological maps of Denmark and religion elsewhere, a further question suggests itself: will this optimism be fulfilled by his more conservative, rather than his more liberal, colleagues?

Acknowledgments

We are very grateful to Pastor Christian Grund Sørensen (Copenhagen), Prof. Peter Øhrstrom (Aalborg University), as well as Peter Fischer-Nielsen and Stefan Gelfgren for their insightful comments and advice, especially in regard to the complexities of the Danish religious landscapes. We further wish to thank Annette Markham (IMV, Aarhus University) for her helpful criticisms and suggestions.

Notes

1. As a further example: in the fall of 2010, the church inaugurated a significant—in some ways, dramatic—rearrangement of its sanctuary, with a view towards reducing the sense of distance between congregants and ministers and to encourage greater interaction between congregants. These and related changes, e.g., greater congregant involvement in worship planning, all point to a more inclusive and egalitarian impetus.
2. According to the most recent Danish national internet statistics, 42 % of the Danish population between the ages of 16 and 74 had a profile on a social network site in 2009, the vast majority (95 %) on Facebook. Accordingly, it is fair to say that Facebook is a well-established and highly popular service in Denmark, likely playing a role in many Danes' everyday lives (Danmarks Statistik, 2009).
3. The age distribution in the group is based on our estimates upon visiting the individual profiles of the group members. Most have restricted privacy settings, allowing only Facebook friends to view their profile information. Thus, we cannot verify the age estimates and the numbers should be viewed with caution.
4. Peter Fischer-Nielsen observes that this may further be an example of what Heidi Campbell (2010) labeled a validating discourse: "The validation discourse seeks not only to affirm certain practices or positions towards the internet, but to promote the group's chosen response and the values it reflects. This means that the internet is used to affirm the community itself" (p. 150).
5. In this context, Facebook Pages should also be mentioned as a very similar functionality on Facebook. Whereas Facebook Groups is meant to facilitate groups that can organize around a topic, and exchange information and viewpoints, Facebook Pages is seen as more of a broadcasting functionality through which companies and celebrities can broadcast themselves to their fans (the users who have pressed the "like" button of the page).
6. This characterization of Facebook is supported from a number of directions, beginning with the notorious debates over Facebook's ideological commitment to transparency and the resulting clashes it has thereby stirred among users over the years regarding perceived violations of privacy—perhaps most notably, its Beacon initiative in 2007 (Ess, 2009, pp. 1–3). While Facebook has ostensibly responded to such complaints by introducing changes in the privacy settings manipulable by its users, the most recent of these offer us a bewildering array (50+) of choices—with the upshot being that most users appear to leave their privacy settings in their default, i.e., largely open, modes. At

the same time, countering these sorts of concerns is an apparently broader movement towards greater transparency online—e.g., through posting of intimate videos, etc. Gabriella David (2009) helpfully characterizes this movement in terms of Mark Federman's neologism "publicy"—i.e., a collapse of the private into the public (p. 86).

References

Baym, N. K. (2010). *Personal connections in the digital age.* Oxford, England: Polity Press.

Baym, N. K. (2011). Social networks 2.0. In M. Consalvo & C. Ess (Eds.), *The handbook of internet studies* (pp. 384–405). Oxford, England: Wiley-Blackwell.

boyd, d., & Heer, J. (2006). Profiles as conversation: Networked identity performance on Friendster. *Proceedings of the Hawaii International Conference on System Sciences (HICSS-39).* Kauai, HI, USA, IEEE Computer Society. doi:10.1109/HICSS.2006.394

Bruns, A. (2008). *Blogs, Wikipedia, Second Life, and beyond: From production to produsage.* New York, NY: Peter Lang.

Campbell, H. (2010). *When religion meets new media.* New York, NY: Routledge.

Campbell, H. (2011). Internet and religion. In M. Consalvo and C. Ess (Eds.), *The handbook of internet studies* (pp. 232–250). Oxford, England: Wiley-Blackwell.

Cheong, P.H., Huang, S.H., & Poon, J.P.H. (2011). Religious Communication and Epistemic Authority of Leaders in Wired Faith Organizations. *Journal of Communication, 61*(5), 938–958.

Danmarks Statistik (2009). Befolkningens brug af internet 2009. Retrieved from http://www.dst.dk/pukora/epub/upload/14039/it.pdf

David, G. (2009). Clarifying the mysteries of an exposed intimacy: Another intimate representation mise-en-scène. In K. Nyíri (Ed.), *Engagement and exposure: Mobile communication and the ethics of social networking* (pp. 77–86). Vienna, Austria: Passagen Verlag.

Donath, J., & boyd, d. (2004). Public displays of connection. *BT Technology Journal, 22*(4), 71–82.

Ellison, N., Lampe, C., Steinfield, C., & Vitak, J. (2011). With a little help from my friends: How social network sites affect social capital processes. In Z. Papacharissi (Ed.), *A networked self: Identity, community and culture on social network sites* (pp. 124–145). New York, NY: Routledge.

Ess, C. (1996). The political computer: Democracy, CMC, and Habermas. In C. Ess (Ed.), *Philosophical perspectives on computer-mediated communication* (pp. 197–230). Albany, NY: State University of New York Press.

Ess, C. (2004). Introduction. In C. Ess (Ed.), *Critical thinking and the Bible in the age of new media* (pp. 3–42). Lanham, MD: University Press of America.

Ess, C. (2007). Cross-cultural perspectives on religion and computer-mediated communication. *Journal of Computer-Mediated Communication, 12*(3), 939–955.

Ess, C. (2009). *Digital media ethics.* Oxford, England: Polity Press.

Ess, C. (2011). Self, community, and ethics in digital mediatized worlds. In C. Ess & M. Thorseth (Eds.), *Trust and virtual worlds: Contemporary perspectives* (pp. 3–30). London, England: Peter Lang.

Finnemann, N. O. (2005). *Internettet i mediehistorisk perspektiv.* Frederiksberg, Denmark: Forlaget Samfundslitteratur.

Fischer-Nielsen, P. (2010). Præstetyper i den danske folkekirke [Types of ministers in the Danish National Church]. *Præsteforeningens Blad, 100*(40), 838–842.

Flyvbjerg, B. (2006). Five misunderstandings about case-study research. *Qualitative Inquiry, 12*(2), 219–245.

Granovetter, M. (1973). The strength of weak ties. *The American Journal of Sociology, 78*(6), 1360–1380.

Haythornthwaite, C. (2005). Social networks and Internet connectivity effects. *Information, Communication & Society, 8*(2), 125–147.

Helland, C. (2007). Diaspora on the electronic frontier: Developing virtual connections with sacred homelands. *Journal of Computer-Mediated Communication, 12*(3), article 10. Retrieved from http://jcmc.indiana.edu/vol12/issue3/helland.html

Jensen, A. K. G. (2011, February 5). Unge uden åndeligt slægtskab med folkekirken [Young people have no spiritual kinship with the national church]. *Kristeligt Dagblad.* Retrieved from http://www.kristeligt-dagblad.dk/artikel/407347:Kirke-tro-Unge-uden-aandeligt-slaegtskab-med-folkekirken

Joinson, A. N. (2008). Looking at, looking up or keeping up with people?: Motives and use of Facebook. *Proceedings of the Twenty-Sixth Annual SIGCHI Conference on Human Factors in Computing Systems,* 1027–1036. doi: 10.1145/1357054.1357213.

Livingstone, S. (2011). Internet, children, and youth. In M. Consalvo and C. Ess (Eds.), *The handbook of internet studies* (pp. 348–368.). Oxford, England: Wiley-Blackwell.

Lüders, M. (2008). Conceptualizing personal media. *New Media & Society, 10*(5), 683–702.

Mullins, P. (2004). Bible study, critical thinking and post-critical thought: Cultural considerations. In C. Ess (Ed.), *Critical thinking and the Bible in the age of the new media* (pp. 269–290). Lanham, MD: University Press of America.

Quan-Haase, A., & Young, A. L. (2010). Uses and gratifications of social media: A comparison of Facebook and instant messaging. *Bulletin of Science, Technology & Society, 30*(5), 350–361.

van Dijck, J. (2010). Users like you? Theorising agency in user-generated content. *Media, Culture & Society, 31*(1), 14–58.

Wagman, I. (2010). Log on, goof off, and look up: Facebook and the rhythms of Canadian internet use. In B. Beaty, D. Briton, G. Filax, & R. Sullivan (Eds.), *How Canadians communicate III: Contexts of Canadian popular culture* (pp. 55–77). Athabasca, Canada: Athabasca University Press.

Walther, J. B., Van Der Heide, B., Hamel, L. M., & Shulman, H. C. (2009). Self-generated versus other-generated statements and impressions in computer-mediated communication: A test of warranting theory using Facebook. *Communication Research, 36*(2), 229–253.

11. Twitter of Faith: Understanding Social Media Networking and Microblogging Rituals as Religious Practices

PAULINE HOPE CHEONG

This chapter discusses a range of communicative uses and appropriations of Twitter in order to deepen the understanding of microblogging as a religious practice, including its benefits and limitations for community building, as well as its heuristic potential for future learning and research. Microblogging has emerged as an increasingly popular phenomenon whereby users engage in composing brief multimedia updates and sending them via web-based applications such as text messaging, instant messaging, email, or on the web. According to a report released by the Pew Internet and American Life Project, 19 percent of online American adults said that they used "a microblogging service" to send messages or "tweets" of no more than 140 characters from a computer or mobile device to family and friends who have signed up to receive them (Fox, Zickuhr, & Smith, 2009). In particular, Twitter has blossomed into one of the most well known microblogging tools. There are 95 million tweets written per day, by 175 million registered users, in multiple languages including English, French, German, Italian, Japanese, and Spanish (Twitter.com, September 14, 2010). At the time of writing, the most recent Pew Internet study that reports data measuring Twitter use exclusively found that 8 percent of online Americans regularly use Twitter, an activity that is particularly popular among "young adults, minorities and those who live in cities" (Smith & Rainie, 2010). Web traffic reports show that Twitter is the ninth most popular site in the world, visited by slightly more than 11 percent of the world's global internet users, according to the three month Alexa traffic rankings (www.alexa.com, April 22, 2011).

Since the first release of the Twitter application in August 2006, the tagline for the site has changed from the simple question, "What are you doing?" to "The best way to discover what's new in your world." By default, tweets are publicly visible, though senders can restrict access to their messages to just their user subscribers, called "followers" or "tweeps." By definition, tweets are limited to 140 characters, but the communicative potential can be extended via the usage of URL-shortening services, such as bit.ly, and content-hosting services, such as Twitpic and Twitvid, to accommodate multimedia content and longer texts. Tweets have been used for a variety of purposes, ranging from episodic communication of social events, campaigns, emergencies, and natural disasters, to the quotidian airing of personal ideas and questions. Microblogging activities also summoned heightened attention in the spring of 2011 for their role in the uprisings and events in the Arab region. To complement semantic analyses of the micro-blogosphere, our understanding of the so-called "Web 2.0" phenomena, such as Twitter, needs to expand beyond the veracity of "scale free network" structures. Accordingly, it is important to attend to the diversity of Twitter behaviors and emerging discourse to support active online groups and networks, including faith believers and seekers.

Religious seekers and believers today are avidly developing microblogging content and symbols to spur sharing, replicating, and searching of faith-related content online. Faithful microbloggers, or in this case, the "Twitness," have emerged to shape the blogosphere, thereby creating new faith connections and flows. The genesis of Twitter and attendant micro social media practices such as the rise of a "remix culture" (Lessig, 2008) raises some crucial questions about the ontological nature of faith communities and their operational mission to spread their beliefs. How is microblogging adopted for religious communication in peoples' everyday lives? To what extent are social media used to promote faith beliefs and missions? As digital media become pervasive in light of multi-media convergence (Jenkins, 2006), what are the ways in which religious networking, blogging, and microblogging practices interact on digital platforms?

This chapter examines the ways in which Twitter is appropriated to develop innovative and interactive forms of online communication, and discusses some of the implications as well as constraints of these new socio-technical practices for religious community building. Congruent with my digital media experiences, this chapter represents a development of my thoughts on digital religion and microblogging, first articulated in 2009 on a series of blogs on *Religion Dispatches,* a daily online magazine dedicated to the analysis and understanding of religious forces in the world today (www.religiondispatches.org/authors/paulinecheong/). By analyzing emerging faith-oriented tweets and the attendant retweet practices, we can gain a sense of Twitter affordances and the activities that inform, reflect, or perhaps even alter and broaden the notion of religious social capital building.

In an earlier publication, I examined blogging practices via a multipronged research process involving 800 blog post content analyses, mapping more than 15,000 hyperlinks, and conducting interviews with 46 religious bloggers. Together with my co-authors, I argued that blogging as a religious practice is an interaction of the personal and communal, banal and sacred, as religious bloggers chronicle how they experience faith in their daily lives. By linking to other believers, fellow bloggers, and digital resources online, outside the realm of the conventional nuclear church, such as mainstream news sites, other non-religious blogs, and collaborative knowledge networks such as Wikipedia, religious-oriented bloggers form connections, relationships, and networks across the websphere (Cheong, Halavis, & Kwon, 2008). Here, I propose that tweeting can serve as various forms of "microblogging rituals" (Cheong, 2010) to help us understand how dimensions of "bonding social capital" are built and maintained within religious communities (Cheong & Poon, 2008) as well as faith-oriented interactants on social networks. The creation and circulation of microblogging rituals, including "faith memes," functions to constitute and fuel the stream of lived sacred experiences, thereby ideologically connecting Twitter believers in real time. Moreover, microblogging rituals also help us to critically comprehend the construction of religious authority and the growth of religious groups as they build distinctive "faith brands" (Cooke, 2008) to publicize their mission and promote loyalty to particular church leadership and organizations.

This chapter proceeds with an examination of several microblogging rituals. First, I examine how Twitter is utilized for viral dissemination to spur evangelization and mobilization of believers across mediated platforms. Next, I discuss how Twitter is appropriated for mobile prayer and mediation, and note how religious organizations have co-opted microblogging to build their brand communities. I conclude this chapter with a discussion of the potentially darker sides of microblogging rituals and the implications of Twitter for the mediatization of religion, with an elaboration on future areas of research in religiously oriented social media networking.

Faith Memes: Retweeting and Spreading the Faith

Given the burgeoning and increasingly diverse user base, one likely vision for Twitter is to be a micro-sharing and mobilization platform for religious communities. Users can group tweets together by topic or type by use of hashtags—words or phrases prefixed with a "#" sign. One can also repost a message from another and share it with one's own followers by using the "RT" retweet function in the message. This open and free message spreading or "retweeting" mechanism can help build memes or replications that spread and enlarge informational networks. A meme can be an idea, catchphrase, instruction, behavior, or story, for which cultural dissemination generates virus-like imitations and reproductions (Blackmore, 1999). For instance, a popular digital meme on Facebook, called "25 things," asks members of the social network to post 25 facts about themselves and to "tag" 25 other people to ask them to do the same thing.

A contemporary development in what Henry Jenkins (2006) dubbed "media convergence" points to the "transmediation" of stories or narratives where they are created, remediated (Bolter & Grusin, 2003), and disseminated across multiple media platforms. With the proliferation of web-based and mobile communication devices, the production and dissemination of viral email, instant messaging, and now religious-related tweets may function as memes to accelerate the speed and intensity of religious message spread and traction.

To this point, multiple faith memes have been developed to raise awareness and to, literally, spread the word about Christianity. One of the first and most popular memes is entitled "Twitter of Faith." In the Twitter of Faith Challenge, one is to write a statement of faith in 140 words and pass it forward:

> What do you believe? You have 140 characters-
> give us your statement of faith in 140 characters. #TOF.

This meme was created on November 22, 2008, when Minister Adam Walker Cleaveland was tasked with composing his statement of faith for his ordination, and his friend Shawn Coons challenged him to condense his beliefs into 140 characters (http://pomomusings.com/2008/11/22/twitter-of-faith/). Subsequently, Minister Cleaveland urged his Twitter friends and followers to respond by composing their own TOF and to add the hash tag #TOF to permit identification and categorization of this tweet. Interestingly, the "Twitter" brand icon was also appropriated to form the accompanying "Twitter of Faith" graphic meme, by inserting the word "faith" capitalized in large yellow font, under the blue Twitter icon.

Within days, multiple #TOF tweets were sent in response through the creation of this viral thread. Many were declarations of faith and summaries of theological truths into punchy, memorable phrases:

> sirmikelittle: #TOF "Life is art. Get to know the Artist."
>
> mattkelley468: #TOF Jesus Christ is the invasion of the infinite into the finite, allowing we who are finite to experience the fullness of God's being.
>
> david_a_zimmerm: One God in three persons created creation and actively pursues its redemption. Redeemed people love God and one another and life itself. #TOF
>
> MattEB: #tof Saved by faith in Christ. Jesus died for my sins. Jesus lives.
>
> ktday: #TOF God was, is, and shall be with us always, and loves us ridiculously. We are called to love one another likewise.

Various other tweets were condensations inspired by verses from the Bible, as in the following cases, from the New Testament book of First Corinthians and the Old Testament book of Micah, respectively:

Josielle: #TOF And now these three remain: faith, hope and love. But the greatest of these is love.

fritzg: Do justice, love mercy and walk humbly with God. #TOF

To further spread the meme, besides composing and sharing their own #TOF, tweeps were also asked to retweet and propagate this "cool social experiment" on multiple social media platforms.

Please post about this on your blog (with a link back to this post here), *feel free to use the above image as well, and Twitter about it or put it on your Facebook.* While some have suggested that this is in fact a sneaky plot to help me with my Statement of Faith—*it could be interpreted in a cool social experiment in sharing your faith with the Twitter world. (website address, italics, mine).*

As with mutating chain letters, the (re)circulation of faith tweets may be conceived of as viral media codes, with the ability to influence a society's agenda with real effects. In this way, microblogging represents a specious portal for thinking about religion, media, and culture. Faith memes introduce religious believers into an emerging form of participatory culture where they are appraised as fellow participants in mediated content creation and are called upon to propagate their beliefs to their networks online. In light of the potential of new media to support digital storytelling among lay publics (Lessig, 2008), creation of digital content now implicates new hybrid groups of producers and consumers or "produsers" (Bruns, 2008). Faith tweets and retweets by religious produsers facilitate the potential agency and channels of everyday lay persons in communicating about religion to new and imagined audiences, and to quick spread faith narratives online.

For instance, to accelerate the transmediation of the #TOF, Presbyterian minister and blogger John Shuck wrote about contemporary proselytization, and praised the progress of the gospel spread via short messages such as tweets. He said: "I think that should be the rule for new statements of faith. If you can't say it in 140 characters, you are way too into words" (http://www.shuckandjive.org/2008/11/twitter-of-faith.html). He then urged fellow believers to circulate faith tweets. "If you want to know how to post yours and get on the Twitter Train, Adam has a ticket." In another case, the #TOF story was further spread by fellow bloggers such as Neal Locke, who retold the origin of the TOF story online on his blog:

Legend has it that one afternoon on November 22nd, Presbymergent founder and about-to-be-ordained-minister Adam Walker Cleaveland was trying to come up with a statement of faith for his Ordination service. So he did the usual thing any 20-something uber geek would do . . . he asked his twitter friends how long a statement of faith should be? After many responses of the usual sort (one page, two page, red page, blue page) fellow presby-geek (and World of Warcraft guru) Shawn Coons tweeted back: "instead of a statement of faith, how about a twitter of faith? Anyone else up to the challenge?" And so it began. . . .

(http://presbymergent.org/2008/11/22/twitter-of-faith/)

As illustrative of the remix culture whereby online participants edit and mash digital content, blogger Locke further clarified the mission at hand, and encouraged other bloggers in his online network to leverage Twitter architecture to enable their faith messages to go viral:

Here's the challenge:

1. If you're not on twitter yet, click here to see what it's all about and why you should be.
2. If you're on twitter (or just joined), log in and tweet your personal statement of faith . . . in 140 characters or less.
3. Add the hashtag #TOF somewhere in your tweet. That will actually make it 136 characters, but it also makes it easy for us to find and compile all of these statements.
4. Encourage your friends to take the "Twitter of Faith" challenge, too — imagine how cool it would be if this meme spreads, proclaiming the gospel across the internets (well, at least across twitter).

Through bloggers such as Shuck and Locke, online users are prompted to act as cultural agents in the circulation of the #TOF meme. In the first case, Shuck framed his invitation to retweet as a ride on the twitter train, reiterating prior associations between new technology and transportation developments (Carey, 1989). In the second instance, Locke asked his readers to envision cultural change via their online evangelism efforts, to "imagine how cool it would be if this meme spreads, proclaiming the gospel across the internets."

Given the fluid and dynamic nature of digital communication, online interactants appropriate data generated on Twitter, and faith messaging takes on a heightened level of "protean mobility" as messages are replicated, modified, and recycled (Jackson, 2009). Here, a further stage of transmediation was observed when the #TOF meme was widened to online social network sites, in particular to a Facebook account entitled #TOF, linked to its creator Minister Adam's blog, pomomusings blog.

Today, a variety of online tools, such as Twitterfeed (www.twitterfeed.com) and SocialOomph (www.socialoomph.com), can facilitate multi-modal connectivity by automatically feeding and integrating updates across social media platforms, for example, connecting tweets to Facebook and vice versa.

But the above examples also show that the replication of memes does not have to be exact in order to reinforce religious beliefs and spur thought contagion. Human imitation can take on many forms, from copying icons, to retelling stories, to adopting ideas. Indeed, the circulation of short but succinct theological messages has precedents in Church history. Some bloggers have recognized the connections between old and new media as they reframe tweets as "byte-sized theology." For example, according to blogger Valhearle, "Barth's tweet is pretty phenomenal," (http://valharle.wordpress.com/2008/12/02/twitter-of-faith/) referring to Karl Barth, who once summarized complex church dogmatics in this concise, oft-quoted phrase: "Jesus loves me, this I know, for the Bible tells me so."

Hence, in this age of media convergence and digital reproductions, developments in the Twitterverse goad movements on other mediated spaces and facilitate social change. As Jenkins (2006) argued, the innovation and creative mixing of content within dynamic production and reception processes aids the "spreadability of values." Burgess (2008) also wrote, "spreadable media content gains greater resonance in the culture, taking on new meanings, finding new audiences, attracting new markets, and generating new values" (p. 3). Faith memes purposefully instigate conversation about spiritual beliefs, thereby permitting the ideational building of an imagined community among microbloggers, bloggers, and other online social media users. As faith memes spread, fellow Twitter users are ascribed a heightened level of bonding social capital around their common interest in religious texts and spirituality. This is perhaps one of the reasons why sites such as Gospelr (http://gospelr.com), which is a "Twitter-integrated microblogging service for Christians," was developed in 2009 to promote "microblogging-as-ministry," where users can tweet from Gospelr but also through the website reference the Bible and discuss religious materials with others. As such, memeing of textual and aesthetic ideas provides a thread to connect like-minded online evangelists in order to influence and spiritually shape the Twitter system to effect informational spread and social change. The next section discusses how religious organizations attempt to harness microblogging rituals of emerging communities to enrich their organizational reach and loyalty.

Pew and Pixel: Prayer on the Go and Tweeting Faith Brands

As the use of Twitter is highly intertwined with the use of other social media, microblogging could be appropriated for larger scale social support networks to mobilize churches and augment their existing organizational links. Prior research points to the pattern of weaving online and offline religious "bonding social capital" among networked believers who are congregants of established religious organizations (Cheong & Poon, 2008).

In terms of microblogging, multiple evangelical Christian groups are harnessing these coincident messaging flows to strengthen their religious communities via synchronized prayer. Popular faith related hashtags include #twurch (Twitter + church), #prayer, #JIL (Jesus is Lord) and #pray4 (as in, #pray4 my mother, or popularly after the Japanese earthquake in March 2011, #prayforjapan). We are now seeing how some individuals and organizations are setting up prayer feeds on Twitter that feature daily updates of prayer requests and recommendations. Consider the Calvin Institute of Worship's set up of an automated Tweeter feed to "pray the hours." Inspired by the Holy Scripture's injunctions to "pray without ceasing" (1 Thessalonians 5:17), users can sign up to receive hourly prayers sent in verses as brief tweets or view a Tweetgrid (www.tweetgrid.com) with a dashboard of all prayer feeds across different topics to prompt continuous prayer or to help those who are unsure of what words to utter or meditate upon in prayer. In this way, contemporary believers may reinvent the century-old practice of praying set prayers from the Bible, hymns, and devotionals. They can match prayer rhythms with fellow believers at designated times of the day. This brings to mind the Pentecostal religious practice of "prayer chains," where lay followers are charged to pray for particular persons, or on particular topics, during set hours and for the same length of time.

In addition, regular online updates or prayer and praise tweet requests can reverberate and contribute to deeper dialogues and a more widespread consciousness of faith (Sanderson & Cheong, 2009). Twitter can serve as a form of "lifelogging" as interactants self-disclose their lived-in moments (Jackson, 2009). Thus, key to innovative practices within religious communities is what some social commentators are now calling the development of "ambient intimacy," whereby one experiences an enveloping social awareness of one's social network. Parishioners, for example, have been exhorted to use Twitter to spread "a sea of prayer." In this sense, microblogging can help to build a portable church where religious performances and texts are woven into the rhythms and spaces of peoples' everyday lives (Cheong, 2010).

A further development is that churches have recently been exhorted to adopt Twitter to build their church "brand." The vigorous promotion of the so-called Web 2.0 communication tools seems particularly strident among megachurches with more than 2000 people in worship services weekly (Thumma, Travis, & Bird, 2005) and/or religious organizations affiliated with the emergent church growth movement. Given the large, sometimes multi-sited, campuses and the strong growth orientation of these churches, mediated activities expressing "tenets of brand faith" (Cooke, 2008), which include the creation story of the church, icons, and rituals, have been robustly encouraged to help build religious community.

In particular, a recently released e-book has earned endorsement from various prominent church leaders in America. Its nomenclature is a clarion call for Twitter action: *The Reason Your Church Must Twitter,* subtitled *Making Your Ministry Contagious.* According to the author, Anthony Coppedge (2009), a minister and self-professed "technology evangelist," "Twitter allows churches to send quick updates, drive traffic to websites and remind people of events more efficiently than ever." In his text, religious organizations are conveyed "solid reasons" that their church staff should be using Twitter, primarily that "Twitter is a free and simple way to connect churches to the cell phones of their congregants, volunteers and staff." According to Coppedge (2009), Twitter in churches can be used primarily as a "megaphone" for updates and announcements or as a "conversation" to spur the sharing of ideas and prayer exchange, illustrating the potential utility of Twitter for building deeper relationships among its congregants.

Hence, on the institutional level, tweeting religious texts is posited to affirm religious community-building, yet particular outcomes depend on if and how these tweets are integrated into the fabric of religious bodies. For instance, a number of churches have incorporated Twitter during their services, where congregational members' tweets may appear as scrolling virtual messages on sanctuary screens. In other churches, tweets are used primarily by leaders to strengthen affiliations and to convert the weak ties that some seekers have developed online to real-life interpersonal attachments, specifically church attendance and participation. For example, in several organizations, religious leaders have urged readers who are inspired by their tweets to listen to their sermons online, to attend church events, and to visit their churches.

Indeed, it is interesting to witness the rise of "holy mavericks," or a cadre of media-savvy religious leaders (Lee & Sinitiere, 2009). Increasingly, these leaders are using microblogs alongside a wide spectrum of older and newer digital media to discursively construct their authority and augment their church's influence (Cheong, 2011). One prominent exemplar of multimodal religious communication is Pastor Rick Warren, the founder of one of the largest churches in America. Besides having millions of bestselling books, and coverage in broadcast television and radio platforms, Rick Warren also composes a weekly electronic newsletter. He maintains a Facebook page and a Twitter account with hundreds of thousands of followers; in May 2011, tweets were sent to more than 310,000 followers (http://twitter.com/#!/RickWarren). He microblogs frequently, and it is not uncommon to see him send several tweets a day. His microblogs have comprised encouraging or uplifting sayings, advertisements of his speaking engagements, prayer requests, endorsements of the publications he has read, and church event reminders. Recently, some of his tweets have been composed in a variety of languages (such as Spanish, Chinese, Korean, and Arabic) and addressed to pastors in his worldwide network of pastor mentees in 195 countries (called the Purpose Driven Pastors Network). Several of his tweets can also be considered faith memes as they are catchy, provocative phrases that have been quickly circulated and retweeted. For example, the tweets below were retweeted more than a hundred times:

> RT @RickWarren: Have you noticed that everyone who favors abortion is alive? (4:06pm, Dec 6th, 2010)

> RT @RickWarren: If people have to earn your love, then you dont really love them. (11:15pm, Mar 19th, 2011)

> RT @ RickWarren: If you prayed instead of worrying, you'd have a lot less to worry about. (4:14pm, March 24th, 2011)

Furthermore, religious organizations can use Twitter to re-enact historical religious events. Followers receive tweets in real time as appointed users perform as "characters" of a particular historical event and communicate from their perspective what is happening. These re-enactments can help initiate reflection related to these historical events, and encourage fresh attention and inject media interest into traditional practices and religious holidays, such as the observation of Lent, Good Friday, and Easter. For example, Wall Street's Trinity Church in New York employed microblogging to re-create Christ's final hours in a Twitter enactment of the Passion Play (http://twitter.com/twspassionplay) on Good Friday, 2009. Over a period of three hours, followers of twspassionplay received frequent updates of 140 characters or less from the main characters: Mary, Joseph, a serving girl, Peter, Pontius Pilate, and, of course, Jesus, whose tweets included: "Let the scriptures be fulfilled," "It is as the prophets wrote," "I am who you say I am," and "it is as the prophets have written: I tell my tale of misery while they look on and gloat."

The church described "what may be the world's first Passion play performed through . . . Twitter," as a "unique Passion Play that marries this timeless Christian tradition with the latest in social networking trends." Comments on the site mostly raved about this new use of microblogging. One follower wrote that it was a "moving experience," while another wrote: "really good and really immediate—never had Passion story so much a part of real life before." Some comments even praised the development of digital technologies itself, for example, one wrote: ". . . I have to say I am proud of technology today."

In this way, twittering the Passion Play represents one more facet of microblogging rituals: dramatization expressed via the tools and symbols of online technologies. But not just a virtual phenomenon, Twitter drama can be utilized to strengthen online and offline religious community-building, as geographically close or dispersed followers connect and participate in experiencing the Passion and the recreation of familiar biblical stories. In the case of Trinity Church, the tweeted Passion Play was part of the larger church programming for Easter, which included both online and face-to-face meetings. Visitors to the church's website were notified of the church's multiple religious service times but were also invited to explore an online "Stations of the Cross," where they could interactively click on a mosaic of black and white photos of a recent staging of the Stations of the Cross in Manhattan to reveal scriptural passages, prayers, and meditative music. In this way, user interactivity is elevated to another level online, with enhanced visual and sensory appeals. Media spectacle here is presented as a web version of the Stations of the Cross, and believers are urged to click and "pray as you go" online.

Communicating, codifying, and commodifying religious experiences is key to faith branding. This is because religious organizations cannot market God, which is a belief, but they can market epiphany as an immediate product (Twitchell, 2007). Hence, contingent on actual Twitter content and the continuity of "social presence" generated (Stieger & Burger, 2009). Microblogs can ultimately extend and enrich bonding social capital within the context of established ecumenical relationships and prayer, Bible study, and support groups in the church to strengthen bonds between followers and devotion to these organizations. For several religious organizations, microblogs are valued within larger and integrated efforts to evangelize, build brand recognition, and achieve church growth targets.

Conclusion: Twitter Tensions and Future Research Considerations

According to Hjarvard (2008), the mediatization of culture and society is effected by a form of "media logic" as the media becomes progressively entrenched within organizing processes of key institutions, including the church, which in turn is, to an increasing degree, dependent on the media. Here, I suggest that tweets play a constitutive role in religion, as microbloggers produce and circulate scripture and its interpretations as well as create new religious practices, including Twitter memes, prayers, and drama. In this way, microblogging practices enabled on Twitter on a variety of mobile platforms can be understood as microblogging rituals, as they facilitate epiphany and a sense of the sacred, which in turn revitalizes communal sentiments and a higher moral purpose through identification and solidarity with other believers. Perhaps a more direct form of mediatization is observed when proselytisation is now performed through interaction with Twitter, blogs, and online social networking sites with others already plugged into existing online networks. Indirect mediatization may be observed in the longer term when Twitter facilitates changes in what it means to experience and build community, aside from, and within, established religious organizations.

These days, rituals are often enacted in and through the media sphere. Indeed, some religious institutions are modifying their operational rules and allocating more resources to the creation of digital communiqués and activities. As discussed above, churches are urged to use microblogs as a megaphone to publicize church events and to galvanize the support of seekers and volunteers. Other organizations are developing new rules of procedure for prayer requests via mobile and "pray as you click" interactive links on church websites and Facebook pages. In this aspect, twitter prayer reflects how the emerging digital media is being promoted as the "religious new normal," dovetailing into the rhythms of peoples' everyday lives and (re)structuring the temporal conditions and sensorium of daily spiritual experiences (Cheong, 2010).

In the transmediation of faith messages across multiple Web 2.0 platforms, this chapter discussed how tweeting and retweeting content of spiritual interest takes up the ancient evangelism and proselytism mandate in innovative ways. With digital mash-up capabilities and online social networking platforms, religious believers can now participate in the creation of their own stories and symbols of piety, as well as sharing faith memes with enlarged new and imagined audiences. The reach of religious microblogging is theoretically far, and wide-ranging. As boyd et al. (2009) noted:

> Though twitter users can access a list of who follows them, this is not necessarily their actual audience. As such, participants must contend with an imagined audience, just as they do when using other social media. This is further complicated when people must account for the overlap in their followers and that of those who they follow. (p. 7)

Therefore, depending on the size of the audience and the robustness of transmediation, the longevity of faith memes may reinforce religious tenets and offer fresh publicity to revered scriptures for the spread of religious worldviews.

While it may be unfeasible to comprehensively account for the traction of faith-oriented microblogs, future research can investigate the offline conditions of what supports religious ideological spread across social media. These investigations include an examination of the motivation of online users and their identity as produsers. How do religious leaders and believers use multiple modes of media for meme transmission? Do they view these activities as their religious duty or as acts of altruism? Are there strong incentives to participate in viral games? In addition, since memes, like viruses, require a host culture to allow mutual interaction and proliferation, what are the cultural contexts that favor the growth and reinforcement of faith-related memetic structures?

As this chapter focuses on data from the North American context, future research should engage in comparative international research to examine the implications of microblogs in other cultures and contexts, with different adoption rates of social media use. For example, future research could investigate the development and circulation of religiously related tweets in contexts where government regulations have tightened control on traditional media. It would also be interesting to find out what sorts of microblogging clones or imitators emerge in contexts, for example in China, where censorship has already been exercised by blocking Twitter.

In the longer term, it would also be interesting to observe the consequences of the use of microblogs and social media on extant church practices. Do more pastors refer to online content, including incorporating tweets in their sermons? Are church services becoming more interactive? Are sermons getting shorter, given the allegedly truncated attention span of today's social media users? If the above outcomes transpire, one could perhaps consider these as vibrant signs of mediatization.

Finally, although the potential for Web 2.0 media to build religious community has been predominantly described as helpful and positive in earlier sections of this paper, I acknowledge that building social capital has its dark side as well. Microblogging rituals may have negative implications for religious groups and organizations as it can lead to the weakening or perversion of existing relational links.

For instance, it is striking to note the promise of utopic revolution behind Twitter's recent promotion as "more than a new techno-fad- it is a near-instant, almost anywhere communication that has the potential to change the face of ministry" (Coppedge, 2009). As with prior celebratory discourse accompanying communication technologies, more grounded investigation is needed to comprehensively assess the ways and extent to which microblogging is adopted by local houses of worship, and to what ends. How do religious leaders balance social media chatter (alongside potential narcissistic self promotion) with the need for quiet reflection and rest that spirituality entails? Are there new rules and compromises for church leadership as they manage the integration of Twitter into existing organizational practices? How do pastors draw the line between the personal and professional in their tweets? Future research could also examine the intended as well as unintended consequences for churches seeking to expand their missionary charge through faith branding and the embrace of microblogging to promote organizational growth.

Moreover, microblogging can contribute to internet radicalization of a more malevolent kind, where we see communication between extremist networked believers who tweet to spread radical views or instigate militant interpretations of faith. In light of media convergence, microblogging and blogging may accelerate Web 2.0 "cyber-herding" and an echo chamber of effect (Sunstein, 2002) among fundamentalist religious ideologues. A recent case in point is the adoption of Twitter by Islamic extremists, the Taliban of

Afghanistan, who sent their first tweet in English on May 12, 2011, about an enemy attack. Their stories are also accompanied by the Facebook Share button, which illustrates their growing presence on social media (Abell, 2011).

Alternative readings of Twitter dramatic enactments also bring up critical thoughts about online faith consumption and rejuvenate concerns about the individualistic character of online spirituality. Vincent Miller, in *Consuming Religion* (2005), discussed how the commodification of religion and the celebrity spectacle supported by mass media, including privatized faith consumption, may both benefit and deform Christianity. Although he seldom referenced the specific role of the internet in creating religious spectacles, we can infer that the ability of religious organizations to attract digital media attention may be beneficial for community growth in the short run. However, it is unknown if the virtual fulfillment of religious sentiments may disorient and blur lines between lived religion and representations of the real. In this vein, concerns about Twitter enactments as online media spectacles revolve around new aesthetics that might abstract original elements of sacred narratives by diluting them into brief, perhaps less meaningful, retweeted messages. Microblogging consequently may serve as a symbolic good that bloggers shallowly use to replace local and sustained communal mediation of religious traditions. More generally, the collective concern is that connections to short texts such as tweets may come to represent an increasingly passive and trivial form of religious info-tainment—in mini byte-sized portions of 140 characters or less.

To be sure, narratives have historically been powerful to satiate human urges for meaning, security, and belonging. Today, the communal nature of religions and the intense need for communication endures, as online storytelling via Twitter takes on novel applications. Microblogging rituals as a recent genre of online communication represents fertile ground for religious community building and provides fascinating new ways to (t)witness the relationships between religion and culture, the empyrean and everyday.

References

Abell, J. C. (2011) Forget Osama's diary: Taliban now tweeting in English. *Wired*. Retrieved from http://www.wired.com/epicenter/2011/05/taliban-tweeting-in-english/

Blackmore, S. J. (1999). *The meme machine*. Oxford, England: Oxford University Press.

Bolter, J. D., & Grusin, R. (2003). *Remediation: Understanding new media*. Cambridge, MA: MIT Press.

boyd, d., Golder, S., & Lotan, G. (2010). Tweet tweet retweet: Conversational aspects of retweeting on Twitter. *Proceedings of the Annual Hawaii International Conference on System Sciences,* Kauai, HI, USA. doi: 10.1109/HICSS.2010.412

Bruns, A. (2008). *Blogs, Wikipedia, Second Life, and beyond: From production to produsage.* New York, NY: Peter Lang.

Burgess, J (2008). "All your chocolate rain are belong to us?" Viral video, YouTube and the dynamics of participatory culture. In G. Lovink & S. Niederer (Eds.), *Video vortex reader: Responses to YouTube* (pp. 101–109). Amsterdam, the Netherlands: Institute of Network Cultures.

Carey, J. W. (1989). *Communication as culture: Essays on media and society.* New York, NY: Routledge.

Cheong, P. H. (2010). Faith tweets: Ambient religious communication and microblogging rituals. *M/C Journal: A Journal of Media and Culture, 13*(2). Retrieved from http://journal.media-culture.org.au/index.php/mcjournal/article/viewArticle/223

Cheong, P.H. (2011). Religious Leaders, Mediated Authority and Social Change. *Journal of Applied Communication Research, 39*(4), 452–454.

Cheong, P. H., Halavis, A., & Kwon, K. (2008). The chronicles of me: Understanding blogging as a religious practice. *Journal of Media and Religion, 7*(3), 107–131.

Cheong, P. H., & Poon, J. P. H. (2008). WWW.Faith.Org: (Re)structuring communication and social capital building among religious organizations. *Information, Communication & Society, 11*(1), 89–110.

Cleaveland, A. W. (2008, November 22). Twitter of faith [Blog post]. Retrieved from http://pomomusings.com/2008/11/22/twitter-of-faith/

Cooke, P. (2008). *Branding faith: Why some churches and nonprofits impact culture and others don't.* Ventura, CA: Regal.

Coppedge, A. (2009, January 5). The reason your church must Twitter [Blog post]. Retrieved from http://www.twitterforchurches.com/

Fox, S., Zickuhr, K., & Smith, A. (2009, October 21). Twitter and status updating, fall 2009. Retrieved from http://www.pewinternet.org/Reports/2009/17-Twitter-and-Status-Updating-Fall-2009.aspx

Hjarvard, S. (2008). The mediatization of society: A theory of the media as agents of social and cultural change. *Nordicom Review, 29*(2), 105–134.

Jackson, M. H. (2009). The mash-up: A new archetype for communication. *Journal of Computer-Mediated Communication, 14*(3), 730–734.

Jenkins, H. (2006). *Convergence culture: Where old and new media collide.* New York, NY: New York University Press.

Lee, S., & Sinitiere, P. (2009). *Holy mavericks: Evangelical innovators and the spiritual marketplace.* New York, NY: New York University Press.

Lessig, L. (2008). *Remix: Making art and commerce thrive in the hybrid economy.* New York, NY: Penguin Group.

Locke, N. (2008, November 22). Twitter of faith [Blog post]. Retrieved from http://presbymergent.org/2008/11/22/twitter-of-faith/

Miller, V. J. (2005). *Consuming religion: Christian faith and practice in a consumer culture.* New York, NY: Continuum.

Sanderson, J., & Cheong, P. H. (2010). Tweeting prayers and communicating grief over Michael Jackson online. *Bulletin of Science, Technology, & Society, 30*(5), 328–340.

Shuck, J. (2008, November 23). Twitter of faith [Blog post]. Retrieved from http://www.shuckandjive.org/2008/11/twitter-of-faith.html

Smith, A., & Rainie, L. (2010). 8% of online Americans use Twitter. Retrieved from http://www.pewinternet.org/~/media//Files/Reports/2010/PIP-Twitter-Update-2010.pdf

Stieger, S., & Burger, C. (2009). Let's go formative: Continuous student ratings with Web 2.0 application Twitter. *Cyber Psychology, Behavior, and Social Networking*, 13(2), 163–167.

Sunstein, C. (2002). *Republic.com* 2.0. Princeton, NJ: Princeton University Press.

Thumma, S., Travis, D., & Bird, W. (2005). Megachurches today 2005. Retrieved from http://hirr.hartsem.edu/megachurch/megastoday2005_summaryreport.html

Twitchell, J. B. (2007). *Shopping for God: How Christianity went from in your heart to in your face*. New York: Simon & Schuster.

Twitter your prayer says Cardinal. (2009, April 27). Retrieved from http://news.bbc.co.uk/go/pr/fr/-/2/hi/uk_news/northern_ireland/8020285.stm

twspassionplay. (2009, April 10). Twittering the story of Christ's final hours from 12 pm to 3 pm on Good Friday 2009 [Twitter feed]. Retrieved from http://twitter.com/#!/twspassionplay

12. Creating Church Online: Networks and Collectives in Contemporary Christianity

TIM HUTCHINGS

Introduction

Online churches are internet-based Christian communities using a wide range of digital media to conduct worship, prayer, religious education, discussion, proselytism, and friendship. The first examples emerged in the 1980s (Burke et al., 1999), and several hundred are active today (Hutchings, 2010a, pp. 14, 23, 28). Online churches have attracted attention from journalists (Feder, 2004), Christian theologians (Estes 2009), and academics (Schroeder, Heather, & Lee 1998; Miczek, 2008), but these treatments have been brief and largely impressionistic. Previous discussions have tended to view these groups as self-contained online entities, ignoring the relevance of offline connections and practices. This article seeks to offer a more detailed, contextual interpretation of the development and significance of online church activity, based on sustained ethnographic studies of five of the best-known examples.

Existing academic research into online churches has focused on three central themes: online ritual, the transformation of religious authority, and the impact of the internet on local church attendance. Observers of ritual from Schroeder et al. (1998) onward have consistently reported that online rituals closely replicate offline forms, and have suggested a range of pragmatic motives for this trend (see below, "The Familiar and the Local"). Studies of authority have been more diverse, shifting from the common early assumption that digital media would undermine religious hierarchy (Helland, 2000) to a more nuanced understanding of the ways in which authority figures and institutions adapt new media to support and enhance their influence

(Campbell, 2010). Studies of local church attendance reported varied findings, including implausible predictions of a mass exodus from the pews (Barna, 1998), but scholarly consensus soon emerged around the observation that online activity supplements the local rather than displacing it (Campbell, 2005).

This chapter seeks to explore these issues in much greater depth, on the basis of long-term participant observation and more than 100 interviews with leaders and participants. I focus attention on three key areas of interest in particular: the interplay of sociological, theological, and technological factors in shaping group development; the prevalence of familiar elements in visual, liturgical, and organisational design; and the location of these groups within wider collectives and networks at both an institutional and an individual level. I referred to "online churches" as "communities" in the first line of this chapter, reflecting both the self-understanding of interviewees and my own perception of these groups as bounded entities with distinctive cultures and a strong sense of belonging, but this is not the only perspective from which they may be approached. Each church also operates within a larger field of practice, connection, and discourse, and—from an individual perspective—as one point of contact in the religious lives of visitors. Greater understanding of these two issues of interplay and location offers a helpful foundation for future research into the social and religious significance of these online groups and practices.

Methods

This article focuses on five specific online churches: Church of Fools,[1] i-church,[2] St Pixels,[3] the Anglican Cathedral of Second Life (referred to hereafter as "the Cathedral"),[4] and Life Church.tv's Church Online ("Church Online").[5] The first two were launched in 2004 and the remainder in 2006; Church of Fools operated for only four months, and was later relaunched as St Pixels, but the other four remain active today. These five groups have selected diverse media platforms and reflect a range of different religious traditions, but each has generated a stable and committed core community of participants and pursues at least some of the same range of practices. This diversity offers an opportunity to assess the significance of theology, media, and offline context for group development, while the relative success of each group at attracting participants highlights the degree to which these churches represent the emergence of lasting and significant practices.

The five groups selected cover a wide variety of media platforms and channels. Church Online operates a video-sharing website, i-church and St Pixels use discussion forums, and Church of Fools, the Cathedral, and Church Online use three-dimensional graphical virtual worlds. Church Online and the Cathedral maintain an official church blog, while St Pixels and i-church host personal blogs for all members. All five use text chat. Facebook is used unofficially by members of the four surviving groups, and has been adopted for official communication and proselytism by Church Online. LifeChurch.tv also operates a range of other websites and a YouTube channel. Each community has organised face-to-face gatherings, and St Pixels in particular has pursued this intensively as a core aspect of group identity.

These churches also reflect diverse forms of sponsorship and oversight. Church of Fools received a grant from the Methodist Council, but operated as an independent, non-denominational worship and conversation space. The Anglican Cathedral of Second Life was launched by a group of lay Christians with no official approval, but the current leadership team is negotiating with an English bishop and his advisers to forge closer ties with the Anglican Communion. i-church is part of the Church of England's Oxford Diocese, led by a web pastor reporting to a Board of Trustees. Church Online is part of LifeChurch.tv, a megachurch based in Oklahoma that operates more than a dozen campuses across the United States, and streams videos of LifeChurch music and sermons.

Ethnography offers a well-established set of methods for charting the culture, practices, and perceptions of a social group, and has regularly and successfully been applied to the study of online activity (Hine, 2000). My own interest in the development of forms and practices in online churches is ideally suited to this approach, which stresses long-term participation and the recording of participants' own perspectives. None of these five groups is bounded by a single field site, however, and my research required a form of 'multi-sited ethnography.' This research model was developed for the study of global cultural formations, and is ideally suited for the complexity of new media. The researcher constructs the object of study by tracing relationships between different regions of activity, discovering relevant areas and connections by following the circulation of people, ideas, or objects. Participants in online churches might focus on one primary interaction space, such as a church website, but understanding of their commitments and practices required exploration of the multiple, often unofficial connections they were also constructing through a wide range of other media.

Multi-sited ethnography encourages the researcher to adapt methods for each new context, without demanding consistent richness or reliability of data. As George Marcus (1995) explained, "multi-sited ethnographies are invariably the product of knowledge bases of varying intensities and qualities," and each location requires "different practices and opportunities" (p. 100). My own research draws on face-to-face, chatroom, email, and telephone interviews, online and offline observations, media reports, publications by participants, and data from the churches' own surveys. This diversity requires careful attention to the strengths and weaknesses of each source, particularly when engaging in comparative analysis, but was a necessary response to the distinctive challenges and opportunities offered by each medium, platform, and social group.

My research was conducted openly, with full disclosure of my identity and intentions in the format best suited to each group. I began by contacting leaders privately to secure their approval, and then announced my presence to the congregation using my Second Life profile, church blog, chat room conversations, or a forum thread. This policy proved most difficult at Church Online, where no permanent interaction spaces were available. A chat room opened during services, but attendance fluctuated greatly and I rarely encountered the same participants more than once. Church volunteers did reappear regularly, however, so I built rapport with those I met and asked them to recommend individuals I could interview. I supplemented this snowball strategy by introducing myself to fellowship groups and making very occasional approaches in the chat room if individuals' stories seemed particularly valuable. Outside interviews, I distinguished public from private interaction spaces—negotiating this decision with participants—and sought permission from authors before quoting any "private" postings. Interviewees signed consent forms, and are referred to by pseudonyms in the discussions below. I have identified all five churches and—where applicable—their pastors, because each has already been identified repeatedly in media coverage.

Making Sense of Online Churches: Social, Technological, and Theological Factors in Group Development

One important variation between the five groups is the size of their congregations, and this apparently straightforward feature offers a useful introduction to the complex dynamics at work in group development. Group size emerges from a complex interplay of factors, a point observed by Quentin Jones (1997). According to Jones, "various features of CMC-tools will be prerequisites for the stable existence of certain social structures in cyber-space," particularly their capacity to sort, filter, and process messages. Online community and ritual are constrained not only by technological factors such as lag, but also by the need for each participant to make sense of what is happening, and "an overabundance of messages may in theory . . . lead to a virtual settlement's destruction."

Technological prerequisites and limiting factors function in relationship with other pressures, including theological commitments, to generate social forms. In i-church and St Pixels, for example, a highly participatory worship style has emerged in which those present contribute their own responses, prayers, and thoughts. This style reflects a theological commitment to dialogue rather than hierarchical teaching, as expressed in St Pixels' statement of faith: "We aim to create sacred space on the internet where we can seek God together, enjoy each other's company, and reflect God's love for the world" (Acorn, 2010). This focus on participation creates a challenge. Both groups use text chat rooms, and conversations with more than a handful of participants become increasingly unintelligible. St Pixels' members with technical skills created a new chat room in 2006 to overcome this problem. "St Pixels LIVE," relaunched in 2010 as "Expressions," offers a range of behind-the-scenes tools to enable the leader to upload images, audio files, and texts. Different sections of the chat room separate these words and images from those of the congregation, helping viewers make sense of the event. This separation of leader from congregation proved controversial, perceived by some as a reintroduction of clericalism, but it made it possible for much larger groups to participate in services. Following the introduction of the new software, average service attendance rose to 30 or more.

Congregation size is also affected by the interplay of theology and technology, a relationship demonstrated particularly clearly in the history of i-church. The Diocese of Oxford initially envisaged i-church as a small, Oxford-based community of highly committed participants following Benedictine monastic teachings (Thomas, 2004), and was shocked when many hundreds of applicants registered to join from all over the world. Rather than abandon their original vision, the diocese restricted membership to a small core group and tried to preserve an emphasis on intimate fellowship through the creation of small "Pastoral Groups" with authorized leaders. An early newsletter (Leslie, 2004) shows the tensions that emerged around this decision. "It is not going to be easy to get the balance on this one," the pastor wrote. "SO many members are eager to get started—yet we want to move at a pace that allows the groups adequate resources, time for learning and access to technical support in the early stages of their development." Some members had even asked her to "slow things down." This caution still prevailed in 2005, as shown by a forum post by the second web pastor (not publicly available):

> It's really important we grow, but at a rate that lets us remain a community where we know one another. . . . I still think it's important we don't overextend ourselves. So I am very wary of doing interviews with the BBC, or posting articles to very popular websites—we're still not in a position to respond to the demand that might create.

We see here an example of software restrictions and intentional practices set in place to preserve a particular theological understanding of community that might appear contrary to widespread norms of internet activity, emphasising stability, commitment, and accountability over fluidity, transience, and individual control.

Church Online shows a quite different understanding of ideal size, spiritual experience, and authentic community, rooted once again in theology and expressed through media design and media practice. Rather than limit membership, Church Online seeks to maximise the impact of its video messages by leveraging the social networks of its congregation—pre-scripted invitations can be posted to Facebook, MySpace, or Twitter at the touch of a button—and by investing in advertising. Google AdWords have been purchased, linking the church website to pornographic search terms. This strategy was highlighted in a sermon in August 2009, received with laughter and cheering by the local and online audience (Groeschel, 2009). According to one email testimony cited, a man who described himself as "lost" was "looking at some girls dancing on YouTube and about to go to a porn site when your ad popped up. I never made it to that other site because I was drawn to LifeChurch instead. I know God was drawing me. Thank you."

This account illustrates a key feature of Church Online that sets it apart from the other four groups. Where St Pixels finds sacred space in company, LifeChurch.tv believes that God works by drawing strangers to events where their lives are changed through exposure to preaching. This is an over-simplification, of course—LifeChurch also encourages participants to join small online "LifeGroups," and to connect to a private chat channel to pray with volunteers—but the different ideas of community and spiritual experience represented here are striking. Christina, an Austrian woman, explained that "I enjoy the community of people [at LifeChurch] who are my age," emphasising the importance of knowing that other people were there with her in the online space, but like many of my interviewees she also explained that "I haven't started to make friends there, and it isn't important to me." Some interviewees even claimed that real friendships could not be found online at all.

Once again, this social form emerges from a combination of technological, theological, and social factors. Interaction between visitors at Church Online is possible only through a chat room that is closed after services, and sustained conversation was actively discouraged during my time of research in 2008 and 2009. On one occasion, for example, a visitor who described himself as an atheist asked a question about the Dead Sea Scrolls. The web pastor quickly intervened, explaining that "this is not the place. . . . This chat is built around this video message to the left. It is to help us engage further with the content there." Another visitor agreed, explaining that "it's really to keep on track with the teaching going on." Both then proposed their email address and Twitter feeds as ways for the atheist visitor to continue the conversation in private. These comments suggest a definition of community that emphasises shared purpose and vision, participation in a movement toward a shared goal, rather than interpersonal relationships.

The interaction of social, technological, and theological factors I have been describing shows clear parallels with Heidi Campbell's (2010) model of "the religious-social shaping of technology" (RSST). RSST draws attention to four key areas: the history and tradition of the group, particularly its historic attitudes toward media; core beliefs and patterns of life; the process of negotiation through which a medium is evaluated and appropriated, with partial reconstruction or innovation where needed; and the framing of the technology in group discourse (pp. 60–61). All four dimensions are important in online churches. The groups I have studied seek to evaluate digital media in light of their theological commitments to particular styles of leadership, experience, and relationship, and to redesign the structure and use of media to support those commitments, as well as contribute to internal and public discourses about their activity through community discussions, leadership statements, participation in Christian conferences, and mass media interviews.

Tales of hostility were a key part of mass media and participant discourse surrounding Church of Fools at its launch, demonstrating the ongoing negotiation of group image and memory that constitutes the fourth stage of Campbell's model. *The New York Times* (Feder, 2004) was one of many to record the hardships faced by the high-profile preacher who addressed the opening service: "Richard Chartres, Anglican bishop of London, is not used to having congregants wandering around in front of him swearing as he preaches." These apparently negative, comic tales were embraced and popularised by the church's leaders, who saw an opportunity for considerable publicity, and helped generate a wave of media attention that greatly added to the number of visitors the church received (Church of Fools, 2004).

The story of Church of Fools lived on in group discourse for at least two years after the virtual environment closed, retold in detail at all face-to-face gatherings I attended. This version of church history emphasised fun, spiritual experience, encounters with curious non-Christians, encounters with hostile visitors, and the intense work required to defend the church against these invasions. These disruptions were viewed as bittersweet, both affirming the good work of the church and undermining it. According to David, one of my interviewees, "it's nice to get a troll [troublemaker] now and then. . . . I loved talking to people who were not church people."

These accounts demonstrate the value of the RSST model, but also one major weakness. Campbell focused on religious communities, but gave no attention to the processes of resistance and contestation that can occur within those groups. Campbell's stage of "negotiation" is portrayed as an undertaking of group leaders, who evaluate the potential value and danger posed by new media and act accordingly. My study of these online churches demonstrates that the negotiation of technology is not always so straightforward or hierarchical, and may be disputed, resisted, and re-negotiated on many levels. The shape of i-church emerged from many years of more or less harmonious discussion, in which diocese, web pastor, and different camps within the community all disagreed over the best direction to take. The visual design and social boundaries negotiated at the Cathedral of Second Life were bitterly criticised by some of my interviewees, particularly those who found their own creations rejected. Paula described one such deletion as an "exorcism" of a designer who fell from favour with group leaders, and claimed that she herself "felt excluded" by the High Church theology she perceived symbolised in the ornate Gothic architecture of the cathedral itself. Church Online, the most tightly regulated group I studied, also struggled to secure support for the structures favoured by its leaders. Small LifeGroups play an important part in LifeChurch philosophy, and Church Online viewers have regularly been encouraged to join LifeGroups online. According to one group leader, "we don't believe anything really significant happens" without them: "to become fully devoted we have to get *connected*, that's the way God designed it. . . . This is where the real church happens." In fact, only a small minority joins these groups, and several group leaders expressed disappointment at the transient interest of those that do. According to Florence, it was hard "seeing so many people come and go. . . . I just haven't seen the stability in our group that I would like, and which I think would be easier to maintain in an RL ('real life') group." Successful long-term, high-commitment fellowship groups have been created online by Church Online visitors—"they're family," one participant enthused—but they remain rare. In this case, a discourse of commitment and accountability strongly promoted by church leaders has been tacitly rejected by online participants, in favour of more individual, self-determined engagement with the video broadcasts. The evaluation and reconstruction of technology is a complex, ongoing process involving many levels of decision-making and mutual influence, and all four stages of Campbell's RSST model must be reconceptualised to account for this contested diversity.

The Familiar and the Local

The discussion so far has addressed the development of diverse styles and structures of online churches through the interaction of social, technological, and theological factors. One clear example of this kind of interaction is the importance of familiarity, a tendency observed throughout the history of online church scholarship (Schroeder et al., 1998; Miczek, 2008). All five churches have preserved familiar elements of design, ritual, and organisation, taken from the offline Christian traditions they represent. Church of Fools, for example, existed in a virtual world designed to look like the inside of a parish church, while the Cathedral re-created a Gothic edifice in Second Life. Church Online also built its own Second Life island, an exact copy of one of the LifeChurch campuses in Oklahoma. Each of the five churches developed a worship style that closely paralleled the offline practices of that theological tradition—rock music and half-hour sermons at LifeChurch, prayers, readings, and set responses for the other four. The Cathedral adapted Anglican liturgies of Evensong and Compline, handing out virtual service sheets to visitors. Leadership patterns also tend to follow familiar lines: i-church is led by a web pastor as part of an Anglican diocese, the Cathedral is attempting to build closer bonds with the Anglican Communion, and Church Online has its own campus pastor just like any other part of LifeChurch.tv.

Theology can play a key role in this close adherence to the familiar. At i-church, for example, several interviewees cited the presence of an ordained minister and inclusion in a diocese as key factors underpinning their confidence in the church. For Esme, "the knowledge that those leading are from a true Church such as the Church of England or another denomination in communion with it [is] 'invaluable.'" I encountered theological defences of the familiar at Church Online, too, where the campus pastor framed the online project as an act of obedience, responding to signs that LifeChurch. tv's ministry format had been divinely blessed with success: "we don't want to do anything outside what you're already doing, God."

More pragmatic reasons also play a role, as noted in several previous academic studies. Schroeder, Heather, and Lee (1998) suggested that a familiar phrase used by the service leader can frame the event in a particular way, inviting participants "to infer the kind of language and practices expected in the meeting," and this idea can also be applied to visual design. Stephen Jacobs (2007) argued a stronger point: "meaning has to be encoded in a way that is recognisable to the interpretative community for whom it is intended." The need to be recognisable did influence at least some design decisions. The founder of the Cathedral, for example, tried to create a space that was "very clearly Christian, an icon, a symbol of Christianity."

These points of familiarity can be used to generate or support new, innovative, and unfamiliar structures and experiences. Familiar elements can act as a platform for innovation in other areas, or be combined in novel ways. Simple and well-known liturgical styles, for example, can be adapted and performed by group members with no prior training or experience, and both i-church and St Pixels have encouraged large numbers of lay participants to take on new leadership roles.

Familiar practices or styles may also be reframed, setting them into new contexts to generate new and potentially critical perspectives. Nadja Miczek (2008) observed a number of instances of "the transformation of ritual gestures" in Church of Fools, including the use of religious avatar gestures in social situations, and non-religious ones during worship. This idea of transformation can be extended to design, liturgy, and leadership: Church of Fools recreated a parish church interior but did so in a cartoon-like manner, undermining the recognisability of the scene by incorporating vending machines, sofas, and comic gestures. The resulting space blends the sincere with the light-hearted, both affirming and gently sending up traditional church culture. This double-edged intent is clear in Simon Jenkins' (2008) account of his design decisions:

> Since our church was going to appear in the medium of computer games, we thought this ecclesiastical style would create atmosphere and give the whole thing a playful, experimental edge. And we were curious to see how people would respond to such a religious-looking environment. (p. 101)

These observations—and indeed all others in this chapter—relate closely to prevalent patterns of belonging. My interviews and conversations suggested that the great majority of participants in all five churches continued to attend a local church as well, combining physical and mediated spaces to seek the kinds of education, experience, and interaction they valued. Additional media resources were sometimes also accessed, including books, radio, television, blogs, and podcasts. This did not necessarily mean that online activity operated merely as a supplement to the local. Instead, each operated as a complement to the other in a fluid, many-layered, digitally infused, religious life.

A substantial minority in each online church were not part of any local congregation. Almost all had once attended a local church, leaving due to theological differences, negative experiences, or the onset of a disability their church could not accommodate, and at least one had subsequently maintained solitary spiritual practices for decades. In each case, the decision to leave was taken long before, or at least independently of, the decision to join an online community. Others suspended their local attendance temporarily, while moving house or during a time of illness. I encountered only two individuals during my research who chose to worship online simply because they preferred it: Christina from Austria, who claimed that Church Online was superior in style and content to her local churches, and Frank from the UK who explained that he lived in the same town as his closest St Pixels friends and met them every month instead of joining a local congregation.

These impressions are supported by a series of internal surveys, conducted independently of my research, by leaders of Church of Fools, i-church, St Pixels, and the Cathedral. These surveys were not systematically administered, reported, or analysed, and seldom phrased questions in quite the same way, making it difficult to assess their reliability or to undertake comparisons, but in conjunction with my own observations and interviews they do at least strengthen the picture I have presented. Church of Fools (2004; see Jenkins, 2008) recorded that 39 percent were not regularly attending a local church, against 34 percent in i-church (2006, not publicly available), 22 percent in St Pixels (2008, not publicly available) and 17 percent at the Cathedral of Second Life (Brown, 2008). i-church reported that 93 percent of the 114 respondents had attended regularly in the past and 96 percent defined themselves as Christian.

None of these surveys explored the possibility that those who do not attend a local church participate differently online from those who do—avoiding online worship, for example, or remaining marginal to the group. The reliance of all five churches on familiar elements of traditional church culture suggests a greater affinity with those already familiar with, and well-disposed toward, that culture, and the small number of self-described non-Christians I encountered bear out this hypothesis. Rachel, for example, described herself as an "eclectic witch," and regularly spent time at the island home of the Cathedral of Second Life. She perceived the island as a space of great spiritual "energy," in just the same way as the local churches she liked to visit in her native Scotland. She refused to attend an online service, however, explaining that "they annoy me on a personal level": she would be expected to sit still and listen, and her more provocative contributions would not be welcome. I interviewed three self-described non-Christians in St Pixels, and they shared Rachel's disinterest. According to one, St Pixels services were "just the same as going to church," with "hymns and prayers and someone saying something"—"not something I enjoy at all."

These discussions of familiarity and belonging demonstrate the complex relationship between context, media, form, and practice. Theology and denominational affiliation can have significant influence over the development of the structures, styles, and activities of these online churches, but this in turn affects the kinds of participants likely to join—a cycle which has limited the ability of all five groups to appeal beyond the boundaries of their parent tradition. Online churches operate within wider religious contexts, given the shape and significance by other connections and activities maintained by their participants.

Conceptualizing the Online Church: Communities, Collectives, Networks

If online churches operate primarily as one part of a broader spectrum of religious connections and practices, then emphasizing their existence as distinct entities—"online communities"—is only one of a number of strategies through which they can be understood. This chapter has so far focused on the culture, connection, and activity emerging within particular online groups, but their role within these wider networks or fields of activity must also be explored. This issue cuts deep into our understanding of the relationship between online and everyday life and connects closely with theories of contemporary social change.

Some online churches are classic examples of "virtual communities" (Baym, 1998; Wellman & Gulia, 1999), constituted as such by stable patterns of social meanings and personal relationships and largely self-contained as bounded groups with distinctive cultures. i-church, for example, has developed a small, stable, highly committed community with relatively little engagement with digital platforms beyond the primary website. The Cathedral of Second Life can also be understood as an online community, with a core membership of regular participants who know one another well, but this group exists within a quite different, much more fluid milieu. Many of those who came to the island for worship, group discussion, or informal conversation were also visitors to, participants in, or leaders of, other Second Life churches, ministries, and Christian sites. We have already met Rachel, who toured a number of pagan, Buddhist, and Christian locations as part of her own spiritual landscape as an "eclectic witch." Paula, also quoted above, visited numerous in-world churches while also creating her own independent ministry, a virtual garden in which Bible passages were represented through animated art installations. I found a similar trend at Experience Island, the Second Life region operated by LifeChurch.tv. Gloria, an American woman with Swedish ancestry, visited a range of Second Life churches to satisfy different aspects of her spiritual tastes and needs: "lifechurch teaches me to grow in my Christian faith and noway church [a Swedish Lutheran church in Second Life] gives me tradition."

These examples indicate the presence of a fluid, loosely networked sphere of Christian activity in Second Life, within which individuals circulate freely to find the people, places, and activities that appeal to them. Nancy Baym (2007) has described the emergence of "networked collectivism" in music fandom, a form of digital sociality that lies "between the site-based online group and the egocentric network, distributing themselves throughout a variety of sites in a quasi-coherent networked fashion . . . members move amongst a complex ecosystem of sites, building connections amongst themselves and their sites as they do." This idea applies easily to the Christian population of Second Life, a kind of "networked religious collective" that incorporates a wide array of often short-lived locations.

My interviews with Church Online attendees suggested that many also engage with a range of other online sites, looking primarily for good-quality preaching suited to their personal theology. Visiting Church Online rarely involves the generation of lasting friendships or sustained commitment, but ideas of community, shared purpose, and participation in divinely blessed success were important for my interviewees. These observations indicate the formation of at least two collectives: LifeChurch.tv itself, understood as a kind of movement focused around the preaching of Craig Groeschel, and the global field of evangelical Christians, loosely connected through a maze of digital channels and platforms in which LifeChurch.tv forms only one small sub-region.

LifeChurch.tv also operates within a number of institutional collectives, each gathering like-minded churches together under a LifeChurch initiative. An annual event, OnePrayer (LifeChurch.tv, 2010a), encourages churches worldwide to distribute video messages, share resources, collaborate on community projects, and give money to a range of causes, and several thousand churches participate each year. LifeChurch.tv also uses the internet to maintain networks of affiliated churches (LifeChurch.tv, n. d.) on three different levels: "United," in which a church "partners with" LifeChurch to become a new campus; "Network," in which the partnering church shows LifeChurch.tv videos instead of a weekly sermon but retains its independence; and "Open," a much looser format in which pastors download resources to use as they wish. More focused connections are encouraged through the inclusion of guest preachers and brief video testimonies from Network and Open pastors, functioning to enhance the reputations of all concerned through public expressions of mutual admiration.

The idea of networked collectivism is a helpful counter-balance to an older, more egocentric idea. "Networked individualism," a concept explored in great detail by Barry Wellman (Wellman et al., 2003), reflects a turn "away from solitary, local hierarchical groups and towards fragmented, partial, heavily-communicating social networks" and is greatly facilitated by the social affordances of digital media. Rather than depending on a neighbourhood or household as the basic unit of sociality, this shift "facilitates *personal communities* that supply the essentials of community separately to each individual: support, sociability, information, social identities, and a sense of belonging." As a result, individuals are now "manoeuvring through multiple communities of choice where kinship and neighbouring contacts become more of a choice than a requirement . . . people operate in a number of specialized communities that rarely grab their entire, impassioned or sustained attention."

Wellman (2001) is careful to contextualise the rise of personalized communities within a historical progression between different kinds of networking, based on different basic units of sociality and different kinds of relationships. Digitally networked religion cannot be contrasted against an imagined past in which all religious resources were received within a single stable local congregation. Meredith McGuire's (2008) research into everyday, lived religion demonstrates that individual religious belief and practice has always been complex, diverse, and constructed from a range of sources and authorities. Fluid appropriation of a range of official and unofficial resources typifies "nearly every sector of the religious population" (p. 67), and has long included mediated and material elements alongside a range of authorities:

> An individual's religion could include an elaborate combination of, say, a denominational tradition . . . , the preaching of a nondenominational church leader and

the particular congregational practices of a nondenominational church, beliefs and practices learned from television or radio evangelists, practices related to objects sold at Christian gift shops, and more. (p. 95)

Online churches can be understood not only as communities or as regions within collectives but also as nodes or clusters of nodes accessed as part of individually generated religious networks, used to secure specific desired goods at specific times according to convenience, taste, and interest. From this perspective, the frustration experienced by those online church leaders who have sought to generate long-term, stable, committed, communities is unsurprising.

The virtual communities, collectives, and networks that operate in, connect with, or subsume the field of online churches can be understood as examples of the mediatization of religion. Mediatization theory, as formulated in recent years by Stig Hjarvard (2008), argues that social institutions have become increasingly dependent on the logic of the media, which operates both as an independent institution in its own right and as the means through which institutions communicate and conduct their affairs. "Religion is increasingly being subsumed under the logic of the media," Hjarvard argued: the media report on religion, but also "change the very ideas and authority of religious institutions and alter the ways in which people interact with one another when dealing with religious issues" (p. 11). Citing Meyrowitz (1985), Hjarvard argued that the media function as conduits, languages, and environments, broadcasting a hybrid of spiritual themes as entertainment, influencing the format of messages and the relationship between sender and receiver, and structuring interaction and communication (p. 12).

All three dimensions are relevant to online churches. Digital media are used to communicate, generating global networks of conversation and resource exchange, but also offer constant access to other communication platforms and channels. The form and context of each communication is shaped by the media through which it is generated and transmitted, forcing careful attention to the design and appropriation of channels and platforms. LifeChurch.tv makes careful use of camera angles, video editing, and graphic design to maximise the appeal and impact of its productions, endeavouring to generate bonds between preacher, online pastor, and audience that will "lead people to become fully devoted followers of Christ" (LifeChurch.tv, 2010b), and struggles to turn casual viewers into committed "partners." As environments, digital media make it possible for participants to shift their attention and attachment between a wide range of communicators, forming collectives and networks as they do so. The mutual-strengthening relationship between digital media and "networked individualism" can be understood as one of the most important aspects of the logic of new media, facilitated by all three dimensions.

Conclusion

Online churches now occupy an extremely diverse range of media platforms and channels, representing numerous theological traditions and institutions. Institutional involvement guarantees the funding for Church Online, the credibility of i-church, and the global attention drawn to Church of Fools, but also brings restrictions and pressures that groups such as St Pixels are seeking to avoid. The shape of a church develops through the negotiation of multiple factors, including theology, ownership, funding, and selected media, and each of these factors generates possibilities and limitations.

A number of key challenges and common strategies have emerged through this diversity. All the churches studied attract a primary audience of local church attendees and develop styles of worship, visual design, and organisation that mirror offline practices and environments. Each is viewed as a community by its participants, and can act as a generative space for spiritual experiences. In each case, as we have seen, there are also dynamics of transformation: the familiar is undercut by parody, community becomes network, and at least a minority of participants now has no connection with local Christian congregations.

These online groups may be viewed as communities, but also as components in wider collectives of digital and local religious activity and as connections in the self-constructed religious networks of their visitors. These additional levels of significance suggest a need for future research, complementing the focus of this chapter through closer attention to these new, digitally infused, religious lifeworlds. Future scholars must find new methodologies and conceptual frameworks to trace and understand the fluid, ever-connected practices and identities of an emerging society of networked religious individuals.

Notes

1. "Church of Fools," http://www.churchoffools.com. Accessed 10-01-10.
2. "i-church," http://www.i-church.org. Accessed 10-01-10.
3. "St Pixels," http://www.stpixels.com. Accessed 10-01-10.
4. "The Anglican Cathedral of Second Life," http://secondlife.com/destination/anglican-cathedral-in-sl. Accessed 10-01-10.
5. "Church Online," http://live.lifechurch.tv. Accessed 10-01-10.

References

Acorn (2010). Our core values. Retrieved from http://www.stpixels.com/article?article=54bdb29d-03f0-4a18-ab65-2dc59c7ff102

Barna, G. (1998, May 5). The cyberchurch is coming: National survey of teenagers shows expectation of substituting internet for corner church. Retrieved from http://web.

archive.org/web/19991010051101/http://www.barna.org/PressCyberChurch. htm

Baym, N. (1998). The emergence of on-line community. In S. J. Jones (Ed.), *CyberSociety 2.0: Revisiting computer-mediated communication and community* (pp. 35–68). Thousand Oaks, CA: Sage.

Baym, N. (2007). The new shape of online community: The example of Swedish independent music fandom. *First Monday 12*(8). Retrieved from http://firstmonday.org/htbin/cgiwrap/bin/ojs/index.php/fm/article/view/1978/1853

Brown, M. (2008, April). Christian mission to a virtual world [Blog post]. Retrieved from http://issuu.com/mbrownsky/docs/virtualmission

Burke, D., Crosbie, C., Beale, N., Byrne, T., Leal, D., Jones, S.P., Pickering, J., Pullinger, D., & Thimbleby, H. (Church of England Board for Social Responsibility) (1999). *Cybernauts awake! Ethical and spiritual implications of computers, information technology and the internet.* London, England: Church House.

Campbell, H. (2005). *Exploring religious community online: We are one in the network.* Oxford, England: Peter Lang.

Campbell, H. (2010). *When religion meets new media.* Abingdon, England: Routledge.

Church of Fools (2004, May 25). 41000 go to church in a single day [Blog post]. Retrieved from http://www.churchoffools.com/news-stories/03_41000.html

Estes, D. (2009). *SimChurch: Being the church in the virtual world.* Grand Rapids, MI: Zondervan.

Feder, B. (2004, May 15). The first church of cyberspace: Services tomorrow. *The New York Times.* Retrieved from http://www.nytimes.com/2004/05/15/nyregion/religion-journal-the-first-church-of-cyberspace-services-tomorrow.html

Glaser, B. G., & A. L. Strauss (1967). *The discovery of grounded theory.* Hawthorne, NY: Aldine de Gruyter.

Groeschel, C. (2009). Behind the curtain, Part 1 [Video file]. Retrieved from http://www.lifechurch.tv/watch/behind-the-curtain/1

Helland, C. (2000). On-line religion/Religion on-line and virtual communitas. In J. K. Hadden & D. E. Cowan (Eds.), *Religion on the Internet: Research prospects and promises* (pp. 205–224). London, England: JAI Press.

Hine, C. (2000). *Virtual ethnography.* London, England: Sage.

Hjarvard, S. (2008). The mediatization of religion: A theory of the media as agents of religious change. *Northern Lights 6*(1), 9–26.

Hutchings, T. (2010). *Creating church online: An ethnographic study of five internet-based Christian communities* (Unpublished PhD thesis). Durham University, England.

Jacobs, S. (2007). Virtually sacred: The performance of asynchronous cyber-rituals in online spaces. *Journal of Computer-Mediated Communication 12*(3). Retrieved from http:///jcmc.indiana.edu/vol12/issue3/jacobs.html

Jenkins, S. (2008). Rituals and pixels: Experiments in online church. *Online— Heidelberg Journal of Religions on the Internet 03*(1). Retrieved from http://archiv.ub.uni-heidelberg.de/ojs/index.php/religions/issue/view/153

Jones, Q. (1997). Virtual-communities, virtual settlements & cyber-archaeology: A theo-retical outline. *Journal of Computer-Mediated Communication 3*(3). Retrieved from http://jcmc.indiana.edu/vol3/issue3/jones.html

Leslie, A. (2004, August). A letter from the web paster [Church newsletter]. Retrieved from http://web.archive.org/web/20040814024824/http://www.i-church.org/news/200408_pastoral.php

LifeChurch.tv. (2007). Open. Retrieved from http://open.lifechurch.tv

LifeChurch.tv. (2010a). OnePrayer 2010. Retrieved from http://2010.oneprayer.com/

LifeChurch.tv. (2010b). Who we are. Retrieved from http://www.lifechurch.tv/who-we-are

Marcus, G. (1995). Ethnography in/of the world system: The emergence of multi-sited ethnography. *Annual Review of Anthropology 24*, 95–117.

McGuire, M. B. (2008). *Lived religion: Faith and practice in everyday life*. Oxford, England: Oxford University Press.

Meyrowitz, J. (1985). *No sense of place: The impact of electronic media on social behavior.* New York, NY: Oxford University Press.

Miczek, N. (2008). Online rituals in virtual worlds: Christian online service between dynamics and stability. *Online—Heidelberg Journal of Religions and the Internet 03*(1). Retrieved from http://archiv.ub.uni-heidelberg.de/ojs/index.php/religions/issue/view/153

Schroeder, R., Heather, N., & Lee, R. M. (1998). The sacred and the virtual: Religion in multi-user virtual reality. *Journal of Computer-Mediated Communication 4*(2). Retrieved from http://jcmc.indiana.edu/vol4/issue2/schroeder.html

St Pixels (2010). Our core values [Blog post]. Retrieved from http://www.stpixels.com/article?article=54bdb29d-03f0-4a18-ab65-2dc59c7ff102

Thomas, R. (2004, March 5). Why internet church? [Blog post]. Retrieved from http://www.thinkinganglicans.org.uk/archives/000499.html

Wellman, B. (2001). Physical place and cyberplace: The rise of personalized networking. *International Journal of Urban and Regional Research, 25*(2), 227–252.

Wellman, B., & Gulia, M. (1999). Virtual communities as communities: Net surfers don't ride alone. In P. Kollock & M. A. Smith (Eds.), *Communities in cyberspace* (pp. 167–194). London, England: Routledge.

Wellman, B., Quan-Haase, A., Boase, J., Chen, W., Hampton, K., Isla de Diaz, I., & Miyata, K. (2003). The social affordances of the Internet for networked individual-ism. *Journal of Computer-Mediated Communication 8*(3). Retrieved from http://jcmc.indiana.edu/vol8/issue3/wellman.html

Part III: Historical and Theological Examinations

13. "Let There Be Digital Networks and God Will Provide Growth?" Comparing Aims and Hopes of 19th-Century and Post-Millennial Christianity

STEFAN GELFGREN

Introduction

The aim of this chapter is to nuance a common view of digital media as something completely new, with specific focus on the use of the media within the Christian sphere. In so doing, the chapter will highlight two different periods of time and contexts; the 19th-century Evangelical revivalist movement (with Pietist and Methodist origins), and the contemporary situation, mainly related to the use of social media within (but not restricted to) Protestant Churches. The chapter is centered around, and compares, aims and goals related to the use of information technology within churches.

Church and media is a huge area of research with many implications, of which it is only possible to study a few in this article. Related issues, for example who is using the media (specific individuals, denominations, or churches); what are the consequences (for people, communities, and institutions); how do transformations in religious faith and practices relate to a changing media landscape; and how does "secular" relate to "Christian" media, are not dealt with here, because that is not the specific aim of this chapter.

There are both similarities and differences between the two periods when it comes to contextual factors, and also when it comes to purposes for using contemporary information technology. Two centuries ago, home visiting and distribution of tracts and other inexpensive publications were the main means for the Evangelical revival to mediate and communicate the word of God.

Today, the internet and its various digital channels are considered by many (not all) Christian churches to be increasingly important tools for reaching people. A historical comparison puts contemporary rhetoric, hopes, and fears into perspective.

It is noticeable how often the contemporary media situation is considered a complete novelty. Digital media is often mentioned as "new media," with everything that came before clustered together as just old. Then there is "social media," including tools for mutual interaction such as Facebook, Twitter, YouTube, Wikipedia, blogs, and so on. In 2009, Paul Levinson published a book called *New New Media*, the title of which refers to social media. From a historical point of view some questions arise: Is the internet and its implications for mankind and society really new? Has the world ever seen anything else similar to what is happening right now? The answer must be both yes and no. Some issues are new, but there are definitely strong resemblances to previous epochs in history.

Different forms of information technology have appeared and been factors in transforming society, for example those pointed out by Walter Ong (1982) in his influential work *Orality and Literacy*—from the spoken language, to the alphabet, codex, various forms of printing, and different electronic means of communication (Ong, 1982). Some internet-related features are indeed new, such as the possibility to instantly bridge and distribute interaction in time and space, but some are not. As a part of society, the Church and its representatives have throughout their history quite rapidly endorsed new ways of communication, which consequently have often had transforming effects on Christian faith and practices. However, the different ways in which the internet changes Christian churches is not the specific focus of this article.

It is relevant to compare the contemporary media situation with the 19th century, especially when it comes to how representatives for different Christian affiliations, denominations, and churches integrate media in their work. There are similarities when it comes to the use, hope, and rhetoric of modern media. There are also contextual resemblances between the two periods. In both cases, society underwent a period of transformative change—turning from rural to industrial during the 19th century, and turning from industrial to post-industrial in the present day. During the 19th century, people were aware of, and imagined, these changes, and took action accordingly, as did Christian representatives.

There are, of course, differences within the Christian sphere regarding attitudes toward digital media, noted for example by Heidi Campbell (2010). She pointed out how different views of community, traditions, and authority affect how media is used within different religious communities. In this short article it is impossible to deal with the whole spectrum of Christian churches and their diverse relation to digital media, so instead, this article focuses on some churches' and Christians' initiatives in relation to contemporary digital media, in an attempt to map a general tendency.

Media and Mission

During the 18th and 19th century, the Evangelical revivals were keen users of the media of the day. The attitude toward media is closely related to the established core of Evangelical values. In a review of the Evangelical movement over the past two centuries, British church historian D. W. Bebbington (1989) highlighted four characteristics, which are still valid today. These are: *biblicism* (reading the Bible and related literature are crucial for Christians); *crucicentrism* (Jesus' atoning death opened the way to God for humanity); *conversionism* (emphasis on the life-changing moment of personal revival); and finally *activism* (the urge to bring the Gospel to others as a consequence of your Christian life).

The mission to bring others to God has been strong throughout the history of Christianity, based in Jesus' Great Commission in Matthew 28:16–20, but was further emphasized within the Evangelical movements of the 18th century and onwards. What Bebbington labeled as activism, in other words the attempts to reach and connect to new people, is one key to understanding the role that various forms of information technologies played, and still play, within especially these movements. Church historian Callum G. Brown (2001) used the expressions "salvation economy" and "salvation industry" to describe the activism and the "ideology" for reaching the unsaved souls, particularly from 1800 onwards (Brown, 2001).

Brown wrote "from the beginning of the nineteenth century, the objective of Christian evangelicalism was to lead every individual on earth to this point [of conversion]" (p. 35).

The need to help others turned into a schematic and almost scientific method. A whole enterprise, with many different agencies appeared. There were both national and local organizations, and at the centre of the local congregations were Sunday schools, prayer meetings for boys and girls, bible classes, temperance societies, social events in general, and . . . tract distributors (p. 38).

Furthermore, Brown pointed out three core agencies for spreading the evangelical values—Sunday schools, tracts, and home visitations. In other words: to reach the young, to spread (mediate) the word, and to build relations. After a look at the situation of today, regarding Church and digital media, one might wonder if the concept of the salvation industry is still relevant.

Even if it might be fairly anachronistic to compare two different periods of time, there are some likenesses, relevant for the perception and use of media, and these are dealt with in the following section.

Contextual Similarities

The 19th century was a period when major social transformations took place, just as is the early 21st century now. In both cases, the religious sphere was/ is affected, and in both cases institutionalised Christianity especially was/is questioned and undermined. Under those circumstances, Christian representatives and churches search for new ways to find and connect to new people, and also to communicate the word of God.

The process of industrialisation begun in early 18th-century England and spread around Europe and Northern America thereafter. Europe turned from mainly a rural society into a modern industrial society, with huge social, economic, and mental consequences for individuals and the society as a whole. The following gives a very brief and generalized introduction to the process of modernity:

Traditional institutions such as the monarchy, the aristocracy, the Church— the Ancient Régime—saw their privileged position undermined. New social classes and professions emerged in the wake of the new economy. Industrial processes made it possible to produce and consume commodities on a larger scale. Working hours were separated from leisure, and novel ways of spending your work-free hours were invented and implemented, especially in the growing cities. At the same time, science evolved, for example within astronomy, geology, physics, chemistry, biology, each posing questions regarding the relevance of metaphysical explanations. Traditional Christianity was disputed on scientific and ideological grounds. The individual was emancipated from the collective and she/he experienced increasing possibilities to reflect upon, and chose his/her trajectory through, life. New ways to answer existential dilemmas were sought and found. Technology developed rapidly in different areas, and new ways to communicate emerged, for example through the telegraph and improved printing presses (for an overview of the process of modernity see Giddens, 1991; Taylor, 1989). The previously relatively homogenous society gradually turned in to a more diverse and pluralistic society.

This process affected Christian institutions, faith, and practices, resulting in a transformation often described in terms of secularization, a concept which, for good reasons, has been put under serious criticism during the last two decades (Brown, 2001; McLeod, 2000). The revival movements were a part of this process (Gelfgren, 2009). Nevertheless, a pluralistic society led to a market situation where different ideologies, religious affiliations, and leisure activities had to compete with each other to find and attract new adherents. The concept of Evangelical activism and the so-called salvation industry of the 19th century should be seen in this perspective.

It is often claimed that our contemporary society is once again going through a transitional phase. Different concepts have been used to describe the state of our contemporary situation—post-modern, post industrial, the information age, to mention a few—and they all imply that present-day society has changed from what it used to be. This transformation affects the religious sphere as well.

Under the umbrella of post-modernity, truth in an objective sense is undermined. Objective narratives and statements are disregarded and replaced by subjective and contextual ones. Truth is seen as constructed through a system of discursive, paradigmatic power structures. Universal claims of, for example, power, science, and religion, are scrutinized and relativized.

At the same time, computer science and communication technology have developed immensely over the last two decades. Society is getting more fragmented as people travel more easily and move around the globe. Modern media are reaching around the world, connecting different areas and people in the process referred to as globalization. Science is still hoping to explain the mysteries of the world and even to solve the most puzzling mysteries of all, such as how life is created and constituted. The secrets of the world have, in one way, become even more profound as more discoveries are made, opening up new possibilities for metaphysical models of interpretation. Consequently, once again, particularly organized religious and traditional dogmas are debated (for example, see Drane, 2008). Again, new forms of constructing answers to existential questions appear, now with a noticeable tendency to pick-and-mix your personal religious system (Heelas & Woodhead, 2005). The process of increasing societal plurality continues.

To conclude, society changes, and consequently the role and expression of religion transforms accordingly. Both during the 19th century and today, Christianity was/is put under pressure and the significance of institutionalized religion was/is questioned. In this situation, different initiatives are taken to reclaim the relevance of Christianity. The use of modern media has been one way to reach out and connect with other people.

Taking Advantage of the Media of the Day

19th century

There are different reasons for Christians to use contemporary media. During the 19th century the outreaching efforts of Evangelical revivalist movements coincided with new and cheaper ways of printing. Huge amounts of so-called tracts and other publications were spread by preachers and colporteurs. In an annual report from a Swedish confessional revivalist organisation, written in 1863, the reason is hinted at. Tracts were supposed to literally rain over the country—and just as water nourishes a plant, tracts gave the prerequisites for spiritual growth (Evangeliska Fosterlands-Stiftelsens årsberättelse och matrikel—EFSAM, 1863).

Tracts comprised from two to 16 pages, approximately, with, for example, an exhortation, a concise sermon, or a so-called true (but actually fictional) story, in which the reader could follow a sinner's spiraling path to disaster, or the tale of a lucky reborn person. The message was simple to understand and the aim was to present the Gospel for ordinary people. Tracts were composed in an easy to understand language; in a way the clergies in the traditional Church institutions did not.

As noted by Callum G. Brown (2001), distribution of tracts was one key agent in promoting and spreading the Christian message. Different tract societies mushroomed, representing the increasingly diverse religious landscape. In Great Britain, there were publishers in many towns, according to Brown. One example is the Stirling-based Drummond Tract Enterprise. For one decade in the mid-19th century it printed approximately 200 different publications, and distributed around eight million copies, an amount that increased over the next decades.

Sweden was a targeted area for British missionaries, and there were close connections between Swedish and British tract societies (Hodacs, 2003). During the early 19th century, distributing tracts was one way of getting around the Conventicle Act, in force between 1726 and 1858. In 1856, inspired by the Pietist and Methodist movements Evangeliska Fosterlands-Stiftelsen was founded (EFS—approx. the Swedish Evangelical Mission Society). EFS distributed around 500,000 to 1 million publications a year during its first few decades of existence (numbers are published in each annual report)—this in a country of around 3.5 million citizens. In the beginning of the 20th century, EFS' publishing house was the largest in the Nordic countries (Rinman, 1951). The amount of tracts distributed could never be high enough to meet the huge demand.

The increasing distribution of tracts was related to an overall growing book market during the 19th century. The strategy behind tract publishing and distribution was actually linked to this process, and one aim was to publish good pious literature instead of cheap secular literature (EFSAM, 1857, pp. 11–12; 1863, p. 22). The tracts adapted to the format of the fiction books and magazines of the time, with the aim to "infiltrate" the Christian message into a well-known format (EFSAM, 1862, p. 25). However, in reality, tracts were often read by already affiliated persons and empowered converted Christians (Gelfgren, 2003).

Faith in tract distributing was, in other words, strong, and there was no reason for not distributing as many tracts as possible. The publications were seen as even more efficient if someone who could build relations with the receiver distributed them. Therefore representatives, often a preacher or a colporteur, made home visits for personal meetings and to talk about God as well as selling and giving away tracts. In that way, relations and trust were built. Good relations were considered important for the success of the tracts.

21st century

The internet has a fairy short history stretching back to approximately the 1960s, when it began as a military project. Later, the network became more user-friendly around the mid-1990s when the web browser was developed. Soon religious activities started through web pages, email lists, and chat rooms, and, around the beginning of the new millennium, also in virtual worlds. Heidi Campbell (2005) gave an overview in her book, *Exploring Religious Community Online: We Are One in the Network*. The internet was used for religious purposes early on, but the real increase in religious activities online, and the movement into mainstream Christianity, seems to have come just recently, with the booming so-called Web 2.0, with collaborative and networking tools, founded upon user-created content such as blogs, wikis, Facebook, Twitter, and YouTube.

When trying to formulate what is happening on the internet and how that affects our life, concepts such as participatory culture, user created content, collaboration, and the creation of relations through networking are mentioned (Jenkins, 2006; Rheingold, 2002). These are features that can be seen as positive for a Church trying to reach and engage people.

Development within interactive digital media has been extraordinary in the last two years. One inspirational force behind this process can be traced back to Barack Obama's successful use of social media to engage the grassroots during his 2008 campaign for the presidency. Obama's campaign is not an isolated example, but his large-scale sensation induced hope for what can be achieved through digital, and especially, social media.

In early 2009 the PR firm Edelman published the report *The Social Pulpit: Barack Obama's Social Media Toolkit* (Lutz, 2009), the main aim of which was to describe how Obama used social media to engage people with his message in order to make them spread the word and make people vote for him. This report, and references to Obama's success at empowering people, was taken up by some Christian bloggers and organizations, which could see the possibilities for church and Christianity (Baker, 2009; M. Brown, 2009b). At the same time, social media tools such as Facebook and Twitter have grown rapidly and become an integrated part of the lives of many individuals, across age, class, and gender.

The increasing number of social media users makes it interesting too, for Christian representatives to commit themselves to the media. The YouTube video *Social Media Revolution* by Erik Qualman (2009), shows in a very persuasive way that social media is revolutionizing our world. It states that it took radio 38 years to reach 50 million users, TV 13 years, internet four years, yet it only took Facebook nine months to reach 100 million dedicated users (Qualman, 2009). Without making any explicit connections to churches, this video appears on different Christian blogs emphasizing the relation between social media and the mission of churches to reach people. Blogger LayGuy said that "I believe that the invention of print, radio and TV combined pale in comparison to the potential online social media has in terms reaching the world for Jesus" (LayGuy, 2009), and on the blog CadillacZac (http://www.zakwhite.com/), pastor Zac claims that "Jesus went where the people who needed him most were. And right now, they use social media" (White, 2009). Both of them refer to the Social Media Revolution video.

There seems to be a strong feeling within Christianity (at least looking at what is happening on the internet) that churches should, and indeed must, engage in digital media. In some cases, as churches experience a process of secularisation and decline, they explore the virtual environment as one way to stay updated and relevant. Pope Benedict XVI (2010) wrote that "[p]riests are thus challenged to proclaim the Gospel by employing the latest generation of audiovisual resources (images, videos, animated features, blogs, websites) which, alongside traditional means, can open up broad new vistas for dialogue, evangelization and catechesis" (Benedict XVI, 2010). Another reason for the Church to explore and engage with the internet is that it is where the largest community of unreached people on Earth is to be found, according to both the Pope, and, for example, Douglas Estates (2009).

The question is, are there similar forces behind the encouraging of the use of new media today as there were in the 19th century? However, seeing the amount of Christian web channels, churches with web pages, Christian networking sites, Christian Facebook groups and fan pages, as well as Twitter accounts for pastors and denominations on different levels, and so on, one can assume this is not a marginal phenomenon.

Shared Themes

In order to compare 19th century use of media and the contemporary situation, this article highlights four different themes. First, there's the *belief* in the inherent power of the word of God, manifested through, for example, the use of tracts, blogs, and Facebook. Second, there's the way in which churches use the *format* of secular media in order to intertwine the Gospel into a format known by the "reader". Third, to utilize the full potential of media there is the importance of building *relations* between the sender and the receiver. Fourth, there's the need to *learn* from the publishing culture related to the use of media. It is possible to compare these key concepts over time, as discussed below.

Belief

A major reason why the churches that engage in digital media actually do so, both during the 19th century and today, is belief in media itself. Judging from the rising amount of Christian blogs, Christian communities in virtual worlds, chat rooms, Facebook fan pages, Twitter accounts, streamed videos, interactive web pages, and so on, there seems to be no limit to the amount of, often innovative, internet activities and materials. A quotation from Wilson and Moore (2008) is illustrative of this, where they claim that "[t]he more digital, participatory, and immersive, the better" (Wilson & Moore, 2008). Even if there is no discussion about the value in itself of mediating the Gospel in as large volumes as possible, there seem to be similar underlying ideas behind the use of modern media today, and two hundred years ago.

Digital media is considered a mere tool for communication, but there is also another aspect—media itself seems to give new modes of communication. As Bill Reichart (2009) on the blog Ministry Best Practices (http://www.ministrybestpractices.com/2009/02/why-should-your-church-invest-in-social.html) puts it: "Social Media must help the church effectively and efficiently communicate its message. Certainly Social Media isn't the only medium. . . . Social Media has some unique benefits all it's own in effectively communicating" (Reichart, 2009). Internet communication is easy and effortless, ubiquitous, converging, and viral, and it also connects people—contrary to previous communication's "one-way" tools. Or as the introductory banner on Church Marketing Online (church marketing online.com) says: "Is your church website fishing with a hook—or is it fishing with the 'Net?" "Get your site fishing with 'The 'Net.'" In other words, the internet is seen as having the potential to connect with people en masse.

Internet based communication is, among the proponents, thought of as being able to bring people together, and thus create relations internally between members of the church, as well as make outreaching contacts. Since people are using Facebook, MySpace, virtual worlds, and other channels for making contact, churches must be able to do that as well. It's almost as if relations come with the media and not by people and content.

The question is, how to use the potential of the internet? But it is interesting to note that there seems to be an allusion of the Net itself, and then especially social media, as autonomously bringing commitment and connections. In *The Blogging Church*, Bailey and Storch (2007) wrote: "Imagine a world where everyone has a voice, access to the marketplace of ideas, and the freedom to say whatever he or she want. With blogs, that world is here" (Bailey & Storch, 2007). It is implied that internet communication can change the world on its own. In *Sim Church*, Douglas Estates (2009) said something similar about churches in virtual worlds. He writes:

This type of church is unlike any church the world has ever seen. It has the power to break down social barriers, unite believers from all over the world, and build the kingdom of God with a widow's mite of financing. It is a completely different type of church from any the world has ever seen (p. 18).

The belief in media is thus comparable to the 19th-century parable of the raining of tracts, thereby soaking and saturating audiences with spiritual wisdom and conversion. In other words, one cardinal principle appears to be this: Let there be network communication and God will provide growth.

Format

Presenting the message in a recognizable format can also be a reason for churches and their representatives to be involved in internet-based communication. The Church is supposed to be where people are (an aspect developed further below), and to communicate in ways that they are familiar with. Since people are spending more and more time on the Net, communicating through mainly social media tools, churches must learn to communicate through media formats that people use, and in a language that they understand (Wilson & Moore, 2008).

Apart from being a format people recognise and use, Facebook also has the benefit of showing that even church representatives are human. Through Facebook status updates it is possible to "see someone's mood, hear what they're up to and get to see behind the curtain. I tell them what I'm up to. If I am reading, watching a movie or ball game," said Greg Atkinson (2008) in the foreword to Chris Forbes' e-book, *Facebook for Pastors* (p. 6). He also said that it is about making the Church transparent, and breaking down walls.

Mark Brown, CEO of The Bible Society, New Zealand, and an Anglican priest, tries to reach people of the digital world with the word of God. Therefore, he started a Facebook group aimed at presenting the Bible in new ways, and he also founded a group for sharing prayers (Praying People). Both groups have connected Twitter accounts. Brown (2009a) concluded that since church attendance is declining and social media is rising, churches need to be actively engaging digital media and using these channels to communicate with people on a regular basis. He represents just one of many Christian entrepreneurs in digital media.

Simultaneously there are indeed examples of how churches are reluctant to adopt "secular" digital media. One way to deal with this dilemma seems to be to close or moderate the interactive features. For example, the Vatican has turned off the comment feature on its YouTube channel. The openness of digital media exposes the Church to sabotage and hostile intervention. For instance, occasionally the Facebook page The Bible (http://www.facebook. com/TheBible) is exposed to hostile intervention. The founder and coordinator Mark Brown wrote in message to the members of the page:

> Over the course of the past 12 or so hours there has been a coordinated attack on the Bible page and my personal page which has been both vicious and sustained. Given the severity I took the decision to close the wall on the two pages down. (Facebook post 2009b December 6, Open letter re: the attacks on The Bible page and my personal page)

The format can obviously be valued, but not the content, so a substitute is sometimes created with the positive features of digital communication technology included and the negative features excluded. Instead of using the same communicative tools as "ordinary" people, there are channels developed as solely Christian. There are Christian networking sites, for example, myChurch (http://www.mychurch.org/), Unifyer (http://www.unifyer.com/), or Faithout (http://www.faithout.com/), which is explicitly marketed as an alternative to Facebook. The video sharing site GodTube/Tangle (http://www.godtube.com/) is promoted as a substitute for YouTube, while Gospelr (http://gospelr.com/) is promoted as an alternative to Twitter, and so on. In these ways, Christian digital channels create alternative, as opposed to secular, systems of communication. Therefore, they can be seen as parts of an evolving potential Christian counter culture (for example, Cox, 2008).

Relations

For churches and their representatives who are involved in digital media for communication, the main impetus seems to be the drive to build relations within the Church and with people who are yet unchurched. This motivation stems in part from a perception that the Church (especially in the Western world) has lost its primacy and relevance in the lives of many people. When looking at networking tools, church representatives see the potential and the possibility to create meaningful relations. Handbooks such as the aforementioned, *The Blogging Church, Facebook for Pastors, The Reason Your Church Must Twitter*, and *SimChurch* all stress the potential to build relations in computer-mediated environments. For example, in *The Blogging Church* authors Bailey and Storch (2007) claim that:

> There is a new passion for authentic communication. People want to be part of an open and honest conversation. . . . One-way communication is no longer enough. . . . [People] are looking for those who are willing to open the door and let others inside. Blogging is a revolution in communication, community, and authentic conversation; a revolution that churches cannot afford to ignore. (Bailey & Storch, 2007, p. xiv)

That is one important reason why the church should use digital media in general and social media in particular.

One important aspect of the "building relations argument" is to have a presence where people actually are. When, for example, the Church of Sweden in 2007 planned to establish a church in Second Life, that was the main reason behind their thinking (Där människorna finns där ska vi också finnas, 2007). In the same way as Jesus met people in the midst of their lives, Church should take the opportunity to meet people where they are. The Church of Sweden must subsequently be available on the internet too since people are spending more and more time on there (an argument valid for other churches as well). Representatives from the Church should, in other words, use chat rooms, Facebook, and other available arenas where people meet and socialise. The Church of Sweden has acknowledged this, and at their national meeting in 2009 it was decided that the Church should have a presence on the web as people spend time there (Kyrkolivsutskottets betänkande, 2009, p. 2).

Digital media is also a means for the Church to get involved in the private lives of people. Through the different web-based channels people share interests and experiences. For example, social networking through digital media is seen as one way to reach out, share stories, develop relationships, and thereby to build sustainable communities.

The idea is that the Church and its representatives, the clergy as well the laity, are made more accessible and also appear more down to earth, as the quotation from *The Blogging Church* above indicates. That is what is considered in building relations. Later, when relations are established, it is possible to use media to show how Jesus is working in your life and also to integrate the Gospel into the lives of others.

Learn

In some cases, the internet and its related culture can work as a source of inspiration for churches. The culture related to digital media and Web 2.0 is said to be one example of individual participation and involvement, creative user-centered content production, networking based on relations, and active production rather than passive consumption—attributes often regarded as positive by many churches. Digital culture can be seen as a way for the Church to re-invent its role and to overcome the often-recognized dilemma with established institutions and inherited and frozen traditions. Internet can be something that the institutions can learn from in order to become more significant to people who are not already included in the sphere of the Church. The concept of "being connected" can, for example, function as a metaphor for how the Church should be connected to people and also individuals to individuals.

In *Thy Kingdom Connected*, the internet is presented as an ideal for the Church. Rather than being dissociated collections of parts, Church should be an integrated whole, like the Net. Friesen (2009) wrote: "The break through theories behind Facebook, MySpace, and the social networking revolution will be explored. . . . Scale-free networks enable us to reimagine the Kingdom of God in terms of being rationally connected with God, one another, and with all of creation" (p. 31). The Internet shows, according to Friesen, that we are all connected to each other, and that the Church and its members should be united like that as well. The word of God, with emphasis on respect and love, is "particularly well suited for helping us understand, adapt to, and even thrive among the challenges of living within a hyper-connected culture" (Rice, 2009). What is seen as the un-institutionalized, anti-hierarchical character of the internet is even said to bear resemblances to the first-century Christian home-based communities. People are leaving the institutions for better and more fulfilling alternatives—the loosely knit communities on the internet (Estes, 2009).

Conclusion

Even though this article tends to focus on various forms of revivalist movements, the arguments are more general than that, involving also, for example (former), State Churches and the Catholic Church too. This article does not deal with all churches, rather with those churches who are proactively responding to what is happening on the Net. Consequently, there are many churches that do not see the internet as something necessary or desirable, quite the contrary, in fact.

However, this article aims at highlighting relations between ideas surrounding use of media within (mainly Evangelical) churches during the 19th century and today in the early 21st century. Of course, there are major discrepancies as well. Two centuries have passed, and contemporary communication technology is much more sophisticated and also much more accessible, both for the sender/producer and for the receiver/consumer. Modern communication technologies seem to blur the relation between the sender and receiver—the institutionalized church and the churchgoers. Anyone has the potential of being both a producer and a consumer of content—to be a so-called prosumer (for example, Tapscott & Williams, 2010). Individual initiatives are also easier to undertake, which contributes to a further pluralized religious situation, in which religious monopoly is inevitably restructured.

Looking at this situation from a historical perspective it is more appropriate to speak of a developing process rather than a sharp break between old and new media. The key to understanding the role of media, in particular the outreaching work of Christian communities, is the concept of "activism," which church historian D. W. Bebbington (1989) pointed out as one of the main characteristics of the Evangelical movement. In that perspective, media, both new and old, are useful means to reach people. Through dividing the use of media into three categories—belief, format, and relation—the aim has been to make a visible link between the two periods of time. A fourth aspect, learn, is used in this article to describe a perspective on media usage.

There are strong beliefs in the power of the mediated word, probably stretching back to the central role of the written and spoken word, especially in different Protestant traditions. Today the word of God is mediated through a vast amount of blogs and on-line communities, almost as if the distribution itself will bring people to God.

There is also an idea behind the use of specific formats. It is considered strategic to use a format that the people that you want to reach will recognize. If people read novels and fictional stories, the Church should present the Gospel accordingly, for example. By the same token, if people use social media, the word of God should be presented through those channels, i.e., channels that they know.

Whether or not one likes to speak of the contemporary situation as a "salvation industry" as church historian Callum G. Brown (2001) did in relation to the 19th-century Evangelical movement is probably in the eyes of the beholder. The amount of Christian blogs, Facebook groups, web pages, networking tools, and so on, might make it relevant to speak about the situation in such terms. Wilson and Moore acknowledge this situation and state, "the online church media market has become flooded with what is often poorly made video clips for worship" (2008). Today, there is no explicit discussion regarding the value of large volumes of Christian content. However, the implications of a pluralistic competitive situation probably stimulate Christian representatives to use media in different innovative ways. Once again, this particular aspect lies outside the scope of this article.

Finally, there is the aspect of building relations between churches and their representatives and people. This is the most important incitement for using digital media today. Many churches in Western societies experience a period of decline and see social media in particular as a way to re-connect to people and have relevance to people's lives. In the 19th century, home visits by preachers and colporteurs were crucial when distributing tracts, today the personal touch and dialogue over the Net is regarded as just as important.

The use of media for spreading the Gospel has been important for churches throughout history, so there is nothing particularly new about that. It is rather a matter of scale. In the mirror of history, it is also possible to see how the use of different media has changed religious faith and practices. We can only discuss and analyze what the consequences are for contemporary use of media, trying to predict the future, but in that process, a historical perspective is necessary.

References

Atkinson, G. (2008). Foreword. In C. Forbes (Ed.), *Facebook for pastors: How to build relationships and connect with people using the most popular social network on the internet* [E-book] (p. 5). Retrieved from http://saddlebackmediawest.s3.amazonaws.com/7073-ebook-facebook-for-pastors-1.pdf?AWSAccessKeyId=02SEKEM7N07K11AZCQ02&Expires=1313354387&Signature=APQi0b13DKLCRsVRPF9kYXFWJN8%3d

Bailey, B., & Storch, T. (2007). *The blogging church.* San Francisco, CA: Jossey-Bass.

Baker, J. (2009, January 23). The social pulpit—Barak Obama gets it [Blog post]. Retrieved from http://jonnybaker.blogs.com/jonnybaker/2009/01/the-social-pulpit-barak-obama-gets-it.html

Bebbington, D. W. (1989). *Evangelicalism in modern Britain: A history from the 1730s to the 1980s.* London, England: Unwin Hyman.

Benedict XVI. (2010, January 24). Message for the 44th World Communications Day. Retrieved from http://www.vatican.va/holy_father/benedict_xvi/messages/communications/documents/hf_ben-xvi_mes_20100124_44th-world-communications-day_en.html

Brown, C. G. (2001). *The death of Christian Britain: Understanding secularisation, 1800–2000.* London, England: Routledge.

Brown, M. (2009a). The Bible in the digital space [E-book]. Retrieved from http://issuu.com/mbrownsky/docs/thebibleinthedigitalspace

Brown, M. (2009b, December 6). Open letter re: the attacks on The Bible page and my personal page [post on The Bible Facebook page]. Paper copy saved by author.

Campbell, H. (2005). *Exploring religious community online: We are one in the network.* New York, NY: Peter Lang.

Campbell, H. (2010). *When religion meets new media.* London, England: Routledge.

Cox, B. A. (2008, November 7). Faithout.com, GodTube.com and our online ivory tower. Retrieved from http://brandonacox.com/2008/11/07/faithoutcom-godtubecom-and-our-online-ivory-tower

Drane, J. (2008). *The McDonaldization of the Church: Consumer culture and the Church's future.* Macon, GA: Smyth & Helwys.

Estes, D. (2009). *SimChurch: Being the Church in the virtual world.* Grand Rapids, MI: Zondervan.

Evangeliska Fosterlands-Stiftelsens årsberättelse och matrikel (Evangeliska Fosterlands-Stiftelsens annual book). (1856–). Stockholm, Sweden: Evangeliska fosterlandsstiftelsen.

Friesen, D. (2009). *Thy kingdom connected: What the Church can learn from Facebook, the internet, and other networks.* Grand Rapids, MI: Baker Books.

Gelfgren, S. (2003). *Ett utvalt släkte: väckelse och sekularisering: Evangeliska Fosterlands-Stiftelsen 1856–1910 (A chosen people: Revivalism and secualrisation—Evangeliska Fosterlands-Stiftelsen 1856–1910)* . Skellefteå, Sweden: Norma.

Gelfgren, S. (2009). Secularisation, revivalism, and religious dichotomisation: The message of nineteenth century religious tracts. *Ideas in History, 4*(3), 63–90.

Giddens, A. (1991). *Modernity and self-identity: Self and society in the late modern age.* Cambridge, England: Polity Press.

Heelas, P., & Woodhead, L. (2005). *The spiritual revolution: Why religion is giving way to spirituality.* Malden, MA: Blackwell.

Hodacs, H. (2003). *Converging world views: The European expansion and early-nineteenth-century Anglo-Swedish contacts.* Uppsala, Sweden: Acta Universitatis Upsaliensis.

Jenkins, H. (2006). *Convergence culture: Where old and new media collide.* New York, NY: New York University Press.

Kyrkolivsutskottets betänkande (Report from the Church of Sweden) (2009). Svenska kyrkans närvaro på internet (The Church of Sweden on internet). Retrieved from http://www.svenskakyrkan.se/default.aspx?id=304742

LayGuy. (2009. September 1). The Church and social media (blog post). Blog no longer available.

Levinson, P. (2009). *New new media.* Boston, MA: Allyn & Bacon.

Lutz, M. (2009). The social pulpit: Barack Obama's social media toolkit [E-book]. Retrieved from http://issuu.com/edelman_pr/docs/social_pulpit_-_barack_obamas_social_media_toolkit

McLeod, H. (2000). *Secularisation in Western Europe, 1848–1914.* Basingstoke, England: Macmillan.

Ong, W. J. (1982). *Orality and literacy: The technologizing of the word.* London, England: Methuen.

Qualman, E. (2009, July 30). Social media revolution [YouTube video]. Retrieved from http://www.youtube.com/watch?v=sIFYPQjYhv8&feature=youtube_gdata

Reichart, B. (2009, February 5). Why should your church invest in social media? [Blog post]. Retrieved from http://www.ministrybestpractices.com/2009/02/why-should-your-church-invest-in-social.html

Rheingold, H. (2002). *Smart mobs: The next social revolution.* Cambridge, MA: Perseus.

Rice, J. (2009). *The church of Facebook: How the hyperconnected are redefining community.* Colorado Springs, CO: David C. Cook.

Rinman, S. (1951). *Studier i svensk bokhandel: Svenska bokförläggareföreningen 1843–1887* (*Studies of Swedish bookstores: The Swedish Publishers' Association 1843–1887*). Stockholm, Sweden: Norstedt.

Skogward, M. (2007, 13 April). "Där människorna finns där ska vi också finnas" (We should be where people are). *Dagen.se.* Retrieved from http://www.dagen.se/dagen/article.aspx?id=133015

Tapscott, D., & Williams, A. D. (2010). *Wikinomics: How mass collaboration changes everything* (Expanded.). New York, NY: Portfolio Trade.

Taylor, C. (1989). *Sources of the self: The making of the modern identity.* Cambridge, England: Cambridge University Press.

White, Z. (2009, August 31). Social media [Blog post]. Retrieved from http://www.zakwhite.com/2009/08/social-media/

Wilson, L., & Moore, J. (2008). *The wired church 2.0* (Illustrated ed.). Nashville, TN: Abingdon Press.

14. "A Moderate Diversity of Books?" The Challenge of New Media to the Practice of Christian Theology

PETER HORSFIELD

What is commonly known as "theology" has been a major agent by which the meaning of Christianity has been developed and expressed, and a central means by which coherence and continuity have been constructed in Christian identities in the diverse contexts in which they have found themselves across different times and in different places.

Though theology can be embodied in a variety of expressive forms or genres, and though it is informed by a variety of affective experiences and sensory inputs, it is primarily an intellectual exercise. Macquarrie (1966) defined theology as "the study which, through participation in and reflection upon a religious faith, seeks to express the content of this faith in the clearest and most coherent language possible" (p. 1). For Tillich (1951), theology is an indispensable element in every religion:

> If taken in the broadest sense of the term, theology, the logos or the reasoning about theos (God and divine things) is as old as religion. Thinking pervades all the spiritual activities of man (sic). Man would not be spiritual without words, thoughts, concepts. (p. 15)

Theology, as the conceptual or propositional interpretation of the contents of a religious faith, arises from, and in turn informs and shapes, the other expressive and affective forms and practices that together make up the ethos of the faith. Boomershine (1991) therefore identified theology as a secondary language among the many forms of language that are involved with, and facilitate, human interaction with an Other. Primary forms of religious language are more direct in their facilitation of personal engagement, such as worship, ethical actions, images, visions, prayer, stories, songs, and witness. As a secondary form of religious language, theology is a critical reflection on the religious experience encountered in the primary languages of the religion. Macquarrie (1966) identified this distinction by drawing a difference between "faith" and "theology":

> While theology participates in a specific faith and does not speak from outside this faith, it has nevertheless taken a step back, as it were, from the immediate experiences of faith. In theology, faith has been subjected to thought. (p. 2)

There is a spectrum of theological opinions as to the specific nature of this theological reasoning. At one end of the spectrum is the view that sees what is done in theology as description, critical reflection, and interpretation of the faith experiences of a particular religious community. At the other end, building on a strong concept of Christianity as the direct result of God's self-revelation, theology is seen as a literal description of the nature and structure of the Divine being(s) as conceptually revealed by God. These differences in thinking about theology arise from the diversity of experiences, practices, contexts, and vested interests in which the theology is developed, and the different purposes for which it is intended.

Williams (1996) attempted to bring some order to this diversity by proposing three basic models of theology based on the major functions that they serve within the life of the Christian community. The first, celebratory theology, is more poetic in its language, to build connections of meaning for the purpose of thanksgiving, worship, and celebration. The second, communicative theology, is more rhetorical in its language, and focused on interpreting the inherent meaning in the Christian faith and the implications to new contexts and practical situations. The third, critical theology, is more scientific or declarative in its language, in establishing fundamentals of the faith to address situations of crisis or challenge. Each, he argued, has its strengths but also its weaknesses, and the interaction of each one's strengths with the challenges to its weaknesses leads to a constantly moving ground of theological thought.

For both philosophical and historical reasons, Christian theology has tended to see itself as a practice that is distinct from other constructions of knowledge, with its own sources of information, foci of study, and bases of reasoning. Common to most theologies are six main identified sources of information with which theology works, though different theological systems give different weight to some over others, or rank them in a different hierarchy of importance. These sources are: human experience, particularly those considered relevant by the theologian; revelation, a particular type of religious experience characterized by a particular mood of meditation leading to an in-breaking experience of a holy presence, followed by a mood of self-abasement, a restorative sense of purpose, and a sense of being called or commissioned; scripture, the authorized written accounts of the selected memory about the foundations of the faith; tradition, the selective history of experiences and inter-pretations of the faith; culture, resources acquired or demands made by the surrounding context; and reason, the intellectual mechanisms for the calculated construction of these disparate sources into a meaningful structure of thought.

While culture is an identified factor in most theological processes, it is largely envisaged in most theological systems as a separate element with which theology needs to engage, or from which it may draw resources. The idea that theology itself may be a particular cultural enterprise, symbiotically enmeshed within wider cultural processes, expectations, power relationships, values, and structures, is one that, until lately, had largely been rejected. Within the Prot-estant traditions of Christianity, the emblematic and influential work in this area was Richard Niebuhr's *Christ and Culture* (1951). Niebuhr's framing of the issue posited a distinctive Christian culture (Christ), which has to be pre-served in its interactions with the wider "worldly" culture (Culture):

> The fact remains that the Christ who exercises authority over Christians or whom Christians accept as authority is the Jesus Christ of the New Testament; and that this is a person with definite teachings, a definitive character, and a definite fate . . . the Jesus Christ of the New Testament is in our actual history, in history as we remember and live it, as it shapes our present faith and action. (pp. 12–13)

Within Catholic scholarship, culture is most actively engaged in the area of the so-called "inculturation" of faith. Here also, the engagement with cul-ture reflects the view that there is an unconditioned, a-cultural truth within Christianity that cannot be amended and must be protected:

> The liturgy has replaceable elements, but not everything may be replaced. In order to know what may be changed and what must stay, it is important to make a dis-tinction, insofar as this is possible, between the theological content and the liturgi-cal form of a rite. . . . The theological content is the meaning of the liturgical text or rite. . . . The liturgical form, which consists of ritual acts and formularies, gives vis-ible expression to the theological content. . . . With this distinction in mind we need to observe a rather rigid principle. If the theological content or the liturgical form is of divine institution, it may not be replaced with another content or form that will modify the meaning originally intended by Christ. (Chupungco, 1992, pp. 41–42)

What is presumed in statements such as these is that particular theologi-cal content or liturgical forms can be considered as divine in institution or as "the meaning originally intended by Christ" and therefore unconditioned, culturally unspecific and unmediated, and free of any form of political, ideo-logical, or institutional influence or interest.

This view, that the theologian's personal cultural position or intellectual approach is of no relevance to the theological enterprise, began to be challenged in the last third of the twentieth century, particularly from more marginalized cultural contexts of race and gender (Hood, 1990; Reuther, 1993; Song, 1984; Tanner, 1997).

While these different aspects of theology's cultural positioning have been challenged in recent decades, the significant influence of the media-culture of theology has been largely unaddressed. To a great extent, this is because most theologians and their critics, from their own media cultural position as literate elites, have considered "media" primarily as instruments for carrying ideas, once the theologians and their educated critics, using their esoteric theological sources and methods, have divined what the ideas are to be.

From within this view, any question of what impact changes in media or the implementation of new media technologies may have on the theological enterprise are addressed as primarily technical questions of adaptation and implementation, rather than as questions of substance. The extensive work that has been done on seeing media not just as instruments, but as technological and cultural phenomena that have social and ideological implications within the context of the complexity and interactivity of cultures, has largely been ignored in theological thinking, even though substantial work has now been done in the area of media and religion (e.g., Edwards, 1994; E. L. Eisenstein, 1983; Goizueta, 2004; Hoover & Lundby, 1997; Horsfield, 2003; Morgan, 1998; Ong, 1982).

An entry into thinking about how the mediation of theology may contribute to the shape of theology can be found in Ong's identification of three main characteristics of media that contribute to different media constructions and communication of human reality. One is the senses that are addressed and activated through the physical characteristics of the medium being used, and the way in which those activated senses shape the selection and experience of reality and the construction of meaning through their different processes of denotation and connotation. Also important in this is the way in which individual media sensory characteristics are extended more widely into cultural practice, industries, and structures. A second is the way in which different media handle and facilitate the storage, retrieval, and reproduction of cultural knowledge. The capacities and limitations of different media for managing and reproducing information become a significant factor in that medium's construction and reproduction of reality, influencing how much information can be handled, what sort of information is selected, how it is organized, the conditions under which it is reproduced, and the ways in which it becomes available for audience use and adaptation. The third is how each medium positions people in relation to each other, and the social relationships and social organizational structures that develop as a result of these requirements. This social positioning requirement influences the construction of social realities not only by specifying how people need to be positioned in order for the medium to work, but also by creating new potentials and new liberties of action, as the scope inherent within the medium is developed.

Bourdieu (1977) identified a fourth relevant characteristic in the relationship between media and theology: the relationship of media and power. He drew attention to the role of symbolic systems and mediated constructions of reality as instruments of knowledge and domination. Symbolic systems are created and maintained, not just to provide a usable picture of the world, but to construct a particular order of the world that serves the purpose of establishing a dominance of one particular group over another. Media become a significant site of conflict in this everyday contest of attempted dominance and resistance. By establishing particular forms of mediation as more legitimate or correct than others, those groups whose expertise lies in that form of mediation gain an advantage through the establishment of greater status, prestige, and legitimacy. As will be seen in what follows, establishing what was to be the "proper" medium for theological construction to benefit particular groups has been a significant site of contest throughout Christianity (Horsfield, 2009). One of the major challenges of digital media to theology today lies in a fundamental challenge to the dominant media within which Christian theology has been developed and preserved.

Media Contests of Christian Theology

The basic medium of theology is language, but the means by which language may be produced are various, and include oral, written, printed, visualized, sung, or screened expression. Within those variations are the various differences identified above: changes in sensory patterns, changes in the storage, organization, and reproduction of information, changes in social organization and relationships, and changes in the power structures of status, legitimation, and authority of different language expressions. While the different mediations of theology within Christianity may be seen as complementary and mutually enriching, they also have been the cause of significant conflicts.

Contests over the construction of the meaning of Jesus, particularly between oral and written expression, were a part of the early shaping of the Christian tradition following the death of Jesus. Theology constructed and performed orally is influenced significantly by its production and reception as a live performance before a living, present, and known audience. The process of oral theological construction is influenced by the characteristics of its construction in performance: the visual and verbal feedback that comes from the audience being present, the limitations of the audience to remember detail of what is said rather than general impression, and the immediate transformation by the audience in their own recounting of what has been said and seen as soon as the performance is over. Power in the production of oral theology was a distributed one, developed in the interaction between the speaker/performer and the audience.

The earliest constructions and mediation of Christian theology were oral. As Jesus and most of his first followers were from the lower classes, and most likely illiterate, the earliest working out and public pronouncement of this new revelation were primarily in oral form, following the patterns of oral performance modelled by Jesus.

Following the death of Jesus, the first Christians communicated their new insights in the streets, market places, and temples through making public speeches, declaring prophecies, recounting dreams and visions, and integrating their new ideas with re-interpretations of old scripture passages and beliefs. And, in the pattern of Jesus, along with their public oratory and personal conversations, they demonstrated the power and truth of what they were saying by performing acts of healing, casting out demons, challenging public authorities, and other acts of seemingly spiritual power. These events in turn were passed on, discussed, and retold by eyewitnesses, bystanders, and other interested people.

As is common in oral-based cultural perceptions of time, there was immediacy in this form of prophetic speech that removed barriers between what had happened in the past and what was happening now. Jesus was spoken of not as a past figure who was dead and gone, but as a continuing presence, alive in those who were speaking and performing. Through his re-energised followers, the public ministry of Jesus that seemed to have ended with his arrest and execution was resurrected. In effect, in the oral speech and performance of his followers, Jesus came alive again. Though not physically present, speaking dramatically about Jesus served to embody Jesus in the speaker. Through these oral devices of speech, performed actions of healing, exorcism, and miracles, and channelling devices of prophecies, dreams, and visions all linked to the presence of a living Jesus, the distance between the past Jesus and the present speaker became erased.

From the very beginning, there was significant adaptation of the sayings and events of Jesus' life in the process of bringing them to life for the people to whom they were being told. In the process of retelling and adaptation, therefore, whatever was the original message of Jesus gained new meaning and new material, as the original Jesus was imaginatively recreated in the process of oral performance in new settings. The Rabbinic and prophetic traditions within Judaism provided a model for this process of change, through adaptation and application to different contexts and circumstances. This process of adaptation in different places and in response to different needs lead to the development of different oral theological traditions within Christianity, often associated with particular charismatic leaders. So, while there were common themes and practices across these different traditions of Christianity, there was also a significant diversity of opinion, understanding, and practice.

This oral theologising from the beginning was challenged by the practice of writing, and by those Christians who were literate. Theology constructed and performed in writing is a more measured construction of theological thought written over a period of time by an individual with likely access to resources of human memory and archived written memory. Though initially read out loud to groups, the earliest written Christian materials were received by the audience as a completed treatise, not as a living "performance in process" to which the audience contributes. Power in the production of written theology lay with that small minority of Christians who had the literary and practical resources to produce documents and get them distributed.

Most of the first Christians were illiterate (some figures suggest only 5 percent of the first Christians could read or write; Crossan, 1994) though most, if not all, of the early Christian communities included someone who could read. As Christianity spread beyond its Jewish context, however, writing became an increasingly important skill and mode of communication. Those who were literate, therefore, acquired an exaggerated importance and power in proportion to their number. Since little attention was given to developing literacy within Christianity itself, these people were those whose schooling was in the classical rhetorical tradition of Greco-Roman education. Their adaptation of Christianity was to the cultural systems they saw as dominant within the Roman world, particularly Platonic idealism and systems of abstract thought. This included the adoption of presumptions and laws of argument common in that cultural rhetorical-dialectical system.

The widespread adaptation of writing within Christianity, and integration of Christianity into the writing culture of the Empire, was a major factor in the fairly rapid development of Christianity from being just a sectarian religious movement to an Empire-wide or "global" religion. The communication, organization, and political advantages that literacy gave to Christianity, along with the deliberate cultivation of their own kind by early Christian leaders who were literate, lead to Christianity steadily becoming a textualised religion. As Mitchell (2006) noted, "The earliest Christians did not just produce texts, they created a literary culture" (p. 191).

In a relatively short time, therefore, the process of theological construction within Christianity had become a strongly literate activity. Significant theologizing was still done in the interpretation of faith in the face-to-face oral activities of churches, but increasingly, the outworking of faith in such things as worship, catechesis, mission, and ethical behaviour became subject to the regulatory doctrines defined in writing-based theology. In difference from the diversity that was possible in oral theology, in which truth was developed and assessed in relation to its relevance and usefulness to specific situations, Christian theology that was written became more fixed in character. It also became more abstract, separated from the changing and diverse practical concerns of daily living in different contexts, in order to be "true" and non-contradictory to a variety of potential audiences and cultural contexts.

In time, therefore, the measure of theological truth shifted from its relevance and usefulness for daily living to the elevation and consistency of its philosophical propositions. As this theological development progressed, and reflecting the philosophical interests of its literate advocates, theology became increasingly complex. The earliest confession asked of those who were about to be baptized was that Jesus was Lord. By the end of the second century, the baptismal confession had grown to a Trinitarian one involving at least 16 different philosophical and doctrinal affirmations.[1] Gradually these questions changed to declaratory statements, with "I believe," used no longer as an affirmation of faith, but as a measure of orthodoxy.

The downside of this was that interpreting the meaning of Christian faith, the theology of the faith, was appropriated by the writing class of Christianity out of the hands of the wider Christian population. As a result, written theology became a reflection of the interests of that class—larger, abstract philosophical questions rather than a focus on the practical issues of living out the consequences of one's faith on a daily basis: a shift, as Küng (1994) noted, from "an apocalyptic temporal scheme of salvation" of the early Jewish movement to a cosmic-spatial scheme "explained in the essential-ontological concepts of contemporary Hellenistic metaphysics" (p. 172).

Even though the parameters of the Christian story were roughly defined and understood, working out how to integrate the elements of the story of Jesus into the details of the adopted Greek philosophical concepts was not an easy task, and continually raised philosophical conundrums. It is hard to know how much, or what, the everyday Christian thought about these things, but as the third and fourth centuries progressed, resolving these philosophical conundrums and boiling down the diversity of Christianity into short, single philosophical creedal summaries became the preoccupation of the educated bishops and Christian intellectuals, and the primary focus of Christian theology. The disagreements were protracted, the conflicts torrid, vicious, and at times lethal, and the resolution came finally not through consensual agreement but through imperial edicts that were enforced militarily.

The result was a significantly changed Christianity, one that Küng (1994) identified as a quite different paradigm. Instead of being explained in the everyday concrete language used by Jesus, theology became a philosophical exercise. The relationship of Jesus to God was recast in the essential-ontological concepts of contemporary Hellenistic metaphysics. Instead of continuing reflections on God's dynamic activity of revelation, the focal point of reflection shifted to a more static consideration of God's self within eternity and God's innermost nature. The exaltation of Christ with an original Jewish stamp, beginning from below and centered in the death and resurrection, was increasingly suppressed by a Hellenistic incarnation of Christology beginning above. And reflecting a fascination with mathematical, magical, religious, and metaphysical numerology, theology took up a fascination with the number three in its endless arguments around Trinitarian thinking.

Küng (1994) commented on the consequences of this particular literate framing of theology:

> Now Christianity was understood less and less as existential discipleship of Jesus Christ and more—in an intellectual narrowing—as the acceptance of a revealed doctrine about God and Jesus Christ, the world and human beings. And it was to be above all the Logos Christology which increasingly forced back the Jesus of History in favor of a doctrine and finally a church dogma of the 'incarnate God. (p. 171)

The invention of printing in the fifteenth century marked another significant media influence on the shape of Christian theology. In the West, the enforced dominant Catholic theological monopoly was broken with the sixteenth century Protestant Reformation. As Eisenstein (1979) and Edwards (1994) both made clear, printing provided an alternative centre of power by which Martin Luther could mount his significant and sustained theological challenge to the distributed institutional and political power of the Roman Catholic Church.

Printing as a medium changed the practice of theology in a number of significant ways that unfolded progressively through the Modern period. The same ideals of the Hellenistic system to integrate knowledge into a single system of non-contradictory propositions continued to guide the theological enterprise. But the integration and standardization of knowledge that printing favored, that found expression in such new authoritative print genres as the encyclopedia, scientific tables, and the dictionary, made more apparent and problematic theological differences between different Christian viewpoints. These lead to the fracturing of Christianity into numerous confessional denominations, each affirming their own absolute, unified, and non-contradictory theological world view. Print's capacity to handle greatly expanded knowledge, which stimulated the sub-division of knowledge into various disciplines of thought, influenced the shape of theology as well, leading eventually to the subdivision of theology according to dominant disciplines.[2]

Another influence of printing on Christian theology was the symbiotic relationship formed between the practices and institutions of Christian theology and the practices and institutions of the publishing and printing industries. This symbiosis began with Martin Luther's close working relationship with the printers and their commercial interests, which influenced, among other things, the format in which he wrote, the language and pitch of his theological writings to the emerging German bourgeoisie, and the distribution of his writings. The printers were also instrumental in Luther's shift from writing in Latin—the language of the church and an already saturated commercial market—to vernacular German—the language of the marketplace, business and public administration, and the publishing market of expanding commercial potential (Edwards, 1994; E. Eisenstein, 1979).

That symbiotic relationship between modern theology and the publishing industries has continued to the present. Christian theology in the modern period, even today, has been dominantly a book-based enterprise, sustained by wider cultural literate practices. Theological education takes place primarily within tertiary institutions in which the library is one of the largest and most expensive resources. Learning takes place primarily through the presentation and discussion of written lectures read by teachers, and through students being assigned reading lists of books and journals that they are required to reference and discuss, before being assessed on their knowledge by writing essays or writing answers to exam questions. Even students who are preparing for what will be a largely local, oral-based ministry are prepared and finally accredited for that ministry, not on the basis of their oral competence or their competence in inter-personal relationships, but by their competence in reading, absorbing, and reproducing printed material.

Theologians and teachers of theology are authorized as theologians likewise by demonstrating their competency in absorbing and producing printed materials. After writing a book-length PhD thesis that is approved by colleagues who have themselves successfully completed a book-length PhD thesis, theologians progress through the ranks, secure a paying job, and advance into higher-paying jobs, by furthering the interests of commercial publishers in writing new theological ideas that are accepted for publication in commercial journals or as commercial books.

This has been the literate-based industry of Christian theology in the late modern period. In direct application of Bourdieu's (1997) concept of legitimization through symbolic authorization, whatever the religious issue, the religious practice, or the ethical situation to be addressed, within most Christian churches one was not seen as qualified to speak authoritatively unless one had been through, and was authorized by, the media system of theological education.

It is this literate-based industry of Christian theology that Martin Marty (1989) in his prescient statement of more than two decades ago, identified as being in a process of change:

> It is time to say that theological expression was reliant upon the stable, purchasable, book-length literary products of theologians in community within free societies. Those were books written by people whose vocation climaxed in reading and writing them. Now they present a fragile, endangered species. (pp. 186–187)

This building of a theology or theological opinion in which one was presuming to describe or account for a universe of knowledge, organized logically in the sequential grammar, ordered divisions, and sub-divisions of a written work that incorporates and engages existing published knowledge on the subject, was possible when there was limited information to process. That literate-based character of theology is now challenged by the development and advances in digital media. Or, as Marty (1989) expressed it, even before the impact of the internet was known:

> Technologically, economically, politically, religiously, and in respect of status, conception, and the use of time, the concept of theology expressed through a moderate diversity of books is called into question by hyper-modern and counter-modern tendencies. (p. 186)

Theology in Digital Media?

I am proposing that, from a media-technological and media-cultural perspective, the characteristics of digital media—their information processing and textual construction characteristics, their technological mediation of reality, their patterns of usage practices, and the economics of their industrial organization—represent a paradigmatically different means of mediated communication than that of print publishing, upon which, until recently, most social practices, including the practices of theology, have been built. Exploring some of the key elements of new media will make some of these differences, and their challenge to theology, more evident.

An important characteristic of digital media is the vastly increased amount of information that they make possible. This comes from the technological capacities of digital media to facilitate the production of information from an almost unlimited number of producers, to store that information and make it accessible through an almost unlimited number of databases, to transform that information into an almost unlimited number of auditory, visual, and tactile expressions, and to distribute that information through an almost unlimited number of distribution and access channels. The practical need to contend with almost unlimited information has led to quite different criteria and social practices for engaging with information. With the greatly expanded orders of categorization, segmentation, and flow of information, new cultural literacies have had to be developed. There has grown a widespread recognition that one cannot know or keep track of everything, even in specific areas of personal interest. What becomes important in engaging with information is knowing how to place oneself within the flow of information in order to keep in touch with what is happening in your areas of interest, to avoid becoming bogged down in the processing of unnecessary or irrelevant detail that is thrust upon us (the "push" of information), and to know how and where to find information when it is needed (the "pull" of information). Crucial in communicating within this system, therefore, is the development of practical and grammatical skills that enable one to contribute one's meaning into the matrix and have it heard.

For the systematic theologian, whose concept of theology has been the building of a universal framework of meaning within which all experiences can be subsumed or at least made sense of, the limitless expansion of information that is to be taken into account poses a significant practical, as well as intellectual, challenge. The cosmos that is emerging from a global system of constantly expanding, changing, and circulating information filtered through the meaning-making of the Google algorithm, requires a quite different process of theological construction and communication than that which has been practiced within elite institutions working with "a moderate diversity of books."

A further challenge to the practice of theology has been the changed nature of text, provoked by the characteristics of digital technology. The flexibility and mutability of digital language and audio-visual texts has led to changes in how the producer of the text conceives what he or she is doing, and how the user of the text receives it. Printed text is a more permanent and less flexible mode of reproduction. When writing something that is to be made available in print, particularly within a culture that has traditions of printed books and journals, one is more conscious of the permanence of the activity and of the ideas being expressed. While the reader may disagree with what is written and may even write something in reply, the disagreement and reply does not change the text itself. A digital text, on the other hand, is infinitely mutable, able in an instant to be processed and republished as a different document or media form. The technologies of new media provide the opportunity and the encouragement for the audience not only to engage with the text, but also to transform it. This is producing a changed attitude to information, as something not simply to be received but to be worked with. This is reflected in the concept of the audience changing from being receivers, the old mass media concept, to *prod-users*, active participants in the creation of textual meaning.

Theologians have commonly understood their task as working in an educated, deliberate, and authoritative way with the sources of revelation and tradition "to express the content of this faith in the clearest and most coherent language possible" (Macquarrie, 1966, p. 1). For many, this is a sacred duty as guardians of the faith. The previous means of media production supported this particular conceptualization of the theological task, with the theologian's printed words remaining discreet and identifiable in the printed text. To have the theologian's considered words capable of being reworked and re-expressed in an instant by someone with no theological education and perhaps little deliberation presents a marked challenge to the concept of theology and the status of theologians. While theologians' ideas have frequently been challenged, prior to the development of digital technologies those challenges were generally expressed in media that were limited in their circulation. Digital media provide the ready means for equal distribution and circulation of theological ideas developed by the theologically uneducated as for the theologically educated.

This changed media situation raises a related question of how theological authority is judged. Throughout the modern period, authority in religious matters was strongly institutional in its ascription. This was supported significantly by the centralized production characteristics of print and its offspring of print-based education, institutions, and industries. Theological authority, which reflected and supported particular patterns of power within Christianity, was created and supported by institutional processes of recognition, including declaring particular positions as authoritative and appointing approved people to those positions, or offices. Processes of censorship and reward (such as status, promotions, titles, and privileges) reinforced those arrangements.

New media structures and processes have significantly undermined these institutional hegemonies, extending further the subversion or containment of religious authority in the processes of modern secularization. Media changes, which have been fundamental in wider cultural changes in the nature of communities, are challenging the dominance of centralized institutional structures in favour of constantly changing functional or online associations and networks. The distributed and decentralized patterns of new media communication have increased the potential for a diversity of voices, rather than an authorized few, to project themselves and their opinions into the marketplace. As a result the social process of declaring what is, or is not, authoritative is shifting from social institutions to media audiences. While traditional religious authorities are increasingly adapting to the demands and possibilities of the internet, in so doing they are recognizing that they must contend with a wider stable of competitors and a new environment in which their previously recognized criteria of religious authority, such as formal qualifications or institutional position, are giving way to more fluid characteristics applied by audiences, such as a person's charisma, accessibility, and perceived cultural competence.

In a similar way, this growth of diversity of voices in the market has changed the criteria by which the value of what may be seen as theology is judged. There is a move away from formal characteristics such as the consistency, rationality, universality, or institutional authorization of what is said to be theology, towards more pragmatic characteristics such as its usefulness and relevance to the issues people are dealing with, its imaginative content, its aesthetic appeal, or the perceived integrity or charisma of the person promoting it.

In what has become an openly competitive media marketplace, part of the judgment of whether theological ideas are valid or not is their perceived ability to be competitive in that marketplace. I have argued elsewhere (Horsfield, 2005) that in an age where digital virtual realities command a good deal of people's attention and resources, theological reflection may productively be understood also as a virtual reality. Far from being just distractions or escapes from real life, virtual realities are conceptual and experiential spaces free from the constraints of fixed time and space in which people explore alternative meanings, possibilities, hopes, and aspirations in a way that allows them to make sense of, and transform, the practical realities with which they deal on a day-to-day basis. Christian virtual realities constructed in such practices as liturgy, meditation, prayer, preaching, and theological systems, have been significant ways by which Christianity in the past has engaged its audiences and offered the means of personal and social transformation. Digital virtual realities now pose a significant competition to what has been offered by Christianity (and by other religious traditions) in terms of their attractiveness, appeal, multi-sensory engagement, and practicality.

If theology has been a primary means of constructing coherence and integration within the diversity of Christian experience, identity, practice, and tradition, what do these changes in media mean for the practice of theology? Will there still be theology? I believe there will be, on the grounds that reasoning about meaning and ultimate questions, and working to formulate that reasoning in connected concepts and conceptual systems, has been part of human civilizations since their beginning. This has been the case in all media systems, from the earliest sophisticated cultures of orality to today's sophisticated globally networked cultures of electronics.

I also believe that as long as there are social institutions of churches, with their structural power rooted in the significant social wealth and resources at their command, the practice of theology as an authorized and authorizing institutional process of religion will continue. Because as a practice it is intertwined with the strongly entrenched symbiotic industries of tertiary education, publishing, and religious institutions, I expect that academic theology will also continue for some time yet.

However, these traditional practices of theology are being significantly changed by the new practices of theology that are developing within new media. The purpose of this historical survey has been to indicate that though the practice of theological reasoning continues, the specific ways in which this reasoning takes place, the forms that reflection takes, and the practices or reasoning that are communally recognized, are conditioned by the cultural conditions within which they take place. These cultural conditions include particular media characteristics by which they are formed—technologies, textual practices, industries, and social structures. When those characteristics change significantly, the practices that have been formed within them also change. I consider that we are in one of those periods of significant change, provoked by a constellation of cultural changes, of which the development of new media is a significant condition. If the practice of theology is changing, what might be some of the new characteristics of theology?

One characteristic is changes to the nature of authority in theology. With changes taking place in the nature and function of social institutions, authority in theology is shifting from that based primarily on institutional authorization, towards that which provides imaginative, attractive, and useful resources to help the human community progress in their human aims and spiritual journeys. Without the captive audience of church attendance, theology that is influential will need to establish itself in the marketplace by being noticed, easily accessible, and by being attractive—in the root sense of drawing people to it—by its aesthetic appeal, imagination, humour, and practical relevance.

Theology that is influential will be more fluid and flexible, more characteristic of oral theology than written theology, easily accessed, easily carried, and adaptable as the market changes.

Theology that is influential will be open for the audience to participate in, to adapt to their own situations, and to make their own contribution. As with the oral parables of Jesus that invited the audience to imagine the meaning, theology in new media will be constructed in the interaction between the performer and the audience. The aim will not be to get it right, but to participate in a particular type of relationship and to engage in a conversation of mutual exploration. As Tanner (1997) suggested, in this new environment, coherence in Christianity may be found not so much in trying to identify a distinctive theological essence of Christianity, but in participating in a particular type of conversation or search.

Notes

1. From the *Apostolic Tradition*, a church manual from the later second century attributed to Hippolytus.
2. That is, historical theology (biblical disciplines, church history, and history of religion), systematic theology (natural theology, apologetics, ethics, and dogmatics), and practical theology, the more technical application of the other "pure" forms of theology to the life and activities of the church.

References

Boomershine, T. E. (1991). Doing theology in the electronic age: The meeting of orality and electricity. *Journal of Theology, 95*, 4–14.

Bourdieu, P. (1977). The economics of linguistic exchanges. *Social Science Information, 16*(6), 645–668.

Chupungco, A. J. (1992). *Liturgical inculturation: Sacramentals, religiosity and catechesis.* Collegeville, MN: The Liturgical Press.

Crossan, J. D. (1994). *Jesus: A revolutionary biography.* San Francisco, CA: Harper.

Edwards, M. U. (1994). *Printing, propaganda and Martin Luther.* Berkeley, CA: University of California Press.

Eisenstein, E. (1979). *The printing press as an agent of change: Volume II: Communications and cultural transformations in early-modern Europe.* Cambridge, England: Cambridge University Press.

Eisenstein, E. L. (1983). *The printing revolution in early modern Europe.* Cambridge, England; New York, NY: Cambridge University Press.

Goizueta, R. (2004). Because God is near, God is real: Symbolic realism in US Latino popular Catholicism and Medieval Christianity. In P. Horsfield, M. Hess, & A. Medrano (Eds.), *Belief in media: Cultural perspectives on media and Christianity* (pp. 33–47). London, England: Ashgate.

Hood, R. E. (1990). *Must God remain Greek? Afro-cultures and God-talk.* Minneapolis, MN: Fortress Press.

Hoover, S. M., & Lundby, K. (1997). *Rethinking media, religion, and culture.* Thousand Oaks, CA: Sage.

Horsfield, P. (2003). Electronic media and the past-future of Christianity. In J. Mitchell & S. Marriage (Eds.), *Mediating religion: Conversations in media, religion and culture* (pp. 271–282). London, England: T & T Clark.

Horsfield, P. (2005). Theology as a virtualising enterprise. *Colloquium, 37*(2), 131–142.

Horsfield, P. (2009). The language of media and the language of faith. In H. Geybels, S. Mels, & M. Walrave (Eds.), *Faith and the media: Analysis of faith and the media: Representation and communication* (pp. 23–35). Brussels, Belgium: P.I.E. Peter Lang.

Küng, H. (1994). *Christianity: Essence, history, and future (The religious situation of our time).* London, England: SCM.

Macquarrie, J. (1966). *Principles of Christian theology.* London, England: SCM.

Marty, M. (1989). The social context of the modern paradigm in theology: A church historian's view. In H. Küng & D. Tracy (Eds.), *Paradigm change in theology* (pp. 174–201). New York, NY: Crossroad.

Mitchell, M. (2006). The emergence of the written record. In M. Mitchell & F. Young (Eds.), *The Cambridge history of Christianity (Vol. 1: Origins to Constantine)* (pp. 177–194). Cambridge, England: Cambridge University Press.

Morgan, D. (1998). *Visual piety: A history and theory of popular religious images.* Berkeley, CA: University of California Press.

Niebuhr, H. R. (1951). *Christ and culture.* New York, NY: Harper and Row.

Ong, W. J. (1982). *Orality and literacy: The technologizing of the word.* London, England; New York, NY: Methuen.

Reuther, R. R. (1993). *Sexism and God-talk: Toward a feminist theology.* Boston, MA: Beacon Press.

Song, C. S. (1984). *Tell us our names: Story theology from an Asian perspective.* Maryknol, NY: Orbis Books.

Tanner, K. (1997). *Theories of culture: A new agenda for theology.* Minneapolis, MN: Fortress Press.

Tillich, P. (1951). *Systematic theology.* Chicago, IL: University of Chicago Press.

Williams, R. (1996, May 24). *Models of theology.* Unpublished lecture given at Trinity Theological College, Parkville, Australia.

15. Clocks and Computers: The Doctrine of Imago Dei, Technologies, and Humanism

SAM HAN

Introduction

A funny thing happened in January 2011. A computer named Watson, built by IBM specifically for the purpose, beat Ken Jennings, a champion of the American game show *Jeopardy!*, who had the most wins in the show's history. To add insult to injury, the score was not even close, with the tally at the end reading: $77,147, $24,000, and $21,600. After the contest was televised a month later, there emerged online, on TV, and in newspapers, a resurgence of the discussion of artificial intelligence and its consequences for the future of not only humanity but also the world. Editorials and articles were largely skewed this way, as headlines such as "*Jeopardy!* invites supercomputer Watson to destroy all humans" (Maerz, 2011) or "Watson: Supercharged Search Engine or Prototype Robot Overlord?" (Goertzel, 2011) could be found everywhere. Jennings even wrote an article for the online publication *Slate,* entitled "My Puny Human Brain" (Jennings, 2011).

The idea that a product of human creativity could mimic specific aspects of humans and then overtake humans is something that has hovered as a specter over human thinking since the gods died, that is, receded in their prominence as guarantors and co-signers of ontological security. But in the era of "mechanical reproduction," as Walter Benjamin once called it, with its increased mechanization and automation, the thrill of modernity became just as much promise as it was threat. As was the case in Shelley's *Frankenstein* (1818) and the Golem of European Jewish folklore, creation would overthrow the creator, or so was the fear. Industrial capitalism, while decreasing the level of human effort in production, was also the driving force of, as Marx well argued, the alienation of humans from nature.

US magazine *The Atlantic* published a well-timed cover article in its March 2011 issue called "Mind vs. Machine." In it, the author Brian Christian (2011), while not directly referring to Watson, reflected on artificial intelligence as it pertained to how we humans defined ourselves. Tracing the various different traits that we humans thought defined us as separate from non-humans, which include the use of language, tools, and mathematics, he asks: "Is it appropriate to allow our definition of our own uniqueness to be, in some sense, reactive to the advancing front of technology? And why is it that we are so compelled to feel unique in the first place?"

Most recently, in the digital, "post-mechanical," age, the computer has been added to this list of potential metaphors.

The aim of this chapter is to investigate the meta-historical and theological significance of various points of convergence between Christianity and technology that pervade the history of the concept *imago Dei*, leading up to the contemporary digital moment wherein the computer has become the dominant conceptual mirror of human existence. The *imago Dei* is the doctrine in which Christian anthropology and the Enlightenment concept of humanism is rooted, in spite of the latter's anti-clericalism. Following Brian Christian, I argue that as far back as the 17th century, the relations of God, man, and nature have always been mediated through engagements with specific technologies, not specific traits.

I borrow this mode of "media archaeology" from the approach of German media theorist Friedrich Kittler (1999) in *Gramophone, Film, Typewriter*, the locus classicus of the German media theory that emerged in the 1980s (Geisler, 1999). Kittler treated those three media objects as key markers not only of technological history, but also of the history of what he calls, after Foucault, "so-called Man."

History and all discourses turned humans or philosophers into God. The media revolution of 1880, however, laid the groundwork for theories and practices that no longer mistake information for spirit. Thought is replaced by a Boolean algebra, and consciousness by the unconscious, which (at least since Lacan's reading) makes of Poe's "Purloined Letter" a Markoff chain. And that the symbolic is called the world of the machine undermines Man's delusion of possessing a "quality" called "consciousness," which identifies him as something other and better than a "calculating machine." For both people and computers are "subject to the appeal of the signifier;" that is, they are both run by programs. "Are these humans," Nietzsche already asked himself in 1874, eight years before buying a typewriter, "or perhaps only thinking, writing, and speaking machines?" (pp. 16–17).

The "media revolution of 1880"—the accomplishment of *recording* attributed by Kittler (1999) to the gramophone—signals a momentous shift in the trajectory of "so-called Man" from the bearer of a special quality of "spirit" to a "program." Though it was covered over ideologically by the West's own self-imaging—namely, humanism, which effectively, as Kittler (1999) rightly suggested, resulted in the deification of the human, of which Hegelian Spirit is perhaps the most egregious example—the human becomes, if anything, in the words of Freud (2005) evoking Nietzsche and Feuerbach before him, a "*prosthetic* god" (p. 76).

I refer to Kittler (1999) for the simple fact that he identifies a crucial point that I see as fundamental: the study of technology necessarily takes into account the metaphysics of a given age, which, since the Enlightenment, has always included "the human," "nature," and "God." In this chapter, I propose that *imago Dei*, the core of Christian anthropology, has historically been mediated through a theologico-technological figuration, leading to some larger questions pertaining to the status of humanism, Christian theology, and technologies today, in a technological moment that is quite unique due to digitization. As I will show, the *imago Dei* is the point d'appui, or stage, upon which the *technological unconscious*[1] of humanism takes hold with theological implications.

I begin with a discussion of *imago Dei* linking it to medieval discourses of technology and humanism, drawing from Augustine, Reinhold Niebuhr, Michael Gillespie, and David Noble. From there, I offer a historical parallel-cum-periodization scheme, comparing the 17th–18th centuries to the 21st century, pointing to key technologies that figure into—sometimes directly, at other times by inference—ideas about God, technology, and the human. Paying particular attention to the computer and artificial intelligence, I conclude with a discussion of some of the theological and technological implications of the overarching trend of these developments, and suggest an *immanentization* of the *imago Dei* in the 21st century.

Imago Dei, *Transcendence, and Technology*

Biblically, most theologians and religion scholars place the doctrine of *imago Dei*, that humans were made in the "image of God" and thus have value and worth, in Genesis 1:26–27:

26. Then God said, "Let us make man in our image, after our likeness. And let them have dominion over the fish of the sea and over the birds of the heavens and over the livestock and over all the earth and over every creeping thing that creeps on the earth."

27. So God created man in his own image,

in the image of God he created him;

male and female he created them. (English Standard Version)

The Creator relinquishes some control over his creation to the human—man, to be exact. This is done through the imposition of a hierarchy wherein the human is the mirror of God, in terms of power and sovereignty over biological life, that is, "every creeping thing that creeps on the earth." The human is, as many theological interpretations put it, the *actualization* of God on earth (hence the importance of Christ's paradoxical status as Son of Man *and* son of God), and the display of ultimate care for his creation. Most critically, this affords the human a specific ontological trait, as a possessor of the ability to reason, as Augustine (1873) famously suggested.

Yet the human soul is never anything save rational or intellectual; and hence, if it is made after the image of God in respect to this, that it is able to use reason and intellect in order to understand and behold God, then from the moment when that nature so marvelous and so great began to be, whether this image be so worn out as to be almost none at all, or whether it be obscure and defaced, or bright and beautiful, certainly it always is (p. 350).

Political theorist Michael Gillespie (2008) summarized the Augustinian view thus: "Humans were made in the image of God, and like God were principally willful rather than rational beings" (p. 28). From this flowed "the original modern vision of a unified theory that could explain the motions of God, man and the natural world thus in his view had to be abandoned" (p. 7). Hence, "creation itself was the embodiment of this reason, and man, as the rational animal and *imago dei*, stood at the pinnacle of this creation, guided by a natural *telos* and a divinely revealed supernatural goal" (p. 14). This of course would form the rationalism of Aquinas and later Galileo, Descartes, and Newton.

But according to the Protestant theologian Reinhold Niebuhr (1964), who was influenced greatly by Augustine, the *imago Dei* is not so much rested upon the "rational and intellectual soul," but on something that he called "self-transcendence" (p. 155). For Niebuhr, while there is undoubtedly a clear Aristotelian logic to Augustine's characterization of reason as *imago Dei*, there is something unsaid by critics of Augustine, which is that his view of man is "something that reaches beyond itself—that he is more than a rational creature" (Niebuhr, 1964, p. 162). Niebuhr claims:

Implicit in the human situation of freedom and in man's capacity to transcend himself and his world is his ability to construct a world of meaning without finding a source and key to the structure of meaning which transcends the world beyond his own capacity to transcend it. The problem of meaning, which is the basic problem of religion, transcends the ordinary rational problem of tracing the relation of things to each other as the freedom of man's spirit transcends his rational faculties. (p. 164)

The *imago Dei* as not only reason but also *transcendence* has been echoed by historian David Noble (1997), with regard to what he labeled "the ideology of technology" in Christianity, and in modern times. Noble viewed the Weberian idea of *Entzauberung* or disenchantment to overlook the "the present enchantment with things technological—the very measure of modern enlightenment—is rooted in religious myths and ancient imaginings" (p. 3). Reading medieval theological texts on technology, Noble suggested that the useful arts or "technics" were associated with the Christian ideas of redemption and transcendence, ideas that were of special interest among medieval theologians. Prior to that, such as in Augustine, transcendence and redemption was only to be garnered through Grace, a formulation reflecting the impact of Paul. Yet, at some point in the Middle Ages, wrote Noble (1997), technology came to be largely viewed within the framework of the Adamic fall, and thus, as a means by which to rectify and compensate for it. He said:

> Technology came to be identified more closely with both lost perfection and the possibility of renewed perfection, and the advance of the arts took on new significance, not only as evidence of grace but as a means of preparation for, and a sure sign of, imminent salvation. (p. 12)

Though humans could not return to the Garden of Eden, they could attempt to create it in this world through the directing of science towards application. Rightly, Noble suggested that this attempt to re-create Eden is a particularly *Christian* endeavor for theological reasons. Judaism, for instance, was far more monotheistic, and could not theologically entertain a God-human hybrid found in the figure of Christ, since it, theologically at least, adhered to an ontological dualism that radically separated God and humans.

This "new" theology of technology was first expressly demonstrated in the work of Erigena, who used the term "artes mechanicae," which Noble noted was a precursor to "useful arts" and "technology." Though influenced by Augustine, Erigena rejected Augustine's bodily disdain by arguing that if humans were indeed the embodiment of *imago Dei*, then bodies, which all humans posses, must have some divine quality about them as well. The physical element, he argued, could be used in the service of salvation, and in turn of the spiritual, allowing him to insist that knowledge of the mechanical arts was innate in man, an aspect of his initial endowment, but had become obscured by sin since the Fall of Adam. The mechanical arts could then recover the prelapsarian dignity of the human being. "In other words, Erigena invested the arts with spiritual significance, as elements of man's God-likeness, and identified them as vehicles of redemption" (Noble, 1997, p. 17).

By the 12th century, centuries after Erigena, the "spiritualized" view of the useful arts became the norm. This theology of technology extended into the late-Middle Ages through many threads, one of which was Christian eschatology. As Noble pointed out, the millenarian conception of transcendence was linked to technology, and with it a new conception of historical time woven into the relation of humans and God. Unlike Augustine's separation of City of God and City of Man, the millenarian concept of redemption awarded human beings the ability to *construct* the City of God. The useful arts could be utilized in preparation for the Second Coming of Christ. This, of course, meant that there needed to be a new figure of Adam, as not just the fallen Father of Sin but as the archetypal artisan, and the Lord of Nature given the power to work the land and name the beasts by God (Genesis 2:20). British Millenarians, such as John Napier, interpreted this as encouraging a view of a new lordly attitude toward nature, anticipating the restitution of Eden.

We can see from Noble's reading that the ideology of technology innate in medieval Christian theology is largely oriented around themes in Christian anthropology—the place or nature of the human in the God-given world. He identified the crucial component of the theological anthropology of technology to be what Niebuhr (1964), in his reading of Augustine, suggested as well—transcendence. Technology, as a product of human ingenuity and reason (and, in turn, of *imago Dei*) takes on a dual purpose: (1) to recover Adamic perfection—articulated as piety, and (2) to imitate the life of Jesus— articulated as asceticism (Noble, 1997, p. 11).

If, as Noble argued, the *imago Dei* served as a fulcrum around which ideas about technology, science, and God swirled, attached, detached, and reattached, in the Middle Ages, then it must also be the case throughout the course of modernity, since it is there that we can find the "origins of modernity" (Gillespie, 2008). We will investigate the dynamics of the triangular relations of the God, the human, and nature in three periods—the 17th–18th centuries, the 19th century, and the 20th century.

The Clock—17th–18th Centuries

Lewis Mumford (1963) famously declared in *Technics and Civilization:*

> The clock, not steam-engine, is the key-machine of the modern industrial age. For every phase of its development the clock is both the outstanding fact and the typical symbol of the machine: even today no other machine is so ubiquitous. Here, at the very beginning of modern technics, appeared prophetically the accurate automatic machine, which, only after centuries of further effort, was also to

prove the final consummation of this technics in every department of industrial activity. (p. 14)

Mumford, while he may be accused of hyperbole, is certainly right on one account. "The clock," as image, as concept, was central to the redefinition of the relations of nature, God, and the human, from the medieval cosmology to early modern Newtonian mechanicism. It was, as he argued, the very height of technological *automation* at the time. This *episteme* of the clock was embodied in the widely influential Clockmaker analogy. It was the clock analogy that provided the basic interpretive image of the world as a perfect machine, autonomous and self-sufficient, with natural causes acting in independence of God. The technological analogy, of Nature as machine (specifically, a clock) and God as Divine Clockmaker, reflects not a "deus ex machina" [God out of the machine] but a "machina ex deo"[machine out of God] in early modern philosophy and science.

Many, including religion and science scholar Ian Barbour (1966), intellectual historian Amos Funkenstein (1989), and sociologist Robert Merton (1938), have supported Mumford's identification of the 17th century as a critical moment. For Barbour (1966), the 17th century is undoubtedly the "century of genius," following Alfred North Whitehead, in which "modern science" was birthed (p. 15). For Funkenstein (1989), the 17th century stands as an exceptional moment of the "secularization of theology," that is, when "theological discussions were carried on by laymen" (i.e., scientists and philosophers) (p. 4). For Merton, it was the period in which science became a full-fledged social force, and began to influence cultural spheres beyond its own borders, such as poetry. The 17th century, then, can be thought of as the beginning of a convergence of an emerging social force—science—with the already-existing, dominant one—religion—which, in fact, was not a single social force among others, but rather *the* force underneath even politics, which heretofore had to appeal to the Divine.

According to Barbour (1966), the 17th century is the period in which physics and metaphysics redefined the views of God's relation to nature and humans' relation to nature from a medieval "world-drama" to the "world-machine." The medieval world-drama saw God as the supreme entity in the hierarchy of being, with the human at the center of the created order. In this view, Nature is subservient to the will of humans, adhering pretty strictly to the doctrine of *imago Dei*, and its subsequent actualization in the narrative of God granting Adam authority via naming the living creatures around him. The move away from this ontological outlook came through Galilean science, which viewed Nature as "the sole source of scientific knowledge . . . along with scripture, a source of theological knowledge, a way of knowing God" (Barbour, 1966, p. 30). For Barbour, the Galilean combination of

mathematical reasoning and experimental observation brought forth the possibility of a natural theology, which saw Nature not as simply subservient to
human will but as a place to find scientific and theological truth.

Building on the Galilean "mathematization of Nature" (Husserl, 1970,
p. 23), Newton suggested that nature was a "law-abiding machine" and
adapted the medieval notion of the universe as a single harmonious order,
but as a structure of forces and masses, not a hierarchy of purposes, which
Galilean science still maintained.[2] Nature was "an intricate machine following immutable laws, with every detail precisely predictable" (Barbour, 1966,
p. 36). In Barbour's narrative of Nature becoming more and more closely
aligned with the divine and humans becoming less and less central to the created order, Newton's mechanical worldview is the critical contribution to the
view of God as First Cause, an attempted reconciliation of a mechanical world
with belief in God. "Newton himself," Barbour (1966) wrote, "believed that
the world-machine was designed by an intelligent creator and expressed his
purpose; to later interpreters, impersonal, and blind forces appeared to be
entirely self-contained, and all sense of meaning and purpose was lost" (p.
36). Thus to find scientific and theological truth in Nature, as the contributions of Galileo had facilitated, was to look for a *mechanism*.

Galilean and Newtonian science were successfully combined in the figure
of the "Divine Clockmaker" who later came to be called the "Watchmaker
analogy" in William Paley's *Natural Theology* ([1804] 2008), who was purportedly a major influence on Darwin. The figure of the Divine Clockmaker
effectively summarized the relationship of science and religion in the 17th
and 18th centuries. Barbour (1966) again:

> It was the clock analogy that provided the basic interpretive image of the world
> as a perfect machine, autonomous and self-sufficient, with natural causes act-
> ing in independence of God. "Divine preservation" started as active sustenance,
> became passive acquiescence, and was then forgotten. Frequent reference was
> made to God's dominion and governance, but the interpretation given to these
> terms made them applicable only to the original act of creation. (p. 42)

He posited two major theological consequences of the figure of the
Divine Clockmaker. First, the medieval idea of divine immanence in nature
was challenged, making God external to the world. Second, God began to be
thought of as First Cause, not a constantly active force in the world. Therefore, by the beginning of the 18th century, Nature, a self-contained machine,
is expunged of God, its creator who dwells—critically—*outside* of the domain
of humans. The image of the Clockmaker, who after he creates his product no longer actively intervenes in it, as Barbour noted, is suggestive of a
strategy widely used among early modern philosophers that he called "God
of the gaps." In other words, when early modern philosophy and science

begin to take shape and develop their respective fields of knowledge, outside the confines of theology, "God" is utilized to fill in unexplained gaps. The technological analogy, of Nature as machine (a clock) and God as Divine Clockmaker, then reflects a "machina ex dei" in early modern philosophy and science. Just as a "deus ex machine" was the means by which ancient Greek drama resolved itself (through the sudden appearance of a god dropped down onto the stage by a crane), the "machina ex dei" is the condition of possibility for the Galilean-Newtonian worldview of the 17th–18th centuries.

In his reading of the Clockmaker analogy, Funkenstein (1989) also emphasizes the *mechanical* nature of the clock, suggesting that the Clockmaker analogy is the figural epitome of the increasingly mechanical view of the world. Funkenstein (1989) says:

> The mechanical clock, in whose perfection the scientists and craftsmen of the seventeenth century invested so much energy, was the most suitable analogue to natural, mental, and social processes for more than one reason. A clock is a machine that, once wound, works of itself. Its work is not a work on something—pulling, pushing or lifting another object. Its work is performed by the very regularity of its motions. So also does the universe—and the universe, moreover, is, by definition, the most precise time-telling device. Organisms are clocks too: a healthy body has a regular heartbeat, and the circulation of the blood had recently been made susceptible to a mechanical explanation. (p. 324)

Differing from Barbour, however, Funkenstein (1989) situated the Clockmaker analogy in a much longer history of mechanical metaphors. As he noted, the comparison of universe to machine goes back to Antiquity and Middle Ages, when "complicated astronomical clocks were designed and built that visualized, represented, and facilitated the computation of celestial orbits." But nevertheless, he argued, the Clockmaker analogy emerged in the 17th–18th centuries because not only was the clock "the most admired man-made artifice [and] the paradigm of a perfect machine" but also because the new scientific insights occasioned an opening for a new explanation of the relation between creator and creation. However, Funkenstein (1989) suggested that there is a difference between the mechanical metaphors of ancient and medieval cosmology and early modern ones. "The irony of the attribution of a 'mechanization of the world picture' to the seventeenth century," he wrote, "lies in the simple, often overlooked circumstance that cosmologies based on the 'new science' of mechanics were incapable of being represented by actual mechanical devices" (p. 318). Thus, the key development in the formation of the technological analogy was, as Mumford (1967) stated, the "transfer of order from God to the Machine." He continued:

> For God became in the eighteenth century the Eternal Clockmaker who, having conceived and created and wound up the clock of the universe, had no further

responsibility until the machine ultimately broke up—for, as the nineteenth century thought, until the works ran down. (p. 34)

By virtue of it being the most advanced device of its time, the clock was, for Mumford, "the typical symbol for the machine as such" (Dohrn-van Rossum, 1996, p. 11). So, we see in the 17th and 18th centuries, amid the shift in the relation of religion and science, the problem of how to keep God in the equation of the mechanical world getting solved by deployment of the technological figuration of the Clockmaker analogy. The "problem" of God becomes solved by a technology—the clock. As the historian of time Dohrn-van Rossum (1996) summarized it: "The demiurge-God [from Plato] became a clockmaker-God, and the 'machina mundi' became the clockwork-like universe, and the starry heavens, the ideal clock" (p. 284).

The Computer—20th–21st Centuries

In the 20th and 21st centuries, another convergence of religion and technology has emerged, which, like the problematic of the clock, has ramifications for the conception of *imago Dei*, and thus also of God, humans, and nature. While, this time, the technology is different, and happens to be the computer, the intellectual crisis and set of challenges to the understanding of the *imago Dei* are nevertheless parallel. Whereas the clock resonated with the growing influence of modern science and mechanical thinking, the computer, or cybernetic machine, exhibits other characteristics, namely "creative reproduction."

According to Robert Geraci (2008), "one of mankind's most cherished dreams—in religious, scientific and artistic circles—has been the creation of humanoid life" (p. 138). While the definition of "humanoid" has often been linked with "intelligence" or "sentience" (think about the use of the latter with regard to the possibility of life on other planets), it seems that today, "robotics and artificial intelligence (AI) hold the most promise for realizing this longstanding dream" (Geraci, 2008, p. 139). Among the many other features of computing, since even its earliest instantiations, such as complex calculation, it has been automation, true automation, that has defined the ethos of computer technology for most people. While some degree of *automation* has existed since the beginnings of industrialization, the kind of automation that is possible within the framework of computing is actually *autonomy*. In other words, industrial automation requires a great degree of human input whereas the computerized automation demands far less.

In *God and Golem, Inc.: A Comment on Certain Points Where Cybernetics Impinges on Religion*, Norbert Wiener (1966), the arguable founder of cybernetics, attempted to quell some of the potential negative religious reaction against cybernetics, and, more broadly, automatization. The book, then, is in part a work of apologia, one which tries to:

> Take certain situations which have been discussed in religious books, and have a religious aspect, but posses a close analogy to other situations which belong to science, and in particular to the new science of cybernetics, the science of communication and control, whether in machines or in living organisms. (Wiener, 1966, p. 8)

The myth of the Golem can be traced to the Jewish ghetto of medieval Prague. Under duress and threat of expulsion or annihilation from the Roman emperor, the Rabbi of Prague constructed a Golem, an anthropomorphic statue, out of clay from the Vltava River, "placing the unspoken name of the Almighty on its forehead," giving it life. "The Golem grows, stretching in size and in weight in the ability to perform great tasks," mostly to guard the townspeople (Kuhns, 1971, p. 15). But it spurred out of control, spreading fear amongst the Jews whom it was supposed to protect. The Rabbi, in response, had to erase the first letter of the name, rendering it still forever. While the Golem may seem like a Frankensteinian story of hubris, for Wiener (1966), the Golem, a result of the human's Godly nature of creation, is an apt illustration of the *imago Dei*'s crucial link to technology, or at least to the figure of the cybernetic machine, which in some ways, the Golem was. It is a story of human extension, of creation.

Wiener's argument in *God and Golem, Inc.* (1966) is to insist on machines' ability to learn and *create* other machines in their self-image, as the Rabbi of Prague had done. This, according to Wiener, is at the heart of the divine quality of the human. As he wrote:

> God is supposed to have made man in His own image, and the propagation of the race may also be interpreted as a function in which one living being makes another in its own image. In our desire to glorify God with respect to man and Man with respect to matter, it is thus natural to assume that machines cannot make other machines in their own image; that this something associated with a sharp dichotomy of systems into living and non-living; and that is moreover associated with the other dichotomy between creator and creature. (p. 12)

As Wiener argued, this idea of creation is at times explained biologically, in the phylogenic and ontogenic terms of procreation, that is, as man making man in his own image. "This seems to be the echo of the prototype of the act of creation, by which God is supposed to have made man in His image," he wrote. But, "can something similar occur in the less complicated (and perhaps more understandable) case of the nonliving systems that we call machines?" (p. 29). The answer for Wiener is clearly, "Yes."

Unsurprisingly, as those who are familiar with cybernetics, and in particular Wiener's work, may well have guessed, the points of resonance between cybernetics and religion are rooted in the process of "learning" and feedback. The Christian anthropological doctrine of *imago Dei*, he argued, unnecessarily excludes the possibility of reproduction in non-living entities, such as machines, or even non-human entities. "Machines," he wrote, "are very well able to make other machines in their own image" (p. 13).

Learning, for Wiener (1966), has a particular meaning as it relates to machines. A learning machine is, according to Weiner:

> An organized system . . . [that] transforms a certain incoming message into an outgoing message, according to some principle of transformation. If this principle of transformation is subject to a certain criterion of merit of performance, and if the method of transformation is adjusted so as to tend to improve the performance of the system according to this criterion, the system is said to *learn*. (p. 14)

But, what then, is a machine? In his words, a machine is a transducer, "a device for converting incoming messages into outgoing messages" (Wiener, 1966, p. 32). Messages, in Wiener's schema, are obviously signals, such as electrical currents. But within them, he suggested, are "images" of reproduction.

> The messages in which the function of a given transducer may be embodied will also embody all those many embodiments of a transducer with the same operative image. Among these there is at least one embodiment with a certain special sort of mechanical structure, and it is this embodiment that I am proposing to reconstruct from the message carrying the operational image of the machine. (p. 37)

Wiener's distinction of operational and pictorial images in mechanical self-reproduction is actually how archive files work in today's computer operating systems. ISO (International Organization for Standardization) and DMG (Disk image) are two of the most widely known and used image file types. An exemplary use of disk images is when large institutions such as university computer labs or libraries create a standard image with the standard software environment (e.g., the programs that should be on all of the computers) in order to quickly "clone"—the term that is used in IT-circles—the disks. This is how all the computers of a given institution have the exact same programs. Disk images of today's computers work exactly as Wiener (1966) described operative images of machines. For Wiener then, creative reproduction, better yet *artificial intelligence*, is the process by which the figures of God, man, and ultimately machine are connected.

Along similar lines, theologian Anne Foerst (1998) argued that the emergence of the science of artificial intelligence and robotics has raised questions about the *imago Dei* (Foerst, 1998). In particular, she pointed to the Cog project of MIT, Wiener's intellectual base, which developed a "humanoid robot," with "embodied artificial intelligence," that has "intuitive self-under-standing." The Cog's researchers and scientists have a different understanding of intelligence than traditional AI. As Foerst described it:

> Intelligence, so their creed states, cannot be implemented on a disembodied machine. On the contrary, intelligence emerges only in bodies and is dependent on bodily features and conditions. An ant has a different body and *lebensraum* from a horse, so they have developed different abilities and intelligence tasks which serve their respective needs. (p. 100)

This translates practically to Cog's hardware, which bears a humanlike body with "a head, a neck, a torso, two arms and two hands," with "degrees of freedom similar to the parts of a human body and are humanlike in shape" (Foerst, 1998, p. 100). Further, it also bears a sensory-perceptual system that mirrors the human sensorium in addition to the ability to act socially.

Though the full functioning of such a machine may be some time away, for Foerst (1998), the philosophical and theological implications underneath the embodied AI of the Cog project offer an occasion to rethink the *imago Dei* to include "humanoids as part of God's creation" (p. 107), including the humanoid robot of the Cog. As Foerst argued:

> Cog is a creature, created by us. The biblical stories of creation describe us and all living beings as creatures created by God. On that ground, God's creative powers are mirrored in Cog. The Cog project also tells us a story about the human creative powers that are a part of the image of God. The Cog project does not necessarily have to be understood as a hubristic attempt to be like God but can be seen as a result of our God-given imagination and courage to create something new. (p. 108)

For her, the "intelligence" in "artificial intelligence" is defined beyond rational computation; it is creative reproduction.

The inclusion of all creatures—biological and technological—initiated by Foerst's (1998) analysis of recent developments in AI points towards a relational ontology, and resonates with recent movements among certain Trinitarian theologians, who might be labeled as "relationalists," that have been critical of the traditional—humanist, rationalist and mechanical—interpretation of *imago Dei*, suggesting that the term aims mostly to provide an ideal picture of the human being as the embodiment of divine rationality, and thus coming dangerously to apotheosis. Figures such as John Zizioulas (Zizioulas & Zizioulas, 1985) and Jurgen Moltmann (1993) have argued for a rethinking of the *imago Dei* in relational terms, that is, "not as an individually held static quality of the mind, but as a relational achievement that is constituted between others-in-relation" (Stephenson, 2005, p. 7), inspired by the *hypostases* in one *ousia* of the Trinity.

In *God in Creation*, Moltmann (1993) argued that the traditional formulation of *imago Dei*, which, by the way, he suggests is not Biblically accurate, "is based on a false inference." According to Moltmann:

> The human being's likeness to God is a theological term before it becomes an anthropological one. It first of all says something about the God who creates his image for himself, and who enters into a particular relationship with that image, before it says anything about the human being who is created in this form. (p. 220)

For Moltmann (1993), the "divine image" is misconstrued by the anthropological reading given to it by the Enlightenment in lieu of the proper theological reading, which he elucidated through a philological distinction between the two meanings behind "image." Moltmann (1993) continued:

> The two definitions of God's image as *selem* and *demuth*, *eikon* and *homoiosis*, *imago* and *similitudo*, already point this possibility, in the process of their translation into other languages: *imago* expresses the ontic participation (methexis), *similitudo* the moral correspondence (mimesis). *Imago* has to do with the nature of human beings in their consciousness, reason and will. *Similitudo* means the human virtue of fearing God and obeying him. If a person becomes a sinner, he becomes disobedient and contends against God. So in sin it is the *similitudo Dei* which is lost; the *imago Dei* can never be forfeited. (p. 230)

Here, in bringing up the distinction between *imago* and *similitudo*, Moltmann (1993) also raised the issue of sin and the fall, in line with Noble's (1997) discussion of transcendence and technology mentioned earlier. In doing so, Moltmann (1993) questioned the Enlightenment view of *imago Dei* as it rests upon an anthropocentricism that views the human being as a special case of divinity, distinguishing "the human being from animals, and interpret[ing] whatever is specifically human about men and women in religious terms as their likeness to God" (Moltmann, 1993, p. 220). Thus, the *imago Dei* has had far greater anthropological importance than theological, lying beneath the generating of what Gillian and Lemert called a "humanist cryptometaphysics" (Gillan & Lemert, 1982). For Moltmann (1993), the alternative way of viewing the *imago Dei* is relational, starting from God's relationship to human beings, and extending to the rest of nature. He wrote: "If we start from God's relationship to human beings, then what makes the human being God's image is not his possession of any particular characteristic or other—something which distinguishes him above other creatures; it is *his whole existence*" (p. 221).

This theological argument is echoed by Lutheran theologian of science Antje Jackelén (2002), who accused the anthropocentrism of the traditional *imago Dei* of "denying the biological unity of humans with the rest of nature" (p. 298). She extended this also to the realm of the technological through the concept of "relationality." She wrote:

> Relationality can be addressed as a crucial feature of the image of God, and it certainly is also an issue relating to AI [Artificial Intelligence] and its various applications. In my view, relational capacity and a creativity that goes together with—and often results from—imperfection are crucial marks of the image of God. (p. 299)

Relationality, or creativity, reflects an understanding of God not as "primarily omnipotent and omniscient," but rather as an "image of a God who creates by means of irregularity, instability, disturbance and sudden inflation—features we recognize from the epic of creation as it is told by contemporary science" (Jackelén, 2002, p. 299). And thus, we end up in a completely different place than where we started. The God of relational theology is irregular and unstable, mirroring the complex, non-linear technologies of the day.

Conclusion

What we see is that *imago Dei*, at least in modern times, becomes the stage upon which theologians, scientists, historians, and sociologists wage the intellectual battle grappling with the definition of the human and God. In the all-too-brief, snapshot-like historical outlines in this chapter, I have argued that the conceptualization of relation of God and the human has been articulated through technological metaphor and analogy through the *imago Dei*. The mechanical 17th–18th century *imago Dei* resulted in an idea of a removed, transcendent God that had, in the mold of Deism, been mostly Creator, allowing its Creation—chiefly the human—to hold dominion in "this" realm. It was the cosmology that preceded humanism. By the 19th century, the mechanical *imago Dei* had become relational, or creative.

In 1954, media theorist Marshall McLuhan wrote of the "revolutionary situation," wherein "the essential function of the universe which is a machine for the making of gods," quoting Bergson's *Two Sources of Morality and Religion*. For McLuhan then, "the new conditions of global inter-communication" were "the new universe" for the making of gods. "And whereas the machine of nature made whatever gods it chose, the machines of man have abolished Nature and enable us to make whatever gods we choose" (McLuhan, 2002, p. 198). However, he identified a paradox, which brings us back to Niebuhr's (1964) critical point about self-transcendence as the point at which *sin* encounters the image of God:

The fall brings about the rise of individual reason and the invention of the instruments of culture and civilization. Reason, the tool-making faculty, is the fruit of evil. And reason is the myth-making power which produces the ruler. The ruler rules by the myth or lie which intimidates men to the point of social obedience. (p. 199)

The "men" who are intimidated, in this case, are those who are also the rule-makers. The very faculty, reason, that linked the human to God, which has facilitated the *making* of technical gods, has also ruled over those who created it. The rule rules over the rulers.

Or so the humanist argument goes. Contrary to this view, which is echoed by even the most brilliant of 20th century scholars of media, if one looks at the history of the relations between technologies and *imago Dei*, there is a clear trajectory, which, I argue, reflects a re-immanentization of the *imago Dei*, bringing down the ontology of the human as the embodiment of earthly dominion to relational with all creatures, as with the medieval era, but with a twist, technologies included. One of the most significant implications of this is its critique of the humanism for which it was a primary technique for so long. In a rather ironic twist of events, the rationalist *imago Dei* of humanism that midwifed the birth of modern science and technology, in the end, ultimately becomes its hospice.

Notes

1. I use this term following Fredric Jameson's work on the political unconscious. See Jameson, F. (1982). *The Political Unconscious*. Ithaca, NY: Cornell University Press.
2. It is important to note that Newton made a distinction between scientific explanation (natural laws) and the purpose of nature.

References

Augustine, A. (1873). *The works of Aurelius Augustine: A new translation* (M. Dods, Ed., A. Haddan, Trans.) (Vol. 7). Edinburgh, Scotland: T. & T. Clark.

Barbour, I. G. (1966). *Issues in science and religion*. Englewood Cliffs, NJ: Prentice-Hall.

Benjamin, W. (1969). The Work of Art in the Age of Mechanical Reproduction. H. Arendt (Ed.), *Illuminations* (217–250). New York: Schocken Books.

Christian, B. (2011, March). Mind vs. machine. *The Atlantic Magazine*. Retrieved from http://www.theatlantic.com/magazine/archive/2011/03/mind-vs-machine/8386/5/

Dohrn-van Rossum, G. (1996). *History of the hour: Clocks and modern temporal orders*. Chicago, IL: University of Chicago Press.

Foerst, A. (1998). Cog, a humanoid robot, and the question of the image of God. *Zygon*, *33*(1), 91–111.

Foucault, M. (2002). *The order of things: An archaeology of the human sciences*. London, England: Routledge.

Freud, S. (2005). *Civilization and its discontents* (J. Strachey, Trans.). New York, NY: W. W. Norton.

Funkenstein, A. (1989). *Theology and the scientific imagination from the Middle Ages to the seventeenth Century.* Princeton, NJ: Princeton University Press.

Geisler, M. (1999). From building blocks to radical construction: West German media theory since 1984. *New German Critique, 78,* 75–107.

Gillan, G., & Lemert, C. (1982). *Michel Foucault: Social theory as transgression.* New York, NY: Columbia University Press.

Gillespie, M. A. (2008). *The theological origins of modernity.* Chicago, IL: University of Chicago Press.

Goertzel, B. (2011). Watson: Supercharged search engine or prototype robot overlord? [Blog post]. Retrieved from http://hplusmagazine.com/2011/02/17/watson-supercharged-search-engine-or-prototype-robot-overlord/

Halpern, O. (2005). Dreams for our perceptual present: Temporality, storage, and interactivity in cybernetics. *Configurations, 13*(2), 283–319.

Husserl, E. (1970). *The crisis of European sciences and transcendental phenomenology: An introduction to phenomenological philosophy.* Evanston, IL: Northwestern University Press.

Is God dead? (1966, April 8). *Time.* Retrieved from http://www.time.com/time/covers/0,16641,19660408,00.html

Jackelén, A. (2002). The image of God as techno sapiens. *Zygon, 37*(2), 289–302.

Jameson, F. (1982). *The political unconscious.* Ithaca, NY: Cornell University Press.

Jennings, K. (2011, February 16). My puny human brain. *Slate.* Retrieved February 20, 2011, from http://www.slate.com/id/2284721/

Kittler, F. A. (1999). *Gramophone, film, typewriter.* Stanford, CA: Stanford University Press.

Kuhns, W. (1969). *The electronic gospel.* New York, NY: Herder and Herder.

Kuhns, W. (1971). *The post-industrial prophets: Interpretations of technology.* New York, NY: Weybright and Talley.

Lash, S. (1999). *Another modernity: A different rationality.* Oxford, England: Blackwell.

Maerz, M. (2011, February 12). "Jeopardy" invites supercomputer Watson to destroy all humans. *Los Angeles Times.* Retrieved from http://latimesblogs.latimes.com/showtracker/2011/02/jeopardy-invites-super-computer-watson-to-destroy-all-humans.html

McLuhan, M. (2002). *The medium and the light: Reflections on religion* (E. McLuhan & J. Szlarek, Eds.). Berkeley, CA: Gingko Press.

Merton, R. K. (1938). Science, technology and society in seventeenth century England. *Osiris, 4,* 360–632.

Moltmann, J. (1993). *God in creation: A new theology of creation and the spirit of God.* Minneapolis, MN: Fortress Press.

Mumford, L. (1963). *Technics and civilization.* New York, NY: Harcourt.

Mumford, L. (1967). *The myth of the machine* (Vol. 1). New York, NY: Harcourt.

Niebuhr, R. (1964). *The nature and destiny of man: A Christian interpretation* (Vol. 1). New York, NY: Scribner.

Noble, D. F. (1997). *The religion of technology: The divinity of man and the spirit of invention*. New York, NY: Alfred A. Knopf.

Paley, W. (2008). *Natural theology*. Oxford, England: Oxford University Press.

Stephenson, B. (2005). Nature, technology and the imago Dei: Mediating the nonhuman through the practice of science. *Perspectives on Science and Christian Faith, 57*, 6–12.

Whitehead, A. N. (1997). *Science and the modern world*. New York, NY: Simon & Schuster.

Wiener, N. (1966). *God and golem, Inc.* Cambridge, MA: MIT Press.

Zizioulas, J. D., & Zizioulas, J. (1985). *Being as communion*. Crestwood, NY: St. Vladimir's Seminary Press.

16. *Toward a Theology of the Internet: Place, Relationship, and Sin*

LYNNE M. BAAB

In a 2002 *Theology Today* article, Graham Ward observed that a number of conceptual categories are undergoing modification in our time, including space and materiality, as well as relational categories such as community, friend, contact, and acquaintance. He also noted that boundaries are being blurred, including the boundary between the real and the virtual (off-line and online) and between human and machine. He maintained, as many scholars do, that new theological reflection is necessary in the light of these changes. In the past decade, most articles and books linking the Christian faith to the internet have focused on practical, not theological, issues. As McDonnell (2009) pointed out, when theologians have tried to make connections between Christian theology and the internet, they have usually focused on the ethical and psychological consequences of new media. Some scholars and theologians, such as Charry (2004), have used the phenomenon of the internet to illuminate theological principles. Generally, however, theological reflection about the internet remains in its infancy, and in this chapter I have endeavored to make new connections between three major areas of theology—theologies of place, relationship, and sin—and the rise of the internet in human communication.

The internet is increasingly viewed as a place where people spend significant amounts of time; it functions like a library, a place for the interchange of information, a casual gathering place and, for some Christians, a place for ministry. Therefore, the first area of reflection is theology of place, which has been a minor but significant strand in theological reflection throughout Christian history. Secondly, theological discussion about human relationships is necessary because the internet presents unprecedented opportunities for connection with others. Humans enthusiastically take advantage of these opportunities because we were inscribed at creation with the drive for connection. We were made in the image of a relational God; we use whatever means are available and convenient to nurture relationships. Yet electronic communication encourages individualism, self-determination, and objectification of others, so the internet, like much of the rest of life on earth, is a place where God can work, but also a place where self-focused and addictive behavior can easily emerge. Therefore, theology of sin is a third area of fruitful reflection.

Theology of Place

The biblical narratives in both the Hebrew Scriptures and the New Testament put significant emphasis on God's work in specific places. Abraham was called by God to leave his home to go to a new land. His descendents lived there for only a few generations before being enslaved in Egypt for several centuries. The Exodus from Egypt involved a generation spent in the wilderness, a place where God worked mightily with the people of Israel. The conquest of a land "flowing with milk and honey" (Exodus 3:8 and many other passages) followed. In the early years in the land, numerous towns and other specific locations were named for a miracle or action of God that occurred in that specific place. Stones were used as markers of places where God had helped the people of Israel (e.g., 1 Samuel 7:12). The pain of the exile in the sixth century was particularly profound because of the people's removal from the places where God had worked in their lives: "By the rivers of Babylon—there we sat down and there we wept when we remembered Zion. . . . How could we sing the Lord's song in a foreign land?" (Psalm 137:1, 4, NRSV). The incarnation of Jesus Christ occurred in a particular place, and the spread of the Gospel around the world began in Jerusalem, with the sending of the Holy Spirit on a specific group of believers in a specific place, with the understanding that the disciples would be witnesses "in Jerusalem, in all Judea and Samaria, and to the ends of the earth" (Acts 1:8, NRSV).

Jesus' words to the woman at the well in John 4:24 about worship in spirit and in truth could be seen as indicating that God's work in specific places would be superseded by an outpouring of the Holy Spirit in all places. However, even though the New Testament testifies to this new reality, that God's presence and activity goes far beyond the land of Israel, the incarnation itself gives weight to the significance of action of God in human life on earth, which occurs in specific times and places. John Inge, in *A Christian Theology of Place* (2003), affirmed that the notion of place retains "vital significance in God's dealings with humanity, since places can be thought of as the seat of relations, or the place of meeting and activity in the interaction between God and the world" (p. 58). T. J. Gorringe (2002) expanded on this specificity of human existence:

> To be human is to be placed: to be born in this house, hospital, stable (according to Luke), or even, as in the floods in Mozambique in 2001, in a tree. It is to live in this council house, semi-detached, tower block, farmhouse, mansion. It is to go to school through these streets or lanes, to play in this alley, park, garden; to shop in this market, that mall; to work in this factory, mine, office, farm. These facts are banal, but they form the fabric of our everyday lives, structuring our memories, determining our attitudes. (p. 1)

Gorringe (2002) went on to argue that theological reflection on the specific locations of human life involves "a discernment of God active in God's world" (p. 7). He noted that the Christian church is, first and foremost, a local community (p. 185), but that challenges for a theology of place in our time come from the postmodern reality that "individuals no longer have a single location, but many have several, and that rather than the city being a mosaic of spatially discrete worlds, there are multiple grids within which identity is formed" (p. 186).

Inge (2003) traced the history of theological reflection on place. He noted that the theological significance of place remained significant, beginning in the Old Testament and continuing through the medieval period, as is evidenced by the medieval emphasis on pilgrimage and the crusades. However, theologians during and after the Reformation placed more emphasis on the significance of time rather than place. Inge (2003) cited Wendell Berry as one of the few contemporary theologians who discuss in detail the significance of place. Inge argued that undifferentiated space becomes a place for us when we become familiar with it because our perception of reality is shaped by what we do, think, and feel in specific places (pp. 1, 26). He advocated for a *relational view of place* because "any conception of place is inseparable from the relationships that are associated with it" (p. 26, italics in original). Jeanne Hallgren Kilde (2008), after having discussed issues of power as they occur in sacred places, affirmed: "The material world is far from neutral; indeed, as we have seen, it is through physical spaces and material objects that many of the power relations we have witnessed are articulated and maintained" (p. 199). Thus Kilde (2008) and Inge (2003) joined Gorringe (2002) in asserting that, even though in many ways God's work, after the coming of the Holy Spirit, transcends place, we remain created beings who live and move and experience relationships with people and with God in specific places.

Can the internet be considered to be one of those specific places? "Place" has traditionally been linked to particular locations or spots, but in our time, people talk about the internet in ways that resemble discussion about particular locations: "I met my boyfriend on the internet," or "I like to spend time with my friends on Facebook." Using Inge's (2003) description of what makes undifferentiated space become a place, the internet has become familiar to many people because of the time they spend there and because relationships are experienced on the internet. Using Gorringe's (2002) descriptions of how places work, the internet is a place where, for many people, identity is formed, memory is structured and attitudes are determined. As Gorringe has noted, people today live in multiple locations, and one of those locations can be said to be the internet. For some Christians, the internet is a place where God is active and ministry is accomplished. Many churches view their websites as places where their congregational ministry is enhanced and expanded. Many Christian bloggers hope to stimulate reflection, discussion, and growth in faith through blogging. Christian online discussion groups and special interest websites provide a place for Christians to connect with each other around specific issues. Some Christians experience worship in online congregations. On Facebook, I see people promising to pray for their friends in times of crisis. These actions play a part in a growing perception that the internet is a place for connection with others and with God, as well as a place to find information.

One way to understand the internet as a place is to consider the concept of a "third place," a term coined by Oldenburg and Brissett (1982), who cited the coffeehouses and public houses of Europe, particularly in previous centuries, as examples of a third place. Neither the home nor the workplace, a third place provides a location for sociability and nondiscursive symbolism, which Oldenburg and Brissett described as idiomatic, spontaneous, colorful, and freewheeling conversation, steeped in stories and emotional expression, in contrast with conversation that is instrumental and pragmatic, used to give directions, solve problems, buy merchandise, write contracts, and talk with clients. A third place can host a spectrum of kinds of personal involvement, and is often a site for informal connections between people of different ethnic or socioeconomic groups. North American society in the late twentieth century had very few third places.

The internet is a place for communication that gives directions, solves problems, purchases merchandise, and involves communication with clients, so, in some of its forms, the internet has qualities that are instrumental and resemble the workplace. However, with the rise in social networking, increased opportunities for extended discussions on blogs and news websites, the possibility of lingering over friends' photos posted on photo-sharing websites, and the ability to play competitive games online while talking with the other players, the internet functions in many ways as a third place, a place where a variety of colorful and freewheeling interactions can take place. In addition, the internet's growing role as a source of information on a vast array of topics makes it increasingly like a library. Thus, the internet functions like a market place, a library, and an informal gathering place where a wide variety of activities take place. Many have argued that the internet is an inferior place for these activities to happen, citing the disruption of geographic communities, increasing tribalization, one-dimensionality, and the marginalization of people with limited internet access (Edwards 2000; Evensen, 2010). However, for good or ill, the internet functions like a place for many people, and theological reflection about God's presence in human places can be extended to a consideration of the internet. The benefit of considering the internet to be a place, and as such, a locus of human activity and God's engagement with us, lies in the possibility of stepping away from the highly dichotomized discussion of the internet that is so common, with some writers and thinkers viewing the internet as evil or approaching evil, while others view it with an almost utopian enthusiasm (Lawson [2001] summarized both sides of the way Christians frame the argument). If the internet is a place, then we need to spend time considering how to bring forth the best kinds of human activity there, just like we would explore that question with any other place. We need to confront human sin on the internet, just as we would confront it in other places. In addition, we need to explore the ways God is working there, in much the same way that God is working in other places.

The idea of a utopian paradise is relevant to this discussion because of the highly dichotomized views about the internet that are so common. Alessandro Scafi, in his 2006 book *Mapping Paradise*, noted that throughout history, human beings have looked for paradise. The utopian language in some of the early literature on internet communication stands in that long tradition of hoping that here, at last, we have found the place where relationships will be free from the taint of role, class, gender, and status (Herring, 2001; Dean, 2000). I recently conducted interviews for a book on friendship in the Facebook age, talking (in person, by phone and email, and on Facebook) with dozens of people ranging in age from 12 to 85. I heard a wide range of opinions about relationships with a significant internet component. Some interviewees were very negative, mirroring the many articles in print and online publications that view social networking as dangerous or even evil. However, some interviewees were uncritical about the ways they communicate online with friends, some of them verging toward a kind of utopian optimism. Some interviewees believed that staying connected with friends as much as possible, through means such as Facebook, instant messaging, Skype, and cell phone texting, makes good relationships happen almost inevitably. To them, the tools for communication that are found in this place, the internet, are uniformly helpful and will certainly build good relationships. The word "utopia," coined by Sir Thomas More in his 1516 book with that title, comes from two Greek words, "no" and "place," and More used the word in a fictional construction indicating his belief that paradise on earth is not possible. As Scafi (2006) pointed out, the search for paradise or utopia on earth has always failed, and the complexities and challenges of the online world make it clear that the internet is already failing as a place for utopian communication. This will become increasingly apparent as we turn to consider further the question of human relationships, beginning with the image of God in human beings and moving on to human sin and the fall.

The Relational Trinity and Human Relationships

Throughout Christian history, the idea that humans are created in the image of God (Gen 1:26) has precipitated much thought and analysis. Theologians over the centuries have proposed numerous answers to the question of what exactly the image of God in human nature consists of. In the twentieth century this question came back to the forefront as a part of the renewed interest among theologians in the nature of the Trinity. These reflections on the Trinity, and the implications for human relationships, shed light on the way we understand relationships with a significant online component.

Stanley J. Grenz (2004) used the words "renaissance" and "rebirth" to describe the rise in interest in trinitarian theology in the twentieth century (p. x). His own work includes three books that focus on the relational nature of the Trinity and the connection to human relationality, and the titles themselves are illustrative of the theological trends related to the Trinity around the turn of the century: *Created for Community* (1996), *The Social God and the Relational Self* (2001), and *Rediscovering the Triune God* (2004). The nature of personhood and the roles of the three persons of the Trinity were often explored by theologians in the last century, and one recurring theme was the roots of human relationality in the Trinity. Grenz (2004) summarized this theological movement:

> By the end of the twentieth century, the concept of relationality had indeed moved to center stage. In fact, the assumption that the most promising beginning point for a viable trinitarian theology lies in the constellation of relationships among the three trinitarian persons had become so widely accepted that it attained a kind of quasi-orthodox status. (pp. 117–118)

Grenz, in his 2001 and 2004 books surveyed the twentieth century theologians who contributed to this relational emphasis, noting that the stage was set by Karl Barth and Karl Rahner, developed further by Jurgen Moltmann, Wolfhart Pannenberg, and Robert Jenson, and then a whole host of other writers followed (Grenz, 2001, p. 118).

Calvin and Luther contributed a great deal to trinitarian theology and our understanding of human beings created in the image of triune God, and contemporary theologians drew on the Reformers (such as Grenz, 2001, pp. 162–170), as well as even earlier sources. John Zizioulas (1985, 1991, 2006), writing from an Eastern Orthodox perspective, had a great influence on Protestant and Roman Catholic scholars in the area of Trinitarian theology. Zizioulas cited the writings of the Cappadocian Fathers, such as Basil the Great, Gregory of Nyssa, Gregory of Nazianzus, and Amphilachius of Iconium, who lived in Asia Minor in the fourth century. Zizioulas argued that the Cappadocian Fathers help us understand that the image of God in humans does not relate to our nature, because we cannot become God, but to our personhood. This personhood is best understood as mirroring the relationships between the persons of the Trinity. "True personhood arises not from one's individualistic isolation from others but from love and relationship with others, from communion" (Zizioulas, 2006, p. 168). Only love, Zizioulas asserted, can generate personhood, and this is true of both God and humans. In fact, relationship is so constitutive of personhood that relationship is not a part of being but is being itself (Zizioulas, 1985, p. 101; 1991).

Kathryn Tanner (2001) noted that it is not enough to say that we as human persons are constituted by our relationships with others. We must also describe what human relationships should be like. "Their shape must also mirror the incarnation and Trinity" (p. 79). Millard Erickson's (1995) words echoed the same idea: "There is mutual submission of each of the members of the Trinity to each of the others. Thus, the type of relationships that should characterize human persons . . .would be one of unselfish love and submission to the other" (p. 333). The longing for deep and loving connection was wired into human beings at creation because of human creation in the image of a social God, whose three persons are characterized by love and mutual submission. Even though God's image in humans is marred by sin, the longing for connection is still there. This longing manifests itself in the relentless efforts to connect personally with others, that are visible in many areas of everyday life, including the internet.

The early years of the telephone and the early years of the internet have some interesting parallels that illustrate the human propensity for personal connection with others, originating in the creation of humans in the image of a relational God. Alexander Graham Bell envisioned people chatting personally on telephones. However, for the first two decades of the twentieth century, when telephones were beginning to become common in homes in North America, telephone executives emphasized the telephone's effectiveness for accomplishing tasks, such as getting information or placing orders with shops. Personal conversations were branded as "trivial," "frivolous," and "unnecessary" (Fischer, 1988, pp. 48, 49). Surveys that observed patterns of telephone use showed that people were increasingly using the telephone for personal relationships as well as accomplishing tasks, so by the mid-1920s advertising and sales strategies shifted toward an increased emphasis on sociability (Fischer, p. 58). In much the same way, email came on the scene in the 1970s for the purpose of allowing researchers to send data to each other (Shannon, 2010). Within a few years, those researchers found themselves sharing personal information and asking personal questions as they shot data back and forth. This move from the functional to the relational resulted, in the 1990s, in the increasing popularity of personal email, online groups, forums, and bulletin boards, which made possible a variety of personal connections online. In the early years of the twenty-first century, social networking provided even more ways to connect personally online. Leonard Kleinrock, a UCLA computer engineer who was involved in 1969 in the creation of ARPANET, the precursor of the internet, said on the fortieth anniversary of its creation that the broad appeal of the internet was something many of its inventors never predicted. "I am surprised, and totally pleased, at how effective the internet has been in allowing communities of people to form, communicate, exchange ideas, and enter their daily lives in so many ways" (Than, 2009).

David Cunningham (1998) expressed reservations about the use of "relationship" in reference to the Trinity because he believed relationality implies separate entities or individuals, and this cannot be said to be true of the three persons of the Trinity. He focused on the virtues of Trinitarian existence, which God has as a part of God's being and which we receive by grace. Cunningham identified one of those virtues as participation: "What I want to stress about the Three is not that they are related to one another . . . but that they participate in one another to such a degree that any attempt to understand them as independent existences is undermined" (p. 10). In the interviews I conducted about friendship in the Facebook age, some people expressed deep gratitude for the connections they are able to nurture with friends and family members far and near using email, Skype, Facebook, special interest websites, and online groups. Several of my teenaged interviewees talked with enthusiasm about the way that online communication, particularly Facebook with its options for chat as well as for asynchronous connection through reading friends' updates and looking at their photos, coupled with frequent cellphone text messages, provided them with the opportunity to stay connected all day long with their friends. They said they are able to participate in their friends' lives frequently and thoroughly. Cunningham's words about participation "to such a degree that any attempt to understand them as independent existences is undermined" has striking resonance with the way teenagers, as well as many people of all ages, talk about using electronic communication to stay in constant contact with their friends.

Numerous people who have used social networking talked to me in interviews about being overwhelmed by too much information about people's lives, making them feel a bit like voyeurs. One man in his thirties talked about his Facebook connections with friends as being "too convenient" and "compartmentalized." Others talked about Facebook as a double-edged sword, with the capacity to nurture healthy connections with others, yet coupled with an onslaught of information that encourages consumerism and individualism in relationships.

Zizioulas's (1985) view of the significance of the sin and the fall sheds light on the compartmentalized, consumeristic, and voyeuristic aspects of online connection. Human personhood is constituted by communion, he argued. We are not persons with an individual identity first; our identity comes from our relationships with God and with others. "The fall consists in *the refusal to make being dependent on communion*" (p. 102, italics in original). This switches the order of things: if we are not willing to be dependent on communion for our being, then we become autonomous beings or objects, who view the world as full of objects like ourselves. We may still try to connect with others, but we do it as autonomous beings rather than as people who know we are constituted by relationships. Zizioulas, writing in 1985, a decade before email was widely used and two decades before social networking became common, argued that this results in "fragmentation, individualization, conceptualization" (p. 106). His words are strikingly similar to the ones I heard in the interviews I conducted with people who use social networking and who expressed their concerns about it. Human sin, then, in Zizioulas's view, turns human beings into objects, and the internet as a communication tool is unprecedented in human history in its ability to encourage the objectification of others. To retain an awareness of "being as communion" (the title of Zizioulas's 1985 book and the main thesis of that book and much of his other writing) requires significant intentional effort in the midst of the barrage of information about other people available online, often unconnected with personal interactions with them.

I heard story after story from people who are exercising intentional practices to nurture healthy and life-giving connections in relationships with a significant online component. They "listen" to what their friends and family members say online, they respond with compliments, words of love, and commitments to pray for the concerns they hear. They share their own thoughts and feelings, and they affirm their friends and family members when they do so. They place a priority on face-to-face connections and view online connections as a way to stay up to date with the details of their friends' and family members' lives so that they can reconnect easily when they see each other. They do not treat their friends and family members as objects; instead, they treat them as precious gifts. All of this requires intention and commitment in any setting, and congregations can, and do, nurture that intentionality in many ways, including Holy Communion, small groups for prayer and Bible study, prayer for people in need, and a commitment to hospitality. In online settings, the challenge is great because the barrage of information encourages objectification. Zizioulas's (1985) view of being as communion encourages internet users to slow down in our consumption of information about others and to do everything possible to place a priority on a loving relationship with God and with others.

Theology of Sin and Addiction

Theologians have described sin and the consequences of the fall in many diverse ways, and some of those views shed light on the issues around internet use. As noted above, Zizioulas's (1985) understanding of the fall has provided one way to understand human sin: humans turn into objects, which encourages fragmentation and individualization, a phenomenon clearly visible in the online world. This objectification results in rupture of relationships, a common way theologians talk about sin. LaCugna (1991) described sin as "broken relationship" and noted that sin "disorders and fractures our capacity for communion" (p. 284). In a similar way, Grenz (1996) described sin as "a failure of 'community'" (p. 90). He described the process:

> Because we are alienated from God, sin alienates us from other humans as well. God designed us to enjoy wholesome, enriching relationships with each other. But we find ourselves exploiting and being exploited. We jostle with each other for power, influence, and prominence. Or we allow others to rob us of our dignity and sense of worth. (p. 100)

The online world has enabled many forms of exploitation and alienation, including rude or verbally abusive blog posts or responses to blogs, online bullying, and sexual predation. These and many more subtle negative forms of online communication result in loss of dignity and sense of worth. Personal websites and blogs all too often seem to take the form of jostling "with each other for power, influence and prominence" (Grenz, p. 100); readers don't need to look far to find arrogant, self-focused boasting, often accompanied by rude responses that rely on personal attacks and vicious put-downs to make their points. Haskell (2010) pointed out that the world of the internet follows the pattern of Genesis 1–3: the desire for beauty and perfection, so apparent in virtual worlds and idealized self-presentation, yet with human sin visible and vivid online as well, in the form of broken relationships, fractured community, and other manifestations of selfishness.

For Tanner (2001), God's love comes to us as a life-changing gift. One aspect of sin, according to Tanner, is that humans want to be ourselves and to be perfect in ourselves, independent of God's gifts to us (pp. 46, 77). The online world provides novel opportunities for self-presentation and self-marketing through such means as personal websites and blogs, personal pages on social networking websites, and photo-sharing websites. Self-presentation of identity online morphs easily into the creation of identity, a phenomenon that was studied by many early internet researchers (e.g., Chandler, 1998;

Baym, 2000), and which is now accepted as a common aspect of life online. This creation of identity by ourselves for our own purposes has overtones of Tanner's view of sin as human independence from God's gifts, a lack of receptivity for the good things God gives to us. We define who we are quite apart from God's view of us and God's gifts to us. LaCugna's (1991) comments about the different forms that sin takes among men and women also relates to this creation of identity online. She wrote, "It is a staple of Christian moral theology to define sin as prideful self-assertion . . . [but] temptation to sin for women is not the same as for men. The typical sin of women in a patriarchal culture is self-abnegation" (p. 311). I frequently see prideful self-assertion, as well as self-abnegation, in online constructions and representations of identity. It would be interesting to examine whether these opposing patterns of online identity presentation and construction are related to gender. It would also be interesting to reflect on the ways that the online environment provides opportunities for people to present themselves as creatures made in the image of a loving and relational God whose abundant gifts to us define our identity.

The growing literature around internet addiction contributes an additional connection with the theology of human sin. Division of the will is one characteristic of addiction, according to Christopher C. H. Cook in *Alcohol, Addiction and Christian Ethics* (2008); a person desires to continue the addictive behavior but also desires to stop it. Many of the comments posted on Facebook about Facebook reveal the presence of this division of the will. "I spend too much time online!" is a common post. Deeply addictive behavior, with its attendant powerlessness and damage to family and work life, is increasingly visible in some internet users, and more frequently is a topic for books and articles (e.g., Struthers, 2010; Young & Klausing, 2007). This deeply addictive behavior includes engagement with internet pornography and internet gambling. In my dozens of interviews about friendship, four individuals used the language of addiction to refer to their internet use. One man, aged 19 years old, described quitting an online game that he had been engaged in for many months. The game and its attendant online relationships with people all over the world were getting in the way of face-to-face relationships with his dorm mates and family members. After he quit, he pondered the connections between his behavior and his understanding of other forms of addiction, such as addiction to work or to alcohol. Two other university students, both women, talked about the individuals in their circle of friends who have left Facebook because they can't limit its use; they functioned like addicts. Another individual, a man in his thirties, described what he called his addictive personality. He found that Facebook triggered his addictive and competitive urges and he found himself checking it many times a day, trying to accumulate more Facebook friends than other people.

Gerald May, in his landmark book *Addiction and Grace* (1988), noted that the "presence of addiction should be suspected whenever interior human freedom is compromised" (p. 31). He described the condition:

> Addiction exists wherever persons are internally compelled to give energy to things that are not their true desires. To define it directly, addiction is a *state* of compulsion, obsession, or preoccupation that enslaves a person's will and desire. Addiction sidetracks and eclipses the energy of our deepest, truest desire for love and goodness. We succumb because the energy of our desire becomes attached, nailed, to specific behaviors, objects or people. *Attachment*, then, is the process that enslaves desire and creates the state of addiction. (p. 14, italics in original)

The objects of attachment, he noted, become preoccupations or obsessions that gain too much power in our lives. In effect, the objects of attachment become idols. Thus, May (1988) saw addictions as a direct outworking of humanity's ongoing willful rebellion against God. Functionally, addictions are the enemy of love because the addicted person focuses intently on the object of attachment, to the exclusion of other aspects of life, including God and God's priorities. Even when the object of attachment is a person, the relationship is not a true love relationship but instead a relationship with a selfish or ego-based agenda.

May's (1988) view of addiction, relevant to many levels of internet addiction, brings us back full circle to Zizioulas's (1985) understanding of the fall as the objectification of human beings. Addiction focuses the addict on an object of attachment, whether that object is a behavior, a thing, or a person. Freedom is lost because the focus on the object is compulsive and obsessive. Being as communion is ruptured, and loving relationships are compromised. May believed that addictions are the enemy of love and can also bring us to our knees in humble acknowledgement of our powerlessness (p. 4). In fact, he argued that all humans have a propensity to addiction, and that facing into our addictions can draw us back into relationship with God, the One who Tanner (2001) identified as the God who pours out abundant gifts on us.

The Need for a Nuanced Approach

Engaging with the internet as a place where people spend time with their friends and look for information enables the internet to be considered as one of the many places on earth where humans engage with each other, where we sin in multiple ways like we do anywhere else, and where God works. Many Christian congregations have adopted this philosophy, at least in part, as they seek to make their websites and blogs places for ministry to members and to people outside the church, places where people can turn for information, spiritual nurture, and connections with others. Many Christian congregations have dived enthusiastically into Facebook and Twitter as ways to get information about activities out and to nurture connections between individuals, and some congregations encourage members to participate in worship online. As Haskell (2010) pointed out, while some congregations and congregational leaders view the internet as a tool for effective ministry, others hold negative views that paint electronic communication as impersonal and detached, and completely unable to nurture the kind of relationships that honor God. The three theological perspectives in this article—theologies of place, relationship, and sin—would indicate that a more nuanced approach is necessary. The internet enables access to remarkable amounts of information and vibrant connection with people across the miles. The internet can also encourage objectification of others and compartmentalization of relationships, and it can enable behavior that is profoundly addictive and destructive. These two disparate realities about the internet coexist, and navigating these two realities will require creativity, discussion, and exploration in congregations.

Because electronic communication is embedded in everyday life for most people, a phenomenon that appears to be magnifying rather than declining, it will increasingly be impossible and ineffective for congregational leaders simply to denounce the internet. Guidelines for effective and appropriate use need to be articulated, taking into account the benefits of the information and relationships that can be nurtured online, alongside the challenges of objectification and addiction. What kinds of support are needed for people who use a computer all day at work and who find internet gambling so seductive that they lose all their savings and go into debt? How can a group of Christian friends, who tend to stay connected with each other online, support people in their midst who find that Facebook arouses all their competitive and addictive instincts and who desire to quit using it? How can congregational leaders talk realistically about the compartmentalization and objectification that can happen in online friendships, while also affirming that many find the internet to be a place where healthy relationships are nurtured?

Kathryn Tanner's (2001) emphasis that the shape of human relationships "must also mirror the incarnation and Trinity" (p. 79), and Millard Erickson's (1995) similar emphasis, rooted in his Trinitarian perspective, on "unselfish love and submission to the other" (p. 333), are relevant to any discussion of human relationships, online or face-to-face. Our online relationships and practices need to be characterized by the kind of love we experience in the Triune God, in the same way that we strive to reflect God's love in face-to-face settings. I believe Christian leaders need to speak, preach, teach, and write more specifically about what love looks like in all settings of life, offline and online. A realistic perspective about the kinds of sin associated with the internet—particularly objectification and addiction—need to be addressed. We need to grow in our ability to think creatively, theologically, and practically about the challenges presented by this new means of communication, this new place, which is embedded in everyday life for so many people, and where so many people spend significant amounts of time.

References

Baym, N. K. (2000). *Tune in, log on: Soaps, fandom, and online community*. Thousand Oaks, CA: Sage.

Chandler, D. (1998). Personal homepages and the construction of identities on the web [WWW document]. Retrieved from http://www.aber.ac.uk/media/Documents/short/webident.html

Charry, E. T. (2004). Virtual salvation. *Theology Today, 61*(3), 334–346.

Cook, C. C. H. (2008). *Alcohol, addiction and Christian ethics*. Cambridge, England: Cambridge University Press.

Cunningham, D. (1998). Participation as a Trinitarian virtue: Challenging the current "relational" consensus. *Toronto Journal of Theology, 14*(1), 7–25.

Dean, J. (2000). Community. In T. Swiss (Ed.), *Unspun: Key concepts for understanding the World Wide Web*. New York, NY; London, England: New York University Press.

Edwards, M. U. (2000). Virtual worship. *The Christian Century, 117*(6), 1262.

Erickson, M. J. (1995). *God in three persons: A contemporary interpretation of the Trinity*. Grand Rapids, MI: Eerdmans.

Evensen, K. (2010). Pastor on Facebook? Not for me. *Word & World, 30*(3), 329, 331.

Fischer, C. S. (1988). "Touch someone": The telephone industry discovers sociability. *Technology and Culture, 29*(1), 32–61.

Gorringe, T. J. (2002). *A theology of the built environment: Justice, empowerment, redemption*. Cambridge, England: Cambridge University Press.

Grenz, S. J. (1996). *Created for community: Connecting Christian belief with Christian living*. Wheaton, IL: Victor Books.

Grenz, S. J. (2001). *The social God and the relational self: A trinitarian theology of the imago Dei*. Louisville, KY: Westminster/John Knox.

Grenz, S. J. (2004). *Rediscovering the triune God: The Trinity in contemporary theology*. Minneapolis, MN: Augsburg Fortress.

Haskell, R. (2010). eVangelism: The gospel and the world of the internet. *Evangelical Review of Theology, 34*(3), 279–285.

Herring, S. C. (2001). Computer-mediated discourse. In D. Schiffrin, D. Tannen, & H. Hamilton (Eds.), *The handbook of discourse analysis* (pp. 612–634). Oxford, England: Blackwell.

Inge, J. (2003). *A Christian theology of place*. Aldershot, England: Ashgate.

Kilde, J. H. (2008). *Sacred power, sacred space: An introduction to Christian architecture and worship*. Oxford, England: Oxford University Press.

LaCugna, C. M. (1991). *God for us: The Trinity and Christian life*. San Francisco, CA: Harper San Francisco.

Lawson, L. L. (2001). Doing religion in cyberspace: The promise and the perils. *The Council of Societies for the Study of Religion Bulletin, 3*(1), 3–9.

May, G. (1988). *Addiction & grace.* San Francisco, CA: Harper and Row.

McDonnell, J. (2009). "The fabric of our lives": Catholic Church perspectives on the internet. *Fieldwork in Religion, 4*(2), 150–167.

More, T. (2003, originally published in 1516). *Utopia.* New York, NY: Penguin Classics.

Oldenburg, R., & Brissett, D. (1982). The third place. *Qualitative Sociology, 5*(4), 265–284.

Scafi, A. (2006). *Mapping paradise: A history of heaven on earth.* Chicago, IL: University of Chicago Press.

Shannon, R. (2010). The history of the net. Retrieved from http://www.yourhtmlsource.com/starthere/historyofthenet.html

Struthers, W. M. (2010). *Wired for intimacy: How pornography hijacks the male brain.* Downers Grove, IL: InterVarsity Press.

Tanner, K. (2001). *Jesus, humanity and the Trinity: A brief systematic theology.* Edinburgh, Scotland: T&T Clark.

Than, K. (2009, October 29). Internet turns 40: First message crashed system. *National Geographic News.* Retrieved from http://news.nationalgeographic.com/news/2009/10/091029-internet-40th-anniversary-birthday.html

Ward, G. (2002). Between virtue and virtuality. *Theology Today, 59,* 55–70.

Young, K., & Klausing, P. (2007). *Breaking free of the web: Catholics and internet addiction.* Cinncinati, OH: St. Anthony's Messenger Press.

Zizioulas, J. D. (1985). *Being as communion.* Crestwood, NJ: St. Vladimir's Seminary Press.

Zizioulas, J. D. (1991). On being a person: Towards an ontology of personhood. In C. Schwobel & C. E. Gunton (Eds.), *Persons, divine and human* (pp. 33–46). Edinburgh, Scotland: T&T Clark.

Zizioulas, J. D. (2006). *Communion and otherness.* London, England: T&T Clark.

17. Conclusion: Religion in a Digital Age: Future Developments and Research Directions

PETER FISCHER-NIELSEN AND STEFAN GELFGREN

Summarizing Thoughts

To study religion and digital media in a justifiable way demands a continuous attention to new developments. This book has distinctively taken up the challenge to describe and analyse the internet as an increasingly popular platform for social religious interaction, and looked for the consequences of the changes for churches and other religious organisations.

One of the aims of the book has been to establish a cross-disciplinary approach to these subjects. Especially, the inclusion of historical and theological perspectives has been a unique contribution in that regard. Stefan Gelfgren and Sam Han have highlighted the importance of a longer historical perspective on the rise of "new" media. In the words of Bernie Hogan and Barry Wellman, this will help researchers to avoid the dangers of *presentism*, which is to think "that the world has started anew with the internet" (p. 46). Thus, a more balanced and less emotional view on the digital media can be established that incorporates the dialectics of digital religion, one that simultaneously takes seemingly opposite but complementary aspects of continuation and change into account.

As noted in the Introduction chapter, this book emerged from the session "Church in Cyberspace" at an overtly theological conference, namely, "Church and Mission in a Multireligious Third Millennium," held at Aarhus University in January 2010. Most of the contributors to our session and members of the audience, however, were scholars of other disciplines such as the sociology of religion, the media, and communication science, as well as practitioners in non-profit organizations and leaders of faith groups. This illustrates the need for thorough conceptual and theological reflections on the new digital media that goes beyond viewing them as merely expedient and utilitarian tools for communicating (oftentimes narrowly conceived as the one way dissemination of) the gospel. Therefore, the contributions of Peter Horsfield and Lynne Baab to this book are important. Horsfield sees the internet as compatible with a fluid, flexible, and engaging theology that might threaten the authority of the church institution, but, on the other hand, corresponds well with the ideals of early Christianity. Baab introduces important theological perspectives on the internet, describing it as a place where "humans engage with each other, where we sin in multiple ways like we do anywhere else, and where God works" (p. 288).

Not only the historical and theological chapters, but also the other theoretical and empirical contributions to this book, reflect a new orientation in the research in church and digital media. Instead of treating church and digital media as an isolated field, the research must move in the direction of doing broader research in *church in a digital age*: so, for instance, Knut Lundby's opening chapter offers a critique of the concept of cyberchurch that makes this point (among others). Digital media is nowadays simply not just a mere tool for communication; it is more fundamentally reshaping our understanding of the world. At the same time, other influences and general societal and religious developments must be taken into account: the media, though a powerful factor, are not the only catalyst for change in key institutions, including the church, in contemporary society. Indeed, Randolph Kluver and Pauline Hope Cheong (2007) documented some of the complex cultural informatization of society and technological modernization processes in Asia that follow on Christian, Buddhist, Hindu, Muslim, and Taoist religious organizations appropriating the internet for recruitment, teaching, mobilization, and encouragement in Singapore. Here, Peter Fischer-Nielsen in his chapter further relates what is happening with the contemporary church to a more general and wide-ranging process of secularization within the Danish context, offering varied challenges and opportunities to the growth of the church. Rich insights culled from an in-depth survey analysis from pastor responses in the Evangelical Lutheran tradition illustrate the conjoinment of evolving pastoral practices and vigorous new and social media adoption, amidst the secularization process in the interrelationship between state and church, and between the individual and the church.

In this concluding chapter, we will discuss what future and pioneering developments in digital media and society might mean for religion, religious organisations, and religious communication, and propose multiple pathways for future research in this growing field of study.

Looking Ahead: Some Anticipated Future Developments

This book has dealt with some of the latest developments within digital media and proposed theoretical directions in the study of these media. It is, however, also fitting to look ahead for emerging research themes. At least six developments call for increased scholarly attention: digital media become increasingly mobile; digital media become even more personalized; new technology will provide more sophisticated environments online; the power struggle will become more complex; the commercialisation of religion online will increase; and finally, digital media will penetrate the third world.

Digital media become increasingly mobile

In the early days, the internet was accessed primarily through stationary computers. Today, laptops, tablet computers, smartphones, internet-enabled TV and radio, and other devices are changing the picture and will probably continue to do so. The internet is integrated into many gadgets and routines of everyday life, and web-surfing is not as much a separate activity but something that is increasingly combined and multitasked into a diverse range of daily endeavours. To illustrate this mobile development, a Pew report showed that 38 percent of Americans used their cell phones to access the internet in May 2010 (an increase from 25 percent the year before), and among the 18–29-year-olds, as many as 65 percent went online from their cell phone (Smith, 2010). Another example can be observed from Sweden, where the Stockholm diocese is discussing opening up the opportunity to live-stream funerals. Through web services such as Bambuser and Ustream, anyone can stream whatever they want from, and to, different mobile devices. Whether this possibility will be a replacement or complement to existing church memorial activities in the physical reality is still to be discovered.

As emphasized in "the third age" of Internet Studies (so Wellman, 2011) and the corresponding "third wave" of studies of religion online (Campbell, 2011), it is increasingly clear that users' experience of websites and applications cannot be isolated from the various contexts within which they are accessed. Correspondingly, there are several tasks on the research agenda in this regard: First, there is a need for further empirical descriptions of the ways that the digital media are mobilised religiously, both for the individual in his or her daily life, and for the church or religious groups as the new opportunities physically and mentally become integrated into their routines and liturgies. Second, the short and longer term consequences of these changes must be studied. How do the mobile devices affect the individual user's religious life, and how do they influence the beliefs, traditions, values, and authorities of the church or the religious group? In consonance with the broader thematic raised in the introduction chapter regarding the weaving of new media with older media, especially literacy-print, as core for the Protestant Reformation as well as the modern liberal-democratic state (pp. 11, 17), related questions here include:

Will the use of digital media strengthen and expand the religious communities—and perhaps even call attention to the local church through location-based applications such as Foursquare or Facebook Places—or will they just add confusion and distraction to the devotional and ritual space as people are updating their Facebook and Twitter profiles while participating in services or ceremonies? Will it lead to a reintegration of religion in the different "non-religious" spheres of daily life, or will religion simply appear on the individual's smartphone as pieces of popular entertainment on an open, competitive market, not demanding any specific religious commitment?

When the internet becomes mobile and an integrated element of ordinary routines and activities, researchers of new media, religion, and culture must accordingly extend the scope of their research loci. It is no longer possible to study internet users only through a computer. Researchers must systematically study and observe people and contexts, if they want to reach a fuller understanding of the consequences of the evolving digital media landscape. This book has shown some examples of broader methodologies, such as participant observation and personal interviews (Lomborg & Ess), online and penned questionnaires (Cantoni et al.; Fischer-Nielsen) and multi-sited online and offline ethnography (Hutchings). More methodological approaches that draw on innovative methods from various fields will probably develop as the internet becomes increasingly visible in previously non-digitalised and thereby understudied contexts and situations.

Digital media become more personalized

Compared with the contemporary internet and smartphone user, the pre-digital media consumer could palpably be viewed as much less influential. Of course, as the reception of media products has always varied from person to person and from context to context, and also in relation to "old" media, there is a need to study "the creative reworking of the text at the site of the audience" (Clark & Hoover, 1997, p. 32). Still, the consumer of mass media products before the internet did not have much direct influence on the product. He or she could take it or leave it—and if too many chose to leave it, the producer had to adjust the product. The appearance of the internet marked a radically new development—and from being a mere user the individual web-surfer can now more accurately be described as a *produser* (a combination of producer and user—Bruns, 2008) or *prosumer* (producer and consumer—Ritzer & Jurgenson, n.d.). The hybrid produser/prosumer can use and choose between millions of websites and products, and at the same time he or she can potentially become the creator of content that can be applied and reconstructed by other users. Notwithstanding that this new portmanteau might overinflate the current, more active, production of media, as many still prefer passive consumption, some of these new opportunities have been documented in this book: both the chapters of Mark D. Johns and Stine Lomborg and Charles Ess show how Facebook groups and pages today function as a way to mark a religious identity. Pauline Hope Cheong describes how Twitter is being used by religious people to rephrase and reformulate Christian statements, and both Jørgen Straarup and Tim Hutchings deal with virtual spaces such as Second Life and cyberchurches as places where people engage with religion online.

In spite of these examples, future research also needs to address why relatively few internet users make use of the digital opportunities to produce and remix religiously related content. We note that van Dijck (2010) pointed out that less than 20 percent of internet users actually move from more passive consumption to more active production (p. 44); thus future research could examine the motivations and practices of lay digital remix and recycling, particularly in the realm of religious communication.

As the power of the individual produser/prosumer grows in the contemporary media landscape, more effort is being put into the development of content, applications, and devices that can satisfy her wishes and expectations. In a world where the flow of information is theoretically endless, filtering is becoming crucial, and highly dependent on individual preferences. Today, a multiplicity of personalized web tools have been launched to ensure that people get what they like and demand, and consequently "redundant" information is sorted out. A striking religious example of this development is the emergence of search engines such as Seekfind.org (Christian), Jewogle.com (Jewish), and Imhalal.com (Muslim)", that are designed to give people with a specific religious orientation information that is considered relevant to them. Likewise, the internet has fostered a wide range of religious portals (such as Christianity Today.com, Buddhanet.net, Islam Today.net, and Chabad.org) that provide the religious followers with "trustworthy" information. Also, social networking sites exclusively targeted at distinctive religious communities, such as GodTube.com or Faithout.com, and dating sites such as Muslima.com, contribute to this development.

This increasing personalization is indeed interesting to follow closely from a religion scholarly perspective. In the early days it was hoped that the internet could "make a unique contribution to global fellowship in the frequently volatile area of interreligious understanding" (Brasher, 2001, pp. 6–7). These dialogical hopes have since then vanished, as empirical studies have shown that conflicts between and within religions groups thrive online, and that "the possibility of fruitful diversity might be overpowered by the need for a shared,

social identity" (Lövheim & Linderman, 2005, p. 134). There is a possibility that the personalized web will lead to even more "faith astroturfing,"
division, and narrow-mindedness. These patterns appear to be examples of a
larger tendency towards fragmentation as facilitated by online venues—what
Cass Sunstein identified early on in terms of "the daily me," i.e., precisely our
use of the internet to reinforce, rather than challenge, our extant preferences
and beliefs (Sunstein, 2001; cf. Stromer-Galley & Wichowski, 2011).

Within religious contexts, it is conceivable to envisage a bifurcated world
in which Muslims only get their information on Christianity from Muslim
sources, and Christians just learn about Islam from Christian websites, since
the information will probably be rather biased. Researchers must both study
the logics guiding these different personalized applications and analyse how
religious people apply them. Who is attracted by the purportedly safe and manageable religious search engines and websites, and how are they being used? Do
they function as a supplement to other sources of information, or do they—for
some users—entirely replace these and promote closed sectarian milieus?

New technology will provide more sophisticated environments online

In the mid-2000s the interest for virtual worlds peaked through the success of,
for example, Second Life. Initiatives were taken to create virtual churches in 3D
virtual environments. Thereafter there has been a noticeable decline in interest for virtual worlds after not fulfilling initial high expectations. The decline
of interest in virtual worlds has also coincided with the implementation and
wider use of social media and smartphones, and their cheaper, less complicated,
technology (e.g.,Terdiman, 2010). However, today, 3D-technology is still in
use, and some virtual worlds have developed, for instance LEGO Universe,
PlayStation Home, Open Simulator, Entropia Universe and IMVU. At the
time of writing, a Christian multiverse alternative is also on the way—The Universe of Faith. The future of ever-complex and sophisticated 3D virtual worlds
is difficult to predict based upon experiences from the last few years, but we
have probably not seen the end of virtual worlds (cf. Ess & Thorseth, 2011).

In due time, the different virtual worlds will probably both move into
mobile devices and possibly also become seamlessly connected. Related to
this is the possibility to interact with the digital interface without keyboards
and other physical objects. At the same time we experience how the virtual
and the physical worlds are merging together in what is called an augmented
reality, where the digital and the physical worlds are simultaneously accessible
and supplement, instead of replace, each other. Such merging raises interesting possibilities, both for users and researchers. For example, will it be possible to see, through your mobile device, who in your digital social network is
attending church, and who the rest of the congregation (present and absent)

are, including their digital persona? Can you access information about the building, its art and previous services, or can the pastor project visualisations of the sermon for you to download and take with you when leaving church, etc.? A combination of GPS-enabled tools, social media tools, face recognition, and augmented reality technology can make it possible. We have so far only seen the beginning of the process.

In a church context, one can only speculate about the possible effects. Technology has in the past, as one of many components, contributed to an overall process toward decentralisation and "de-hierarchisation" of established institutions. As noted in the Introduction, the role of the printing press in the Reformation process is one historical example in that regard. In the digital age of today we must ask what the consequences will be for a traditional Christian locality-based community, when people can replace physical church attendance with a presence in a virtual world or some sort of web-service. In keeping with the broader observation that internet usages are increasingly interwoven with our day-to-day, real-world lives, so as to complement and supplement these, rather than replace them (cf. Introduction, pp. 12–24)— so far the conclusion has been that religious experiences online only for a minority function as a replacement for religious life in a church or a mosque (Larsen, 2004, p. 18; Campbell, 2005, p. 161; Hutchings, 2010, p. 295). But an improved quality of the online religious experience due to more advanced technology may change this picture.

Even if the digital religious opportunities continue to be nothing but a supplement to the Sunday service and social life of the local community, they will have an influence that must be observed. How does it, for instance, affect the role of the ordained local priest or clergy as authority and interpreter of the word of God, when anyone instantly (and even from the pew) can access "better" preachers on the internet or instantaneously check any claims made by the preacher against other sources of information in wired religious campuses?

Simultaneously, it is possible that we will see a countermovement opposing the "technologisation" of the religious sphere, and there will probably be initiatives to emphasise the strength of face-to-face meetings, "going back to the basics" in terms of interpersonal communication and interaction.

These issues are not entirely new to the study of religion and the internet, but it will be increasingly challenging for researchers to gather relevant source material for making well-grounded analysis. More sophisticated and visual environments demand new methods, which must be combined with more traditional approaches in order to encompass what is happening in the increasingly fluid field of online and offline modes. At the same time, as the boundaries between the physical and the virtual world dissolve, researchers themselves must be able to move between worlds, and it will become even more apparent how these two realities are related to each other. The now classic division between online religion and religion online will be further dissolved as Christopher Helland pointed out in 2005, and may even be merged together. This development will demand more intense involvement in higher degrees of multi-disciplinary approaches to interpret transformations within the religious sphere overall. In particular, traditional perspectives stemming from disciplines such as church history and sociology of religion must be combined with perspectives from media studies and digital humanities.

The power struggle will become more complex

One recurrent theme in research regarding church and digital media in this volume is the question about changing power structures between the institutions and their representatives, on the one hand, and people without conventional authority, on the other hand. Traditional boundaries are blurred and dissolved under the influence of the internet. Whether this development is favoured or not often depends upon theology and traditions.

As previously mentioned, the church and its congregation can be, and are distributed and now reaching beyond the constraining walls of a building to a higher degree than ever before. In many churches there has traditionally been a division between an appointed leadership and the parishioners. In our digital age, the line between those who produce and the consumers is potentially mixed—hence the concept of the prosumer/prosumer. This has happened before throughout history (Ekström et al., 2011), in church, for example, in relation to various revivalist movements driven by laypeople, but the possibilities are far more elaborate today through digital media and the internet.

The internet has made it possible for anyone with internet access and some technical skills to make his/her voice heard through blogs, Facebook, and YouTube, or to start Twitter-based prayer groups, or even to plant a church in a virtual world or build a community through a web page. Anyone can, for example, start a Twitter account or a blog and gather followers, but when a well-known person such as pastor Rick Warren does it, he is swiftly liked and followed by thousands of people. Consequently, researchers must look beyond the pitfalls of internet-related hopes and fears. As Wellman and Hogan point out in their article, the internet has been viewed both with utopian and dystopian perspectives. So after claiming that internet undermines power structures, it must be said that internet already relies on existing structures, and new piggy-back structures will be constructed.

Different web-based initiatives are, however, taken by private entrepreneurs driven by their own interest to spread the word of God, or by churches willing to take on the challenges they are facing in a digital age, but also by companies and media corporations that see the possibilities to attract users and make money in the relatively large faith and spirituality markets. In a world where digital communication is becoming increasingly important, the initiative to communicate the Gospel is potentially transferred from the established leadership of a church to its technology or communication department. To what degree are the church and its representatives taking over the worldview of consultancies and companies in the hope of a remedy to an experienced ongoing process toward extinction? The discussion about diminishing structures and new power struggles must take into account the complex nature of the question—and usually there is not simply a one-directional process requiring only one answer, but multiple factors in play that must be taken into account.

The commercialisation of religion online will increase

In the US, religion has more or less always been competing in a non-regulated market. In Europe, on the contrary, many countries have a long tradition of state-supported churches—a tradition that amounts to (at least in part) regulating and even suppressing other religious alternatives. In some countries (for example, in Scandinavia), therefore, the population has religiously been quite homogeneous.

A number of international developments are gradually changing this situation. People are becoming more mobile due to cheaper and easier travel possibilities; immigration has introduced foreign cultures and religions, transnational religious communication has circumvented national regulations and censorship of religious content to enable the global spread of faith messages via multiple media and personal conduits (Cheong & Poon, 2009); and secularization has shaken the strength and authority of established religious institutions and paved the way for competing worldviews, a process related to the rise of the modern society. All this has led, or is leading, to a market situation where churches and religious groups must promote their messages in constantly new and creative ways in order to be seen, heard, and followed. The new media landscape might radicalize these tendencies as religious promoters enter into heavy competition, not only with each other, but also with secular products and experiences that can be found when searching on the internet or browsing through smartphone applications.

Bala Musa and Ibrahim Ahmadu speak in this book of *church brandversation* as a necessary task for religious organisations in pluralistic and democratic societies. Peter Fischer-Nielsen shows how marketing terms such as "branding" and "profiling" appear in the statements of Danish pastors when they speak about the church's online communication, and also Cheong, Huang, and Poon, in a recent article (2011) describe how Buddhist leaders in Singapore develop multimodal competencies to initiate multimedia marketing campaigns to promote Buddhist teaching. This commercialisation not only affects the group, but also the individual consumer who uses commercial products to "demonstrate their true faith and their unique authenticity as persons" (Clark, 2007, p. 27).

As we saw in the Introduction, there are increasing concerns more broadly in Internet Studies regarding how far our ever-growing engagement with commercially driven and proprietary environments may lead to the reduction of all human selfhood and activities to the logics of commodification (including self-commodification: see p. 7). Future research must continue to take this theme of online commercialisation seriously and observe how the development affects religion both on a collective and an individual level. When studying churches, religious groups, and movements, their ways of adapting to the terms of the new media marketplace must be followed. Which organisational types and theologies thrive on the internet, and which ones suffer? Can a church, for instance, communicate its "brand" in social media without losing control over it? Maybe, as Peter Horsfield suggests in his chapter, one of the answers is to accept that dialogue and fluency really could be a central part of the Christian brand. Heidi Campbell has in this book underlined the importance of studying negotiation processes within religious groups. Continuing in this direction, researchers must examine how churches and religious organisations negotiate the market conditions and whether this leads them to market adjustment, adaptation, or rejection? Also, there is a need for studying how the commercialisation of religion takes place online outside the domain of religious groups. How are religious symbols and terms used to promote entirely secular products and experiences—and with what consequences?

On the individual level, there is a need to more closely study how individual users of digital media combine products from both the religious and the secular marketplaces. Is it possible, in a meaningful way, to distinguish between actions of shopping for goods and "shopping" for spiritual content, and if so: how does the user distinguish between the two situations? Finally, differences due to age and gender will continue to be an important element in the future research on individual religious web-shopping.

Digital media will penetrate the Third World

The internet has so far most heavily penetrated North America, Oceania, and Europe. According to Internetworldstats.com, 77 percent of North Americans, 61 percent of Oceanians, and 58 percent of Europeans were internet users by 2010. In contrast, only 11 percent of Africans, 22 percent of Asians, and 30 percent of the Middle Eastern population can be classified as such. Yet the growth in these regions is remarkable. In Africa, for instance, the growth from 2000 to 2010 was 2,357 percent, while in North America, at the other end of the scale it was only 146 percent. It is expected that this growth will continue as internet technology develops and costs are reduced. Africa will be able to skip the step of land-based communication and instantly enter the world of wireless communication.

Though a few studies have been done on Buddhist, Hindu, Jewish, and Islamic online-expressions in Asia and the Middle East (see examples in *Online—Heidelberg Journal of Religions on the Internet*, www.online.uni-hd. de), most of the academic work on religion and the internet has focused on North America and Europe, and virtually none of it has dealt thoroughly with Sub-Saharan religious expressions online and integration of new digital media in traditional religious contexts. (The same can be said about how the changing role of contemporary religion is interpreted—i.e., different secularisation theories.) Generally, when the internet-poor regions have been in focus it has primarily been the well-wired part of the population that has been described.

As the internet in the future will be ever-more accessible for people in developing countries, it will be necessary for scholars to pay attention more closely to this development. How will access to new media shape people's religious identities and lives? How will the development affect the established religious traditions, institutions, and authorities? And most interestingly: Will the development look the same as what we have seen in Europe and North America, or will differences in culture, societal values, and traditions mean that internet use looks different, and might lead people in other directions? Scholars must approach these and other questions open-mindedly and with a variety of methodological approaches.

Concluding Remarks

Doing studies in religion and the internet is no longer a desk job (if it ever has been). Researchers cannot expect to reach a full understanding of religious web use only from our computers. We must meet people wherever and whenever they go online: in the church and on the street, in the West and in Africa, from their computers or from their smartphones. We must watch them combine and integrate online and offline activities, observe their web searches, and watch them move from site to site. We must observe how they use and produce religious content online and ask them about their dispositions and intentions.

The fact that people are living their lives on the internet to an increasing extent, and hence leaving "public" traces of their personal lives in blogs, Facebook status updates, tweets, and comments on various web pages, and that they also leave their movements through different GPS-based services, and so on, calls for an ethical awareness. To what extent can the researcher use material that is retrieved through communication in chat rooms and virtual worlds while remaining anonymous behind a nickname or an avatar?

What is public and what is personal in such a world? What kind of source material can researchers use without been giving consent by the informants (cf. McKee & Porter, 2009)?

To these ends, new methodological approaches are needed that go beyond website analysis and apply methods from various fields. It has indeed been a major point throughout this book that research in religion and digital media should be a multidisciplinary endeavour. Another important dialogue that this book might push forward is the one between academia and church. On the one hand, research carried out by more or less secular scholars will help churches and other religious groups to navigate in an increasingly complex digital landscape. On the other hand, the religious practitioners can provide valuable data material, statistics, reflection, and perspectives that will strengthen the researchers' possibilities to carry out meaningful research. This book sprung out of a conference where both scholars and church representatives took part, and it is our belief that similar multi-voiced gatherings should be promoted in the future to benefit all parties.

A recent report shows that 80 percent of 895 internet stakeholders agree with the statement that "the hot gadgets and applications that will capture the imaginations of users in 2020 will often come 'out of the blue'" (Elon & Pew, 2010). In the Introduction, we have highlighted the example of emerging faith-related mobile apps. In this concluding chapter we have tried to point to some of the developments that are challenging scholars in religion and digital media, but we are also looking forward to being surprised. The research area is constantly changing and demands continuous attention, creative research agendas, and new theoretical reflections.

References

Bruns, A. (2008). *Blogs, Wikipedia, Second Life, and beyond: From production to produsage.* New York, NY: Peter Lang.

Campbell, H. (2005). *Exploring religious community online: We are one in the network.* New York, NY: Peter Lang.

Campbell, H. (2011). Internet and religion. In M. Consalvo & C. Ess (Eds.), *The Blackwell handbook of internet studies* (pp. 232–250). Oxford, England: Blackwell.

Cheong, P.H., Huang, S.H., & Poon, J.P.H. (2011). Cultivating online and offline pathways to enlightenment: Religious authority in wired Buddhist organizations. *Information, Communication & Society, 14*(8), 1160–1180.

Cheong, P.H., & Poon, J. P. H. (2009). Weaving webs of faith: Examining internet use and religious communication among Chinese Protestant transmigrants. *Journal of International and Intercultural Communication, 2*(3), 189–207.

Clark, L. S. (2007). Introduction: Identity, belonging, and religious lifestyle branding (Fashion bibles, Bhangraparties, and Muslim pop). In L. S. Clark (Ed.), *Religion, media, and the marketplace* (pp. 1–34). New Brunswick, NJ: Rutgers University Press.

Clark, L. S., & Hoover, S. M. (1997). At the intersection of media, culture, and religion: A bibliographic essay. In S. M. Hoover & K. Lundby (Eds.), *Rethinking media, religion, and culture* (pp. 15–36). Thousand Oaks, CA: Sage.

Ekström, A., Jülich, S., Lundgren, F., & Wisselgren, P. (Eds.). (2011). *History of participatory media: Politics and publics 1750–2000*. New York, NY: Routledge.

Elon University & Pew Internet Project (2010). Imaging the internet: A history and forecast. Retrieved from http://www.elon.edu/e-web/predictions/expertsurveys/2010survey/default.xhtml

Ess, C. & Thorseth, M. (2011).*Trust and virtual worlds: Contemporary perspectives.* Oxford, England: Peter Lang.

Helland, C. (2005). Online religion as lived religion: Methodological issues in the study of religious participation on the internet. *Online—Heidelberg Journal of Religions on the internet 1.1.* Retrieved from http://archiv.ub.uni-heidelberg.de/volltextserver/volltexte/2005/5823/pdf/Helland3a.pdf

Hutchings, T. (2010). *Creating church online: An ethnographic study of five internet-based Christian communities.* (PhD dissertation, Theology and Religion). Durham University, England.

Kluver, R., & Cheong, P.H. (2007). Technological modernization, the internet, and religion in Singapore. *Journal of Computer-Mediated Communication, 12*(3), 1122–1142. Retrieved from http://jcmc.indiana.edu/vol12/issue3/kluver.html

Larsen, E. (2004). Cyberfaith: How Americans pursue religion online. In L. L. Dawson & D. E. Cowan (Eds.), *Religion online: Finding faith on the internet* (pp. 17–22). New York, NY: Routledge.

Lövheim, M., & Linderman, A. G. (2005). Constructing religious identity on the internet. In M. T. Højsgaard & M. Warburg (Eds.), *Religion and cyberspace* (pp. 121–137). London, England; New York, NY: Routledge.

McKee, H., & Porter, J. (2009). *The ethics of internet research.* Oxford, England: Peter Lang.

Ritzer, G., & Jurgenson, N. (n.d.). *Production, consumption, prosumption: The nature of capitalism in the age of the digital "prosumer"* (Paper). Retrieved from http://www.georgeritzer.com/docs/Production%20Consumption%20Prosumption.pdf

Smith, A. (2010). Mobile access 2010. Retrieved from http://www.pewinternet.org/~/media//Files/Reports/2010/PIP_Mobile_Access_2010.pdf

Stromer-Galley, J., & Wichowski, D. (2011). Political discussion online. In M. Consalvo & C. Ess (Eds.), *The Blackwell handbook of internet studies* (pp. 168–187). Oxford, England: Wiley-Blackwell.

Sunstein, C. R. (2001). *Republic.com.* Princeton, NJ: Princeton University Press.

Terdiman, D. (2010, February 26). Where virtual worlds once ruled, Farm Ville dominates. Retrieved from http://news.cnet.com/8301-13772_3-10460293-52.html

Van Dijck, J. (2010). Users like you? Theorizing agency in user-generated content. *Media, Culture and Society, 31*(1), 14–58.

Wellman, B. (2011). Studying the internet through the ages. In M. Consalvo & C. Ess (Eds.), *The Blackwell handbook of Internet studies* (pp. 17–23). Oxford, England: Blackwell.

Contributors

Ahmadu, Ibrahim M. (PhD, University of Jos, Nigeria) is Associate Professor of Religious Studies, Department of Religious Studies, University of Jos, Nigeria. He is an expert in New Testament Theology, Christian Ethics, Church History, and World Religions. He is a past National Vice-President and, currently, a National Board Member in the Reformed Christian Church of Nigeria (RCCN). He formerly chaired the Department of Religious Studies at the College of Education, Jalingo, and the Department of Religious Studies at the University of Jos. Ahmadu has served as editor of several theological journals. He has published numerous scholarly journal articles and book chapters on the role of religion in social, cultural, and political change. Contact: ahmadum@unijos.edu.ng

Arasa, Daniel (PhD, Pontifical University of the Holy Cross, Rome, Italy) is Associate Professor of Digital Communications at the Pontifical University of the Holy Cross as well as member of the Board of Directors of *Rome Reports TV News Agency*. His main research interest is online religious communication, particularly the internet communication of Catholic institutions. He is author of *Church Communications Through Diocesan Websites: A Model of Analysis* (Rome: Edusc, 2008), and co-editor of *Religious Internet Communication: Facts, Experiences and Trends in the Catholic Church* (Rome: Edusc, 2010) and *Church Communication & the Culture of Controversy* (2010). Contact: arasa@pusc.it

Baab, Lynne M. (PhD, University of Washington, Seattle, USA) is a Presbyterian minister and a lecturer in pastoral theology at the University of Otago in Dunedin, New Zealand. Her PhD research focused on identity presentation and persuasion on the websites of American Protestant congregations. She currently researches Christian spiritual disciplines and con-gregational life, with particular focus on the ways relationships are nurtured and listening is facilitated using digital media. She is the author of numer-ous books, most recently *Friending: Real Relationships in a Virtual World* (Downers Grove: InterVarsity Press, 2011), *Reaching Out in a Networked World* (Herndon: The Alban Institute, 2008), *Sabbath Keeping* (Downers Grove: InterVarsity Press, 2005). Contact: lynne.baab@otago.ac.nz; www.lynnebaab.com

Campbell, Heidi (PhD, University of Edinburgh, Scotland) is Associate Professor of Communication at Texas A & M University where she teaches in media studies, global and popular culture, and religion. Her research focuses on religion and the internet and the influence of digital and mobile tech-nologies on religious communities. She is author of *Exploring Religious Com-munity Online* (New York: Peter Lang, 2005), co-editor of *A Science and Religion Primer* (Grand Rapids: Baker Academic, 2009) and *When Religion Meets New Media* (London: Routledge, 2010). Her work has appeared in publications such as the *Journal of Contemporary Religion, Journal of Com-puter-Mediated Communication, The Information Society, New Media and Society and Religion Online* (London: Routledge, 2004). Contact: heidic@tamu.edu; http://comm.tamu.edu/people/campbell.html

Cantoni, Lorenzo (PhD, Università Cattolica, Milan, Italy) is Profes-sor and Dean at the Faculty of Communication Sciences, Università della Svizzera italiana, Lugano, Switzerland. He is vice-director of the Institute of Public and Educational Communication, and scientific director of the laboratories webatelier.net, NewMinE Lab: New Media in Education Lab, and eLab: eLearning Lab. His research interests are where communica-tion, education, and new media overlap, ranging from computer mediated communication to usability, from eReligion to eLearning, from eTourism to eGovernment. He has edited and authored several books and articles on communication issues; among others, he is co-editor of *Religious Inter-net Communication. Facts, Experiences and Trends in the Catholic Church* (Rome: Edusc, 2010) and co-author of *Internet (Routledge Introductions to Media and Communications)* (London: Routledge, 2006). Contact: lorenzo.cantoni@usi.ch; newmine.blogspot.com

Cheong, Pauline Hope (PhD, University of Southern California, Los Angeles, USA) is Associate Professor at the Hugh Downs School of Human Communication and an affiliate faculty with the Center for the Study of Reli-gion and Conflict at Arizona State University. She is researching how reli-gious leaders are appropriating digital media to construct their authority and communities. Her two other book projects include lead co-editing the vol-ume *New Media and Intercultural Communication: Identity, Community and Politics* (New York: Peter Lang, in press, 2012) and co-authoring *Narrative*

Landmines: Rumors and the Struggle for Strategic Influence (Brunswick, NJ: Rutgers University Press, in press). She has presented more than 60 papers at international conferences and has more than 40 publications in books and flagship journals on digital media and communication, including *New Media and Society, The Information Society, Information, Communication and Society, Journal of Communication, Journal of Computer-Mediated Communication,* and *Journal of Media and Religion.* Contact: Pauline.Cheong@asu.edu; www.paulinehopecheong.com

Ess, Charles (PhD, Pennsylvania State University, University Park, USA) is Professor MSO at the Department of Information and Media Studies, Aarhus University, Denmark, and Professor of Philosophy and Religion, Drury University (Springfield, Missouri, USA). He has also served as a guest professor at IT-University (Copenhagen, Denmark), Trier University (Germany), the Norwegian University of Science and Technology (Trondheim, Norway), and Nîmes (France). He has received awards for excellence in both teaching and scholarship, and has published extensively in both philosophy and media studies, including as guest editor for special issues of *The Journal of Computer-Mediated Communication, Ethics and Information Technology,* and *New Media and Society.* Recent books include (with Soraj Hongladarom), *Information Technology Ethics: Cultural Perspectives* (Hershey: IGI Global, 2007); *Digital Media Ethics* (Cambridge: Polity Press, 2009); (with Mia Consalvo), *The Blackwell Handbook of Internet Studies* (Oxford: Wiley-Blackwell, 2011); and (with May Thorseth) *Trust and Virtual Worlds: Contemporary Perspectives* (New York: Peter Lang, 2011). Contact: charles.ess@gmail.com

Fischer-Nielsen, Peter (PhD, Aarhus University, Denmark) is head of communications at the Danish IT company KirkeWeb. He has published articles on new media in relation to religion, Christianity, and church especially in a Danish context. Furthermore, he has been member of the editorial staff at the influential website www.religion.dk for a number of years. His dissertation of 2010 was on the internet communication of the Evangelical Lutheran Church in Denmark. Contact: pfn@kirkeweb.dk; www.e-religion.dk.

Gelfgren, Stefan (PhD, Umeå University, Sweden) is Associate Professor and research coordinator at HUMlab & Department of Historical, Philosophical and Religious Studies at Umeå University. Gelfgren has a background in the History of Ideas, and the History of Christianity (Birmingham University, England), and he is currently working on the project *Pinocchio Goes to Church: The Religious Life of Avatars,* dealing with churches in virtual worlds and how holiness is created in these worlds. He has published in books and journals mainly on the relation between social and changes within the Christian sphere from the 16th century until today. He has also published articles on revivalism and adult education, and pedagogy in virtual worlds. Contact: stefan.gelfgren@humlab.umu.se; churchandinternet.wordpress.com

Han, Sam (BA, Wesleyan University, Middletown, USA) is Instructional Technology Fellow of the Macaulay Honors College and a PhD candidate in Sociology at the Graduate Center of the City University of New York (CUNY). He writes in the fields of social and cultural theory, media studies, religion, and race. He is author of *Web 2.0* (London: Routledge, 2011), *Navigating Technomedia: Caught in the Web* (Lanham: Rowman & Littlefield, 2007) and co-editor of *The Race of Time: A Charles Lemert Reader* (Boulder: Paradigm Publishers, 2009). He is at work on a thesis manuscript entitled *Technologies of Spirit: The Digital Worlds of Contemporary Christianity*. Contact: samhan.samhan@gmail.com; sam-han.org

Hogan, Bernie (PhD, University of Toronto, Canada) is a Research Fellow at the Oxford Internet Institute at the University of Oxford. Hogan's research focuses on the relationship between technologically mediated social cues (such as friend lists, real names, address books, etc.), social identity, and network structure. In pursuing this research, Hogan has also focused on novel techniques for the capture and analysis of online social networks. His recent work is featured in *Information, Communication & Society, City & Community, Field Methods, Bulletin of Science Technology & Society* and several edited collections. He is currently working on identity and social conflict on Wikipedia and cross-national perceptions of social norms in online dating. Contact: bernie.hogan@oii.ox.ac.uk; http://www.oii.ox.ac.uk/people/?id=140

Horsfield, Peter (PhD, Boston University, USA) is Professor of Communication and Associate Dean (Writing and Communication) in the School of Media and Communication at RMIT University, Melbourne, Australia. He was a member of the International Study Commission on Media Religion and Culture and is Chair of the Porticus Fellowship Program for Research in Media Religion and Culture. He has published widely in media and religion. His early work, *Religious Television: The American experience* (London; New York: Longman, 1984) is seen as one of the classic works on televangelism. Among his recent publications are the co-edited volume *Belief in Media: Cultural Perspectives on Media and Christianity* (Aldershot: Ashgate Press, 2005) and "Media" in *Key Words in Religion Media and Culture* (London; New York: Routledge, 2008). Contact: peter.horsfield@rmit.edu.au; bit.ly/ijPzR9

Hutchings, Tim (PhD, Durham University, England) is a Postdoctoral Research Fellow at the HUMlab digital humanities research laboratory, Umeå University, Sweden, where he studies the role of new media in Christian recruitment and disaffiliation. His PhD thesis, titled *Creating Church Online: Five Ethnographic Case Studies of Online Christian Community* (2010), focused on community, ritual, authority, and the relationship between online and offline activity. He has subsequently undertaken research into Christian music festivals, the impact of new media on death and memorialisation, and the mediatisation of religious emotion. His work has been published in *Information, Communication and Society, Online—The Heidelberg Journal of Religions and the Internet, The Australian Religious Studies Review, The Expository Times* and *Studies in World Christianity*. Contact: tim.hutchings@humlab.umu.se; tim.hutchings@gmail.com

Johns, Mark D. (PhD, University of Iowa, Iowa City, USA) is an Associate Professor of Communication Studies at Luther College in Decorah, Iowa, USA. An ordained Lutheran minister, his research interests are dealing with religion and the media in general, as well as in the adaptation of research methods and research ethics to new media environments. He is co-editor of *Online Social Research: Methods, Issues, and Ethics* (New York: Peter Lang, 2004) and of *Social Media Campaigns: Methods and Issues* (forthcoming). He is also Director of the Carl Couch Center for Social and Internet Research, and of the Luther Study Centre in Nottingham, UK for 2011–12. Contact: mjohns@luther.edu

Lomborg, Stine (MA, Aarhus University, Denmark) is a PhD candidate in the Centre for Internet Research at the Department of Information and Media Studies at Aarhus University. Her primary research area is social media, including how mundane online practices play a pivotal role in how ordinary users manage relationships and negotiate selves in everyday life. Her PhD dissertation examines social media as communicative genres, focusing empirically on personal blogs and twittering as collaborative, ongoing negotiations, and accomplishments of genre. She has presented her work at several international conferences, and her work has appeared in international journals such as *Philosophy and Technology* and *First Monday*. Contact: imvsl@hum.au.dk

Lundby, Knut (PhD, University of Oslo, Norway) is Professor of Media Studies in the Department of Media and Communication, University of Oslo. His doctoral degree is in sociology of religion. He was the founding director of the InterMedia, University of Oslo, researching digital environments. He has a long-standing interest in research on the relation between media, religion, and culture, e.g., from *Rethinking Media, Religion, and Culture*, co-edited with Stewart M. Hoover (Thousand Oaks; London: Sage, 1997). Among his recent books are *Digital Storytelling, Mediatized Stories. Self-representations in New Media* (Ed.) (New York: Peter Lang, 2008) and *Mediatization: Concept, Changes, Consequences* (Ed.) (New York: Peter Lang, 2009). Contact: knut.lundby@media.uio.no; www.hf.uio.no/imk/personer/vit/knutl/index.html

Musa, Bala A. (PhD, Regent University, Virginia Beach, USA) is Professor and Chair of Communication Studies at Azusa Pacific University. His research interests include media and religion, media ethics, political communication, development communication, intercultural communication, communication and conflict management, and communication and human rights. He has published in, and serves on the editorial board of, many scholarly journals. He is also the series editor for the *Communication, Society, and Change* series (Lanham: University Press of America). He is author of *Framing Genocide: Media, Diplomacy & Conflict* (Palo Alto: Academica Press, 2007); and co-editor of *Emerging Issues in Contemporary Journalism* (Lewiston: Edwin Mellen Press, 2006); *Communication in an Era of Global Conflicts* (Lanham: University Press of America, 2009). Contact: bmusa@apu.edu

Rapetti, Emanuele (MAed, Università Cattolica, Milan, Italy) is a PhD candidate at NewMinE Lab, New Media in Education Lab, Faculty of Communication Sciences, Università della Svizzera italiana, Lugano, Switzerland. His thesis explores how eLearning and ICTs are changing the way people learn in the knowledge society. His research interests are pedagogy and educational issues for the third millennium, eLearning, media education, and qualitative methods in educative-social research. Contact: emanuele.rapetti@usi.ch; materialieducativi.blogspot.com.

Straarup, Jørgen (ThD, Uppsala University, Sweden) is full Professor of Religious Studies with a special interest in expressions of religion in contemporary culture and society, at Umeå University, Sweden. Trained in sociology of religion, he has earlier held positions at Uppsala University, the research department of the Church of Sweden, Luleå University of Technology and University of Gävle. His publications are centered on religious expressions of population majorities, mainly in Sweden. His present project, *Pinocchio Goes to Church*, funded by the Swedish Research Council, lies behind his contribution to the present volume. Another project in progress is about local parish trajectories, where a more or less glorious past (in religious terms) corresponds poorly with a rather inglorious present. Contact: Jorgen.Straarup@religion.umu.se; www.idesam.umu.se/om/personal/religion/jorgen-straarup/

Tardini, Stefano (PhD, Università Cattolica, Milan, Italy) is researcher at the Faculty of Communication Sciences, at Università della Svizzera italiana, Lugano, Switzerland. He is also the managing director of eLab: eLearning Lab. He is developing his research in three interrelated directions: ICT mediated communication from a socio-historical perspective, the impact of the introduction of eLearning activities and tools into given communities, and a semiotic approach to online communities and social networks. He has co-authored, together with Lorenzo Cantoni, the book *Internet (Routledge Introductions to Media and Communications)* (London: Routledge, 2006). Contact: stefano.tardini@usi.ch

Vannini, Sara (MA, University of Bologna, Italy) is a PhD candidate at the NewMinE Lab, Università della Svizzera italiana, Lugano, Switzerland. Her research interests focus mainly on the field of ICTs for International

Development. She is currently working at the project RE-ACT (social REpresentations of community multimedia centres and ACTions for improvement), a research project aimed at investigating conceptualizations of CMCs—Community Multimedia Centres—in Mozambique. The research is in collaboration with the Universidade Eduardo Mondlane, Maputo, Mozambique. Contact: sara.vannini@usi.ch; http://www.people.usi.ch/vanninis/phd/index.html

Wellman, Barry (PhD, Harvard University, Cambridge, USA) is the S.D. Clark Professor of Sociology and Director of NetLab at the University of Toronto. He studies the triple revolution: the turn to social networks, the personal internet, and mobile accessibility to communication and information. His most recent publication is *Networked: The New Social Operating System* (with Lee Rainie) (Cambridge: MIT Press, 2011). Wellman's current research studies the triple revolution as well as networked organizations. He has written more than 200 articles, including "The Community Question" (1979), "Different Strokes from Different Folks" (with Scot Wortley, 1990) and "Physical Place and Cyber Place: The Rise of Networked Individualism" (2001). Contact: wellman@chass.utoronto.ca; homes.chass.utoronto.ca/~wellman

Person Index

Index

Acknowledgments

We would like to our publishing and production team at Peter Lang for their industrious partnership in this project. We would also like to thank Areopagos, a non-profit foundation, for their kind sponsorship of the formatting costs of this book. Our hearty appreciation to Jørn Henrik Olsen for kindly providing us with the painting, "Gateway to Jerusalem" for the cover art material.

Pauline wishes to thank her family (especially Simon) and friends for their *joie de vivre*, encouragement and prayers. She is also happy to acknowledge her colleagues at the Hugh Downs School of Human Communication and the Center for the Study of Religion and Conflict, Arizona State University, for their dedicated scholarship and support. Special thanks to Kerstin Radde-Antweiler and Kocku von Stuckrad for their kind hospitality and invitation to lecture in the Netherlands and discuss with them and their graduate students some of the ideas that have nourished the development of this introduction chapter.

Peter is thankful to his wife (Bente) and children (Johan, Gertrud and Valdemar) for their love, support and daily inspiration. He also wishes to thank Viggo Mortensen (Aarhus University), Morten Thomsen Højsgaard (the Christian Daily/the Danish Bible Society) and Birger Nygaard (Areopagos) for their guidance, critique and wise suggestions during the last three years of research in church and new media. He is grateful for being part of an inspiring and generous teamwork at the Centre for Contemporary Religion, Aarhus University. Likewise, he appreciates the gatherings in the Nordic Network on Media and Religion that has been a great context for reflecting on themes related to this book and for engaging in numerous stimulating conversations with religion and media scholars.

Stefan first and foremost would like to thank his family (Ulrika and his three kids—Svea, Kalle and Knut) for love and support for their sometimes absent-minded, late evenings working, husband and father. He is also most thankful to all the colleagues at HUMlab, Umeå University, where it is always possible to meet open and cross disciplinary minded people there, coming from a wide range of disciplines and backgrounds. He would also like to thank staff at Faculty of Arts, in general, for keeping him in rooted in the various disciplines of traditional humanities, and project colleague Jørgen Straarup in particular, for collaboration within this interesting field.

Charles wishes to thank first of all his colleagues at the Department of Information- and Media Studies, Aarhus University, for their exceptional support and hospitality; these have been key to his participation in both the initial conference track on Church and Cyberspace, and in the subsequent development of this volume. As well, he gratefully acknowledges Maja van der Velden (Informatics, University of Oslo) and Knut Lundby (Department of Media and Communication, University of Oslo) for their kind invitation to lecture and critically discuss with them and their students some of the central ideas that have shaped this introduction. Your and your students' comments and criticisms have been invaluable. Finally, he is very grateful indeed to those in Denmark, from university professors to pastors to congregants, who have graciously shared your insights and views, and, even better, who have exemplified the primary virtues of the Abrahamic traditions by offering us strangers and foreigners warm welcome, generous hospitality, and fast friendship—along with patience, good humor, compassion, and forgiveness for our inevitable blunders and errors in struggling to learn new languages and ways of being.

General Editor: *Steve Jones*

Digital Formations is the best source for critical, well-written books about digital technologies and modern life. Books in the series break new ground by emphasizing multiple methodological and theoretical approaches to deeply probe the formation and reformation of lived experience as it is refracted through digital interaction. Each volume in **Digital Formations** pushes forward our understanding of the intersections, and corresponding implications, between digital technologies and everyday life. The series examines broad issues in realms such as digital culture, electronic commerce, law, politics and governance, gender, the Internet, race, art, health and medicine, and education. The series emphasizes critical studies in the context of emergent and existing digital technologies.

Other recent titles include:

Felicia Wu Song
  Virtual Communities: Bowling Alone, Online Together

Edited by Sharon Kleinman
  The Culture of Efficiency: Technology in Everyday Life

Edward Lee Lamoureux, Steven L. Baron, & Claire Stewart
  Intellectual Property Law and Interactive Media: Free for a Fee

Edited by Adrienne Russell & Nabil Echchaibi
  International Blogging: Identity, Politics and Networked Publics

Edited by Don Heider
  Living Virtually: Researching New Worlds

Edited by Judith Burnett, Peter Senker & Kathy Walker
  The Myths of Technology: Innovation and Inequality

Edited by Knut Lundby
  Digital Storytelling, Mediatized Stories: Self-representations in New Media

Theresa M. Senft
  Camgirls: Celebrity and Community in the Age of Social Networks

Edited by Chris Paterson & David Domingo
  Making Online News: The Ethnography of New Media Production

To order other books in this series please contact our Customer Service Department:

(800) 770-LANG (within the US)
(212) 647-7706 (outside the US)
(212) 647-7707 FAX

To find out more about the series or browse a full list of titles, please visit our website:

WWW.PETERLANG.COM

The emergence of e-sourcing

business guide

Editorial director: **Stuart Rock**
Editor: **Jo Reeves**
Associate editor: **Alison Jones**
Sub-editor: **Vicki Jackson**
Art editor: **Gary Hill**
Production executive: **Matt McGinty**
Advertisement director: **Kate Cazenove**
Circulation manager: **Cassandra Donovan**
Chief executive and publisher: **Mike Bokaie**

Published by Caspian Publishing Ltd, Millbank Tower, Millbank, London SW1P 4QP
Editorial: **020 7828 0744**
Advertising & production: **020 7828 0733**
Fax: **020 7828 0737**
e-mail: **mgmt@caspianpublishing.co.uk**
Web: **www.caspianpublishing.co.uk**

This guide is produced in association with IBM UK Ltd. IBM Global Services is the world's largest information technology services provider, with approximately 150,000 professionals serving customers in 160 countries and annual revenue of approximately $35bn (2001). IBM Global Services integrates IBM's broad range of capabilities – services, hardware, software and research – to help companies of all sizes realise the full value of information technology. For more information visit: www.ibm.com/services/uk or call 0870 010 2503.

Parties interested in sponsoring other guides in this series should contact Jeremy Knight; in the first instance on 020 7592 8905
Additional titles are available at a cost of £15 (plus £1 p+p)
Contact Cassandra Donovan on 020 7592 8903

Printed in England.
ISBN 1 901844 35 8

1

Contents

Philip Guido,
General manager, e-business hosting, IBM Global Services, EMEA

Introduction

As enterprises everywhere struggle to come to grips with what is now a changed and uncertain world, they are faced with a host of new, critical issues. Budget restrictions, a dubious economy and apprehensive consumers are placing pressure on companies to do more with less, accommodate unpredictable demands, respond quickly to the market and launch new initiatives if they are to survive and win in their own industries.

The drive to stay competitive is forcing many businesses to integrate incompatible systems, adopt new technologies, integrate and distribute information, and adjust rapidly to enterprise and marketplace restructuring.

In this changed environment, maintaining an e-business infrastructure that is ready to support new conditions and requirements can drain a company's financial, human and technological resources – assets that could be better directed toward strengthening core competencies and establishing differentiation.

IBM has launched a new model of providing IT infrastructure, applications, business processes and know-how on demand, called e-business on demand™. It offers a holistic approach that "connects all the dots" – management, technologies, processes and cost – in a profit-focused e-business. This guide aims to explain the business and technology drivers for e-business on demand and to give an insight into experiences of early adopters.

I hope you find this guide valuable and interesting, and that it opens up to you new ways of gaining competitive advantage.

Digby Jones
Director-general, Confederation of British Industry

Foreword

The hype over e-commerce may have subsided over the past two years, but a new chorus of promises can be heard about the potential benefits of the internet. Those chanting the new mantra are not the dot-commandos of the nineties, who are now taking refuge, but the providers of computer hardware, software and internet services.

IT companies now and in the future will provide a computing utility service, which means you can access e-business applications via the internet – on a "pay as you go" basis. Just as the water companies preside over an infrastructure of mains, pipes and sewerage outlets to deliver water, and the electricity companies maintain a series of substations and copper cabling to deliver energy to your door, so too will information technology companies deliver e-business applications to your desktop, laptop, PDA or cell phone.

It's a practical and economical idea that one day will simply be taken for granted, and will be as easy as turning on a tap to run water.

Hundreds of millions of pounds have been invested to create the infrastructure needed to make this new IT approach work. And as this investment continues, over the next two to three years, a steady stream of new, internet-based services will come online, providing significant cost savings over traditional internal systems. Using IT as a utility will provide new opportunities for collaboration among companies, with huge cost savings for service providers and end users.

It's another exciting and important step in our internet-focused society. I do hope this guide serves as a useful tool, and will excite you as to the wealth of business possibilities that lie ahead.

5

1

Paul Bailey, market strategist, IBM EMEA market intelligence
Tosca Colangeli, worldwide director of e-sourcing solutions, IBM Global Services

Come the revolution

IBM e-business on demand is set to make e-business
services as flexible and easy to access as any other utility

Bloodshed and battles do not always typify revolutions. When water first
became a commodity in 310 BC with the construction of the Roman
aqueduct system this, more than commerce or military strength,
enabled Roman civilisation to expand and dominate the Italian peninsula.

When electricity became available to factories in the 1880s, it sparked
what historians have dubbed the "second Industrial Revolution". Electricity
in the workplace meant factories and plants no longer had to be built next
to rivers or other sources of water-based power – something that helped
industrial output expand exponentially.

What these examples make clear is that it's not the invention or the technology in itself that bring revolutionary change, but the availability of the
technology, on demand, in a standardised, scalable way. That requires
infrastructure.

For instance, the first telephone device was created in the late 1870s, and
in just five years there were a quarter of a million telephones in existence.
But what good is a telephone without a network? And it's that network that
laid the foundation for global telecommunications and e-business.

So, what does this history lesson have to do with modern business

6

technology? Well, we are set for another revolution, and this time it will be the IT industry at the forefront.

Introducing The Next Utility™

The idea really is a simple one. In much the same way as water and electricity, IT and IT services will become the next utility. And, just as the introduction of electricity and gas revolutionised industry and changed the way we live, the delivery of e-business as a utility will have the same kind of revolutionary impact.

Benefits of utilities

The nature of utilities is that they are shared, simultaneously serving multiple customers in a flexible, automated fashion. Electrification became more affordable and widespread once the power grid was in place because factories no longer had to build and maintain their own power generators. This creates a more efficient infrastructure, because of the shared cost of ownership.

Utilities are standardised, which means they require little customisation or integration. You flip a switch or open a tap and use what you need. We take utilities for granted because they are reliable – the water, lights, gas and dial tone are almost always there when we need them, with supply to spare. When this basic level of service is automatic, resources are freed up to focus on other priorities.

And utilities are scalable – you get as much capacity as you need, when you need it, and customers are billed according to how much they consume. When usage is metered, there is more control over spending. You can plan for periods of peak consumption, so cost becomes predictable. In IT, the internet makes all of these characteristics – shared infrastructure, standardised tools and scalability – more widely available than ever before.

So why now?

Over the past century, technology (and now IT) has been the major source of initiatives creating business value. Initially, IT was used to solve basic automation issues which helped to improve productivity. This improved efficiency enabled companies to rationalise their operations and spend more time and effort on developing new management systems. As IT developed, it became the agent for change itself, with new business models, such as business process engineering, being developed around technology.

As IT became the key enabler for meeting increasingly demanding market requirements, it very quickly became a "must have". New technologies were actively sought and companies offering new technologies, applications and business solutions saw record growth. But it quickly became ubiquitous. Many technologies that had once seemed world-beating now became utility functions of the business.

We now know that merely owning technology does not bring competitive advantage. Functions such as processing capacity, data storage and basic business applications are all necessary to run a business. We cannot do without these elements, but we gain no advantage from having them.

As a result, businesses are now looking to new ways to create "business value". This newly-emerging business landscape has IT at its heart but places a higher value on the management and application of knowledge to the market place as a means of creating new opportunities. It is not the accumulation of technology that creates competitive advantage, but the way in which it is used – differentiating between utility functions and those technologies which will optimise knowledge sharing.

The market is ready

The market research IBM commissioned last year indicated that almost half of large and medium-sized enterprises have already bought into the knowledge economy and are taking advantage of some kind of IT utility.

About a third of this is web hosting, a market that has tripled in size over the last three years. Another quarter is e-commerce. But increasingly, customers are exploring supply chain and storage utilities, e-mail, systems management, and network-delivered applications. The accelerating growth in packaged software also indicates a growing market acceptance of standardised applications, which clearly lend themselves to utility-type delivery. According to research company IDC, spending worldwide on packaged applications will grow 46 per cent over the next three years, approaching $100bn; meanwhile custom application development will remain flat, at just over $20bn. By 2003, eight out of ten companies expect to be employing an e-utility solution to some aspect of their e-business operations.

What's driving the utility model?

There are a number of key trends that are driving the IBM e-business on demand model:

- *Cheaper bandwidth.* One hundred million miles of fibre optic lines were laid in the last two years. With this glut of capacity has come falling prices. The cost of internet access today is less than a third of what it was in 1999, and prices are expected to drop another 15-25 per cent by the end of 2002 (source: Morgan Stanley). Spot prices for bandwidth on exchanges continue to reach new lows, and some major routes (such as New York to Los Angeles) have dropped more than 80 per cent over the last couple of years. That's not such good news for the telecommunications carriers and network technology suppliers who invested the $35bn it took to create what is now an under-used infrastructure. But it is part of a recurring pattern. When new networking technologies come around, investors who see the potential impact pour money into build-out. Both the telegraph system and the railroad system were built out well in advance of demand. In the case of the telegraph, it was 15 years before the system was profitable. But once the infrastructure is ready and waiting, businesses will quickly find ways to use it. The need for distributed architectures has taken on increasing importance in the wake of September 11th. Companies recognise the value of distributing their operations to be in a better position to resume business in the event of catastrophe.

■ *Server and storage virtualisation.* Today a large server can have many virtual machines running side by side on its processors. In an e-sourcing context that means, for instance, that an application provider can set up virtual partitions that separate the applications delivered to different customers, giving the company economies of scale and reducing costs to the customer. There's also a software component to this, because there has to be middleware that can enable and manage virtualisation. Storage systems, too, can incorporate multiple, distinct spaces, providing flexibility for e-business on demand.

Grid computing – the final driver

The easiest way to think about grid computing is to think about the relationship between the internet and the world wide web. Before the web, the internet was merely a vast network of computers linked together that made it easier for universities and research agencies to pass text files back and forth. It was a bland, slow, cumbersome system. The web introduced open-source software, shared protocols and conventions that enabled us to transform the internet into what it is today – a rich trove of images and text that anyone with a PC, wireless or any other device can access. What the web did to revolutionise content on the internet, the grid will do to revolutionise computing.

"Utilities are scalable – you get as much capacity as you need, when you need it – and customers are billed accordingly"

Like the web, the grid is a set of software tools using standard protocols that will give users access to shared applications, shared data, shared storage and other shared computing resources, all available over the internet. It will be as though the internet were transformed into a vast, global supercomputer that businesses, universities and government agencies could tap into when they need the resources.

This vast computing facility will potentially be millions of times more powerful than the existing internet. Although the focus of current grid activity is in the scientific community, it also holds great promise for e-business.

Business drivers

Just as IBM have always said that e-business is about business and not about technology, the same is true for e-sourcing. The real drivers are the business demands our customers are facing. We surveyed a group of customers last year to gauge their interest in IT services delivered in a utility-like model and to discover the things that caught their interest. Above all, customers see utilities as a means of developing new capabilities quickly. Utilities can help businesses achieve speed to market and competitive advantage. Speed also implies a higher level of service performance, which contributes to customer satisfaction and loyalty.

Cost-effective

The cost-saving aspect is also important. With IBM e-business on demand, an enterprise can acquire new infrastructure and process capabilities without a huge upfront investment. Similarly, companies save on the cost of hiring and training staff. Utilities have intellectual capital built in, so there is access to skills and expertise that wouldn't otherwise be available, particularly with the persistent shortage of IT skills in the market. Many customers told us that technology is advancing so quickly that maintaining that expertise internally is just not time- or cost-effective. Utilities can be a vehicle for taking advantage of best practices in the industry. Finally, customers recognise the benefits of utilities in terms of economies of scale and being able to better manage unpredictable demand.

"What the web did to revolutionise content on the internet, the grid will do to revolutionise computing"

We validated our 2001 research at the beginning of 2002. In a cross-industry survey of IT executives, we found that all of these business drivers still resonate, but four in particular rose to the surface:

- ■ *Reducing upfront investment.* In addition to initial capital outlays, customers are burdened by the high cost of managing and maintaining their current e-business systems.

- *Acquiring new capabilities quickly.* The need for speed is persistent, and complicated by systems that are not easily scalable, are not interoperable, and offer little flexibility. Said one customer, the CTO of a large technology company: "I want to be able to point to a database, point to an application, and get results."
- *Gaining expertise.* The ongoing skill shortage raises the cost of high-demand talent. The overall cost of IT skills is frustrating to many companies that have to invest in something that is not a core competency.
- *Economies of scale.* Many customers have told us they already run a tight, efficient shop; but they are ready for the next turn of the crank that will enable them to reach higher levels of efficiency.

As part of our research, we also asked customers to specify the business and IT capabilities that they would be most likely to adopt as a utility service. Based on that research, as well as what we know about business demands and the future course of technology, we created a three-part model that illustrates how we expect e-business on demand will evolve, and the types of services and capabilities the market can expect from providers.

e-business on demand combines IT utilities...

At the infrastructure level are two major sets of services – core infrastructure services that deliver capacity on demand, and management services that manage and administer the infrastructure. These services are supported by an underlying technical platform that meets all the requirements of a utility service – it's a shared infrastructure, it's scalable, and it's standardised.

Core infrastructure services represent the first wave of the IBM e-business on demand model. These cover the basic infrastructure assets of an IT utility platform – processors, storage and bandwidth. Many of the services at this level, such as web hosting and load balancing, are already well established and growing.

Management services offer assistance in areas such as security, the number one issue that customers in every industry raise when asked about accessing IT infrastructure as a utility. They also include capabilities such as application integration, monitoring and reporting, backup and recovery, and remote systems management. These services eliminate the need for customers to deploy expensive administrative tools, and eliminate or reduce the cost of hiring, training and retaining the skilled personnel needed to run their infrastructure and applications.

...and business process utilities

Riding atop this infrastructure are two kinds of network-delivered business processes – "horizontal" business services, which are processes and functions that are common across all industries, and "vertical" business services, which are applications unique to specific industries.

Given the market demand for packaged applications and the recent interest in shared services such as e-markets, we believe the e-business on demand market will embrace both horizontal and vertical business services.

Horizontal services, such as procurement, e-commerce and HR, which are often standardised across industries, are particularly suited to e-business on demand. E-procurement is particularly hot. Aberdeen Research has estimated that e-procurement solutions can be implemented 23 per cent faster and at 60 per cent lower cost than in-house deployments. IBM developed in-house expertise when we re-engineered our own procurement process and moved it online three years ago. E-procurement has enabled us to save close to $1bn since 1998.

In terms of vertical business processes, several leading-edge companies are beginning to pursue the revenue potential of new IT intensive, web-delivered business services that improve cycle time and the cost of key business processes for their customers and business partners. Companies that have developed

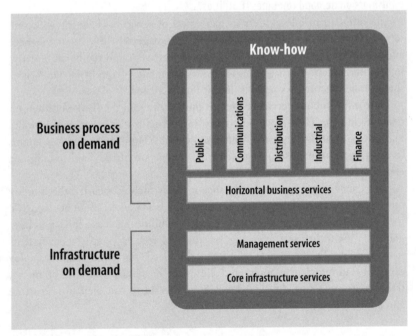

particular expertise are looking to codify their knowledge and provide it to others in their industry, or related industries, as a utility service.

An important benefit to companies with industry-specific expertise that do not have a core competency in technology is that the infrastructure that underlies their utility solution is standardised and shared. Not having to invent the infrastructure to deliver a utility-like service allows them instead to focus on their particular area of expertise.

...wrapped in "know-how"

The third component of this model is what we call "know-how" – the knowledge of business processes and industries that becomes codified in the business process utilities of level two above, and the technical expertise to integrate, run and manage these services at the infrastructure level.

Know-how is also the rare combination of business insight, process knowledge, and technical expertise and research capabilities you need to conceive and create new e-business on demand services.

conclusion

As we move into a more knowledge-based era, future battles for competitive advantage will be fought over knowledge, not IT. Companies need to consider how to better apply technology to meet business needs while freeing up the intellectual capabilities of the business. The challenge now is to understand how to manage technology, to understand what technology contributes to the business and how to manage resources between utility technologies, strategic technologies, and the creation of business value that accumulation and application of knowledge across the organisation will bring.

Paul Bailey works as a market strategist within IBM EMEA market intelligence, looking at emerging business opportunities in the technology-enabled market place. A particular area of focus he has been considering is the emerging market landscape for technology-enabled business value delivery. Tosca Colangeli is the worldwide director of e-sourcing solutions at IBM Global Services.

John R Patrick
Author, *Net Attitude*

Taking the internet for granted

Internet technology will soon be so pervasive,
reliable and transparent that its use will become the norm

The internet we use today is undergoing a massive evolution, bringing about far more change in the next few years than in the last ten. The next generation of the internet, or NGi, will make today's internet seem primitive! Many parts of the NGi are here already. Everyone doesn't have it yet but millions do. There is no arrival date but each day we get a step closer. Not only will the next generation internet be orders of magnitude faster but it will also be always on, everywhere, natural, intelligent, easy, and trusted. The impact of these characteristics on organisations of all kinds will be dramatic. Many people expect or hope that the NGi is going to bring us incredible speed for surfing the web. Speed is in fact one of the characteristics of the NGi, but all seven of the following characteristics are profoundly important.

Fast
Adam Smith's invisible hand is at work on bandwidth (the speed of the internet). Competition among cable, telecom, satellite and other media to provide internet access, as well as technology advancements, will assure the rapid expansion in bandwidth. Using the NGi will be a dramatically

different experience compared with using the internet of today. High-quality, jitter-free, full-screen video will enable experts to appear on video walls in hospitals and classrooms from thousands of miles away.

Always on

No more logging on; you will just be on. You don't log on to the power grid to use your toaster, and you won't log on to the internet to tap the vast resources that it offers. They will just be there. We will begin to think of the internet as a powerful communications network that is not just for surfing the web. Since it will be always on, we will use it to monitor real-time data from weather stations, industrial processes, and even medical monitoring equipment attached to real people.

Everywhere

The era of the PC as the centre of the web is over. Mobile phones, kiosks, PDAs, pagers and new wireless devices will enable the internet to be everywhere and not limited to PCs. Digital signatures will enable us to wire money, transfer securities, and sign contracts electronically from wherever we are: at home, on a train, walking down the street, or in an airplane moving at five hundred miles per hour. When we walk down the Champs-Élysées in Paris, our mobile phone will vibrate and remind us that we are walking by a store that happens to have that rare wine we have been looking for.

Natural

Imagine a real-time multilingual intercom for customer service. Integrated telephony and voice recognition within web pages will enable us to ask a question of customer service in the language of our choice and have that question be routed to the most knowledgeable expert, who will answer the question in her native language and then enable us to hear the answer in our own language. All forms of media, in fact our entire collection of pictures, sound and movies, will fit in a pocket for easy transportation.

Intelligent

A new web standard called XML (extensible markup language) will add context to web pages that will enable people to find things and will enable application software programs to be seamlessly integrated with each other. Finding things on the web will no longer be an exercise in frustration. Instead of millions of matches, we will get a few relevant ones. A new design for computers called autonomic computing will enable systems and networks to become self-healing and self-managing, much like the human body.

Easy

A software system called Linux, developed by a student in Finland, is changing how computers operate. From Beijing University students to Taiwanese entrepreneurs, Linux is taking Asia and the rest of the world by storm. As more and more computers use Linux and more and more students come from school with Linux skills, e-businesses will be much easier to build and maintain. A new approach to creating software – web services – will allow web sites to do much more than "click here to buy". Web sites will do much more for us and we will stand in fewer lines in the physical world and have to endure fewer telephone call centres that want to control us. Fulfilment models at our favourite retailer's web site will result in the staple goods we need showing up outside the garage door when we need them.

"Web sites will do much more for us and we will stand in fewer lines in the physical world and endure fewer telephone call centres"

Trusted

Security is not going to be the biggest issue. Authentication is. Who is that web server you are dealing with? How do the people know it is really you they are doing business with? The NGi will use digital IDs so that we can have authentication, in other words, be able to establish that we are who we say we are and without having to go to a notary or a bank. We will also know that web sites we visit really are who they say they are. We will be able to send messages to friends and businesses that only they can read, be assured that no messages were changed, and allow our financial transactions on the web to stand up in a court of law. Once we establish who we are, we will also be able to establish the level of privacy we would like to have. [See *Protecting your business*, CBI business guide, December 2001/January 2002].

The potential of the internet is much greater than meets the eye. As the internet evolves into the NGi, it will be so pervasive, reliable, and transparent that we will take it for granted. It will be part of our life, like electricity or plumbing. We know that the internet is already transforming business, education, and entertainment. Even larger changes are coming as the internet becomes more reliable and robust. Net attitude will help you get comfortable with the seven characteristics of the NGi and allow you to start planning for how to take advantage of them.

Next-generation attitude

Building a successful e-business requires insight about what the next-generation internet will make possible, as well as an e-business strategy that is deeply embedded in the fabric, the culture and all the operational systems of the company. Also required are a solid business plan, a robust technology plan, and in-house or outsourced human resources with all the latest skills. But even having all of these things at your disposal is not enough to build a successful e-business. All the technology and money on the planet won't enable you to meet people's expectations if you don't have the right attitude. It is essential to have a "next-generation" attitude imbued in management at all levels of the organisation, company, university, hospital or government. They need to be prepared to think and act in new ways that meet the rising expectations of customers and constituencies

Part of "net attitude" is looking to the future, following the internet standards, and anticipating new technology. But a bigger part of it emanates from the grassroots thinking that was part of the evolution of the internet itself. It is a way of thinking that is extroverted in nature, very people oriented. A net attitude is hard to describe, but you will know it when you see it. Young people tend to have it, but it is not really an age thing. An increasing number of seniors have it too. The masses of people in the middle layers of large organisations often don't have it. It is not that there is anything wrong with them as people, but the bureaucracies of large organisations have shielded them from the new way of thinking. And in some cases Darwinian instincts have caused them to bring up their own shields. Net attitude includes the ability to think globally but act locally, to think big but start simple, to think outside in instead of inside out, be able to accept "just enough is good enough", engage in "trial by fire" and transform to a model of "sense and respond" instead of the traditional model of "plan, build, deliver".

Extracted from *Net Attitude: What Is It, How To Get It, and Why Your Company Can't Survive Without It* by John R Patrick (ISBN 185788299-7) published by Nicholas Brealey Publishing (www.nbrealey-books.com) at £19.99 and available at this price (including postage and packing for pre-paid orders) from orders@nbrealey-books.com. John Patrick is a founding member and chairman of the Global Internet Project, a founding member of the World Wide Web consortium at MIT, and formerly vice president of internet technology at IBM Corporation. His website is at http://ibm.com/patrick.

Colin Tyler
Partner, The McKenna Group

Technology comes of age

As IT matures and becomes more pervasive, it is time to think about merging technology and business strategies

As IT has matured over the years it has developed from being used in just a few important areas of business to being an integral part of every business process. With the relentless advance of Moore's Law, better, cheaper, faster IT intelligence is now invading almost all aspects of a business's internal and external processes. Everything from online order placement and HR record keeping, to monitoring delivery vehicles now takes place with IT assistance. However, in a business environment where cost control remains the bottom line, the IT function is now being forced to redefine how its pervasive role can begin to deliver true business value.

A pervasive presence

Despite the pervasiveness of IT, in the vast majority of cases, today's businesses have changed neither the role of the IT function, nor how the business looks at IT. As chairman of the McKenna Group Regis McKenna points out: "New technologies don't simply replace old ways of doing things; they also replace old models of thinking."[1] The fact that IT is now within every business function causes the boundaries between IT strategy and business strategy to blur.

Few substantial IT purchases are now solely within the remit of a lone CIO (especially in today's tight fiscal conditions) and, increasingly, senior managers are IT-literate – a generation of managers brought up on personal computers is gradually taking the reins.

From an IT perspective the change may appear subtle but the impact is huge. The old models of thinking are being replaced; more than ever, IT strategy must become intertwined with business strategy. Solving today's business challenges is becoming today's IT requirement.

Facing up to the challenge

Business challenges come in many shapes and sizes. Some are transitory, for example, efficiently handling integration following mergers and acquisitions, or supporting the launch of new products and services. Others are permanent, such as driving down operating costs, improving yield from existing customers, capturing market insight, gaining new customers or ensuring business continuity. Although each challenge calls for a specific solution, four IT capabilities will form the cornerstone of a new model of IT as it becomes fully pervasive across business functions:

- *Flexibility.* Remaining flexible to unforeseen needs, new innovations and evolving requirements becomes a key IT capability and is essential to handle future uncertainty. For example, businesses who adopted early ERP packages with visionary zeal became leading innovators in the ERP space. However, few considered the difficulties of finding themselves locked into a technology platform that would rapidly be leapfrogged – with no easy migration path. The innovators of yesterday rapidly became the laggards of today. Handling organic growth, mergers, acquisitions, new innovations, all depend on building flexibility into the fabric of the business and (by association) a more flexible approach to IT.
- *Integration.* We live in the era of integration; IP-based technology has brought remote "economically unviable" customers and partners within reach. However, many organisations are struggling to integrate disparate systems acquired over a lifetime of disconnected decision-making or a legacy of corporate acquisitions. The apocryphal story of a financial services company refusing car insurance to a customer, without realising that he was actually the most valuable customer to their life and home insurance divisions, is too close to the truth for many organisations. Gaining a single view of customers across multiple, disparate divisions is only one example of how integration will become a vital IT capability for building more intelligence into business, and the only way to extract full value from the customer base.

- *Reliability.* When asked to choose, few organisations would now prefer their e-mail service to be "down" rather than their fax line. Most become paralysed when sophisticated network connectivity drops or a virus attacks; and many carry the expense of massive capacity redundancy to minimise the impact of IT failures. As IT increasingly permeates the business, so the need for reliable IT capabilities is becoming an implicit requirement.
- *Cost efficiency.* In tightened economic climates, IT must begin to understand the business demands of capital and operating cost efficiency. More than any other capability it is within cost efficiency that the old models of IT will be broken most completely. Identifying where businesses can invest in IT to deliver true competitive advantage must be accompanied by tougher decisions regarding where even the most sophisticated IT solution only allows a business to deliver merely equivalent functionality.

Divide and conquer

In this new world, IT decisions will get driven into three categories, each of which has contrasting objectives and must be relentlessly pursued. Businesses have always been forced to make trade-offs between their business requirements and available resources. As IT has become more pervasive, a "divide and conquer" approach will

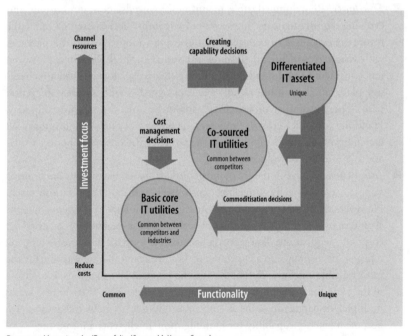

Figure one: Managing the IT portfolio (Source: McKenna Group)

increasingly be used. In leading businesses the very function of IT will be split into the following three categories and managed aggressively. At the same time the strategic skill will be to constantly re-assess responsibilities to understand which functions can be transferred between categories as available technology matures.

The three main IT categories

Increasingly, there will be three principal categories of IT investment.

■ *Basic core IT utilities.* Many IT functions are already so universally embedded that their very performance becomes invisible. System administrators who run and manage a web site or an e-mail server only ever get cursed when it appears to be "down"; the allocation and re-allocation of storage arrays for massive ERP databases remain invisible to almost every end user; and the provision of patches, upgrades and security features to most client-side applications is increasingly transparent. Every industry competitor will spend IT resources on these things but few, if any, will see them as fundamental to delivering unique value to customers. These have become core IT commodities, to be managed for cost (at appropriate reliability and flexibility levels) but basically recast as utilities and, wherever possible, releasing capital and skills to be invested in areas of greater business advantage.

In the next few years, basic core utilities will probably include the web-based technology that was cutting edge just a couple of years ago. Similarly, the wireless technology of today will soon be commonplace. How this will manifest itself in end-user equipment is still unclear, but what is clear is that the billions of users, be they customers, employees or co-workers, will all require applications to access data, to allocate stock or to find local services. These will all require an infrastructure to support the billions of users, as companies strive to maintain their competitive edge.

■ *Co-sourced IT utilities.* Look inside some of the fiercest industry competitors and you'll find many of their business processes to be remarkably similar. Widespread espionage could be to blame, but more likely are the many drivers that tend to lead competitors to find the same business solution. Often, specialist process suppliers are relatively few. For example, in the travel industry the dominance of only three global players (Galileo, Amadeus & Sabre) meant that fiercely competitive hotels and airlines all had reservation processes that conformed to a common approach.

Other factors such as regulatory controls, process consultants hawking knowledge between competitors, and widely accessible new technologies all contribute to a growing category of processes where, although the approach is specialised, the ultimate business advantage delivered is minimal. For these utilities the challenge for IT is to provide the specialist capability at industry performance standards but at lower total cost. The emerging solution to this dilemma comes from co-operating with competitors in domains that can be co-sourced – a trend already seen in call centre operations where West TeleServices and others provide highly customised solutions but with costs from infrastructure, personnel and facilities shared across multiple competitors. Within these utilities, the leading businesses will define these new services themselves and gain new revenues by offering them as specialised, co-sourced utilities to their fiercest competitors.

■ *Differentiated IT assets.* Stripping away all the common processes, knowledge and systems across competitors reveals just a handful of IT assets that deliver genuine differentiated value. For example, for pharmaceutical companies these assets might include the drug discovery algorithms, for retailers, the processes for optimising profits on markdowns or shelf layouts – truly the "jewels" of a business. These unique processes are almost always proprietary, held closely in-house. Any complementary new innovations will frequently be acquired and immediately integrated into these processes. Remarkably, however, the advantages such processes accrue to their owners are at best transitory, mainly due to the ever-advancing edge of technology. In less than a decade, equivalent search technology to that originally developed by leading information archives such as LexisNexis, Dialog or Westlaw in the eighties, had become available to almost anyone with internet access at many free search engine sites. The boundary of differentiation is constantly advancing. In its wake, tough decisions will need to be taken about whether IT processes become recast as utilities or can still deliver true differentiation.

The portfolio of functions that IT supports will always span all three of these categories. The CIO's skill will be in spotting when one part of the portfolio requires a radically different approach; shifting resources to the more differentiated IT assets or unlocking new value by leading the industry into co-sourcing increasingly undifferentiated processes.

conclusion

As IT strategy becomes bound inseparably with business success, how the CIO responds to these changing opportunities will increasingly dictate overall corporate success. Leading CIOs will become portfolio managers, understanding where they are wasting IT time and resources by retaining control of increasingly undifferentiated utility processes, and instead diverting investment towards the IT assets that deliver real business advantage. The true visionaries will go beyond this and capture the structural advantages available to those who lead the development of a new wave of co-sourced utilities. Implicitly, CIOs will need to handle the cultural change of accepting external partnerships and new providers as a legitimate route to providing some of their traditional IT functions.

1. Regis McKenna, *Total Access*, Harvard Business School Press, 2002

Colin Tyler is a partner at The McKenna Group, the North American technology partners of OC&C Strategy Consultants. He can be reached at ctyler@mckenna-group.com or colin.tyler@occstrategy.com

Niall Andrews
Chief technology officer, 7C

Are your customers being served?

Advances in technology are making robust CRM solutions available to more businesses

The challenge of building robust CRM solutions, coupled with the high cost of failure, is discouraging many companies from pursuing the advantages of CRM. However, a new business model that provides access to robust CRM technologies on a pay-as-you-go basis, could be the solution.

Facing the challenge

The prizes awaiting companies that pursue and achieve best practice CRM are considerable: a powerful combination of loyalty-boosting customer service improvements, significantly increased revenue from the customer base, and improved customer acquisition performance.

Given such significant rewards, one would expect every company to be pursuing this course. Sadly, the evidence tells us this is not the case. 7C's research shows that 82 per cent of FTSE and Global 500 companies don't have a company-wide CRM solution in place. Worse still, more than a third believe achieving such a thing is impossible.

The CRM investment risk can be high. Industry experts estimate that a full CRM implementation – embracing front and back end systems, providing a 360-degree view of the customer across all channels and introducing analytical capability that makes one-on-one marketing possible – could possibly take more than two years to implement and cost as much as $4m. While such forecasts can never be exact, it's clear that the task is considerable.

Given this scenario it can hardly be surprising, especially in a tough economic climate, that many companies are daunted and decide that, despite the potential rich rewards, the cost and risk involved make attempts to pursue best practice CRM simply not worth it.

Also, given that the number of mobile phones in the UK exceeds the number of PCs, and with the growth of other mobile devices likely to follow a similar growth pattern, companies who pride themselves on their abilities to target-market should take note. A best-of-breed CRM solution – one that can access more customers and prospects more of the time – must be able to react and provide customer service whenever and however the customer wants it.

Making CRM work for you

Technology has already brought CRM a long way. The benefit of a best practice CRM implementation to any marketing manager cannot be overstated. It is customer knowledge that drives marketing and product development. But the quality of that customer knowledge will depend on how well disparate systems have been integrated over the years (for example, call centres, online orders or e-mail queries) and how efficiently any customer knowledge captured has been used to build personal customer profiles (see figure one).

As we discussed in chapter three, it is now beneficial for a business to integrate IT strategy with its overall business strategy. It follows, therefore, that by exploiting advances in recent technology, a marketing manager should be seeking to synchronise IT and marketing to maximise CRM best practice at the lowest possible cost.

The challenge for CRM service providers, therefore, is to offer clients a wholly new route to best practice CRM – one that reduces the upfront investment, lowers the cost, reduces the time to implement and removes the investment risks that, at present, are proving to be such powerful deterrents.

What is needed is a solution that provides immediate access to a proven suite of CRM technologies on a pay-as-you-go basis, with a guarantee that those technologies will be future-proof and keep pace with new developments in applications and channels of delivery. The emergence of e-sourcing provides the perfect platform for CRM technologies to make that a reality.

The road less travelled

The issues surrounding the time and cost of implementing a CRM solution that

Achieving best practice CRM – A three step approach

Step one: Getting started	Step two: Building knowledge	Step three: Achieving best practice
Starting point:	**Starting point:**	**Starting point:**
■ You barely know your customers and contact them via disparate systems.	■ You've integrated systems and can capture customer info across all channels.	■ You know your customers and can predict their behaviour.
■ You have call centres, perhaps web-enabled, but they're not linked to your static, incomplete customer databases.	■ You recognise customers however they make contact.	■ You can deliver individually targeted sales propositions to customers.
■ You may be offering online services but they're not linked to other systems or channels.	■ You can capture info from every interaction and use it to build personal customer profiles.	■ You capture responses to every proposition, building a cycle of test and learn.
		■ Customer knowledge drives marketing and product development.
The challenge:	**The challenge:**	**The challenge:**
■ Capture customer info across all channels – via integrated systems.	■ Understand what you know – use database analysis and intelligent decision making.	■ You're ahead, now stay there.
■ Keep customer knowledge current via links to database management systems.	■ Put customers at the heart of your business – synchronise IT and marketing.	

Figure one: A three-step approach to achieving best practice CRM

were discussed earlier are just part of the problem. Hiring and training staff in the necessary skills, integrating CRM applications with existing legacy systems and ensuring that all customer data collected will be held securely are also thorny issues.

One solution would be to outsource CRM. 7C has built a comprehensive platform of CRM applications, called "Incenta", which integrates technologies from Siebel Systems, E.piphany, Cisco and Vitria, that can be implemented on a client's behalf within as little as four to six weeks, depending upon the level of customisation of the platform required.

By utilising e-sourcing technology, businesses now have a genuine alternative to the formidable task of building their own CRM technology platform. Outsourcing in this way also massively reduces the ongoing time, risk and cost involved in keeping pace with the many new emerging technologies.

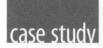

case study Airline solutions

Through a joint venture company, 7C Italia, 7C is working with Italy's national airline to meet two clear objectives: to create high standards of customer service while reducing its cost to serve, and to introduce advanced technologies that will facilitate direct sales and advanced ticketing operations.

Today, 7C Italia handles telephone and online customer service and ticket reservations for customers across Italy and is about to launch its first direct sales programme, which will use the internet, e-mail and SMS messaging to open up new opportunities in Italy's huge SME business market.

The joint venture with Alitalia has created Italy's second largest outsourced CRM business. 7C Italia opened its first customer contact centre in Palermo in Spring 2001, initially with 200 employees, which should rise to 1,400 by the end of 2002. It aims to be a major player in Italy's fast-growing CRM marketplace, which is expected to treble in size by 2005.

For some companies, however, the thought of outsourcing CRM, with the risks to all-important customer data integrity they perceive to be involved, is simply too frightening. However, as Incenta integrates with the clients' own systems at an application level, those client systems themselves act as "gatekeepers" for the data, enforcing integrity rules and preventing loss or damage. Clients can choose to adopt only those elements of the platform that their existing business needs dictate and are able to add more later, as their CRM programmes increase in sophistication.

case study Customer contact

One of the first clients to make use of the outsourcing platform in its entirety is Cisco. On their behalf Incenta supports a series of e-marketing initiatives across Europe, the Middle East and Africa. Directly linked to the Cisco web site, multilingual customer service agents are able to communicate with Cisco customers via Web Chat, Click-to-Talk, web collaboration and e-mail, as well as the more traditional phone and fax.

Nick Hurst, Cisco's business development director for the UK and Ireland, recognises the opportunity Cisco has to revolutionise the way it interfaces with customers. "Through Incenta we're able to provide customers with a fast, direct and flexible interface to our disparate sales and service operations across our complete product range, helping them get the information they want quickly and easily. We believe the service will be particularly beneficial for small and medium sized businesses, whose reliance on the internet as a fact finding and buying tool is increasing. Moreover, we've been able to achieve this in record time. From signing the contract with 7C to implementing the service took only five weeks."

The infrastructure issue

Of course, a suite of CRM applications is only one part of the story. For any company operating on an international basis or, indeed, one that simply needs to provide customer service and support from more than a single site, the question of a technology infrastructure through which CRM applications can be delivered 24x7 on an international basis while remaining cost effective is a key issue.

New developments in VOIP (Voice Over Internet Protocol) and the arrival of robust, internationally deployable Virtual Private Networks (VPN) make significant telephony cost reductions immediately achievable. The customer support and outbound sales provided to Cisco's clients across Europe, the Middle East and Africa are done so from a single, UK-based location but with much reduced international communications costs. VOIP solutions from Cisco Systems and a Virtual Private Network from Worldcom ensure that all calls, wherever they're destined, are passed over a single 7C infrastructure.

The savings from such an infrastructure are considerable, as is the reduction in deployment times, but for many companies the cost and complexity of building such an infrastructure could be prohibitive. As with its CRM platform, 7C provides immediate access on a pay-as-you-go basis to a proven technology infrastructure that can flex to meet almost any volume of demand.

conclusion

The e-sourcing model, which delivers pre-integrated technology applications over a readily available and scalable network, is one which can be applied to a number of business areas. Why are such solutions not more readily available and from more sources? The answer, to my mind, is simple. The CRM challenge will not be overcome by technology alone. A strong CRM solution calls for a combination of technology, operational infrastructure and expertise (in terms of call centres and the people who staff them), plus advanced marketing skills.

Niall Andrews is chief technology officer of 7C, Europe's largest independent outsourced customer management company where he has been responsible for the development and building of the company's advanced multi-channel technology platform, Incenta. Niall previously held roles with PA Consulting, PricewaterhouseCoopers and Accenture.
If you would like to know more about how 7C can help you achieve best practice CRM contact: Clare Roberts on 0207 505 6105 or e-mail clare.roberts@7c.net or visit the 7C web site at www.7C.net

Nick Goodall, communications consultant, IBM Global Services
Neil Hawkins, EMEA Lotus Notes architect, IBM Global Services
Martin James, EMEA HR service centre manager

5

When demand meets supply

HR, procurement, groupware and e-mail – IBM e-business on demand can supply all the requirements of business

Technology might be better, faster and more intelligent than it has ever been but in spite of all the advances in IT and the potential they offer, the size of the problem facing businesses has, if anything, increased, as has the overall cost of ownership. What is needed is a way of maximising the benefits of technology's promise of efficiency without shouldering the burden of ownership.

Changing the goalposts

How can a company plan for future business strategically when technological change moves faster than business strategies, and introduces shifting budgetary problems? The answer is to recognise that technology has moved so much into the centre of successful business that it has become almost invisible. So why not supply information technology in exactly the same way that all essential services are supplied to business – as a utility?

IBM e-business on demand is the model to supply that constant flow of information to people's fingertips, just in time and on demand. The key to making a service culture work is partnership, just as the key to making e-business work within companies is partnership between departments – and,

29

vitally, between departmental systems such as human resources (HR), procurement and shared functions, such as groupware and e-mail.

Working the network

Web services is not a technology in itself, but a set of standards to facilitate application-to-application communication. It is a group of technology components that are dedicated to enabling the free-flowing and intuitive spread of information around a company's network of component departments, systems and personnel.

All networks are a virtual model of the enterprises they serve, so an integrated network means an integrated organisation that can plan strategically with every factor, every cost and every process predictable, and every point of access to that information included in the loop. In such a system, any piece of information and, therefore, any business process, can be amended and sent in any direction, almost *ad infinitum*.

Integrating technologies

IBM e-business on demand is about treating each technology or application component – representing an e-business function – as a utility. When a business wants a particular component it simply "switches" it on, either using the traditional "shrink wrapped" licensing model, or as part of a hosted service. In the latter case, non-core business competencies are outsourced to the people who know how to do them best – the customer's technology partners.

The result is a simplified management process for technology that integrates with the customer's internal systems and business processes, on demand and just in time. Web services allows you to deploy a process by implementing the components of that process as a service. It can be distributed across a complex, legacy-defined organisation, precisely because the technology is built on open standards.

Service with a smile

With e-sourcing, we also regard the infrastructure as something that can be delivered as a service. In this way, customers can focus on their business strategies, giving themselves increased speed to market, improved resource usage and an improved alignment of IT investments with an optimal business return.

Internal e-sourcing

In 1992 IBM started to reduce its IT spending. In order to do this it consolidated its world-wide production data centres from 155 in the nineties down to 13 at the end of 2001. The operation of these centres has been outsourced to IBM Global Services, which manages them and supports all of IBM on a global basis. During this period over 31 private and separate data networks were consolidated into a single Global Wide Area Network and also outsourced for seamless global management.

In 1991 there were hundreds of hardware and software configurations for employee workstations. Today there are just four standard configurations, which make maintenance and support highly efficient and cost effective. These configurations are updated on an ongoing basis and deployed on a rolling three year cycle.

Employee e-mail (Lotus Notes), real time office communications (Lotus Sametime) and Help Desk Support are also managed by IBM Global Services. A common, scalable architecture called the "Global Notes Architecture" (GNA) ensures consistent and highly reliable connectivity and performance from anywhere in the world. GNA operates consistently across all three of IBM's e-Server platforms.

A Global Web Architecture (GWA) is used to ensure consistency and cost effectiveness for all web-based applications across IBM. Development and deployment of all IBM applications and solutions is now managed through a common corporate process called Business Transformation Management System (BTMS). This ensures the rapid, cost efficient and highly successful implementation of new solutions which comply with the common architectures and standards needed to balance workload on a global basis.

In the mid-nineties there were approximately 16,000 applications running within the company, of which one third lacked clear ownership. Today there are less than 6,400 applications in the IBM portfolio; all have clearly identified owners who continually update and further consolidate these assets.

Spending is targeted and managed at the corporate level based on full cost recovery for IT services used. Common services are recovered through consistent "rated service offerings" while employee-based spending (for example, voice services, employee workstations and staff) is managed at the departmental level.

How IBM meets specific business requirements

E-mail

E-mail and groupware were two of the first examples of technology as a service. We wanted to provide better support for our growing number of remote and mobile employees, enable timely and effective information sharing, establish a consistent set of application enablers, promote external awareness and connectivity and enhance productivity among both user and skill groups (two of the categories into which staff are segmented). All these, of course, are shared aims with the burgeoning areas of e-sourcing and web services.

The introduction of Lotus Notes gave us the capability of rich text formatting and a convenient way to exchange file attachments, but its groupware functionality – built on the notion of sharing information throughout the enterprise and establishing communities of users – gave the company and its customers much more than e-mail.

In parallel with the move to Lotus Notes, IBM moved to an internet protocol (IP) network infrastructure. This facilitated widespread use of an intranet to communicate with employees, and also the use of Notes "team rooms", discussion databases, document libraries, and simple applications. We also now use "e-meetings" and instant messaging across a wide range of devices – again, functionality shared with the wider group of IBM e-business on demand services.

Today, any business process can be made available anywhere in the network, and across a complex, technologically divergent organisation. Even a message, once it has become electronic, becomes infinitely accessible, however an employee chooses to send or receive it. However, at the same time, an employee must be assured that information contained in an e-mail will remain secure. All these are tools that employees use – as well as e-mail itself – to collaborate with each other, and all are concerned with personal and group productivity.

E-procurement

Under our own e-procurement initiative, we sourced and procured nearly $40bn-worth of goods and services over the internet through the 2001 financial year, yielding cost-savings of $405m. By web-enabling the procurement process, we found the key was reducing complexity, not just in the number of business processes that became seamlessly web-enabled, but in numerous other areas, as well.

First, the potential for human error (including "maverick buying") is reduced at every stage of the process, since once a requisition is automated, it becomes available at every point of the information chain. Second, purchase order process time, according to our statistics, is down to an average of one hour. Beyond this, internal employee satisfaction has increased by 45 per cent and – last but not least – the average length of procurement contracts has been reduced to just six pages.

These are just some of the unexpected benefits of deploying a business process as a service: even the human elements of the procurement process, such as employee satisfaction and the minutiae of supplier contracts, can be improved by IBM e-business on demand.

Whether for buying or selling, a just-in-time e-procurement environment is designed to help minimise costs and drive greater efficiency, from requisition through to payment.

For example, we use a suite of subscription and transaction-based procure-

We at IBM Global Services hope that you found this business guide to be of interest. In order to evaluate the effectiveness of our communications, we would be grateful if you would take a minute to complete and return this short feedback form.

Your overall opinion of the guide:

☐ Very good ☐ Good ☐ Average ☐ Poor

How could we make the guide more relevant to you?

_____

_____

_____

_____

_____

_____

Where did you actually read the guide?

☐ Home ☐ Office ☐ Train/Plane ☐ Other

Are there other topics you would like to see in future editions of this guide?

_____

_____

_____

_____

_____

_____

Please keep me updated on the following IBM Services:

☐ E-commerce

☐ E-business/Mobile E-business

☐ Hosted Business Applications

☐ Business Management Services/ERP

☐ Customer Relationship Management

☐ Business Intelligence

☐ Supply Chain Management

☐ Business Consulting

☐ IT Consulting

☐ E-business on Demand

Name: _____

Position: _____

Company: _____

Address: _____

_____

Postcode: _____

Telephone: _____

Please send me future information about IBM products and services by e-mail. My e-mail address for this purpose is: _____

This data may be used to provide you with information from IBM organisations worldwide about products and services that may be of interest to you.

☐ Please do not use the information collected here for future marketing or promotional contacts or other communications beyond the scope of this transaction.

ment services, designed to provide access to pre-enabled supplier relationships and sourcing expertise to deliver the benefits of e-procurement faster. This increases purchase control, works with preferred suppliers, reduces procurement cycle times, standardises purchase procedures and rules, offers reporting and analysis to track purchasing data, and supports multiple languages and currencies.

Human resources

HR is a cost centre offering services that range from straightforward administration to complex strategies to driving business performance through good people management. It needs both to provide high level services to top management and also be easily accessible for anyone within the organisation.

"Even the human elements of procurement, such as employee satisfaction, were improved by IBM e-business on demand"

We've already looked at groupware and its possible benefits across the organisation, which include HR, in the form of employee notice boards or "e-meetings" of employee groups. So how else can e-sourcing and web services improve HR?

In IBM's case, the traditional organisation and delivery model, based on an HR adviser covering all topics for a defined area of the business, was totally inadequate for the needs of the business. The HR adviser was swamped with administrative issues, and was frequently unavailable to answer even the simplest of questions. In addition, it was impossible to give enough time to the high level needs of the top management of his/her business area. As a result, managers were wasting time trying to interact with HR, and customer satisfaction was low.

We found that HR requests and queries usually fell into one of several categories – simple advice (on some aspect of company policy), transactions (getting mandatory paperwork through the system) or more higher level consultation (about, for example, effecting a change of corporate policy, or how to roll out an HR programme across a business unit).

Based on these findings, IBM moved to a more radical, customer-centric HR model, building a service centre and an intranet to deal with the straightforward tasks, and introducing an HR strategy partner to focus on the needs of top management. The service centre and web site were designed to meet the differing needs of employees – whether desk-based, mobile or involved in manual work.

Such an e-HR model was perfect for the benefits of the IBM e-business on demand and web services technologies, providing user friendly routes to HR service for all types of employee and manager, and greatly reducing the time they had to spend interacting with the HR back office.

conclusion

We found that some 85 per cent of employee interactions could be handled by either the simple interaction level – ie. not requiring the advice of HR professionals – or by the technology level alone (intranet, telephony, back-office HR systems and infrastructure). The end result was a massive cost reduction of 57 per cent, an HR head count reduced by an even larger percentage and, tellingly, a 90 per cent satisfaction rating from employees. Despite the wide potential for e-sourcing, web services technologies and their usage, the common factors are clear: on demand means a seamless web of services, integration across a diverse legacy network, greater efficiencies and, essentially, improved user satisfaction. With IBM e-business on demand, end-to-end e-business really can be as accessible, affordable and as easy to use as water, gas, telephone or electricity. After all, we should know, it's a solution we deploy ourselves to help our own business.

URLs
www.lotus.com
www.ibm.com/services/uk/ondemand

Nick Goodall is communications consultant for IBM Global Services, Europe, Middle East and Africa. In this role he plans the delivery of information about internal IT to IBM employees. Neil Hawkins is the EMEA Lotus Notes architect for IBM's internal Lotus Notes service. Martin James is the EMEA HR service centre manager.

Allan McKenzie,
Head of business development (Foreign Exchange) Dresdner Bank

6

Laying the financial foundations

The e-sourcing model applies to virtually every facet of financial services – and lends itself well to the sector

The fantastic pace of technological development during the past ten years now means that many larger corporations – particularly in the financial services sector – are presiding over disparate technologies, a mishmash of software applications, all spread across offices around the world.

Meanwhile, in order to make all these different systems work together, companies have invested huge amounts of money in highly complex Enterprise Resource Planning systems (ERPs) which offer suites of interlinked applications. ERPs have solved the problem but they remain inflexible and lock companies into set processes, making innovation and opportunism difficult. IT is supposed to serve business, but progressively the tail is wagging the dog.

Enter e-sourcing – the utility platform that applies to nearly every facet within the financial sector. Financial services is based on a series of processes or tick boxes – if all the boxes can be ticked, the transaction can be completed – and in this sense it works well on any given software application, as long as the broadband delivery platform is in place.

However, the e-sourcing model will only perform if enough users and suppliers subscribe to the basic premise that it is a utility that requires a delivery infrastructure that everyone needs to plug in to. Currently, it looks likely that the financial services market will quickly fragment into the haves and the have-nots.

In this sense, the utility service platform will evolve over the next couple of years and will play an important role in helping business communities – especially in the financial services sector – build a shared meaning in terms of software languages, such as XML, and in business protocols. This is because a set of utilities will be established to help the future development of a set number of trading standards.

> "It looks likely that the financial services market will quickly fragment into the haves and the have-nots"

Crucially, the new infrastructure will provide a platform for companies to offer their core competencies as a service to other companies. Shrewd IT executives in the City and other financial centres will not just consume web services, they will also be selling them.

The bank processing the transaction must maintain a hefty infrastructure of technologies, often linked to third parties on expensive communication networks employing a variety of software. After all, the deal is often transacted over the phone or through the post.

Increasing efficiency

With e-sourcing, the whole process becomes more flexible, more efficient and is automated. Costly leased lines are replaced by the internet, XML and SOAP (an electronic envelope for wrapping up messages to be sent from one computer to another, often across the internet) take the place of proprietary software making the loan cheaper to transact. E-sourcing represents a much more efficient way to manage information technology, by allowing companies to purchase only the functionality they need when they need it, substantially reducing investment in IT assets.

Meanwhile, by shifting responsibility for maintaining systems to outside providers or utilities, it reduces the need for huge numbers of IT support staff and reduces the risk of obsolete systems because if the utility wishes to remain competitive it will have to invest in the most up-to-date technology.

Many companies are already embracing the new utility. A recent paper by Harvard Business School, *Your Next IT Strategy*, points to Merrill Lynch, which is currently testing a series of initiatives designed to take advantage of e-sourcing. One such innovation is the creation of a portfolio analysis system for use by brokers and selected customers. By using XML to link up disparate systems within the bank as well as to integrate information from partner organisations, the new system will tie together customer information, product information and real-time market data drawn from third-party providers.

The system is flexible and low cost, giving brokers access to real-time, integrated information that allows them to quickly address customer needs at any given moment.

Taking a step forward

So what's holding the rest of us back? Well, in the fiercely competitive financial markets, companies are still jostling for position and are afraid to commit to the utility model as to do so, they believe, is tantamount to relinquishing control of a process, and possible competitive advantage. This misses the point. The utility is simply the medium by which companies will deliver a service – whether it be trading futures or equities or processing bank loans.

The only reason existing companies need fear e-sourcing is that it will improve transparency for the consumer, and those companies that deliver a poor quality, costly service will be quickly found out.

This will be another benefit of e-sourcing: certain sectors will become increasingly collaborative. In the financial services arena it should allow a multitude of suppliers offering standard unitised products or tradable assets to share systems and processes, releasing the benefits inherent from economies of scale, reducing costs and allowing greater focus on the quality of the offering. The physical settlement process is near identical for like products from one institution to another.

Client communities

Ultimately the client is king and a group of like-minded clients are truly mighty. So it is here that the client or client communities must enter the game if they want their suppliers to collaborate rather than merely compete for his attentions. The debate now moves on from supply-client relationship, because both sides can equally enjoy the advantages. In the new outsourced world, we are all clients.

It is likely that we are too early in the evolutionary process of collaboration to immediately trust our arch competitors with elements of our process. This in itself endorses the position of market-neutral, trusted providers of systems and services and such companies will be the e-sourcing utilities of the future.

conclusion

For this new utility model to be sustainable there must be real value-added benefits for all users. Added value to the supplier would be the same as value added to the client, reduced costs through streamlined processes. The utility company will make its living by charging less than the combined saving of its two customers for facilitating their savings.

The advent of e-sourcing signals a major change in how companies make use of their existing technology and how quickly they can adapt their businesses to this new model. Either way they will ignore it at their peril.

Allan McKenzie is head of business development (Foreign Exchange), Dresdner Bank. A 20-year veteran of the FX market, he came to the e-commerce environment in 1997, having traded for the bank as chief dealer in London. Prior to this he spent several years working in other mainstream international banks, both in Europe and for three years in the US.

Kate Oakley
Associate director, Local Futures Group

7

Becoming an e-citizen

What are the implications of an e-community where
everyone has equal access to services and information?

ook into the future. If we look far enough there will come a time when
the "digital divide" has been bridged and broadband, high-quality and
reliable information technology is available in every household in the
UK, over a variety of media – computers, PDAs and hand-held devices, or
via the TV. Using the internet and e-mail will be like using the phone –
everyone will do it without giving a second thought to how it works or
worrying about whether it is beyond their skills capabilities.

Once we reach such a stage, technology, e-business and the internet will
no longer just be the domain of the section of the population who have
access to computers. This will then open up a massive potential market for
e-commerce and e-government services. Just as in the real world we exist as
citizens in communities, we need to develop a notion of e-citizenship –
citizens of a digital world.

How do we become e-citizens?

This might seem like a pipe dream, but if we take "IT as a utility" seriously,
then the dream might not be far from reality. However, although businesses
are already beginning to reap the benefits of e-sourcing, this debate has yet

to be had in the public sphere, which understandably remains preoccupied with issues of unequal access to technology.

It is clear, however, that the vision of "e-governance" (a set of technology-mediated partnerships between government, businesses and the community to deliver social goods, such as education, healthcare or democratic services) needs to be underpinned by the notion of "e-citizenship on demand". In other words, we need to think about what it means to be a citizen in this new world. What skills are needed to participate electronically as well as in person? What level of access do people need? What rights and responsibilities should govern access to information, both personal and public? If information technology really does become ubiquitous then we can start to reap the benefits of collective learning and economies of scale from the massive "social experiment" that is already taking place in several European countries, under the rubric of e-government, e-communities, e-learning and e-health.

"We need to think about what it means to be an e-citizen in this new world. What skills are needed to participate electronically?"

However, having the technology available will not automatically put this dream into action. It is clear that information and communications technology (ICT) in itself will not immediately make e-citizens of us all. Like all social phenomena, it simply opens up new patterns of possible outcomes – those outcomes are dependent on how we decide to shape them.

Bridging the digital divide

Debates about the social impact of technologies have for the last ten years at least concentrated on inequality of access, the so-called "digital divide". Access to the internet, particularly via a PC, currently follows the outlines of relative prosperity and advantage.

Internet access is largely determined by socio-economic status. The more affluent the neighbourhood the more home access it is likely to have. Under current circumstances this "geography" of wealth and opportunity looks "hard-wired in" for the next generation.

The benefits of e-communities

But what if Public Wireless LANs become far more common? Wireless LANs at commercial premises could enable a large number of previously disenfranchised people to participate without the relatively large expense of buying a PC and having to find room at home. This becomes more apparent at schools and colleges, where the infrastructure is provided and will give access to a large amount of people from one point of contact. Once the practicalities of creating an e-community are resolved, we can begin to see the benefits and possibilities of what this will allow us to do:

- Harness the benefits of the huge public sector investment in IT and really start to "join-up" e-services such as e-learning, health, benefit payments or council tax payments, for the citizen. Clearly disparate legacy systems, incompatibility and complexity has slowed down progress in this arena so far – but maybe developments in autonomic computing (see chapter twelve) offer some hope for faster progress here.
- Aggregate resources within an entire IT infrastructure, for example, across a health authority or a city's schools. The proposed scheme to create electronic patient records would ensure that UK citizens have their medical files kept electronically in one place and be accessed from anywhere in the country. The possibilities of grid computing (see chapter ten) hold out further hope for online, holistic medical care, available anywhere in the country.
- Aggregate public sector demand for applications, particularly in e-learning or e-health, which would have the added benefit for content producers of stimulating an otherwise fragile market.
- Contribute towards environmental sustainability, for example, by allowing for greater telecommuting and remote working, thereby keeping more cars off the road. This will also have knock-on social (and consequently economic) benefits. It is increasingly accepted that home working can improve the work-life balance making workers more relaxed, happy and productive!
- Start to reduce the current gaps between urban and rural areas in terms of access to services and help with the regeneration of the rural economy. If the rural business community sometimes feels isolated, as e-citizens they will have greater technological access, allowing individuals and small businesses to address national and international markets from wherever they are.
- Above all perhaps, bridging the digital divide and enabling everyone to become e-citizens by buying as much or as little computing power as we need (rather than the whole "kit") can be used to promote a more democratic and inclusive society. The spread of technology could provide forums for people to air their views and complaints directly to either government or businesses. It could change the relationship between governors and the governed, by allowing citizens access to information that has previously been the preserve of a selected few and release the creative and problem-solving abilities of people and communities.

The notion of public-sector or community-led initiatives is not as unlikely as it might sound. After all, one of the earliest examples of grid computing is SETI@home, established by the Search for Extra Terrestrial Intelligence (SETI) Institute, a not-for-profit organisation (see chapter ten). Academia, particularly in research, has also blazed the trail and it is easy to see how ubiquitous computing has a role to play in the increasing number of collaborative research exercises from the human genome onwards. Indeed the very nature of grid computing demands collaboration, rather than competition.

In a "networked economy", the importance of social relationships, which are sometimes referred to as "social capital", becomes a key determinant of the success of e-governance. If ubiquitous computing can enhance those social relationships and build connections between communities – linking people to networks of jobs, ideas and opportunities – then it will be a truly powerful force for social good.

The skills race

Access to technology, even at a reasonable price, is only part of the battle. One of the main causes of the digital divide is skills, confidence and above all, a reason to want access. For a lot of people in the UK, these fundamentals are simply not in place.

On the skills side, a large amount of public money is being invested via UK Online and other initiatives in ICT skills. If information technology in all its forms does soon become so pervasive and easy to use, it may be that the notion of ICT skills as such will become redundant. We would then be able to con-centrate on adopting a far broader range of skills through the technology available. From basic skills such as literacy and numeracy, to content production of all sorts, including interactive, communicative and facilitation skills, all sorts of social skills will be available in cyberspace for those who want to log in.

If the "age of access" is to be Utopian, then we need to ensure that cyberspace is a democratic space. This means that myriad voices must have access to it and that it does not become dominated by a few, well-funded voices. The ICT sector has always resisted broadcasting-type regulation, arguing that as cyberspace is potentially infinite, there is less reason to worry about domination of that space in the way that there is with a traditional broadcasting medium. While this is true in theory, in reality, larger marketing budgets and "gatekeeper" control via search engines have led to what many see as a "commodification" of cyberspace, with the result that unpopular or marginal voices have been weakened. Only when access to cyberspace has become a sort of public right, will we perhaps be able to re-balance the debate.

conclusion

Ubiquitous computing can give us a platform on which to develop this notion of "e-citizenship", but it is only an opportunity – seizing it and making it happen means taking decisive action. It means weaving technology into our existing lives and communities – not being driven by it. It means helping people to develop new skill sets in which soft skills, including communications skills, will be accorded their rightful place. It means the development of new institutions that permit openness and dialogue and encourage informed debate. There are possibilities for increased scrutiny of both companies and government – but civic organisations and citizens must be enabled to take advantage of the opportunity first. This requires access to the same technology and the same skill sets as those they seek to scrutinise. It is an opportunity, above all, to start erasing the legacy of the "rich but divided" society we currently inhabit.

Kate Oakley is an associate director of the Local Futures Group and an associate of the independent think-tank Demos. She writes on the knowledge economy, entrepreneurship and e-governance. She can be contacted at kate.oakley@localfutures.com

Jean A. Lorrain, chief technology executive, e-business hosting services, IBM Global Services
Tony Cox, storage and assessment services business manager, IBM Global Services

Turning technology into a utility

How the evolution of core IT technology is making IBM e-business on demand a reality

Information technology is becoming increasingly critical to businesses as they automate and integrate their processes, interconnect them with their suppliers and give online access to their customers. Pervasive computing devices and wireless technologies will increase the ability to be able to access any application and data from anywhere and at any time. In effect, data and applications need to be unlocked from a physical machine (such as a PC) and become part of "the network" if this type of access is to be achieved (for example, accessing the corporate ERP system from a cell phone while at a customer location to check on the availability of an item). The pace of technical change and the scarcity of skilled resources to deal with an increasingly complex system will favour those who are beginning to buy IT based on the utility model. The development of three key technology areas make this possible: virtualisation of resources, network bandwidth and distributed architectures.

Virtualisation of resources
Over the past three decades, mainframes have hosted thousands of virtual servers, while providing extremely high levels of availability. Sophisticated

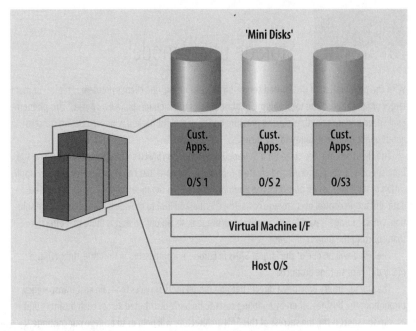

Figure one: Virtual server and storage resources (IBM eServer – zSeries)

workload management techniques allow virtual machines to be created on demand, guaranteeing each machine a certain amount of resources and allowing it to use free cycles beyond that level, if any are available (not all applications peak at the same time), thus saving much "white space" (unused cycles procured for peaks). An entire server farm of virtual Linux machines can thus fit into a single box, saving on electricity, network hardware and space. The most dramatic effect, however, is the saving on people costs.

Likewise, very large storage systems are now delivered with built-in availability functions normally not found in discrete server storage. These devices can be accessed through different networking technologies (Storage Area Networks, IP networks). Associated storage management software allows hundreds of servers to be dynamically allocated storage "volumes" on these systems, providing users with very fast provisioning of additional space, aggregated storage capacity planning (rather than doing it on a per server basis), and greatly reduced operational costs.

case study   Storage utility model

With the proliferation of distributed server-based computing, one client's problem is typical of many larger organisations:"The total volume of our data storage is quadrupling every year." This phenomenal speed of data growth is placing pressure on the overnight backup window, causing concern about application availability to the business.

The client has decided to adopt a Storage Area Networks (SANs) strategy. SANs remove storage from specific server platforms and create a central pool of data that can be accessed from any application or database server platform. The approach enables an organisation to remove duplicated data and attain control over storage costs. The client asked IBM to provide a managed storage solution, where storage is paid for on an allocated/usage basis, an option that is more cost effective than sourcing the project in-house.

The result will be one of the largest SANs in Europe, encompassing mainframe, Unix, NT and many different storage products.

The storage utility provides a direct charging model for IT services to attain cost transparency throughout the business, thereby enabling costs to be fairly distributed across each business unit.

"In the short term, the success of this SAN architecture will help us to achieve our contingency and recovery goals. Looking forward, we will have a storage management infrastructure that provides excellent control over our storage management, enabling the business to manage costs in line with their own specific needs," says the sponsor.

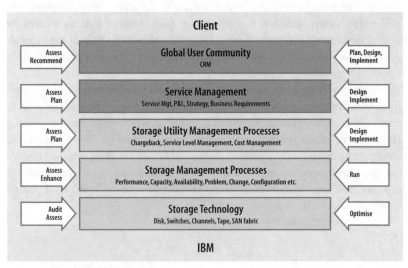

Figure two: Storage utility – service delivery process model

Network bandwidth

What makes it feasible to physically separate the servers from the storage is the very high bandwidth available cheaply on LANs. The cost of wide area network bandwidth has fallen dramatically for very high speed connections in some markets. In fact, we have technically (if not necessarily economically) now reached the point where even storage could be delivered over Wide Area and Metropolitan Area networks.

Beyond cheaper bandwidth in network backbones, a revolution is happening in network access facilities for end users. Cheap, high-speed, "always on" data packet services are available on telephone lines (ADSL), cable TV (cable modems) and soon will be available on mobile devices (cell phones, PDAs and wireless LANs). Secure "tunnels" can be established over the internet, so that intranets and extranets can be extended to homes, hotels, and people on the road.

As bandwidth becomes much cheaper, many corporations have undertaken drastic exercises in "server consolidation", as well as "data centre consolidation", because, in many cases, the computing resources no longer need to be local to the users. The benefits can be huge and far exceed the obvious savings in hardware, software and maintenance. The keys to consolidation are:

- *Standard hardware and, more importantly, standard software.* A centralised team supporting very few platforms is the largest saving. (see chapter five) Furthermore, standard processes (change and problem management, for example) can be created out of the "best practices" in the corporation.
- *A different way to organise, and pay for, IT services.* Consolidation requires that budget authority be removed from individual departments and business units, and handed out wholesale to a single organisation. Cost recovery is obtained by charging each unit based on its usage of IT: it could be charged at cost per seat (such as for mailboxes), per consumed MIPS (million of instructions per second) or storage, or cost per transaction.

If well managed, the centralisation will, in turn, provide the CIO with the scale needed to invest on redundancy, tools, skills and automation, which in the end will deliver a far higher level of service quality. As well as freeing-up skilled IT resources to focus on unique applications that give true competitive advantage.

Distributed architectures

Distributed architectures allow functions to be distributed to where they are more cost-effective. Exploiting the low cost of processing and storage, distributed architectures are routinely used to improve end user response time by placing data or even applications as close to the end user as possible – sometimes on the user's PC. Distributed architectures can significantly reduce the amount of bandwidth required in networks, improve availability and even allow processing in disconnected mode (as is typically the case with e-mail).

The industry trend is to literally "graft" processing and storage capabilities throughout the network, into "network appliances", ie. fixed function computers that do not need to be individually managed and can serve many users and applications. The next frontier in distributed architectures is grid computing (see chapter ten). A good example of distribution through grid middleware is a new US nationwide system, built by the University of Pennsylvania and IBM, to store, access and analyse mammograms and locating the images where hospitals and doctors can best access them.

What is a "utility"?

The definition of a utility is that it delivers a totally standardised service to a massive number of users, through a pervasive network and using a relatively small number of very large plants. Utilities are pre-built ahead of actual user demand and are available all the time (there are no maintenance windows and it is not necessary to shut off a whole neighbourhood to add a new user). Users typically pay for the service based on a subscription fee that reflects their expected peak demand, plus a variable charge reflecting their usage.

When IBM introduced Lotus Notes (see chapter five), it moved the IT func-

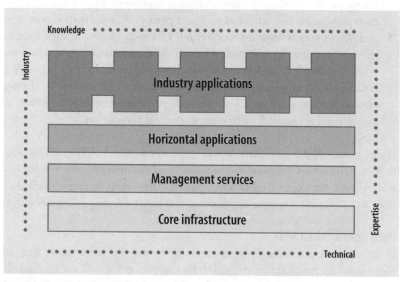

Figure three: The IBM e-business on demand framework

tionality into "the network", making it accessible from anywhere at any time. It replaced hundreds of small departmental IT power generating units with a few very large networked IT power plants. The larger the user base, the more cost-effective the model. Subsequently, as more businesses see IT needs satisfied through shared IT services, the parallel with utilities such as electricity and water becomes increasingly apparent.

E-sourcing

The industry is buzzing with numerous names to convey variations of this utility concept: e-sourcing, e-utilities and computing on demand are among the more popular. IBM has recently introduced this e-sourcing vision:

> *IBM e-business on demand is the delivery of standardised processes, applications, and infrastructure over the network, as a service (with both business and IT functionality).*

IBM e-business on demand is a new model, where IT services are bought on a business value (or usage) basis, rather than being custom built from hardware and software components and price-based on the cost of these elements, regardless of how much they get utilised. Many different hardware and software technologies and delivery processes will be used to support that model. IBM e-business on demand will be delivered as:

- *IBM infrastructure on demand:* virtual servers and virtual storage, content and application distribution services, and management services. These services offer a new way for businesses to quickly acquire infrastructure capacity, without large upfront investment costs.
- *IBM business process on demand:* companies will be able to procure entire business processes on a usage basis. These can be "horizontal" applications, such as e-mail, payroll or customer relationship management, or industry "vertical" processes such as reservation systems or logistics for the transportation industry, or risk management in financial services.
- *Business transformation, consulting and system integration:* these are based on industry sector expertise and are intended to help corporations re-engineer and procure business processes.

The most promising area concerns the wholesale shifting of business processes to the utility model, as it best matches the current concerns of businesses. A recent customer survey indicates that the IT "pain points" for businesses go far beyond mere cost reduction and often have to do with gaining competitive advantage through speed and quality. Of the customers polled, 81 per cent want to acquire new capabilities quicker; 76 per cent want improved service performance; 73 per cent want reduced upfront investment; and 73 per cent want to gain expertise not available internally.

conclusion

While e-sourcing is made possible by new technologies, and will require continued technology advances (such as grid computing and web services), it is not a new technology. Like many industries before it, information technology is about to embark on a massive industrialisation period, with mass production of standard services and processes replacing custom built, one of a kind solutions, for all but the most specialised needs.

There are some IT utilities already available (for example, e-mail, EDI and payroll). But, unlike existing utilities, IT services cannot easily be reduced to one standard commodity (for example, electricity). There will be different IT functions and business processes that will need to be assembled for specific customers, all delivered on massively scalable and shared processing and storage infrastructures. As fully distributed architectures take hold, managing the vast array of computing resources and providing non-stop service will require new concepts in self-managing (autonomic) systems (see chapter twelve). Yet, as long and tortuous as the e-sourcing journey might be, the train has already left the station.

URLs
www.ibm.com/e-business/uk/ondemand
www.ibm.com/services/uk

Jean Lorrain is chief technology executive, e-business hosting services, IBM Global Services.
Tony Cox is storage and assessment services business manager, IBM Global Services.

Dusan Rnic
Chief technology officer, Netengines

9

Untangling web services

Web services is a revolutionary advance that is set
to change the way business is conducted over the web

Web services is, in many ways, the group of technologies that comes closest to mimicking the intuitive, free-flowing nature of information processes in people's heads. Web services often refer to a long, still unfinished, list of standard protocols but it is more than that. In effect, web services is a new IT model, where computers talk to other computers to automate tasks that, up until now, have required manual intervention.

Speaking the same language
The explosive success of the web was made possible by standards. Basically, this means we can view information on a variety of devices without having to care about the software or hardware details of the server from which the web pages originated.

Let's look at a business example of using the web. If you want to buy a washing machine, you can use a search engine to find the many sites where they are sold. By viewing the web pages, you can decide on where to get the washing machine you need at the best price. However, wouldn't it be easier to have the computer do that for you?

Now let's suppose that those companies selling washing machines provided another kind of interface into their systems. This interface would not be for people, but would rather be for other software to ask questions about the types of washing machines that were available, their prices, their availability, and so forth. There would be no HTML to interpret because the conversations between the software making the inquiries and the software providing the information about the washing machine would be very precise and the data described in a standard format. The software providing the information about the washing machine is a "web service" and a new set of standards for computers to talk to computers is being finalised.

"Web services describe a new IT model – computers talk to other computers to automate tasks"

In April 2000, IBM, Microsoft and others introduced "simple object access protocol", (SOAP) 1.1, the first XML-based building block for web services.

What business advantages can web services provide?

The sky's the limit. Through web services, companies and their computers can "offer", "sell" or just give other computers access to data, content, computational tasks or business processes. Web services perform encapsulated business functions, from simple request-reply to full business process interactions.

One place where web services is proving to be useful is within corporations in order to interconnect heterogeneous systems that were never designed to communicate with each other.

- SOAP is an electronic envelope for wrapping up messages to be sent from one computer to another, often across the internet. SOAP is now being standardised in the World Wide Web consortium (W3C).
- WSDL (Web Services Description Language) allows you to define precisely what messages you understand and how you will respond to those messages. WSDL is the key web services standard because it describes exactly how you talk to a web services application. WSDL was jointly created by IBM and Microsoft based on previous work that each had done and was submitted for standardisation to the W3C in January, 2001.
- XML (EXtended Markup Language) allows information to be structured into self defined "fields" (tags) like product name, product price, telephone number, and so on.
- UDDI (Universal Description, Discovery, and Integration) is an industry standards effort started by IBM, Microsoft and Ariba to create registry standards for services on a network. There are public registries available on the internet from IBM, SAP and others, and many companies are starting to deploy private UDDI registries inside their enterprises.

This is an example of enterprise application integration (EAI) where a company can progressively implement "straight through" processing by linking the customer relationship management system, and the customer information data bases, with the product catalogue and price lists, and the Enterprise Resource Processes (ERP). Thanks to their self-defining nature, and their potential to automatically and dynamically find each other, web services bring flexibility to system interconnections.

B2B integration

Web services are also starting to find application in the area of business-to-business (B2B) integration.

One B2B use of web services is the linking of ERP and procurement systems of a company with the ordering systems of its suppliers, including the capability to electronically monitor the status of the order. Our washing machine example above might be expanded into this. The purchase may be part of a larger set of transactions or workflow, where we are also using web services to check catalogues and inventory, and arrange financing, and shipping.

There are many other examples where web services might be used for B2B:

- stock quotes/stock charting
- credit card verification/payment processing
- integrated travel planning
- bid process/auctions

Personal advantage

While businesses are the short-term beneficiaries from this new integration technology, the average internet user is also likely to benefit enormously. Microsoft launched the concept of the .NET initiative, and in particular .NET My Services. It was originally described as a "digital safe-deposit box", where end users could have their personal data safely kept, and from where that data could be automatically extracted for these questionnaires end users have to keep filling in. There is no need to ever again enter your telephone number or e-mail address or to remember and manage passwords. In other words, with the help of a large array of web services on the internet, allowing computers to communicate easily with one another, web services could permit our personal computers to automate a number of things for us. For example, we could ask it to find the cheapest airline fare, or the best digital camera.

case study Staffing solutions

One industry where e-sourcing and web-services could save billions of pounds is the highly frag-mented world of staffing and services procurement.

Recruitment is, in essence, just another form of procurement. But unlike the procurement of paper clips, stationery, computer hardware or software, people are not mere commodities to be acquired, used up and disposed of. So, is there something unique about people and the recruitment process itself, that means the usual procurement processes no longer apply?

I believe that whatever the nature of what is being procured the "process behind the process", as it were, lends itself to automation. The demand within a company is identical, whether it is for peo-ple or paper clips, but there are differences with the nature of what is being supplied.

As far as recruitment is concerned, staff are rarely sourced from a single supplier, but the tradi-tional automated procurement process for commodities, for example, assumes the existence of one approved supplier. Staff recruitment is a complex, multi-tiered process, which is where the unique, integrating benefits of web services come into play. People supply is tiered because people come from many sources. They can't be "catalogued" in the same way as a pen.

Within recruitment, our solutions use web services to do the "plumbing" to integrate the flow of information around all the expensive legacy systems that most large organisations have invested in over the last ten years.

A construction company could, for example, map out its recruitment needs as an integral part of a project at the outset, and feed that information into their planning and management systems. Because the technology is open (platform independent) and scalable, it can link in with dozens of suppliers' legacy systems directly.

Obviously, companies will still source staff themselves, whether it is via agencies, headhunters or newspaper advertising. But with "contingent workers" (temps and contractors) taking up 80 to 90 per cent of the cost of recruiting staff, millions of pounds could be saved annually in timesheet pro-cessing alone if all the logistics and administration were to be handled automatically between the agencies' and buyers' systems.

The problem with multi-tiered organisations is that there are so many opportunities for human error. In the recruitment and employment sector, for example, every time a timesheet is re-entered into the system, there's a potential for error. But once this sort of process is automated throughout – in other words, once a basic requisition has become electronic – it can be moved and amended *ad infinitum*.

Before, where there was the lurking potential for error at every point of the recruitment process, now there is the recurring potential for greater efficiency and quantifiable cost savings across the business. One example is that companies could move towards early payment discounts from their many recruitment suppliers, saving hundreds of thousands of pounds in a financial year.

Business technology analyst Robin Bloor says that web services technology has benefits that "stretch from cutting costs dramatically to removing lags and inefficiencies in the whole [recruitment] process. For some organisations, the benefits will also embrace the issues of compliance and the correct use of competencies."

Yet you cannot take people out of the process. There is always a human element. A temp receptionist might have 150 jobs in a year, but a Java programmer only two. But if I can track their performance when they work for me, then I can also monitor their agency's performance. Web services can allow organisations to track what actually happens in the real world more efficiently, and at every stage of the process. It allows you to build a database of existing staff or potential staff against their performance. Then you can make it pay.

conclusion

Web services isn't just another buzzword – it genuinely constitutes a revolutionary advance that will fundamentally change the way companies conduct business over the web. Web services technology is an evolution of what we have learned about building distributing systems inside enterprises and also about the power of the web to connect people and business. As basic web services systems are now in place and, as in recruitment, are shown to be working incredibly well, it won't be too much longer before the standards are available to carry out more complex connections. Web services may be new, but they will have a significant impact on how we build and deploy applications on the internet and in intranets.

Prior to joining Netengines in May 2000, Dusan Rnic worked as a senior technical architect for Netscape Communications Ltd. Widely known and respected in European internet and e-commerce circles, he became the public face of Netscape in the UK. From his origins as a developer of Artificial Intelligence (AI) systems he progressed to managing the implementation and delivery of AI systems to large enterprises. Dusan has 15 years' industry experience, spanning most of the major IT disciplines.

Ian Baird
Chief business architect, Platform Computing

The international grid

Grid computing promises new opportunities for
sharing information and resources on a global basis

With today's tough economic climate there is constant pressure on organisations to reduce their research and development costs, speed up their time-to-market, increase throughput and improve the quality of their products. Typically, removing resource constraints by increasing an organisation's processing power would address these challenges. However, vast amounts of computing capacity within a typical existing IT infrastructure remain untapped, and dramatic reductions in IT budgets close the door to any unjustified technology spending.

Introducing distributed computing

Distributed computing addresses workload challenges by aggregating and allocating computing resources from across a business to provide unlimited processing power. In the last ten years, it has grown from a concept that would enabled organisations to simply balance workloads across diverse computer resources, to a ubiquitous solution that has been embraced by some of the world's leading organisations across multiple industry sectors.

Distributed computing ensures that all computing services are reliable and deliver "always-on" availability despite scheduled maintenance, power outages, and unexpected failures. It also helps eliminate the problem of users wasting precious time trying to locate available computer resources to process workloads, while many other systems within an organisation remain idle.

And while distributed computing harnesses the full potential of existing computer resources by effectively matching the supply of processing cycles with the demand created by applications, even more importantly it has paved the way for grid computing – a more powerful, yet global approach to resource sharing.

What is grid computing?

An evolution of distributed computing, grid computing represents enormous opportunities for organisations to use processing cycles from networks of computers spanning multiple geographical boundaries.

To understand grid computing, think of the peer-to-peer (P2P) computing model made popular by Napster's file-sharing community. In much the same way that Napster enabled users to access and share music between desktop computers, distributed computing uses a similar model to pool the resources available in separate clusters of desktop computers, servers or supercomputers. Grid computing elevates these clusters to the next level by connecting multiple clusters over geographically dispersed areas for enhanced collaboration and resource sharing.

Benefits of grid computing

- Grid computing enables organisations to aggregate resources within an entire IT infrastructure no matter where in the world they are located. It eliminates situations where one site is running on maximum capacity, while others have cycles to spare.
- Organisations can dramatically improve the quality and speed of the products and services they deliver, while reducing IT costs by enabling transparent collaboration and resource sharing.
- Grid computing enables companies to access and share remote databases. This is especially beneficial to the life sciences and research communities, where enormous volumes of data are generated and analysed during any given day.
- Grid computing enables widely dispersed organisations to easily collaborate on projects by creating the ability to share everything from software applications and data, to engineering blueprints.
- A grid can harness the idle processing cycles that are available in desktop PCs located in various locations across multiple time zones. For example, PCs that would typically remain idle overnight at a company's Tokyo manufacturing plant could be utilised during the day by its North American operations.

A new era in distributed computing

Defined as the coordinated, transparent and secure sharing of IT resources across geographically distributed sites, grid computing is built on industry standard protocols and open source reference platforms for maximum interoperability.

Essentially, grid computing provides the ability to lower the total cost of computing by providing, on demand, reliable and inexpensive access to available computer resources.

Initially embraced by academia, grid computing is very quickly emerging as a means for corporate enterprises to collaborate, share data and software, store more information than on existing networks, and access vast amounts of processing power without spending significant sums of money on expensive supercomputers.

One of the earliest examples of grid computing is SETI@home, established by the Search for Extraterrestrial Intelligence (SETI) Institute. In the quest to find signatures that might indicate the existence of extraterrestrial intelligence, SETI@home utilised the internet to establish a virtual "supercomputer". By bringing together the processing power of more than 500,000 personal computers from around the world, SETI@home ensured it had sufficient processing power to analyse terabytes of data collected from a radio telescope – all without the added expense of a "supercomputer".

> "Grid computing is emerging as a means for corporate enterprises to collaborate without spending significant sums of money"

Beyond the world of academia, corporate enterprises, such as ENEA (see page 59) and Texas Instruments, are already recognising the true potential of grid computing and are adopting it at a phenomenal rate. Today, any organisation that engages in research or delivers value through processing computer-intensive workloads can benefit from grid computing.

While initial grid implementations – which focus on providing an organisation with seamless access to globally available computer resources that exist behind a single firewall – may seem almost simplistic, the potential is enormous.

Grid computing, while still in its infancy, is rapidly emerging into another dimension with the development of public or utility grids that will sell or lease computing resources, including bandwidth, applications and storage, over the internet, charging on a per use or customised service basis, in much the same way as hydro companies charge for electricity.

ENEA

The Italian National Agency for New Technology, Energy and the Environment (ENEA) is a public organisation that conducts research and development on behalf of the scientific community, electrical power industry and environmental groups across Italy. For the past three years, ENEA has used grid computing to connect and harness the processing power of heterogeneous computer resources across 12 geographically dispersed ENEA Research Centres.

DoD

The US Department of Defence (DoD) High Performance Computing Modernisation Program (HPCMP) deployed a production grid that connects five DoD shared resource centres across the United States.

The DoD's production grid will ultimately provide 1.1 million "supercomputer" processor hours per year by enabling the effective utilisation of geographically distributed processing cycles that would otherwise go unused.

Propelling the concept of grid computing

As grid computing necessitates increased collaboration between all stakeholders, standardisation efforts such as the following are of increasing importance:

- *The Globus Project* (www.globus.org) is a multi-institutional research and development effort creating fundamental technologies for computational grids. A primary product of the Globus Project is the Globus Toolkit, an open architecture, open source set of protocols, services and tools that enable secure, distributed, multi-vendor grid computing.
- *Global Grid Forum* (www.globalgridforum.com) is a community-initiated forum of individual researchers and practitioners focused on the promotion and development of grid technologies and applications via the development and documentation of "best practices", implementation guidelines and standards, with an emphasis on rough consensus and running code.
- *The New Productivity Initiative (NPi)* (www.newproductivity.org) is a global industry consortium of leading software and hardware companies, including Platform Computing, Compaq, HP, Cadence and Aurema. Established in 2000 by Platform, a company that has been implementing production grids since 1996, NPi is dedicated to defining and developing industry standard APIs for distributed and grid computing.

The grid potential

The earliest and simplest form of grid computing began with the concept of distributed computing. But today, grid computing is viewed as the next generation IT infrastructure, and is expected to transform computation, communication and collaboration. A multitude of grids will exist, each within its own context, shared by communities within the same industry or with the same interests. Grids will be service-driven, with organisations accessing computing resources over the internet on an as-needed, or utility, basis.

Companies such as Platform Computing estimate that widespread adoption of grid computing will take a three-phased approach, spanning between five and ten years.

The first phase, Enterprise Grids, will see the commercial implementation of production grids within major corporations that have a global presence or a need to access resources outside a single corporate location. These corporations will benefit from virtual collaboration and the sharing of available resources that are located behind a corporate firewall.

The second phase, Partner Grids, will emerge as organisations operating within similar industries and areas of interest collaborate on projects, and use each other's resources as a means to reach a common goal. For example, life sciences organisations working together could accelerate their research time by harnessing the computer potential of available systems or by sharing large amounts of data within partner organisations.

The third phase, Service Grids, will occur as users adopt the grid as a utility model. Much in the same way as consumers are now more confident in their use of the internet, widespread recognition of the benefits of grid computing will take it to the next level of adoption. This final phase, where computer resources are leased on a per use or as-needed basis, will only occur once the grid computing model is proven to be reliable, secure and based on widely accepted standards and protocols.

conclusion

For grid computing to emerge as a successful resource-sharing model, strong partnerships need to be established between the software companies that design grid technologies, the hardware vendors that manufacture the systems that grids will run on, and the application developers that will utilise the capabilities of the grid. Additionally, open standards and specifications need to be established to ensure interoperability between the heterogeneous open source and proprietary solutions that will provide businesses with a broad range of options to choose from.

Fortunately, there are many companies who are already committed to the development of grid computing and are working hard to lay the foundations for its widespread commercial use. For example, IBM has its sights set on building the first public utility grid, and together with The Globus Project, is developing a new set of specifications that will align web services with grid computing and allow businesses to share both applications and computing resources over the internet. Another example is Platform Computing, which launched Grid Suite, a comprehensive commercial grid computing solution that integrates its proprietary distributed computing software with open source components from the Globus Toolkit and external data management components. Additionally, hardware manufacturers are planning to make grid solutions, such as Platform's Grid Suite, available on high performance servers to deliver a completely "grid-enabled" solution.

Experts agree – grid computing has the potential to revolutionise the world of information technology, much in the same way as the internet completely transformed the way people and businesses communicate and share information. It is these and other initiatives that will accelerate the adoption of grid computing beyond scientific and technical applications to everyday business use.

URLs

The Globus Project www.globus.org
Global Grid Forum www.globalgridforum.com
New Productivity Initiative (NPi) www.newproductivity.org
SETI www.setiathome.ssl.berkeley.edu
Platform www.platform.com

11

Vicki Jackson
Freelance business and technology journalist

E-sourcing: in practice

American Express and cahoot use IT as a utility
to meet their business needs

I n an increasingly volatile economic environment since September 11th businesses are looking for ways to move forward competitively without taking unnecessary risks. Cost is always at the sharp end of any business decision but now such decisions have taken on a more urgent edge. Investing heavily in technology at a time like this might be considered risky but this has to be weighed against the need to keep a business competitive. Companies might consider outsourcing some or all of their technology, such as online bank cahoot has done. This gives them the security of knowing exactly what their financial outlay will be from one month to the next. Or, adopting e-sourcing might suit a business better, an option recently taken up by financial services giant American Express. This utility-based service provides the required technology and services on demand, which are paid for on a per usage basis. This chapter will look at how both models can be of huge benefit to a company, depending on its current business and technology strategies.

Outsourcing versus utility

So what is the difference between traditional outsourcing and the utility model? With the outsourcing model the customer orders a dedicated, tailor-made technology system and services, which is then installed as a one-off deal. The "lump" charge for the entire outsourced system will then be repaid at a set amount each month over the life of the contract. However, the customer does have the option to add further services or technology at a future date at pre-defined contractual rates.

The utility model is a much more variable arrangement. From the beginning, the customer and supplier establish a "menu" of services that are available on demand with pre-defined unit costs. Customers are then able to ask for what-ever they want, when they want it, and pay only for what they use. The onus is on the supplier to provide that service within the customer's given timeframe. The technology and services in a utility-based model can be shared within the company across different departments and service areas, depending on where the demand is at the time. This system allows the customer to plan ahead – they will know that they will always have access to the appropriate systems or soft-ware when the need arises.

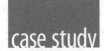 In cahoot with technology

A new entrant to the finance arena is cahoot, an online bank that is a division of Abbey National. cahoot was established in 2000 and already has a customer base of nearly 350,000. When it was set up it was decided to buy in expertise as and when it was needed and outsource key parts of the operation, while maintaining the core systems and infrastructure in-house.

"At the time we considered what was the best option for buying in technology," says Tim Sawyer, director of business development and marketing at cahoot. "We considered using a utility model but it wasn't quite right for us at that time and we opted to outsource. This meant high costs for us at the outset but the benefit for us now is that we know exactly how much we are spending each month – there are no hidden bills or extras that we might have to budget for. Moving towards e-business on demand is something that we are definitely looking at for the future," he says.

By outsourcing so much of its technology cahoot was up and running in just nine months. Alongside speed to market, Sawyer considers its transparency as one of the biggest benefits. "As a customer you know exactly what you're getting and the price doesn't shift. Also, if things go wrong you have a huge knowledge base to rely on for help."

Yet, although Sawyer believes that establishing cahoot so successfully wouldn't have been as easy without outsourcing, he has a word of warning. "Outsourcing can become problematic when co-ordinat-ing the services of different providers," he says. "Our IT staff have found that you have to choose your providers carefully. cahoot's working relationship with IBM has been extremely successful. We have been able to make our products more accessible to customers, easier to use and allow our customers to take control of their financial affairs because of the versatility and reliability of the service provision.

"It can be harder sometimes to use outsourced technology – there should be no illusions about that," he adds. "But in my opinion it's definitely worthwhile. Put in some research right at the beginning to ensure you sign up with the right partners – you need someone who is on the ball and who will make the right decisions with you, consulting you all the way.

"Outsourcing technology has benefited cahoot and its customers by allowing it to react more quickly to bringing in new technologies; it has allowed us to develop a much more efficient system and, therefore, to lower our costs, passing on cost savings to customers in the form of lower interest rates. Be aware, however, that it might not all be completely problem-free. But the potential is there, with the right partners, to put in place an extremely effective technology solution."

Utilising utilities

American Express has signed a deal with IBM Global Services in which vast amounts of its technology services will be acquired through e-business on demand. American Express will remain in control of core technology competencies including information technology strategy, strategic technology relationships, networks, the development and maintenance of applications and databases, and the management of technology portfolios. But a key portion of its IT will be bought in on an on-demand basis. For example, PCs, mainframes, web hosting, IT help desks, mid-range technology, data centres, servers and technical support will all be provided within the utility model and paid for only as it is used. American Express is placing itself at the forefront of a new computer services paradigm, which gives it the flexibility to draw on all the computing resources, skills and technologies required to support future growth.

How it works

American Express is a world leader in charge and credit cards, traveller's cheques, travel, financial planning, business services, insurance and international banking and, therefore, has diverse global technological demands. Adopting a utility-based IT provision model means that it will save money immediately and will have the ability to implement new and improved IT technology on a global basis in the future without huge cost layouts.

IBM e-business on demand will allow American Express access to huge potential increases in capacity but they need only use that capacity as and when its business needs dictate. Therefore, monthly payments will vary according to the demands the company has made during a certain period, but as it is only ever paying for what it needs and uses, it automatically saves money.

"The deal allows American Express to buy into any of IBM's resources and skills," says Nigel White, strategic partnership executive, IBM. "For example, if there is a project which needs extra consolidation of equipment or requires buying a number of new PCs, that is then dealt with and put in place by us. If a new application is needed, the equipment and infrastructure necessary can be put in place and running within a very short time."

The utility model gives them the flexibility to make their IT capabilities match what the business wants by flexing up or down.

Cost benefits

In both the short and long term, using a utility-based technology model can save huge amounts of money. In the long term, economies of scale mean that a provider such as IBM, who has huge resources at its disposal, can offer the technology at lower costs than would be generated by putting together the necessary systems, infrastructure and software in-house.

There is also an immediate cost benefit in that 2,000 American Express staff worldwide will transfer to comparable positions at IBM, therefore, American Express immediately avoids the massive spend on salaries and benefits. Transferring staff in this way is the usual procedure in such a project, according to White.

"IBM would need these staff to continue to provide the necessary services for American Express," he says. "We don't have 2,000 people sitting around ready to take over those services!" White says the response from American Express' staff has been incredible. "I think they realise that they are getting the best of both worlds. It's good for their careers to be working for such a mainstream and reputable IT services company, but they can fulfil their loyalty to American Express because they are still providing services for them. It's important from a HR perspective to create that kind of atmosphere, but also such enthusiasm and a boost to morale are hugely beneficial to both parties with positive knock-on effects to productivity and efficiency."

conclusion

From the customer's perspective e-sourcing could well be a win-win situation. It isn't just about implementing technology – it is about allowing a business to match its IT capabilities to its business strategy. The utility model allows management to meet those needs quickly, maintain competitive advantage and all on a pay-as-you-go basis. It also allows businesses to get a lead on the competition by implementing the latest technologies almost immediately. Utility-based computing takes the risk and cost out of developing IT infrastructure but the business maintains overall control of the strategic direction of IT operations – it can have its cake and eat it too!

12

Dr Paul Horn,
Senior vice president and director of research, IBM Corporation

Autonomic computing

An effective and competently designed computing system should be capable of running itself as well as adjusting to varying circumstances

Sometimes it seems strange that the IT industry continues to create increasingly powerful computing systems. But making individuals and businesses more productive by automating key tasks and processes is done with good reason – by relegating life's mundane requirements to being "automatically handled" we can free our minds and resources to concentrate on previously unattainable tasks.

To use a simple analogy, few of us worry about harvesting the grain to grind the flour to bake the bread – we buy it at a nearby store – or about how we'll connect with a friend halfway across the globe – we simply pick up the phone. But evolution via automation also produces complexity as an unavoidable by-product. Computing systems have proved this to be true. Follow the evolution of computers from single machines to modular systems to personal computers networked with larger machines and an unmistakable pattern emerges: incredible progress in almost every aspect of computing – microprocessor power up by a factor of ten thousand, storage capacity by a factor of 45,000 and communication speeds by a factor of one million.

But there is a price.

Along with the growth has come increasingly sophisticated architecture governed by software whose complexity now routinely demands tens of millions of lines of code. Some operating environments weigh in at over 30 million lines of code created by over four thousand programmers! As computing evolves, the overlapping connections, dependencies and interacting applications call for administrative decision-making and responses faster than any human can deliver.

The internet adds yet another layer of complexity by allowing us to connect – some might say entangle – this world of computers and computing systems with telecommunications networks. In the process, the systems have become increasingly difficult to manage and, ultimately, to use – just ask anyone who's tried to merge two IT systems built on different platforms or consumers who have tried to install or troubleshoot aDSL service on their own. Up until now, we've relied mainly on human intervention and administration to manage this complexity. Unfortunately, we're starting to gunk up the works.

How autonomic computing can help

The way system infrastructure should be managed can be likened to the workings of the human body. Think for a moment about the autonomic nervous system; it tells your heart how fast to beat, checks your blood's sugar and oxygen levels and controls your pupils so that the right amount of light reaches your eyes. But, most significantly, it does all this without any conscious recognition or effort on your part. That's precisely how we need to build computing systems – an approach known as autonomic computing. It's time to design and build computing systems capable of running themselves, adjusting to varying circumstances and preparing their resources to handle most efficiently the workloads we put upon them.

As a proliferating host of access devices becomes part of the corporate computing infrastructure, enterprises must transform both their IT systems and the business processes to connect with employees, customers and suppliers. Companies must also manage the very products they produce, such as network-enabled cars, washing machines and entertainment systems, as part of this integrated "system", extending the system concept well beyond traditional corporate boundaries. This demands a reliable infrastructure that can accommodate rapid growth and hide system complexity from its users.

Imagine, for example, a large retail chain with hundreds of outlets, a network of warehouses, delivery fleets, employee services, customer service call centres, web interfaces and more. An autonomic computing system manages all these distinct (and quasi-independent) IT systems as one and provides integrated, time sensitive functionality, as well as "always available" access through web interfaces.

How it works

To extend the body analogy, our bodies have a hierarchy of self-governance, from single cells to organs and organ systems. Each level maintains a measure of independence while contributing to a higher level of organisation, culminating in the organism – us. We remain thankfully unaware, for the most part, of the daily management of it all, because these systems take care of themselves and only "escalate" to a higher level function when they need help. So, too, with an autonomic computing system. In the end, its individual layers and components must contribute to a system that itself functions well without our regular interference to provide a simplified user experience.

Such a high-level system could be described as possessing at least eight key elements of characteristics:

- *Identity:* To be autonomic, a computing system needs to "know itself" and comprise components that also possess a system identity. It will need to know the extent of its "owned" resources, those it can borrow or lend, and those that can be shared or should be isolated.
- *Configuration:* An autonomic computing system must configure and reconfigure itself under varying and unpredictable conditions. This must occur automatically, as must dynamic adjustments to that configuration to best handle changing environments.
- *Self-optimisation:* An autonomic computing system never settles for the status quo – it is always looking for ways to optimise its workings. It will monitor its constituent parts and fine-tune workflow to achieve predetermined system goals, much as a conductor listens to an orchestra and adjusts its dynamic and expressive characteristics to achieve a particular musical interpretation. This consistent effort to optimise itself is the only way a computing system will be able to meet the complex and often conflicting IT demands of a business, its customers, suppliers and employees. And since the priorities that drive those demands change constantly, only constant self-optimisation will satisfy them.
- *Healing:* An autonomic computing system must be able to recover from routine and extraordinary events that might cause some of its parts to malfunction, such as the September 11th attacks. It must be able to discover problems or potential problems, then find an alternate way of using resources or reconfiguring the system to keep it functioning smoothly. Of course, certain types of "healing" have been part of computing for some

TURNS OUT YOU ARE A TECHNOLOGY EXPERT.

 INTRODUCING E-BUSINESS ON DEMAND
THE NEXT UTILITY

You understand hot/cold, you know how to turn a knob and flip a switch. Congratulations, you are now an e-business expert. Because e-business just became as reliable, flexible and manageable as a utility. With e-business on demand, everything from installation and security to delivery and upkeep are managed for you. You don't make huge upfront investments. You just get a predictable monthly bill. It's The Next Utility. Turn it on. Watch it flow. Visit **ibm.com**/e-business/uk/ondemand or ask for 'on demand' at **0870 010 2503**.

time, such as error checking and correction, but the growing complexity of today's IT environment makes it more and more difficult to locate the actual cause of a breakdown, even in relatively simple environments.

But as we use more intelligence in computing systems, they will begin to discover new rules on their own that help them use system redundancy or additional resources to recover and achieve the goals specified by the user.

■ *Self-protection:* Autonomic computing must be able to detect, identify and protect itself against various types of attacks to maintain overall system security and integrity. Before the internet, computers operated as islands. It was fairly easy then to protect computer systems from attacks that became known as "viruses". As the floppy disks used to share programs and files needed to be physically mailed or brought to other users, it took weeks or months for a virus to spread. The connectivity of the networked world changed all that. Attacks can now come from anywhere. And viruses spread quickly – in seconds – and widely, since they're designed to be sent automatically to other users. The potential damage to a company's data, image and bottom line is enormous. More than simply responding to component failure, or running periodic checks for symptoms, an autonomic system will need to remain on alert, anticipate threats, and take necessary action. Such responses need to address two types of attacks: viruses and system intrusions by hackers.

"The way the system infrastructure should be managed can be likened to the workings of the human body"

■ *Context-sensitivity:* An autonomic computing system knows its environment and the context surrounding its activity, and acts accordingly. This context-sensitivity includes improving service based on knowledge about the context of a transaction. Autonomic computing will also provide useful information instead of confusing data. For instance, delivering all the data necessary to display a sophisticated web page would be obvious overkill if the user was connected to the network via a small-screen cell phone and wanted only the address of the nearest bank. Or a business system might report changes in the cost of goods immediately to a salesperson in the middle of writing a customer proposal, where normally weekly updates would have sufficed.

■ *Open connectivity:* In nature, all sorts of organisms must coexist and depend upon one another for survival. In today's rapidly evolving computing environment, an analogous coexistence and interdependence is unavoidable. Businesses connect to suppliers, customers and partners. People connect to their banks, travel agents and favourite stores regardless of the hardware they have, or the applications they are using. As technology improves, we can only expect new inventions and new devices – and an attendant proliferation of options and interdependency.

Current collaborations in computer science to create additional open standards have allowed new types of sharing: innovations such as Linux, an open operating system; Apache, an open web server; UDDI, a standard way for businesses to define themselves and connect to others; and from the Globus Project, a set of protocols to allow computer resources to be shared in a distributed manner, known as Grid computing. These community efforts have accelerated the move toward open standards, which allow for the development of tools, libraries, device drivers, middleware, and applications for these platforms.

■ *Anticipation:* When faced with a potentially dangerous or urgent situation, our autonomic nervous system anticipates the potential danger before we become aware of it. It then "optimises" our bodies for a selection of appropriate responses. The net result: our body is superbly prepped for action, but our conscious mind remains unaware of anything but the key pieces of information required to decide whether to stay and act (the "flight" response) or run for the hills. An autonomic computing system will allow for that kind of anticipation and support. It will deliver essential information with a system optimised and ready to implement the decision users make and not needlessly entangle them in coaxing results from the system.

conclusion

Realistically, such systems will be very difficult to build and will require significant exploration of new technologies and innovations. Progress needs to be made along two tracks: making individual system components autonomic and achieving autonomic behaviour at the level of global enterprise IT systems.

We know there are also many interim challenges: how to create the proper "adaptive algorithms" – sets of rules that can take previous system experiences and use that information to improve the rules. Or how to balance what these algorithms "remember" with what they ignore. We humans tend to be very good at the latter – we call it "forgetting" – and at times it can be a good thing: we can retain only significant information and not be distracted by extraneous data. Still another problem to solve: how to design an architecture for autonomic computing systems that provides consistent interfaces and points of control while allowing for a heterogeneous environment. We could go on, as the list of problems is actually quite long, but it is not so daunting as to render autonomic computing another dream of science fiction.

Indeed, progress is already being made in key areas. First, many established fields of scientific study will contribute to autonomic computing. What we've learned in artificial intelligence, control theory, complex adaptive systems and catastrophe theory, as well as some of the early work done in cybernetics, will give us a variety of approaches to explore. Current research projects at laboratories and universities include self-evolving systems that can monitor themselves and adjust to some changes, "cellular" chips capable of recovering from failures to keep long-term applications running, heterogeneous workload management that can balance and adjust workloads of many applications over various servers, and traditional control theory applied to the realm of computer science, to name just a few.

IBM's Project eLiza™ uses technology to manage technology

- Project eLiza™ is IBM's internal autonomic computing initiative, to make all of its products and services self-configuring, self-healing, self-protecting and self-optimising.
- The project involves building servers, software and storage which can completely manage themselves in a heterogeneous e-business infrastructure, without human intervention.
- Servers will be able to define themselves "on-the-fly". This aspect of self-managing means that new features, software and servers can be added to the enterprise infrastructure with no disruption of services.
- Recovery from a failing component will be possible – firstly by detecting and isolating the failed component, taking it off-line, fixing or isolating the failed component, and then re-introducing the fixed or replacement component into service without disruption.
- It will define and manage the access from users to all the resources within the enterprise, protect against unauthorised resource access, detect intrusions and report these activities as they occur, as well as providing backup/recovery capabilities which are as secure as the original resource management systems.

URL
www.ibm.com/research

Dr Paul M. Horn is senior vice president of the IBM Corporation and director of research. He is responsible for IBM's worldwide research programme and helps guide IBM's overall technical strategy. His main priority as head of the research division is to stimulate innovation in key areas of e-business. Dr Horn has also published over 85 scientific and technical papers and is a member of numerous professional committees.

 **INTRODUCING E-BUSINESS ON DEMAND**
THE NEXT UTILITY

Need more heat? Turn up the thermostat. Need water? Turn on the tap. Need to expand? Build a server farm, buy a solution, integrate it all. Or use e-business on demand. It lets you avoid huge upfront investment and gets you up and running fast. It includes everything from procurement to storage solutions. Eminently reliable. Rapidly scalable. Whatever happens, with The Next Utility, you'll be ready. Visit **ibm.com**/e-business/uk/ondemand or ask for 'on demand' at **0870 010 2503**.

 TURN IT UP WHEN YOU NEED TO.

Glossary

aDSL

Asymmetric Digital Subscriber Loop. An optional service that can be added to a regular telephone local loop to add a broadband (up to 1.5 megabits per second), always on, packet service that can be used to have a permanent internet connection, without interferring with the telephone service.

Autonomic computing

A dynamic system of interconnected computing resources that can adjust to changing environments, optimise itself and its response to changing workloads, heal and bypass failures and assure its own security. eLiza is the name of IBM's initiative in this field, which is believed to be an essential ingredient to managing the complexity of grid computing. .

Business-to-business (B2B)

The electronic links between corporations and their suppliers, corporate customers and partners.

Business-to-consumer (B2C)

The generic model whereby corporations or organisations offer their customers or end users online access to information and applications through the internet, using a browser.

Business-to-employee (B2E)

This is traditional IT, delivered over a corporate "intranet." With employees increasingly working from home, or needing to access the corporate applications when they are on the road, intranets are now increasingly accessed through the internet, but using very tight security and encryption measures.

Capacity on demand

A pricing model for servers and storage, whereby more processors or disks are shipped into the machine than are required by the customer. Upgrades can be made very fast through remotely enabling more processors or disks to be used. Customers only pay for what is actually activated.

CIO

Chief information officer.

Consumer-to-consumer (C2C)

This is substantially identical to peer-to-peer, whereby internet users directly exchange information, and can engage in commercial transactions without any intermediaries (or just play games or swap music).

Content distribution networks (CDN)

A CDN is a collection of distributed network appliances that bring content as close as possible to the end users. Unlike proxy caches which keep content after a user has asked for it once, CDNs typically push content as it gets created or modified ahead of any end user demand.

CTO

Chief technology officer.

Edge of the network

The edge of the network is the delineation mark between the network infrastructures of the Internet Service Providers (ISPs) and the user subscriber line (last mile). It can be the head-end of a cable system, or the telephone line (local loop). Delivering contents and applications from the edge provides the fastest possible response time, and avoids the costs and bottlenecks of the ISP backbone networks.

e-mobile

Refers to the use of wireless technologies for giving people access to e-business data and applications while they are on the move, without land-line connections. The access device can be a cell phone, a PDA or a notebook computer, and the wireless connection can be any of the wireless technologies in existence (mobile phone network, WiFi).

e-sourcing

This is the industry terminology for information technology delivered on a utility model. It refers to the delivery of standardised IT processes, applications and infrastructure over a network, as a service. E-sourcing places the focus on the procurement model, rather than any given technology.

e-utilities

This has substantially the same meaning as e-sourcing, but with more focus on the technical characteristics of the IT services, such as high availability, cycles or storage on demand.

GPRS

General packet radio switching, also referred to as 2.5 G (midway between Generation 2 GSM and Generation 3 UMTS), is an upgrade to the current GSM mobile phone systems. While GSM is a circuit switched system (one dials to establish a connection), GPRS adds a permanent packet connection for data communications.

GSM

The "group special mobile" created the standard for the second generation of mobile phones based on digital technology. This acronym now means "global system for mobile communications".

Grid computing

The co-ordinated, transparent and secure sharing of IT resources across geographically distributed sites. Grids are built on standards-based interoperability to deliver integrated solutions that allow virtual collaboration.

IBM business processes on demand

The delivery of business processes (for example, payroll, e-mail, CRM and ERP) through a network, in a standardised way (minimum customisation), and charged per usage.

IBM e-business hosting

The infrastructure and management services required to deliver highly reliable and scalable hosting of business processes on the internet. The services are delivered from e-business hosting centres, and range from co-location services (the customer manages his equipment) to fully managed hosting services, where the service provider is responsible for running the sites to agreed service levels.

IBM e-business on demand

IBM's branded response to the e-sourcing market-place. A new way for customers to acquire, outsource and access e-business infrastructure, applications and business processes over the network, as a service, on a pay-as-you-go basis.

IBM infrastructure on demand

The delivery of server cycles, storage capacity, bandwidth, security or management over a network (LAN, MAN or WAN), with pricing on a per usage basis.

ICT

Information and communications technology.

Managed storage services

Combines "storage on demand" with remote management services. Can be delivered on customer premises or at a hosting centre (storage location).

DON'T GO THERE.

INTRODUCING E-BUSINESS ON DEMAND
THE NEXT UTILITY

You don't wrestle with electrical wires. You don't wrestle with plumbing. You don't wrestle with telephone cables. So why wrestle with e-business infrastructure? Leave it to the specialists. e-business on demand from IBM takes care of storage solutions, business applications, hardware, integration and consulting. You just close the door and walk away. Good news. Good business. It's The Next Utility. Visit **ibm.com**/e-business/uk/ondemand or ask for 'on demand' at **0870 010 2503**.

Network attached storage (NAS)

Describes file servers that can be accessed over any IP network. Unlike SANs which provide data block access (and thus are viewed as real disks), NAS appliances only give access to files, using a variety of industry standard protocols, such as Network File System.

NGi

Next generation internet.

PDA

Personal digital assistant, eg. IBM work pad.

Peer-to-peer computing (P2P)

P2P is the capability for end user systems to directly exchange data or provide collaborative computing (for example, shared workspaces or applications), without relying on central servers for the data exchange.

Resource virtualisation

Virtual resources (servers, storage, bandwidth) are resources that appear to their user as fully dedicated stand-alone resources, but are in fact a small portion of a much larger resource, carved out by software, and providing another option to deliver "computing on demand".

SOAP

An electronic envelope for wrapping up messages to be sent from one computer to another, often across the internet. SOAP is now being standardised in the World Wide Web consortium (W3C).

Storage area networks (SAN)

High speed (gigabit) networks, associated data transfer protocols, and mass storage devices which provide any attached computer with access to remote disk storage space. The prevailing networking technology uses FCS (fibre channel standard). A recent standard, iSCSI (IP small computers system interface), carries these protocols over any IP network.

UDDI

Universal Description, Discovery, and Integration is an industry standards effort started by IBM, Microsoft and Ariba to create registry standards for services on a network.

UMTS

The Universal Mobile Telephone System, also known as 3G, is the standard for the next generation of cell phones. It is using a high speed (megabit per second) transmission, and provides an always on IP packet service. With UMTS even voice is transmitted as packets, departing from today's circuit switching technology used on all cell phones (as well as existing telephone systems).

Utilities

There are only four services that are considered utilities: electricity, water, gas and telephone. For example, the electricity grid is a network of powerful electric power plants (nuclear, thermal, hydroelectric) that deliver electricity to households and businesses thanks to a distribution network. Electricity is totally standardised, paid for on a per usage basis, and assumed to be totally available.

Web services

A set of standard protocols intended to facilitate the interconnection of traditionally disparate applications over the internet. It is expected that web services will allow businesses to, for example, directly link into their suppliers' data bases, or sell some IT services (such as credit checking).

WiFi (Wireless Fidelity)

The Wi-Fi logo is a trade-marked logo from the Wireless Ethernet Compatibility. WiFI can be used as an alternative to traditional Ethernet on wires, but is also increasingly deployed in public places (for example, airports, hotel lobbies) to provide easy hook-up to the business travellers.

Workload pricing for software

Software licences are generally based on the total power of the machine over which the software runs. Workload pricing is on a "pay for what customer's use" model.

WSDL

Web Services Description Language allows you to define precisely what messages you understand and how you will respond to those messages. WSDL is the key web services standard because it describes exactly how you talk to a web services application. WSDL was jointly created by IBM and Microsoft based on previous work that each had done and was submitted for standardisation to the W3C in January, 2001.

XML

EXtended Markup Language allows information to be structured into self defined "fields" (tags) like product name, product price, telephone number, and so on.

Notes